Children Act 1989

AUSTRALIA
The Law Book Company Ltd.
Sydney : Melbourne : Brisbane : Perth

CANADA
The Carswell Company Ltd.
Toronto : Calgary : Vancouver : Ottawa

INDIA
N. M. Tripathi Private Ltd.
Bombay
and
Eastern Law House Private Ltd.
Calcutta
M.P.P. House
Bangalore

ISRAEL
Steimatzky's Agency Ltd.
Jerusalem : Tel Aviv : Haifa

PAKISTAN
Pakistan Law House
Karachi

Children Act 1989

with annotations by

Judith Masson
M.A. (Cantab), Ph.D. (Leicester), Lecturer in Law,
University of Leicester

LONDON
SWEET & MAXWELL
1990

Published in 1990 by
Sweet & Maxwell Limited of,
South Quay Plaza,
183 Marsh Wall, London,
and printed in Great Britain
by The Eastern Press Limited
of London and Reading

British Library Cataloguing in Publication Data

Masson, Judith
    The Children Act 1989 : an annotated guide. — (Current law series)
    1. England. Children law
    I. Title   II. Series
    344.202'87

    ISBN 0–421–41970–9

CONTENTS

Children Act 1989

References are to page numbers

Table of Cases vii
Table of Statutes xi
Table of Statutory Instruments xxvii

Part I:	Introductory	41–5
Part II:	Orders With Respect to Children in Family Proceedings	41–22
Part III:	Local Authority Support for Children and Families	41–36
Part IV:	Care and Supervision	41–66
Part V:	Protection of Children	41–91
Part VI:	Community Homes	41–114
Part VII:	Voluntary Homes and Voluntary Organisations	41–120
Part VIII:	Registered Children's Homes	41–126
Part IX:	Private Arrangements for Fostering Children	41–130
Part X:	Child Minding and Day Care for Young Children	41–136
Part XI:	Secretary of State's Supervisory Functions and Responsibilities	41–147
Part XII:	Miscellaneous and General	41–153

Schedules 41–178
Index .... [1]

TABLE OF CASES

References are to sections and Schedules

A. *v.* Liverpool City Council [1982] A.C. 363; [1981] 2 W.L.R. 948; (1981) 121
S.J. 396; [1981] 2 All E.R. 385; (1981) 79 L.G.R. 621, H.L. .. s.8, s.10, s.33, s.100
Att.-Gen. *v.* Hammersmith and Fulham London Borough Council (1979) *The Times*, December 18 .... s.22
Att.-Gen. *ex rel* Tilley *v.* Wandsworth London Borough Council [1981] 1 W.L.R.
854; (1981) 125 S.J. 148; [1981] 1 All E.R. 1162; (1980) 78 L.G.R.; (1981)
11 Fam. Law 119, C.A.; affirming *The Times*, March 21, 1980 .... s.17, s.24

B. (A Minor) (Wardship: Guardian at litem), *Re* [1989] 1 F.L.R. 268 .... s.41
B. (A Minor) (Wardship: Sterilization), *Re* [1988] A.C. 199; [1987] 2 W.L.R.
1213; (1987) 131 S.J. 625; [1987] 2 All E.R. 206; [1987] 2 F.L.R. 314;
(1988) 86 L.G.R. 417; (1987) 17 Fam. Law 419; (1987) 84 L.S.Gaz. 1410;
(1987) 137 New L.J. 432; (1987) 151 L.G.Rev. 650, H.L.; affirming (1987)
137 New L.J. 291, C.A. s.100
B. (Infants), *Re* [1962] Ch. 201; [1962] 3 W.L.R. 694; 105 S.J. 682; 59 L.G.R.
475; *sub nom.* Baker (Infants), *Re* 125 J.P. 591; [1961] 3 All E.R. 276,
C.A.; affirming *sub nom.* Baker (Infants), *Re* [1961] Ch. 303; [1961] 2
W.L.R. 626; 125 J.P. 403; 105 S.J. 282; [1961] 2 All E.R. 250; 59 L.G.R.
317 .... s.36
Baker, *Re. See* B (Infants), *Re* s.36
Bradford City Metropolitan Borough Council *v.* K (1989) *The Times*, August 18 s.41, s.96

C. (No. 2), *Re* (1989) *The Times*, April 27 .... s.97
C. (A Minor) (Adoption Order: Conditions), *Re* [1988] 2 W.L.R. 474; (1988) 132
S.J. 334; [1988] 1 All E.R. 705; [1988] F.C.R. 484; [1988] 2 F.L.R. 159;
(1988) 152 L.G.Rev. 771; (1988) 18 Fam. Law 428; (1988) 138 New L.J.
64; (1988) 152 J.P.N. 430, H.L.; reversing *sub nom.* C. (A Minor)
(Adoption: Contract with Sibling) [1987] 2 F.L.R. 383; (1988) 18 Fam.
Law 13, C.A. s.8
Cocks *v.* Thanet District Council [1983] A.C. 286; [1982] 3 W.L.R. 1121; (1982)
126 S.J. 820; [1982] 3 All E.R. 1135; (1983) 81 L.G.R. 81; (1984) 24
R.V.R. 31, H.L. s.22

D. (A Minor) (Wardship: Sterilisation), *Re* [1976] Fam. 185; [1976] 2 W.L.R.
279; (1975) 119 S.J. 696; [1976] 1 All E.R. 326 .... s.100
D. (A Minor), *Re, sub nom.* D (A Minor) *v.* Berkshire County Council [1987]
A.C. 317; [1986] 3 W.L.R. 1080; (1987) 151 J.P. 313; (1986) 130 S.J. 984;
[1987] 1 All E.R. 20; (1987) 85 L.G.R. 169; [1987] 1 F.L.R. 422; (1987)
151 L.G.Rev. 268; (1987) 17 Fam. Law 202; (1986) 136 New L.J. 1184;
(1987) 151 J.P.N. 190; (1987) 84 L.S.Gaz. 574, H.L.; affirming [1986] 3
W.L.R. 85; (1986) 130 S.J. 467; [1987] 1 All E.R. 20; (1986) 136 New L.J.
513; (1986) L.S.Gaz. 1720, C.A. s.31
Dean *v.* Dean [1987] 1 F.L.R. 517; (1987) 17 Fam. Law 200; (1987) 151 J.P.N.
254; [1987] 1 F.C.R. 96, C.A. s.14
Dipper *v.* Dipper [1981] Fam. 31; [1980] 3 W.L.R. 626; (1980) 124 S.J. 775;
[1980] 2 All E.R. 722; (1979) 10 Fam. Law 211, C.A. s.2
Dyson Holdings *v.* Fox [1976] Q.B. 503; [1975] 3 W.L.R. 744; 119 S.J. 744;
[1975] 3 All E.R. 1030; 31 P. & C.R. 229; 239 E.G. 39, C.A. s.17

TABLE OF CASES

Gillick v. West Norfolk and Wisbech Area Health Authority and the D.H.S.S.
[1986] A.C. 112; [1985] 3 W.L.R. 830; (1985) 129 S.J. 738; [1985] 3 All
E.R. 402; [1986] Crim.L.R. 113; (1985) 135 New L.J. 1055; (1985) 82
L.S.Gaz. 3531, H.L.; reversing [1985] 2 W.L.R. 413; (1985) 129 S.J. 42;
[1985] 1 All E.R. 533; (1985) 15 Fam. Law 165; (1985) 135 New L.J. 81;
(1985) 82 L.S.Gaz. 762, C.A.; reversing [1984] Q.B. 581; [1983] 3 W.L.R.
859; (1983) 127 S.J. 696; (1983) 147 J.P. 888; [1984] 1 All E.R. 365; (1984)
14 Fam. Law 207; (1983) 80 L.S.Gaz. 2678; (1983) 133 New L.J. 888   s.3, s.8, s.10,
s.20, s.22, s.35, s.38, s.43, s.100
Guevara v. Hounslow London Borough Council (1987) *The Times*, April 17 ..... s.17, s.22

H., Re [1989] 2 All E.R. 353 .... s.4
H., Re, K., Re [1989] Fam. Law 388; (1989) *The Times*, June 9 .... s.7, s.96
Hopes v. Hopes [1949] P. 227; [1949] L.J.R. 104; 64 T.L.R. 623; 113 J.P. 10; 92
S.J. 660; [1948] 2 All E.R. 920, 46 L.G.R. 538, C.A. s.68

J.S. (A Minor), Re [1981] Fam. 22; [1980] 3 W.L.R. 984; (1980) 124 S.J. 881;
[1980] 1 All E.R. 1016; (1980) 10 Fam. Law 121, C.A. s.4
J. v. C. [1970] A.C. 668; [1969] 2 W.L.R. 540; [1969] 1 All E.R. 788; *sub nom.*
C. (An Infant), Re (1969) 113 S.J. 164, H.L. s.1

K. (A Minor), Re (1978) 122 S.J. 626 .... s.3
K.D. (A Minor), Re [1988] A.C. 806; [1988] 2 W.L.R. 398; (1988) 132 S.J. 301;
[1988] 1 All E.R. 577; (1988) 18 Fam. Law 288; [1988] 2 F.L.R. 139;
[1988] F.C.R. 657; (1988) 152 J.P.N. 152 J.P.N. 558, H.L. s.1
K.D., Re [1987] 2 F.L.R. 365 .... s.34
Krishnan v. Sutton London B.C. [1970] Ch. 181; [1969] 3 W.L.R. 683; 113 S.J.
774; [1969] 3 All E.R. 1367, C.A. s.3

Lee v. Lee (1983) 127 S.J. 696; (1984) 12 H.L.R. 68, 114; (1984) 14 Fam. Law
243; (1983) 80 L.S.Gaz. 2678, C.A. s.1
Leeds City Council v. West Yorkshire Metropolitan Police [1983] A.C. 29; [1982]
2 W.L.R. 186; (1982) 126 S.J. 79; [1982] 1 All E.R. 274; (1982) 74
Cr.App.R. 336; [1982] Crim.L.R. 364; (1982) 80 L.G.R. 401, H.L. s.90
Liddle v. Sunderland Borough Council (1983) 13 Fam. Law 250 .... s.22

M. and H. (Minors), Re (Local Authority: Parental Rights) [1988] 3 W.L.R. 485;
[1988] 3 All E.R. 5; (1988) 18 Fam. Law 468; [1988] 2 F.L.R. 431; (1988)
152 J.P.N. 818; [1988] L.S.Gaz., September 7, 37, H.L.; affirming [1987] 3
W.L.R. 759; (1987) 131 S.J. 1155; [1987] 85 L.G.R. 844; [1988] 1 F.L.R.
151; (1988) 18 Fam. Law 57; [1988] F.C.R. 97; (1988) 152 J.P.N. 126;
(1987) 84 L.S.Gaz. 2360; (1987) 151 L.G.Rev. 1027, C.A. s.10, s.21, s.34
M. v. M. (Child: Access) [1973] 2 All E.R. 81, D.C. s.34
M. v. Westminster City Council (1985) 15 Fam. Law 39, D.C. s.31
M'Reight v. M'Reight (1849) 13 I.Eq. 314 .... s.3
May v. May [1986] 1 F.L.R. 325; (1985) 16 Fam. Law 106, C.A. s.1

Northamptonshire County Council v. H. (A Minor) [1988] Q.B. 205; (1988) 86
L.G.R. 357; [1988] 2 W.L.R. 389; (1988) 132 S.J. 263; [1988] 1 All E.R.
598; [1988] 1 F.L.R. 529; (1988) 18 Fam. Law 295; (1988) 152 J.P.N. 303;
[1988] F.C.R. 378; (1988) L.S.Gaz. 34 .... s.95
Nottinghamshire County Council v. Q. [1982] 2 W.L.R. 954; (1982) 126 S.J. 309;
[1982] 2 All E.R. 641; [1982] Fam. 94; (1982) 12 Fam. Law 145, D.C. s.46

O'Reilly v. Mackman; Millbanks v. Secretary of State for the Home Department
[1983] A.C. 237; [1982] 3 W.L.R. 1096; (1982) 126 S.J. 820; [1982] 3 All
E.R. 1124, H.L.; affirming O'Reilly v. Mackman; Derbyshire v. Same;
Dougan v. Same; Millbanks v. Home Office [1982] 3 W.L.R. 604; (1982)
126 S.J. 578; [1982] 3 All E.R. 680; (1982) 79 L.S.Gaz. 1176, C.A.;
reversing (1982) 126 S.J. 312 .... s.22

P., *Re* [1986] 1 F.L.R. 272 .... s.100
P. *v.* W. [1984] Fam. 32; [1984] 2 W.L.R. 439; (1984) 128 S.J. 171; (1984) 148
    J.P. 161; [1984] 1 All E.R. 866; (1984) 14 Fam. Law 208; (1984) 81
    L.S.Gaz. 745, D.C. s.14
Pasmore *v.* Oswaldtwistle Urban District Council [1898] A.C. 387 .... s.84
Patterson *v.* Walcott. *See* P. *v.* W.

R. (B.M.) *v.* R. (D.N.) [1978] 2 All E.R. 33 .... s.33
R. *v.* Birmingham City Council, *ex parte* Birmingham Juvenile Court [1988] 1
    W.L.R. 337 .... s.38
R. *v.* Birmingham Juvenile Court, *ex parte* P. and S. [1984] F.L.R. 343 .... s.38
R. *v.* Birmingham Juvenile Court, *ex parte* S. (A Minor) [1984] Fam. 93; [1984] 3
    W.L.R. 387; (1984) 148 J.P. 700; (1984) 128 S.J. 447; [1984] 2 All E.R.
    688; (1984) 14 Fam. Law 279; (1985) 83 L.G.R. 105; (1984) 81 L.S.Gaz.
    1598 .... s.68
R. *v.* Campbell (1982) *The Times*, December 10 .... s.96
R. *v.* Croydon Juvenile Court, *ex parte* N. [1987] 151 J.P. 523; [1987] 1 F.L.R.
    252; (1987) 17 Fam. Law 199; (1987) 151 J.P.N. 255 .... s.38
R. *v.* G. and Surrey County Council [1984] Fam. 100; [1984] 3 W.L.R. 667;
    (1984) 128 S.J. 662; [1984] 3 All E.R. 460; (1985) 15 Fam. Law 155;
    (1984) 81 L.S.Gaz. 2168, C.A. s.31
R. *v.* Hampshire County Council, *ex parte* K. (1989) *The Independent*, November
    15 .... s.42
R. *v.* Hayes [1977] 1 W.L.R. 234; [1977] 2 All E.R. 288; (1976) 64 Cr.App.R.
    194, C.A. s.96
R. *v.* Norfolk County Council, *ex parte* M. (1989) *The Times*, February 27 .... s.71
R. *v.* North Yorkshire County Council, *ex parte* M. [1989] 1 All E.R. 143 .... s.22
R. *v.* Northampton Juvenile Court, *ex parte* Hammersmith and Fulham London
    Borough [1985] Fam. Law 125 .... s.25
R. *v.* Secretary of State for the Environment, *ex parte* Ward [1984] 1 W.L.R.
    834; (1984) 128 S.J. 415; [1984] 2 All E.R. 556; (1984) 48 P. & C.R. 212;
    (1983) 82 L.G.R. 628; [1984] J.P.L. 90; (1984) L.S.Gaz. 2148 .... s.84
R. *v.* Tower Hamlets London Borough Council, *ex parte* Monaf; Same *v.* Same,
    ex parte Ali; Same *v.* Same, *ex parte* Miah; Same *v.* Same, *ex parte* Uddin
    (1988) 20 H.L.R. 529; (1988) 86 L.G.R. 709, C.A.; reversing in part
    (1987) 19 H.L.R. 577; (1988) 152 L.G.Rev. 329, D.C. s.17
R. *v.* Wallwork (1958) 122 J.P. 299; 42 Cr.App.R. 153, CCA s.96
Ready Mixed Concrete (South East) *v.* Minister of Pensions and National
    Insurance [1968] 2 Q.B. 497; [1968] 2 W.L.R. 775; *sub nom.* Ready Mixed
    Concrete (South East) *v.* Minister of Pensions and National Insurance;
    Minister of Social Security *v.* Greenham Ready Mixed Concrete; Minister
    of Social Security *v.* Ready Mixed Concrete (South East) [1968] 1 All E.R.
    433; 4 K.I.R. 132 .... s.68
Rice *v.* Connolly [1966] 2 Q.B. 414; [1966] 3 W.L.R. 17; 130 J.P. 322; 110 S.J.
    371; [1966] 2 All E.R. 649, D.C. s.62
Richards *v.* Richards [1984] A.C. 174; [1983] 3 W.L.R. 173; [1983] 2 All E.R.
    807; (1984) 12 H.L.R. 68, 73; (1983) 13 Fam. Law 256; (1983) 133 New
    L.J. 725; (1983) 80 L.S.Gaz. 2134, H.L. reversing [1983] 2 W.L.R. 633;
    (1983) 127 S.J. 52; [1983] 1 All E.R. 1017; (1983) 13 Fam. Law 84, C.A. ... s.1, s.8
Riley *v.* Riley (1975) 151 J.P. 650 .... s.11

S.W. (A Minor) (Wardship: Jurisdiction), *Re* [1986] 1 F.L.R. 24; (1985) 15 Fam.
    Law 322 .... s.9, s.31
S. (A Minor) (Adoption or Custodianship), *Re* [1987] Fam. 98; [1987] 2 W.L.R.
    977; (1987) 131 S.J. 133; [1987] 2 All E.R. 99; 151 J.P. 577; (1987) 85
    L.G.R. 505; (1987) 17 Fam. Law 238; [1987] 2 F.L.R. 331; [1988] F.C.R.
    57; (1988) 152 L.G.Rev. 269; (1987) 151 J.P.N. 239; (1987) 84 L.S.Gaz.
    497, C.A. s.8
Santos *v.* Santos [1972] Fam. 247; [1972] 2 W.L.R. 889; 116 S.J. 196; [1972] 2 All
    E.R. 246, C.A. s.68

TABLE OF CASES

T. *v.* West Glamorgan County Council (1989) *The Times*, October 12 .... s.34

Thompson *v.* Thompson [1975] 1 F.L.R. 212 .... s.7

W.G. 31/1075, *Re* (1976) Fam. Law 210, C.A. s.33

W. *v.* A. (1980) 124 S.J. 726; (1980) *The Times*, July 30, C.A.; *sub nom* W. *v.*
A. (Child: Surname) [1981] Fam. 14; [1981] 2 W.L.R. 124; [1981] 1 All
E.R. 100; (1980) 11 Fam. Law 22, C.A. s.33

W. *v.* Hertfordshire County Council [1985] 2 All E.R. 301; *sub nom.* W. (A
Minor) (Wardship: Jurisdiction), *Re* [1985] A.C. 791; [1985] 2 W.L.R. 892;
(1985) 149 J.P. 593; (1985) 129 S.J. 347; (1985) 83 L.G.R. 669; (1985) 15
Fam. Law 326; (1985) 135 New L.J. 483; (1985) 82 L.S.Gaz. 2087, H.L.;
affirming (1985) 129 S.J. 269; [1985] 1 All E.R. 1001; (1985) 5 Fam. Law
325; (1985) 135 New L.J. 269; (1985) 82 L.S.Gaz. 924, C.A. s.8, s.10, s.33

W., *Re. See* W. *v.* Hertfordshire County Council.

Wilde *v.* Wilde (1988) 18 Fam. Law 202; [1988] 2 F.L.R. 83; [1988] F.C.R. 551;
(1988) 152 J.P.N. 559, C.A. s.1

X. (Wardship: Jurisdicton), *Re* [1975] Fam. 47; [1975] 2 W.L.R. 335; *sub nom.*
X. (A Minor) (Wardship: Restriction on Publication), *Re* [1975] 1 All
E.R. 697, C.A. s.1

TABLE OF STATUTES

1774 Life Assurance Act (14 &
        Geo. 3, c.48) .... Sch. 8
1837 Wills Act (7 Will. 4 & 1 Vict.
        c.26) .... Sch. 14
        s.1 .... Sch. 13
        s.9 .... s.5
1891 Custody of Children Act (54
        & 55 Vict. c.3) s.3, s.108,
                          Sch. 12, Sch. 15
1918 Wills (Soldiers and Sailors)
        Act (7 & 8 Geo. 5, c.58) ... s.3
1925 Administration of Estates Act
        (15 & 16 Geo. 5,
        c.23)—
        s.46 .... s.3
1933 Children and Young Persons
        Act (23 & 24 Geo. 5,
        c.12) s.2, s.48, s.83
        s.1 .... s.3, s.68
        (1) .... Sch. 13
        (2)(a) .... Sch. 12
        s.3(1) .... Sch. 13
        s.4(1) .... Sch. 13
        (2) .... Sch. 13
        s.10(1A) .... Sch. 13
        s.11 .... Sch. 13
        s.14(2) .... Sch. 15
        s.17(1) .... Sch. 13
        (2) .... Sch. 13
        s.25(1) .... Sch. 13
        s.34(1) .... Sch. 13
        (7) .... Sch. 13
        (8) .... Sch. 15
        s.37(7A) .... Sch. 13
        s.38 .... s.96
        s.39 .... s.97
        s.40 ...... s.35, s.47, s.48, Sch. 12,
                          Sch. 14, Sch. 15
        s.53 .... s.81, Sch. 2
        s.55(1) s.90
        s.104 .... s.58
        s.107(1) .... Sch. 13, Sch. 15
        Sched. 1 .... s.31
1944 Education Act (7 & 8 Geo. 6,
        c.31) s.3, s.63, s.87, s.105,
                          Sch. 3
        s.35 .... s.36
        s.36 .... s.36, Sch. 3
        s.37 .... s.31, s.36, s.91, Sch. 3
        (1) s.91
        (2) s.36
        (5) s.36
        s. 39 .... s.36, Sch. 3
        (2) s.36
        s.40 .... s.31, s.36
        (1) .... Sch. 12, Sch. 15
        (2) .... Sch. 13
        (2A) .... Sch. 13
        (3) .... s.36, Sch. 13
        (3A) .... Sch. 13

1944 Education Act—cont.
        s.40(3B) .... Sch. 13
        (4) .... s.36, Sch. 13
        (5) .... Sch. 13
        s.53 .... Sch. 9
        s.71 .... s.87
        (1)(e) .... Sch. 13
        s.76 .... s.36, Sch. 3
        s.95 .... s.36
        s.99 .... s.84
        s.100 .... Sch. 9
        s.114(1) .... s.36, Sch. 15
        (1D) s.36
        (1D)–(1F) .... Sch. 13
1948 National Assistance Act (11
        & 12 Geo. 6, c.29) s.17
        s.21 .... s.17
        (1) .... Sch. 1
        s.29 .... s.17
        (1) .... s.17, Sch. 13
        Children Act (11 & 12 Geo.
        6, c.43)—
        s.1 .... Sch. 14
        s.2 .... Sch. 14
        Nurseries and Childminders
        Regulation Act (11 & 12
        Geo. 6, c.53) s.77, s.108,
                          Sch. 15
        s.1(1)(a) .... Sch. 14
        (b) .... Sch. 14
1949 Marriage Act (12, 13 & 14
        Geo. 6, c.76)—
        s.3 .... s.2, Sch. 12, Sch. 14
        (1) .... s.33, Sch. 12, Sch. 15
        (1A) .... s.9, Sch. 12
        (1B) .... Sch. 12
        (2) .... Sch. 14
        s.78(1A) .... Sch. 15
        Sched. 2 ..... s.2, Sch. 14, Sch. 15
1951 Reserve and Auxiliary Forces
        (Protection of Civil
        Interests) Act (14 & 15
        Geo. 6, c.65)—
        s.2(1)(d) .... Sch. 13
1953 Births and Deaths Registra-
        tion Act (1 & 2 Eliz. 2,
        c.20) .... Sch. 14
        s.10 .... Sch. 12
        (1)–(3) .... Sch. 12
        (1A) .... Sch. 12
        s.10A .... Sch. 12
        (1), (2) .... Sch. 12
1954 Mines and Quarries Act (2
        & 3 Eliz. 2, c.70)—
        s.182(1) .... Sch. 13
1955 Army Act (3 & 4 Eliz. 2,
        c.18)—
        s.31(8) .... Sch. 12
        s.91 .... Sch. 12

1955 Army Act—*cont.*
    s.101 .... Sch. 12
    s.151 .... Sch. 12
       (1A)(*a*) .... Sch. 12
    Sched. 5A .... Sch. 12
      para. 7(3) .... Sch. 14
        (3A) .... Sch. 12
        (4) .... Sch. 12
        (5)(*c*) .... Sch. 12
          (i) .... Sch. 14
      para. 8(1) .... Sch. 12
    Air Force Act (c.19)—
    s. 151(1A) .... Sch. 12
    Sched. 5A .... Sch. 12
      para. 7(3) .... Sch. 14
        (5)(*c*)(i) .... Sch. 14
      para. 8(2) .... Sch. 12
        (3) .... Sch. 12
        (4) .... Sch. 12
1956 Sexual Offences Act (4 & 5
    Eliz. 2, c.69)—
    s.19(3) .... Sch. 12
    s.20(2) .... Sch. 12
    s.21(3) .... Sch. 12
    s.28 .... Sch. 12
      (3), (4) .... Sch. 12
    s.38 ..... Sch. 12, Sch. 14, Sch. 15
      (3) .... Sch. 14
    s.43 .... Sch. 12
      (5), (6) .... Sch. 12
    s.46A .... Sch. 12
1957 Naval Discipline Act (5 & 6
    Eliz. 2, c.53)—
    Sched. 4A .... Sch. 12
      para. 7(5)(*c*)(i) .... Sch. 14
    Sched. 5A,
      para. 7(3) .... Sch. 14
1958 Adoption Act (6 & 7 Eliz. 2,
    c.5)—
    s.4 .... Sch. 12
    s.22(2) .... Sch. 10
    s.23(4) .... Sch. 10
    s.37 .... Sch. 10
    s.53 .... Sch. 12
    Maintenance Orders Act (6
    & 7 Eliz. 2, c.39) .... Sch. 13
1959 Mental Health Act (7 & 8
    Eliz. 2, c.72)—
    s.8 .... Sch. 13
    s.9 .... Sch. 13, Sch. 15
1960 Administration of Justice Act
    (8 & 9 Eliz. 2, c.65)—
    s.12(1)(*a*) .... Sch. 13
    Matrimonial Proceedings
    (Magistrates' Courts)
    Act (8 & 9 Eliz. 2,
    c.48) .... Sch. 14
    s.2(1)(*e*) .... Sch. 14
       (*f*) .... Sch. 14
       (*h*) .... Sch. 14
1961 Factories Act (9 & 10 Eliz. 2,
    c.34)—
    s.176(1) .... Sch. 13
1962 Education Act (10 & 11 Eliz.
    2, c.12)—
    s.9 .... s.36

1963 Children and Young Persons
    Act (c.37) s.17, s.83
    s.3 .... Sch. 12, Sch. 15
      (1) .... Sch. 14
    s.23 .... Sch. 15
      (5) .... Sch. 14
    s.29(1) .... Sch. 15
    s.53(3) .... Sch. 15
    s.63(3) s.108
    Sched. 3,
      para. 11 .... Sch. 15
1964 Administration of Justice Act
    (c.42)—
    s.38 .... Sch. 11, Sch. 15
    Perpetuities and Accumula-
    tions Act (c.55) .... Sch. 14
1965 Matrimonial Causes Act
    (c.72) .... Sch. 14
1967 Criminal Justice Act (c.80)—
    s.67(1A)(*c*) .... Sch. 13
1968 Health Services and Public
    Health Act (c.46) .... Sch. 14
    s.60 .... s.108, Sch. 15
    s.63(3)(*b*)(vii) .... Sch. 15
        (viii) .... Sch. 15
        (x) .... Sch. 15
    s.64(3)(*a*)(vi) .... Sch. 15
        (vii) .... Sch. 15
        (ix) .... Sch. 15
        (xv) .... Sch. 15
        (xx) .... Sch. 13
    s.65(3)(*b*)(xxi) .... Sch. 13
    Social Work (Scotland) Act
    (c.49) .... s.31, s.108, Sch. 8
    s.1(2) .... s.105, Sch. 2
      (4)(*a*) .... Sch. 15
    s.2(2)(*k*) .... Sch. 13
    s.5(2)(*c*) .... Sch. 13
      (*d*) .... Sch. 15
    s.16 .... Sch. 13
    s.21(3) .... Sch. 13
    s.61 .... Sch. 9
    s.71 .... s.51
    s.74(6) .... Sch. 13
    s.75(2) .... Sch. 13
    s.86(3) .... Sch. 13, Sch. 15
    Sched. 8,
      para. 20 .... Sch. 15
    Civil Evidence Act (c.64)—
    s.12(5)(*b*)(iv) .... Sch. 13
    s.18 .... s.96
1969 Family Law Reform Act
    (c.46)—
    s.6(3) .... Sch. 1
    s.7 .... s.100, Sch. 15
      (2) .... Sch. 14
      (4) .... Sch. 13, Sch. 14
    Children and Young Persons
    Act (c.54) s.35, s.39, s.83,
      Sch. 12, Sch. 13, Sch. 14
    s.1 ...... Sch. 13, Sch. 14, Sch. 15
      (2) ... s.31, s.90, Sch. 13
      (*a*) s.31, s.68
      (*bb*) .... Sch. 15
      (*d*) s.31
      (*f*) s.90

1969 Children and Young Persons
       Act—*cont.*
       s.1(3)(*b*) .... Sch. 14
            (*c*) .... Sch. 14
       s.2 .... s.47, Sch. 13, Sch. 15
            (4) s.95
            (5) s.95
            (9) s.95
            (10) s.38
            (12) .... Sch. 13
            (13) .... Sch. 15
       s.3 .... s.31, Sch. 15
            (8) .... Sch. 13
       s.5(2) .... Sch. 12
       s.7 .... Sch. 15
            (7) .... s.90, Sch. 12
            (*a*) .... s.90, Sch. 14
            (*b*) s.31, s.90, s.105,
                        Sch. 3, Sch. 8, Sch. 14
            (*c*) .... Sch. 12
            (7A) .... Sch. 15
            (7B) .... Sch. 12
       s.8(3) .... Sch. 15
       s.9(1) .... Sch. 15
       s.11A .... Sch. 15
       s.12 .... Sch. 12
            (4) .... Sch. 12
            (5) .... Sch. 12
       s.12A .... Sch. 12
            (1) .... Sch. 12
            (2) .... Sch. 12
            (3) .... s.90, Sch. 12
       s. 12AA .... s.21, s.90, Sch. 12
            (3) s.90
            (4) .... Sch. 14
            (6)–(10) s.90
            (6)(ii) s.90
       s.12B .... Sch. 12
            (1) .... Sch. 12
            (2) .... Sch. 12
       s.12C .... s.36, Sch. 3, Sch. 12
       s.13 .... s.35
            (2) .... Sch. 12
       s.14 .... s.16
       s.14A .... s.35, Sch. 15
       s.15 .... s.99, Sch. 12, Sch. 14
            (1) ...... s.90, Sch. 14, Sch. 15
            (*a*) .... Sch. 12
            (2) .... Sch. 15
            (2A) .... Sch. 12, Sch. 15
            (3)(*e*) .... Sch. 12
            (4) .... Sch. 12, Sch. 15
       s.16(3) .... Sch. 12
            (4) .... Sch. 12
            (5) s.99
            (*b*) .... Sch. 12
            (*c*) .... Sch. 12
            (6)(*a*) .... Sch. 12, Sch. 15
            (8) .... Sch. 13, Sch. 15
       s.17(*a*) .... Sch. 15
            (*b*) .... Sch. 15
       s.20 .... s.89, Sch. 13, Sch. 15
            (3)(*a*) .... Sch. 14
       s.21 .... Sch. 15
            (1) .... Sch. 14
            (2) .... Sch. 14, Sch. 15

1969 Children and Young Persons
       Act—*cont.*
       s.21(4) .... Sch. 13
            (5) .... Sch. 13
       s.22 .... Sch. 15
            (1) s.95
            (1)–(8) .... Sch. 12
            (4) .... Sch. 15
            (6) .... Sch. 15
       s.23(1) s.21
            (5) .... Sch. 14
       s.25 .... s.101, Sch. 14
       s.26 .... s.101, Sch. 14
       s.27(4) .... s.26, Sch. 15
       s.28 .... Sch. 14, Sch. 15
            (1) .... s.44, Sch. 14
            (2) .... s.46, Sch. 13
            (3) s.46, s.52
            (4) s.46
            (5) .... Sch. 15
            (6) .... s.46, Sch. 14
       s.32 .... s.50, Sch. 14
            (1) .... Sch. 12
            (1A)–(1C) .... Sch. 12
            (2A) .... Sch. 12
            (3) .... s.51, Sch. 12
            (4) .... Sch. 12
       s.32A .... s.41, Sch. 15
            (1) s.41
       s.32B .... s.41, Sch. 15
       s.32C .... Sch. 15
       s.34(1) .... Sch. 12
            (2) .... Sch. 15
       s.65 .... s.58
       s.70(1) .... Sch. 12, Sch. 15
       s.73 .... Sch. 12
            (4)(*a*) .... Sch. 12
            (6) .... Sch. 12
       s.106(2)(*a*) .... Sch. 14
       s.124A(2) s.21
       Sched. 5,
       para. 12(1) .... Sch. 15
       para. 37 .... Sch. 15
       para. 47 .... Sch. 15
       para. 48 .... Sch. 15
1970 Administration of Justice Act
       (c.31)—
       Sched. 8,
       para. 6 .... Sch. 13
       Marriage (Registrar Gen-
       eral's Licence) Act
       (c.34)—
       s.3(*b*) .... Sch. 15
       Local Authority Social Ser-
       vices Act (c.42) s.22, s.36,
                        s.42, s.105
       s.2 .... s.22
       Sched. 1 ..., s.22, Sch. 13, Sch. 15
       Chronically Sick and Dis-
       abled Persons (c.44) s.17,
                        Sch. 2
       s.28 .... Sch. 13
       s.28A .... Sch. 13
1971 Guardianship of Minors Act
       (c.3) s.14, s.15, s.97, s.108,
                        Sch. 13, Sch. 14, Sch. 15

1971 Guardianship of Minors
Act—*cont.*
Pt. VI .... Sch. 14
s.1 .... s.22
(1) s.1
s.3 .... s.5, Sch. 14
s.4 .... s.5, Sch. 14
s.5 .... s.5, Sch. 14
s.6 .... s.5, s.6
s.9 .... Sch. 12
(1) .... Sch. 13
s.10(1)(*a*) .... Sch. 13
s.11(*a*) .... Sch. 13
s.11B .... Sch. 12
s.13(1) .... Sch. 14
s.64(7) .... Sch. 14
Courts Act (c.23)—
Sched. 8,
para. 59(1) .... Sch. 15
Sched. 9,
Pt. I .... Sch. 13
Attachment of Earnings Act
(c.32)—
Sched. 1,
para. 7 .... Sch. 13
Tribunals and Inquiries Act
(c.62)—
Sched. 1,
para. 4 .... Sch. 13
Banking and Financial Deal-
ings Act (c.80) s.105
1972 Maintenance Orders
(Reciprocal Enforce-
ment) Act (c.18)—
s. 41 .... Sch. 15
Parliamentary and Other
Pensions Act (c.48) .... Sch. 14
Local Government Act
(c.70)—
s.102(1) .... Sch. 13
s.250(2) s.81
(3) s.81
(4) s.81
(5) s.81
Sched. 12A,
Pt. III,
para. 1(1)(*b*) .... Sch. 13
Sched. 23,
para. 4 .... Sch. 15
para. 9(3) .... Sch. 15
Criminal Justice Act (c.71)—
s.51(1) .... Sch. 15
1973 Matrimonial Causes Act
(c.18) .... s.8, s.15, Sch. 14
s.23 .... Sch. 1
s.25(1) s.1
(4) s.3
s.27 .... Sch. 1
s.41 .... Sch. 12
s.42 .... Sch. 15
(1) .... Sch. 13
(2) .... Sch. 13
(3) .... Sch. 12, Sch. 14
(6) .... Sch. 15
s.43 .... s.1, Sch. 13, Sch. 14,
Sch. 15

1973 Matrimonial Causes Act—
cont.
s.43(1) ...... s.31, Sch. 13, Sch. 14
(5)(*a*) .... Sch. 14
s.44 ..... Sch. 13, Sch. 14, Sch. 15
s.52(1) .... s.8, s.10, Sch. 12,
Sch. 15
Sched. 2,
para. 11 .... Sch. 15
Employment of Children Act
(c.24)—
s.2(2)(*a*) .... Sch. 13
(2A) .... Sch. 13
Guardianship Act (c.29) .. s.2, s.15,
Sch. 13, Sch. 14, Sch. 15
s.1(2) s.2
(3) s.8
s.2(2) .... Sch. 13
(*a*) .... Sch. 14
(*b*) .... Sch. 13, Sch. 14
(3) .... Sch. 14
s.4(*b*) .... Sch. 13
(4)(*a*) .... Sch. 14
(5) .... Sch. 13
Domicile and Matrimonial
Proceedings Act
(c.45)—
Sched. 1,
para. 11(1) .... Sch. 13, Sch. 15
(3) .... Sch. 13, Sch. 15
Powers of Criminal Courts
Act (c.62)—
s.13(1) .... Sch. 15
s.51(3)(*c*) s.58
Sched. 3,
para. 3(2A) ... Sch. 13, Sch. 15
para. 8 .... Sch. 3
para. 18(1) .... Sch. 3
1974 Rehabilitation of Offenders
Act (c.53)—
s.1(4)(*b*) .... Sch. 15
s.5 .... Sch. 14
(5)(*e*) .... Sch. 15
(10) .... Sch. 15
1975 Inheritance (Provision for
Family and Dependants)
Act (c.63)—
s.2 .... Sch. 1
Children Act (c.72) . s.8, s.15, s.26,
s.41, Sch. 14, Sch. 15
s.14 .... Sch. 12
s.25 .... Sch. 12
s.33 .... s.10
s.34(5) .... Sch. 13, Sch. 14
s.36 .... Sch. 14
(3) .... Sch. 13
(*b*) .... Sch. 14
(5) .... Sch. 14
s.37 .... s.8
(1) s.8
s.41 .... s.10
s.43(1) .... s.14, Sch. 14
s.53(1) .... Sch. 10
s.68(4) .... Sch. 14
(5) .... Sch. 14
(7) .... Sch. 14

1975	Children Act—*cont.*	
	Sched. 3,	
	para. 13	Sch. 14
	para. 43	Sch. 14
	para. 46	Sch. 14
	para. 47	Sch. 14
	para. 77	Sch. 14
1976	Legitimacy Act (c.31)—	
	s.1	s.2
	s.2	s.2
	Adoption Act (c.36)	s.8, s.66, s.88,
		s.92, Sch. 11
	Pt. III	s.105
	s.1	s.105, Sch. 8, Sch. 10
	s.2	Sch. 10
	s.3	Sch. 10
	s.6	s.8
	s.11	Sch. 10
	(2)	Sch. 10
	(5)	Sch. 15
	s.12	Sch. 10
	(1)	Sch. 10
	(2)	Sch. 10
	(3)	Sch. 10
	(a)	Sch. 10
	(b)	Sch. 10, Sch. 15
	(4)	Sch. 10
	(5)	Sch. 10
	(7)	Sch. 10
	s.14(1)	Sch. 10
	(1A)	Sch. 10
	(1B)	Sch. 10
	(3)	s.8, Sch. 15
	(18)	s.88
	s.15(1)	Sch. 15
	(4)	s.8, Sch. 15
	s.16	s.2, Sch. 10
	(1)	Sch. 10
	(2)(c)	Sch. 10
	s.18	s.2, s.12, s.33, s.100,
		Sch. 10, Sch. 12
	(2A)	s.88
	(5)	Sch. 10
	(7)	s.88, Sch. 10
	(8)	Sch. 10
	s.19	Sch. 10
	(2)	Sch. 10
	s.20	Sch. 10
	(1)	Sch. 10
	(2)	Sch. 10
	(3)	s.88, Sch. 10
	(3A)	Sch. 10
	s.21	Sch. 10
	s.22	Sch. 10
	(1A)	s.88, Sch. 10
	(1B)	Sch. 10
	(4)	Sch. 10
	s.25(1)	Sch. 10
	s.26	Sch. 14, Sch. 15
	s.26(1)	Sch. 14
	(b)	Sch. 13
	(2)	Sch. 14
	s.27	Sch. 10
	(1)	Sch. 10
	(2)	Sch. 10

1976	Adoption Act—*cont.*	
	s.28	Sch. 10
	(1)	Sch. 10
	(2)	Sch. 10
	(2A)	s.88
	(3)	Sch. 10
	(5)	Sch. 10, Sch. 15
	s.29	Sch. 10
	(1)	Sch. 10
	(2)	Sch. 10
	s.30	Sch. 10
	(1)	Sch. 10
	(3)	Sch. 10
	s.31	Sch. 10
	(1)	Sch. 10
	(2)	Sch. 10
	(3)	Sch. 10
	s.32	s.88, Sch. 10
	(2)	Sch. 10
	(3)	Sch. 10
	(3A)	Sch. 10
	(4)	Sch. 10
	s.33	s.102
	s.34	Sch. 15
	(1)	Sch. 14
	s.35(1)	Sch. 10
	(2)	Sch. 10
	s.36(1)(c)	Sch. 15
	s.37(1)	Sch. 15
	(3)	Sch. 15
	(4)	Sch. 15
	s.39	s.2
	s.51	s.88, Sch. 10
	(1)	Sch. 10
	(3)(a)(ii)–(iv)	Sch. 10
	(d)	Sch. 10
	(7)	Sch. 10
	s.51A	s.88, Sch. 10
	s.55	s.12, s.33, Sch. 10, Sch. 12
	(1)	Sch. 10
	(3)	Sch. 10
	(4)	Sch. 15
	s.56	Sch. 2, Sch. 10
	(1)	Sch. 10
	(3)	Sch. 10
	s.57(1)	Sch. 10
	(c)	Sch. 10
	(2)	Sch. 15
	(3A)(b)	Sch. 10
	(4)	s.88, Sch. 10
	(4)–(10)	Sch. 15
	(5)(b)	Sch. 10
	s.57A	s.88, Sch. 10
	s.59	Sch. 10
	(1)	Sch. 10
	(2)	Sch. 10
	s.60	Sch. 10
	s.62(5)(b)	Sch. 10
	s.65A	s.88, Sch. 10
	s.65A(2)	s.88
	s.72(1)	Sch. 10, Sch. 15
	(1A)	Sch. 10
	(1B)	Sch. 10
	s.74(3), (4)	Sch. 10
	Sched. 2,	
	para. 1	Sch. 14

1976 Adoption Act—*cont.*
    Sched. 3,
        para. 8 .... Sch. 15
        para. 11 .... Sch. 15
        para. 19 .... Sch. 15
        para. 21 .... Sch. 15
        para. 22 .... Sch. 15
    Domestic Violence and
    Matrimonial Proceedings
    Act (c.50) s.7, s.8
    Race Relations Act (c.74) s.17
    s.3(1) s.22
1977 Criminal Law Act (c.45)—
    s.58(3) .... Sch. 15
    National Health Service Act
    (c.49) .... s.105, Sch. 10
    s.21(1)(*a*) .... Sch. 15
    s.76 .... s.81
    s.84 .... s.81
    Sched. 8 .... s.17
        para. 1(1) .... Sch. 15
        para. 2(2) .... Sch. 15
        para. 3(1) .... Sch. 15
            (4A) .... Sch. 12
    Sched. 15,
        para. 10 .... Sch. 15
        para. 25 .... Sch. 15
1978 Domestic Proceedings and
    Magistrates' Courts Act
    (c.22) .. s.8, s.14, s.15, Sch. 14
    Pt. I .... Sch. 1
    s.2 .... Sch. 13
        (1)(*c*) .... Sch. 13
    s.3(4) s.3
    s.6 .... Sch. 13
    s.7 .... Sch. 13
    s.8 .... Sch. 13
    s.9 .... Sch. 13, Sch. 14
    ss.9–15 .... Sch. 15
    s.10 .... Sch. 14, Sch. 15
        (1) .... Sch. 13
    s.11(4) .... Sch. 14
        (8) .... Sch. 14
    s.14(3) .... Sch. 13
    s.16(5)(*b*) .... Sch. 11
        (*c*) .... Sch. 11
    s.19 .... Sch. 13
        (1) .... Sch. 15
        (ii) .... Sch. 13, Sch. 15
        (2) .... Sch. 13, Sch. 15
        (3A)(*b*) .... Sch. 13
        (4) .... Sch. 15
        (6) .... Sch. 15
        (7) .... Sch. 15
        (9) .... Sch. 15
    s.20 .... Sch. 13
        (4) .... Sch. 13
        (9) .... Sch. 13
        (12) .... Sch. 13
    s.20A .... Sch. 13
    s.21 .... Sch. 13, Sch. 15
    s.23(1) .... Sch. 13
    s.24 .... Sch. 15
    s.25(1)(*a*) .... Sch. 13
        (*b*) .... Sch. 15

1978 Domestic Proceedings and
    Magistrates' Courts Act
    —*cont.*
    s.25(2)(*c*) .... Sch. 15
        (*d*) .... Sch. 15
    s.29(4) .... Sch. 15
        (5) .... Sch. 13
    s.33 .... Sch. 14, Sch. 15
    s.34 .... Sch. 15
    ss.36–53 .... Sch. 15
    ss.64–72 .... Sch. 15
    s.73(1) .... Sch. 15
    s.74(1) .... Sch. 15
        (3) .... Sch. 15
    s.88(1) .... s.8, Sch. 11, Sch. 15
    Sched. 2,
        para. 22 .... Sch. 15
        para. 23 .... Sch. 15
        para. 27 .... Sch. 15
        para. 29 .... Sch. 15
        para. 31 .... Sch. 15
        para. 36 .... Sch. 15
        para. 41 .... Sch. 15
        para. 42 .... Sch. 15
        para. 43 .... Sch. 15
        paras. 46–50 .... Sch. 15
    Adoption (Scotland) Act
    (c.28) s.88, s.108
    s.1 .... Sch. 8, Sch. 10
    s.3 .... Sch. 10
    s.11(2) .... Sch. 10
    s.12 .... Sch. 10
        (2) .... Sch. 10
        (3) .... Sch. 10
        (4) .... Sch. 10
    s.22(4) .... Sch. 10
    s.14(1A) .... Sch. 10
        (1B) .... Sch. 10
    s.16(1)(*a*) .... Sch. 10
    s.18 .... Sch. 10
        (5) .... Sch. 10
    s.19 .... Sch. 10
    s.20(3) .... Sch. 10
        (*c*) .... Sch. 10, Sch. 15
    s.21 .... Sch. 10
    s.23(4) .... Sch. 10
    s.27 .... Sch. 10
    s.28 .... Sch. 10
    s.29 .... Sch. 10
    s.30 .... Sch. 10
    s.31 .... Sch. 10
    s.32 ...../.................. ... Sch. 10
    s.45 .... Sch. 10
        (2) .... Sch. 10
        (5) .... Sch. 10, Sch. 15
        (6) .... Sch. 10
        (7) .... Sch. 10
        (9) .... Sch. 10
    s.49 .... Sch. 10
        (1) .... Sch. 10
        (3) .... Sch. 10
        (4) .... Sch. 15
    s.50(1) .... Sch. 10
    s.53 .... Sch. 10
        (1) .... Sch. 10

1978 Adoption (Scotland) Act —
cont.
s.53(2) .... Sch. 10
(b) .... Sch. 10
s.65(1) .... Sch. 10, Sch. 15
National Health Service
(Scotland) Act (c.29) s.19,
Sch. 9
Interpretation Act (c.30)—
s.7 .... s.105
Sched. 1 .... Sch. 15
1979 Justices of the Peace Act
(c.55) .... Sch. 1, Sch. 12
s.16(5) .... Sch. 11
s.17(3) .... Sch. 11
s.38(2) .... Sch. 11
s.58(1) .... Sch. 11
1980 Child Care Act (c.5) s.2, s.22, s.108,
Sch. 13, Sch. 15
Pt. I .... Sch. 12
Pt. V s.29
s.1 .... s.17, s.24
s.2 .... s.20, s.23, Sch. 14
(1) .... Sch. 14
(c) s.20
(3) s.17, s.20, s.23
(4) s.20
s.3 .... s.31, Sch. 14
(1)(b)(i) s.31
(d) s.31
(8) s.31
s.4(3) s.22
s.5(2) .... Sch. 14
s.10(3) s.22
s.12A–F s.32
s.12A–G s.34
s.12C .... Sch. 14
s.12E .... s.34, Sch. 14
s.13 .... s.20, s.49, Sch. 12
s.14 .... s.49
s.15 .... s.50, Sch. 14
s.16 ... s.49, s.50, Sch. 14, Sch. 15
(1) .... Sch. 14
s.18 .... s.17, s.22
(1) s.22
(2) s.22
(3) s.22
s.19 .... s.22
s.20 .... s.26, s.49
s.21 .... s.17, Sch. 13
(1) s.23
(a) .... Sch. 14
(2) .... Sch. 14
s.21A s.25
(1) s.25
s.22A .... s.23, Sch. 14
s.24 .... Sch. 12, Sch. 14
s.27 .... s.24
s.28 .... s.24
s.29 .... s.24
s.30 .... s.30
s.31 .... s.53, Sch. 13
s.32 .... Sch. 13, Sch. 14
ss.35–39 .... s.53
s.36(5) s.53

1980 Child Care Act—cont.
s.40 .... s.54
s.42 .... s.55
s.43 .... s.56
s.43A s.57
s.44 .... s.58
s.45 .... Sch. 10
s.47 .... Sch. 13
s.51 .... Sch. 13
s.56 .... s.60, Sch. 13
s.57 .... Sch. 13
(1)–(6) s.60
(8)–(11) s.60
ss.57A–57D s.60
s.59 .... s.60
s.60 .... s.60
s.62 .... Sch. 14
s.64 .... Sch. 12, Sch. 14
(7) .... Sch. 14
s.64A s.61
s.65 .... Sch. 12, Sch. 14
s.68 .... s.62
(1) s.62
(2) s.62
(2A) s.62
(5) s.62
s.69 .... s.24
s.72 .... s.20
s.74 .... s.80
s.75 .... s.80
s.76 .... s.81
s.77 .... s.83
s.78 .... s.82
s.79 .... s.83
s.80 .... s.82
s.82 .... s.58
s.87 .... Sch. 12
Sched. 4,
para. 1 .... Sch. 14
Sched. 5,
para. 19 .... Sch. 13
para. 20 .... Sch. 13
para. 26 .... Sch. 14
Foster Children Act (c.6) .. Sch. 15
s.3(3) .... s.67, Sch. 14
ss.4–6 .... s.66
s.7 .... s.65, s.68
(2) s.68
s.8 .... s.67, Sch. 13
s.9 .... s.66
s.10 .... s.69
(3) s.69
s.11 .... s.66
s.12(1) .... Sch. 14
s.15 .... s.66
s.16 .... s.70
s.19 .... s.66
Education Act (c.20)—
s.6 .... s.36, Sch. 3
s.7 .... s.36, Sch. 3
Magistrates' Courts Act
(c.43)—
s.37 .... Sch. 12
s.58 .... s.29

1980 Magistrates' Courts Act—
cont.
s.59(2) .... Sch. 13
s.60 .... s.15
s.62(5) .... Sch. 13
s.63 .... s.11, s.43
    (2) s.92
    (3) s.14
    (4) s.14
s.65(1) ...... s.92, Sch. 11, Sch. 15
        (ii) .... Sch. 11
    (2) .... s.92, Sch. 11
        (a) .... Sch. 11
    (3) .... Sch. 11
s.66(1) .... Sch. 11
    (2) .... Sch. 11
s.67(1) .... Sch. 11
    (2) .... Sch. 11
    (3) .... Sch. 11
    (4) .... Sch. 11
    (5) .... Sch. 11
    (6) .... Sch. 11
    (7) .... Sch. 11
    (8) .... Sch. 11
s.68(1) .... Sch. 11
    (2) .... Sch. 11
    (3) .... Sch. 11
s.69(1) .... Sch. 11
    (2) .... Sch. 11
    (3) .... Sch. 11
    (4) .... Sch. 11
s.70(2) .... Sch. 11
    (3) .... Sch. 11
s.71 .... s.97
    (1) .... Sch. 11
    (2) .... Sch. 11
s.72(1) .... Sch. 11
s.73 .... Sch. 11
s.74(1) .... Sch. 11
s.81(8) .... Sch. 15
s.97 .... s.42
s.120 .... Sch. 12
s.121(8) .... Sch. 11
s.127(1) s.70
s.128(7) .... Sch. 12
s.143(2)(i) .... Sch. 15
s.144 .... s.97
s.150 .... s.29
    (1) ... Sch. 1, Sch. 2, Sch. 11
Sched. 7,
    para. 78 .... Sch. 15
    para. 83 .... Sch. 15
    para. 91 .... Sch. 15
    para. 92 .... Sch. 15
    para. 110 .... Sch. 15
    para. 116 .... Sch. 15
    para. 117 .... Sch. 15
    para. 138 .... Sch. 15
    para. 157 .... Sch. 15
    para. 158 .... Sch. 15
    para. 165 .... Sch. 15
    para. 166 .... Sch. 15
    para. 199 .... Sch. 15
    para. 200 .... Sch. 15
    para. 201 .... Sch. 15

1980 Education (Scotland) Act
        (c.44) .... s.78, s.105, Sch. 9
s.6 .... Sch. 9
1981 Contempt of Court Act
        (c.49)—
s.17 .... s.14
Supreme Court Act (c.54)—
s.18(1)(h)(i) .... Sch. 13
        (ii) .... Sch. 13
s.41(2A) .... Sch. 13
s.90(3) s.41
Sched. 1,
    para. 3 .... Sch. 11
        (b)(ii) .... Sch. 13
Armed Forces Act (c.55)—
s.14(9A) .... Sch. 13
Education Act (c.60) ... s.28, s.105,
                            Sch. 2
s.3A .... Sch. 12
s.7 .... s.63
s.11(3)(a) s.63
Sched. 3,
    para. 9 .... Sch. 15
1982 Children's Homes Act (c.20) .. s.63,
                            s.64, Sch. 15
s.1 .... Sch. 13
s.2(2) s.63
ss.4–8 .... s.63
s.10 .... s.65
    (4) s.65
Civil Jurisdiction and Judg-
    ments Act (c.27)—
Sched. 4 .... Sch. 13
Sched. 5,
    para. 5(a) .... Sch. 13
Criminal Justice Act (c.48)—
s.2 .... Sch. 12
ss.22–25 .... Sch. 15
s.27 .... Sch. 15
Sched. 14,
    para. 45 .... Sch. 15
    para. 46 .... Sch. 15
1983 Matrimonial Homes Act
        (c.19) s.7
s.1 .... s.8
    (3) s.1
s.9 .... s.8
Mental Health Act (c.20) s.31, s.66,
                            s.105, Sch. 8
Pt. III .... Sch. 3
s.12 .... Sch. 3
s.26(5)(d) .... Sch. 15
s.27 .... Sch. 13
s.28(1) .... Sch. 15
    (3) .... Sch. 13
    (4) .... Sch. 13
s.116 .... s.83
s.131(2) .... Sch. 13
Sched. 4,
    para. 12 .... Sch. 15
    para. 26(a) .... Sch. 15
        (b) .... Sch. 15
        (c) .... Sch. 15
    para. 35 .... Sch. 15
    para. 44 .... Sch. 15

1983   Mental Health Act—*cont.*
Sched. 4—*cont.*
    para. 50 .... Sch. 15
    para. 51 .... Sch. 15
Health and Social Services
  and Social Security
  Adjudications Act (c.41) .. s.23
s.4(1) .... Sch. 15
s.5 .... Sch. 15
s.6 .... Sch. 15
s.11(2) .... Sch. 15
s.17 .... s.17
s.19 .... s.17
    (1)–(5) .... Sch. 15
Sched. 1 .... Sch. 15
Sched. 2,
    para. 3 .... Sch. 15
    paras. 9–14 .... Sch. 15
    paras. 20–24 .... Sch. 15
    para. 27 .... Sch. 15
    para. 28 .... Sch. 15
    para. 34 .... Sch. 15
    para. 37 .... Sch. 15
    paras. 46–62 .... Sch. 15
Sched. 4,
    paras. 38–48 .... Sch. 15
Sched. 9,
    para. 5 .... Sch. 15
    para. 16 .... Sch. 15
    para. 17 .... Sch. 15
1984   Registered Homes Act (c.23) . s.60,
      s.80, s.87, s.105, Sch. 9
Pt. III .... Sch. 13
s.1(5)(*d*), (*e*) .... Sch. 13
s.39(*a*), (*b*) .... Sch. 13
Sched. 1,
    para. 5(*a*) .... Sch. 15
    paras. 6–8 .... Sch. 15
County Courts Act (c.28)—
s.25 .... Sch. 1
Sched. 2,
    para. 56 .... Sch. 15
Mental Health (Scotland) Act
  (c.36)—
s.10 .... s.83
s.54 .... Sch. 13
Child Abduction Act (c.37) s.1, s.2,
             s.13
s.1(2) .... Sch. 12
    (3) .... Sch. 12
    (4) .... Sch. 12
    (5A) .... Sch. 12
    (7) .... Sch. 12
s.2 .... s.50, s.51
    (1) .... Sch. 12
    (2) .... Sch. 12
    (3) .... Sch. 12
s.3 .... Sch. 12, Sch. 15
Sched. .... Sch. 12
    para. 1(1) .... Sch. 12
        (2) .... Sch. 15
    para. 2(1) .... Sch. 12
    para. 3(1) .... Sch. 12
        (*e*) .... Sch. 15
        (2)(*a*) .... Sch. 12
    para. 5 .... Sch. 12

1984   Matrimonial and Family Pro-
    ceedings Act (c.42)—
Pt. III s.8
Pt. V .... Sch. 11
s.38(2)(*b*) .... Sch. 13
s.44 .... Sch. 11
Sched. 1,
    para. 19 .... Sch. 15
    para. 23 .... Sch. 15
Foster Children (Scotland)
  Act (c.56) s.78, s.108
s.1 .... Sch. 12, Sch. 15
s.2(2) .... Sch. 12
s.7(1) .... Sch. 12, Sch. 15
s.10 .... Sch. 9
Sched. 2,
    paras. 1–3 .... Sch. 15
    para. 8 .... Sch. 15
Police and Criminal Evidence
  Act (c.60)—
s.17(1)(*e*) s.48
s.37(14) .... Sch. 13
    (15) .... s.21, Sch. 15
s.38 .... s.21
    (6) .... s.21, Sch. 13
    (6A) .... Sch. 13
    (6B) .... Sch. 13
    (8) .... Sch. 13
s.39(4) .... Sch. 13
    (5) .... Sch. 15
s.52 .... Sch. 15
s.118(1) .... Sch. 15
Sched. 2 .... Sch. 13, Sch. 15
Sched. 6,
    para. 19(*a*) .... Sch. 15
    para. 22 .... Sch. 15
1985   Prosecution of Offences Act
    (c.23)—
s.27 .... Sch. 15
Surrogacy Arrangements Act
  (c.49)—
s.1(2)(*b*) .... Sch. 13
Child Abduction and Custody
  Act (c.60) s.1, s.108
s.9(*a*) .... Sch. 13
    (*c*) .... Sch. 15
s.16 .... s.35
s.20(2)(*a*) .... Sch. 13
    (*b*) .... Sch. 15
    (*c*) .... Sch. 15
s.25(1)(*a*) .... s.35, Sch. 3
    (*b*) .... s.35, Sch. 3
    (3) .... Sch. 15
    (5) .... Sch. 15
s.27(4) .... Sch. 13
Sched. 3,
    para. 1 .... Sch. 13
        (2) .... Sch. 15
Housing Act (c.68) s.17, s.20, s.105
1986   Children and Young Persons
    (Amendment) Act (c.28)
             Sch. 15
Disabled Persons (Services,
  Consultations and Rep-
  resentation) Act (c.33) .. Sch. 2
s.1(3) .... Sch. 13

1986 Disabled Persons (Services, Consultations and Representation) Act—*cont.*
s.2(3)(*a*) .... Sch. 13
(5) .... Sch. 12
(*bb*) .... Sch. 13
(*cc*) .... Sch. 13
(7)(*b*) .... Sch. 13
s.16 .... Sch. 13, Sch. 15
Insolvency Act (c.45) ..... s.17, s.24, s.29, Sch. 2
s.281(5)(*b*) .... Sch. 11, Sch. 15
(8) .... Sch. 11
Social Security Act (c.50)—
Sched. 10,
para. 51 .... Sch. 15
Family Law Act (c.55) .. s.13, s.108
Pt. I s.48
Pt. I,
paras. 63–71 .... Sch. 13
s.1(1) .... Sch. 13
(2) .... Sch. 13, Sch. 15
(3) .... Sch. 13
(4) .... Sch. 13
(5) .... Sch. 13
s.2(1) .... Sch. 13
(2) .... Sch. 13
(3) .... Sch. 13
s.2A(1) .... Sch. 13
(2) .... Sch. 13
(3) .... Sch. 13
(4) .... Sch. 13
s.3(1) .... Sch. 13
(2) .... Sch. 13
(3) .... Sch. 13
(4)–(6) .... Sch. 15
(3A) .... Sch. 13
(3B) .... Sch. 13
(5) .... Sch. 13
(6) .... Sch. 13
(7) .... Sch. 13
(8) .... Sch. 13
s.4 .... Sch. 15
s.7(*a*)–(*d*) .... Sch. 13
s.11(2) .... Sch. 13
s.13(5)(*a*) .... Sch. 13
(6) .... Sch. 13
(*a*)(i) .... Sch. 13
s.14(2) .... Sch. 13
s.19(2) .... Sch. 13
s.20(3)(*a*) .... Sch. 13
(6) .... Sch. 13
s.21(4)(*a*) .... Sch. 13
(5) .... Sch. 13
s.22(2) .... Sch. 13
s.23(4)(*a*) .... Sch. 13
(5) .... Sch. 13
s.32 .... Sch. 13
s.33 .... s.48, s.50, s.98
s.34 .... s.50
(3) .... Sch. 13
s.35(1) .... Sch. 15
s.40 .... Sch. 13
s.42(4)(*a*) .... Sch. 13
(6) .... Sch. 13, Sch. 15
(7) .... Sch. 13

1986 Family Law Act—*cont.*
Sched. 1,
para. 10 .... Sch. 15
para. 11 .... Sch. 15
para. 13 .... Sch. 15
para. 16 .... Sch. 15
para. 17 .... Sch. 15
para. 20 .... Sch. 15
para. 23 .... Sch. 15
Education (No. 2) Act (c.61)—
s.5(4) .... Sch. 13
(2) .... Sch. 13
(6) .... Sch. 13
s.31 .... Sch. 13
s.65(1) .... Sch. 13
Sched. 2,
para. 7(6) .... Sch. 13
1987 Family Law Reform Act (c.42) s.29, s.34
s.1 .... s.2, s.105, Sch. 12
(2) s.2
(3) s.2
s.2(1)(*f*) .... Sch. 12
(2) .... Sch. 14
(8) .... Sch. 14
s.3 .... s.2, s.3, Sch. 15
s.4 .... s.4, Sch. 12, Sch. 15
(1) .... Sch. 14
s.5 .... Sch. 14, Sch. 15
(1) .... Sch. 14
(7) .... Sch. 14
(9) .... Sch. 14
s.6 .... Sch. 15
s.7 .... Sch. 15
ss.9–16 .... Sch. 15
s.10(4)(*c*) .... Sch. 14
(5)(*c*)(i) .... Sch. 14
(5A) .... Sch. 14
s.15 .... s.15
s.16 .... s.15
(2)(*bb*) .... Sch. 14
s.18(1) s.3
s.20(9)(*a*) .... Sch. 14
s.23 .... s.2
(4)(*c*) .... Sch. 14
s.27(1) s.2
s.28 .... s.2
s.34(1)(*cc*) .... Sch. 14
s.44(11)(*dd*) .... Sch. 14
(13)(*dd*) .... Sch. 14
s.46(10) .... Sch. 14
Sched. 1,
para. 1(1) .... Sch. 14
para. 14(1) .... Sch. 14
Sched. 2,
para. 11 .... Sch. 15
para. 14 .... Sch. 15
para. 51 .... Sch. 15
para. 67 .... Sch. 15
para. 68 .... Sch. 15
para. 94 .... Sch. 15
para. 95 .... Sch. 15
para. 82 .... Sch. 15

1987 Family Law Reform Act—
     cont.
     Sched. 3,
         para. 11 .... Sch. 15
         para. 12 .... Sch. 15
1988 Local Government Act
     (c.9)—
     Sched. 1,
         para. 2(4) .... Sch. 13
     Criminal Justice Act (c.33)—
     s.34 .... s.96
     Legal Aid Act (c.34) . s.99, Sch. 14
     s.3(4)(c) .... Sch. 15
     s.15 .... s.99
         (3A) s.99
         (3B) s.99
     s.19(5) s.99
     s.27 .... s.99, Sch. 15
     s.28 .... s.99, Sch. 15
     s.30(1) .... s.99, Sch. 15
         (2) .... s.99, Sch. 15
     Sched. 2,
     Pt. I,
         para. 2 .... Sch. 12
             (a) .... Sch. 15
             (b) .... Sch. 15
     Education Reform Act
     (c.40)—
     s.52(3) .... Sch. 9
     s.53(8) .... Sch. 13
     s.54(2) .... Sch. 13
     s.58(5)(k) .... Sch. 13
     s.60 .... Sch. 13
     s.61 .... Sch. 13
     s.110 .... s.30
     s.111 .... s.30
         (5) s.30
     Housing Act (c.50)—
     s.39 .... s.17
1989 Children Act (c.41)—
     Pt. I .... s.8, Sch. 14
     Pt. II .... s.8, Sch. 14, Sch. 12
     Pt. III s.21, s.26, s.27, s.46,
         s.47, s.62, s.64, s.67, s.80,
         s.85, s.90, s.105, Sch. 2,
             Sch. 13, Sch. 14
     Pt. IV ... s.1, s.8, s.26, s.62, s.75,
         s.95, s.98, Sch. 12, Sch. 13,
             Sch. 14
     Pt. V... s.21, s.26, s.41, s.62, s.75,
         s.95, s.98, Sch. 12
     Pt. VI s.60, s.87, s.88
     Pt. VII s.2, s.17, s.47, s.87,
         s.88, Sch. 5
     Pt. VIII s.2, s.17, s.47, s.60,
         s.63, s.87, s.88, Sch. 6,
             Sch. 14
     Pt. IX... s.2, s.17, s.47, s.60, s.63,
         s.87, s.88, Sch. 8, Sch. 14
     Pt. X ... s.2, s.18, s.47, s.71, s.78,
         s.80, s.108, Sch. 9, Sch. 14
     Pt. XI s.88
     Pt. XII s.2
     s.1 ...... s.1, s.10, s.17, s.31, s.39,
             s.91
         (1) ... s.4, s.10, s.16, s.37, s.43,
             s.50

1989 Children Act—cont.
     s.1(2) s.7, s.32, s.38
         (3) s.4, s.5, s.31, s.39,
             Sch. 14
         (4) s.4, s.31
         (5) s.4, s.5, s.8, s.10, s.13,
             s.16, s.31, s.34, s.38
     s.2 .... s.2, s.4, Sch. 14
         (1) s.10, s.11
         (2) s.4, s.5
         (8) s.1, s.3, s.8, s.33, s.43
         (9) s.4
     s.3 .... s.3, s.4, s.105, Sch. 10
         (2) s.17
         (5) s.2, s.3, s.4, s.8, s.20,
             s.22, s.43, s.46
     s.4 ... s.1, s.4, s.7, s.8, s.12, s.91,
             Sch. 12
         (1) .... s.91, s.105, Sch. 10
             (a) s.2
             (b) s.2
     s.5 ...... s.1, s.2, s.5, s.6, s.7, s.8,
             s.10, s.11, s.91, s.105,
             Sch. 14
         (1) s.2, s.91
         (3) s.91
         (4) s.91
         (7) s.10
         (8) s.2, s.10
         (11) s.3
     s.6 .... s.6, s.8
         (1) s.5
     s.7 .... s.7, s.41, s.45
         (1) s.1
             (b)(ii) s.16
     s.8 ...... s.1, s.2, s.3, s.7, s.8, s.9,
             s.10, s.16, s.31, s.34, s.39,
             s.48, s.88, s.91, s.100,
             Sch. 13, Sch. 14
         (1) s.105
         (3) s.4, s.31, s.105
             (a) s.10
         (4) s.7, s.9, s.31
     s.9... s.8, s.9, s.10, s.16, s.20, s.31
         (1) s.8, s.33, s.100
         (2) s.8
         (3) s.10, s.31, s.100
         (4) s.10
         (5) s.2, s.8, s.100
         (6) s.8, s.91
         (7) s.1, s.8
     s.10 .... s.3, s.8, s.9, s.10, s.17,
             s.20, s.39, s.93, s.100,
             Sch. 10
         (1) s.1, s.8, s.31, s.34
             (b) s.1, s.4, s.5, s.8
         (2) s.8
             (b) s.8
         (4)(a) s.4
         (5) s.2, s.5, s.31, s.100
             (b) s.9
             (c)(ii) s.9
         (8) s.13, s.34, s.100
         (9) s.5
             (d)(i) s.9
     s.11 .... s.11, s.13
         (4) s.8

1989 Children Act—*cont.*
s.11(5) s.8
   (6) s.8
   (7) s.8, s.13
s.12 .... s.11, s.12, s.78
   (1) s.2, s.11
   (2) s.8
   (3) s.2, s.4, s.8, s.10
   (4) s.4
s.13 ... s.1, s.2, s.3, s.8, s.13, s.78,
                              s.91
   (2) s.8
s.14 .... s.3, s.14, Sch. 13, Sch. 14
s.15 .... s.15, Sch. 1
s.16 ..... s.1, s.16, s.17, s.37, s.38,
                   s.39, s.91, Sch. 13
   (2) s.105
s.17 ... s.17, s.29, s.33, s.37, s.47,
                   s.62, s.105, Sch. 2
   (1) s.20, s.22, s.24
   (3) s.29
   (4) s.104
   (6) s.24, s.29, s.37
   (7) .... s.24, s.29, Sch. 2
   (8) .... s.24, s.29, Sch. 2
   (9) .... s.24, s.29, Sch. 2
   (10)(*a*) s.31
   (11) s.105
s.18 ... s.17, s.18, s.19, s.29, s.37,
                        s.105, Sch. 2
   (1) s.17, s.22, s.29
   (2) s.29
   (3) s.17, s.29
   (4) s.29
   (5) s.29
   (6) s.47
s.19 .... s.17, s.19, s.108
   (13) s.35
s.20 ... s.17, s.20, s.22, s.29, s.37,
                   s.67, Sch. 2, Sch. 13
   (1) s.17, s.29
     (*c*) s.17, s.75
   (2) .... s.30, Sch. 2
   (3) s.24, s.29
   (4) s.24
   (5) s.24, s.25
   (7) s.3
   (8) ...... s.3, s.4, s.25, Sch. 10
   (10) s.2
s.21 ... s.17, s.21, s.22, s.44, s.90,
                              Sch. 2
   (1) s.29
   (2)(*a*) s.29
     (*b*) s.29
   (3) s.30
s.22 ... s.17, s.22, s.23, s.26, s.33,
                 s.39, s.46, s.62, s.64, s.84,
                   s.89, s.105, Sch. 13
   (3) ... s.9, s.23, s.29, s.34, s.61
     (*a*) s.23
     (*b*) s.23
   (4) s.20, s.44, s.61
     (*d*) s.26
   (5) s.44, s.61
s.23 ... s.17, s.22, s.23, s.33, s.38,
                        s.59, Sch. 13

1989 Children Act—*cont.*
s.23(2) s.22
     (*a*) .... s.24, s.59, Sch. 2,
                              Sch. 14
     (*c*) s.62
     (*f*) .... s.59, Sch. 2
   (3) s.62, s.105
   (4) .... Sch. 2
   (5) . ... s.33, s.34, s.38, Sch. 2
   (6) s.23
     (*a*) s.23
     (*b*) s.23
   (8) s.23
s.24 ... s.17, s.22, s.24, s.33, s.37,
                 s.64, s.67, s.85, s.86, Sch. 2
   (1) s.17
   (2) s.20
   (4) s.62
   (7) s.29
   (8) s.29
   (10) s.29
   (12) s.62, s.64
s.25... s.22, s.25, s.31, s.99, Sch. 4
   (7) s.90
   (8) s.108
s.26 ... s.22, s.26, s.33, s.59, s.63,
                        s.84, Sch. 6
   (1) s.37
   (3) s.17, s.20, s.23, s.34
     (*b*) s.31
     (*e*) s.22
   (5) s.26
   (6) s.26
   (7) s.26
   (8) s.26
s.27 .... s.8, s.27
   (2) s.29
s.28 .... s.27, s.28, s.46
s.29 .... s.17, s.29, s.93
   (1) s.17, s.18
   (2) s.17
   (5) s.17
   (7) s.30
   (8) s.30
   (9) s.30
s.30 .... s.30
   (2) s.29
s.31 .... s.2, s.8, s.9, s.16, s.17,
                 s.20, s.31, s.43, s.44, s.67,
                 s.74, s.90, s.91, Sch. 13,
                              Sch. 14
   (1) s.22, s.45
   (2) s.36, s.37, s.38, s.39,
                   s.47, s.90, s.100
   (3) s.22
   (6) s.33
   (7) s.47
   (8) .... Sch. 13
   (9) s.33, s.45, s.47, s.105
   (10) s.17, s.105
   (11) .... s.38, s.105, Sch. 13
s.32 .... s.32, s.36, s.38
s.33 .... s.22, s.33, s.38
   (3) s.2
     (*b*) s.34

1989 Children Act—*cont.*

s.33(6) s.2
(7) s.2
s.34 ..... s.8, s.32, s.34, s.41, s.43,
s.44, s.46, s.91, s.100,
Sch. 14
(1) s.4, s.8
s.35 ... s.33, s.35, s.38, s.39, s.91,
Sch. 3
s.36 ... s.8, s.17, s.31, s.36, s.105,
Sch. 3, Sch. 13
(3) .... Sch. 13
(6) .... Sch. 14
(8) s.28
(9) .... Sch. 13
s.37 .... s.36, s.37, s.47
(1) s.38, s.41
(4) s.38
(6) s.47
s.38 .... s.31, s.35, s.38, Sch. 12
(1) s.37
(3) s.39
s.39 .... s.35, s.39
(1) s.9
(b) s.10
(2) s.35
(4) s.41
s.40 ... s.31, s.34, s.35, s.39, s.40,
s.94, s.100
s.41 .... s.39, s.41
(6)(g) s.45
(9) s.88
(10)(c) s.32
(11) s.45
s.42 .... s.41, s.42, s.93
s.43 ..... s.9, s.21, s.31, s.35, s.41,
s.43, s.44, s.91
(2) s.105
(6) s.44
(8) s.38, s.44
s.44 ...... s.3, s.9, s.20, s.21, s.31,
s.34, s.41, s.43, s.44, s.46,
s.62, s.66, s.75, s.87, s.90,
s.100, s.105
(1) s.43
(a) s.38, s.46
(b) s.43, s.47
(c) s.43
(4)(c) s.45
(13) s.52
(15) s.48
s.45 .... s.44, s.45
(3) s.46
(4) s.52
(8) s.52
(11) s.46
s.46 ... s.21, s.31, s.44, s.45, s.46,
s.49, s.50
(1) s.48
(3)(f) s.21
(7) s.45, s.47, s.52
s.47 ... s.17, s.31, s.37, s.46, s.47,
s.62
(1) s.31
(b) s.16, s.43, s.44

1989 Children Act—*cont.*

s.47(2) s.36
(3)(c) s.46
(4) s.36, s.43, s.44, s.62
(9) s.27
(10) s.27
(11) s.27
s.48 .... s.44, s.48, s.98
(9) s.62, s.67, s.76, s.86
(9)–(13) s.102
s.49 .... s.48, s.49, s.50, s.51
(1) s.50
s.50 ... s.41, s.50, s.51, s.98, s.108
(13) s.108
s.51 .... s.46, s.51
s.52 .... s.52
(1) s.93
(3) s.31
(b) s.47
s.53 ... s.53, s.105, Sch. 4, Sch. 13
(3) s.45
s.54 .... s.54
(2) s.58, s.104
s.55 .... s.55
s.56 .... s.56
(3) s.58
(4)(a) s.58, s.104
s.57 .... s.57
(3) s.58, s.104
(4) s.88
(5) s.58
s.58 .... s.58, s.82, s.106
s.59 .... s.59
s.60 ... s.60, s.105, Sch. 5, Sch. 13
(5) s.86
s.61 .... s.61, s.64, Sch. 9
ss.62–67 .... s.76
s.62 .... s.60, s.62, s.64, s.102
(1) s.59
(5) s.67
(6) s.67, s.76, s.87
s.63 .... s.63, s.66, s.105, Sch. 13
(1) .... Sch. 6
(6) .... s.87, Sch. 6
(10) .... Sch. 14
(11) .... Sch. 6
(12) .... s.66, Sch. 7
s.64 .... s.64, s.102
(4) s.60, s.62
s.65 .... s.60, s.65, Sch. 5
s.66 .... s.66, s.105, Sch. 8
s.67 .... s.24, s.60, s.67, s.102,
Sch. 13
(3) s.70
s.68 .... s.65, s.66, s.68, s.70,
Sch. 8, Sch. 12
(2) s.71
(3) s.70, s.71
s.69 .... s.66, s.68, s.69, Sch. 8
(3) s.66
(5) s.66
(6) s.66
s.70 .... s.68, s.70
(1)(d) s.68, s.78
(2) s.68

1989 Children Act—*cont.*
s.71... s.71, s.74, s.77, s.87, s.105,
Sch. 9
(1) s.18
(*a*) s.72, s.74, s.78,
Sch. 14
(*b*) ... s.19, s.73, s.74, s.78,
s.80, Sch. 9, Sch. 14
(3) s.73
(7) s.74, s.78
(12) s.105
s.72 ... s.72, s.73, s.74, s.75, s.77,
s.78, Sch. 9
(2) s.73
s.73 ... s.73, s.74, s.75, s.77, s.78,
Sch. 9
s.74 .... s.74
s.75 .... s.74, s.75
s.76 .... s.76, s.102, Sch. 9
(4) s.71
s.77 .... s.73, s.75, s.77
(2) s.71, s.72, s.74
(6) s.72, s.74
s.78 .... s.78
s.79 .... s.19, s.79
s.80 .... s.60, s.80, s.102
(1)(*c*) s.60
(*h*) s.108
(*i*) s.108
(2) s.108
(3) s.108
(4) s.60
(5) s.60
(*a*) s.108
(*b*) s.108
(*h*) s.108
(6) s.60
(6)–(12) s.108
s.81 .... s.81
s.82 .... s.58, s.82
(2) s.106
(3) s.58
(4) s.58, s.106
(5) s.23, s.58, s.59, s.81
s.83 .... s.83
(9) s.82
s.84... s.17, s.18, s.84, s.100, s.104
s.85 ... s.17, s.24, s.47, s.60, s.85,
s.86
(1)(*a*) .... Sch. 14
s.86 ... s.17, s.24, s.47, s.60, s.86,
s.102
(1)(*a*) .... Sch. 14
s.87 ... s.47, s.60, s.63, s.66, s.87,
s.102, Sch. 13
s.88 .... s.88, s.108, Sch. 10
s.89 .... s.89, s.108
s.90 .... s.90
(2) .... Sch. 14
s.91 .... s.13, s.91, s.92, Sch. 3,
Sch. 14
(1) s.8, s.39
(2) s.8, s.34
(7) s.4
(8) s.4

1989 Children Act—*cont.*
s.91(10) s.8, s.10
(11) s.8
(12) .... Sch. 14
(14) s.1
(15) s.39, s.43
(17) s.34
s.92 ... s.25, s.31, s.34, s.77, s.92,
Sch. 11
s.93 ..... s.1, s.34, s.38, s.40, s.42,
s.52, s.93
s.94 ... s.25, s.31, s.35, s.94, s.100
(2) s.92
(10) s.92
s.95 .... s.95
s.96 .... s.7, s.41, s.45, s.96
(3) .... Sch. 14
(3)–(7) s.108
s.97 .... s.97
(4) s.104
s.98 .... s.98
s.99 .... s.25, s.99
s.100 .... s.20, s.31, s.45, s.100
(2) s.8, s.9
(*b*) s.20
(3) s.8, s.9, s.36
s.101 .... s.101
(1)(*b*) s.108
(2) s.108
(4) s.91
(5)(*a*)(i) s.108
s.102 .... s.62, s.67, s.86, s.102
(6) s.76
s.103 .... s.103
s.104 .... s.80, s.104, s.108
(3) s.17
(4) s.96
s.105 .... s.105, s.108, Sch. 13
(1) .... s.31, Sch. 13
(3) s.8, s.20
(5) s.21
(8) s.60
(9) s.60
(10) s.60
s.106 .... s.106
s.107 .... s.104, s.107
s.108 .... s.108
(2) s.96, s.104
Sched. 1 ...... s.8, s.15, s.17, s.29,
s.91, s.94, Sch. 1, Sch. 13
para. 1 .... s.3, Sch. 12
(2)(*a*)–(*c*) .... Sch. 13
para. 3(2) s.91
para. 4(3) .... Sch. 12
para. 6 .... s.15
para. 7 .... s.15
para. 15 .... s.100
para. 16 ... s.15, s.105
Sched. 2 .... s.21, Sch. 2
Pt. I s.17, s.47, s.62
Pt. II s.22, s.23, s.33, s.62
Pt. III .... s.29, Sch. 10, Sch. 14
para. 1 .... s.37
(2) s.26
para. 2 .... s.17
para. 4 .... s.17

1989 Children Act—*cont.*
   Sched. 2—*cont.*
    Pt. III—*cont.*
      para. 5 .... s.17, s.44
      para. 6 .... s.17
      para. 7 .... s.17, s.108
          (c) s.25
      para. 8 .... s.17, s.108
      para. 9 .... s.17, s.108
      para. 10 ..... s.17, s.67, s.108
      para. 11 .... s.17, s.22
      para. 12 .... s.23
      para. 13 .... s.23
      para. 14 .... s.23
      para. 15 .... s.23, s.34
      para. 16 .... s.23
      para. 17 .... s.23
      para. 18 .... s.23
      para. 19 .... s.23, s.33, s.40
          (1) s.23
          (2) s.23
          (3) s.23
          (4) s.23
          (5) s.23
          (6) s.23
          (7) s.23
          (8) s.23
      para. 20 .... s.23
      para. 21(6) s.29
      para. 22(5) s.17
      para. 23 ..... Sch. 13, Sch. 14
          (2) .... Sch. 14
      para. 24 .... s.108
      para. 27 .... s.108
   Sched. 3 .... Sch. 3
    Pt. I s.33, s.35, s.39
    Pt. II s.33, s.35, s.39
    Pt. III s.36, s.38
      para. 1 .... s.35, s.39, s.105
      para. 2 .... Sch. 13
      para. 3 .... s.35, s.39, Sch. 13
      para. 4 .... s.35, s.38
          (4) s.35
      para. 5 .... s.35, s.38
          (5) s.35
      para. 6 .... s.35, Sch. 14
          (2) s.35
      para. 7 .... s.35, s.39
      para. 8 .... s.35, s.39
          (1)(b) s.102
          (2)(b) s.102
      para. 9 .... s.35
          (2) s.35
      para. 11 .... s.35
   Sched. 4 .... s.53, s.60, Sch. 4
    Pt. II s.55
      para. 1 .... s.53
          (1) s.104
      para. 2 .... s.53
      para. 3 .... s.53
      para. 4 .... s.53, s.54, s.62
   Sched. 5 .... s.60, Sch. 5
    Pt. I s.60
      para. 6(6) s.60

1989 Children Act—*cont.*
   Sched. 5—*cont.*
    Pt. I—*cont.*
      para. 7... s.25, s.60, s.61, s.62
          (1) s.63
          (2)(c) s.60
          (f) s.60
      para. 8 .... s.60
   Sched. 6 .... s.63, Sch. 6
    Pt. I s.63
    Pt. II s.63
      para. 1(1) s.63
          (2) s.63
          (10) s.63
      para. 2 .... s.63
      para. 3 .... s.63
      para. 4 .... s.63
      para. 5 .... s.63
      para. 6 .... s.63
      para. 7 .... s.63
      para. 8 .... s.63, s.65
          (3) s.65
      para. 9 .... s.63
      para. 10 .... s.25
          (2) s.63
          (3) s.63
   Sched. 7 .... s.63, s.66, Sch. 7,
                          Sch. 8
      para. 2 .... s.63, s.66
      para. 4 .... s.63, Sch. 8
          (3) s.63
          (4) s.63
      para. 5 .... s.63, s.66
      para. 6 .... s.26
          (1) s.63
      para. 8(1)(e) s.63
   Sched. 8 .... s.66, Sch. 8
      para. 1 .... s.66
      para. 2 .... s.66
          (a) s.66
          (2) s.66
      para. 3 .... s.66
      para. 4 .... s.66
      para. 5 .... s.66
      para. 6 .... s.66, s.69
          (3) s.66
          (4) s.66
      para. 7 .... s.66, s.67
      para. 8 .... s.67, s.69
          (6) s.66
          (8) s.66
      para. 9 .... s.66, s.80
      para. 10 .... s.66, s.70
      para. 11 .... s.66
   Sched. 9 .... s.71, Sch. 9
      para. 1 .... s.71
          (2) s.71
      para. 2 .... s.71, s.77, s.78
          (3) s.71
      para. 3 .... s.19, s.71
      para. 4 .... s.19, s.71
      para. 5 .... s.71
      para. 6 .... s.71
      para. 7 .... s.71, s.74
      para. 8 .... s.71

1989	Children Act—*cont.*
	Sched. 10 .... s.88, Sch. 10
	Pt. I s.88
	Pt. II s.88
	para. 3 .... s.88
	para. 4 .... s.88
	para. 6(1) s.88
	para. 8(3) s.88
	para. 10(1) s.88
	para. 14(1) s.88
	para. 20 .... s.88
	para. 21 .... s.88
	para. 25 .... s.88
	para. 29 .... s.88
	Sched. 11 ... s.25, s.31, s.34, s.92, s.100, Sch. 11
	Pt. I s.92
	Pt. II s.92
	para. 1 .... s.92
	para. 2 .... s.92, s.94
	para. 3 .... s.48, s.92
	para. 4 .... s.44, s.92
	Sched. 12 ..... s.90, s.108, Sch. 12
	para. 1 .... s.108
	para. 5 .... s.9, s.33, Sch. 14
	(1) .... Sch. 14
	paras. 7–10 .... s.108
	para. 16(1) .... Sch. 14
	para. 18 .... s.108
	paras. 22–25 .... s.90
	para. 23 .... s.21, Sch. 14
	para. 27 .... s.50, s.108, Sch. 14
	para. 30(*a*) s.108
	para. 35 .... s.34, s.108
	para. 36 .... s.108
	paras. 41–44 .... s.108
	Sched. 13 .... s.108, Sch. 13
	para. 1 .... Sch. 14
	para. 5 .... s.2

1989	Children Act—*cont.*
	Sched. 13—*cont.*
	para. 8 .... s.36
	para. 9 .... s.87
	para. 10 .... s.3, s.36
	para. 11 .... s.17
	para. 12 .... s.36
	para. 13 .... s.36
	para. 14 .... s.36
	para. 15 .... s.36
	para. 16 .... s.36
	para. 18 .... s.36
	paras. 18–23 .... s.108
	para. 19 .... s.36
	para. 21 .... s.108
	para. 22 .... s.108
	para. 27 .... s.17
	para. 32 .... s.108
	para. 46 .... s.108
	para. 47 .... s.108
	para. 50 .... s.108
	para. 53 .... s.21
	para. 57 .... s.35, s.108
	para. 62 .... s.108
	para. 63 .... s.108
	para. 68(*a*)–(*e*) s.108
	paras. 69–71 .... s.108
	Sched. 14 .... s.108, Sch. 13, Sch. 14
	para. 1 .... s.108
	paras. 15–17 .... s.23
	para. 18 .... s.108
	para. 21 .... s.23
	paras. 28–30 .... s.108
	para. 33 .... s.108
	para. 34 .... s.108
	para. 38(*a*) s.108
	Sched. 15... s.21, s.31, s.36, s.108, Sch. 15

TABLE OF STATUTORY INSTRUMENTS

References are to sections and Schedules

1951 Administration of Children's
Homes Regulations (S.I.
1951 No. 1217) s.59, s.60

Local Authorities and Local
Education Authorities
(Allocation of Funding)
Regulations (S.I. 1951
No. 1472) s.30

1965 Rules of the Supreme Court
(S.I. 1965 No. 1766)—
Ord. 53, r.7 .... s.22

1970 Magistrates' Courts (Children
and Young Persons)
Rules (S.I. 1970 No.
1792) s.35, s.41

1972 Community Homes Regulations (S.I. 1972 No. 319) . s.53,
s.62

Health and Personal Social
Services (Northern Ire-
land) Order (S.I. 1972
No. 1265)—
Art. 16 .... Sch. 2, Sch. 10

1977 Matrimonial Causes Rules
(S.I. 1977 No. 344) s.13

1981 Education (Schools and Further Education) Regula-
tions (S.I. 1981 No.
1086)—
reg. 10 .... s.18

Magistrates Courts (Northern
Ireland) Order s.50

1983 Secure Accommodation (No.
2) Regulations (S.I. 1983
No. 1808) s.25
reg. 7 .... s.25
reg. 10 .... s.25

1987 Adoption (Northern Ireland)
Order (S.I. 1987 No.
2203) s.88
Art. 3 .... Sch. 8, Sch. 10
Art. 4 .... Sch. 10
Art. 12 .... Sch. 10
Art. 17 .... Sch. 10
    (1) .... Sch. 10
Art. 18 .... Sch. 10
    (1) .... Sch. 10
Art. 28 .... Sch. 10
Art. 29 .... Sch. 10
Art. 33 .... Sch. 10
Art. 54 .... Sch. 10
Art. 57 .... Sch. 10
Art. 63(1) .... Sch. 10
Income Support (General)
Regulations (S.I. 1987
No. 1967)—
reg. 13A s.24
reg. 40(2) s.17
reg. 53(1) s.24
Sched. 9,
para. 28 .... s.17
Family Credit (General)
Regulations (S.I. 1987
No. 1973)—
reg. 29(2) s.17
Sched. 3,
para. 18 .... s.17

1988 Accommodation of Children
(Charge and Control)
Regulations (S.I. 1988
No. 2183) s.23, s.32
Boarding Out of Children
(Foster Placement)
Regulations (S.I. 1988
No. 2184) s.20, s.23, s.59, s.62
r. 5(4) s.22

CHILDREN ACT 1989*

(1989 c. 41)

ARRANGEMENT OF SECTIONS

PART I

INTRODUCTORY

SECT.
1. Welfare of the child.
2. Parental responsibility for children.
3. Meaning of "parental responsibility".
4. Acquisition of parental responsibility by father.
5. Appointment of guardians.
6. Guardians: revocation and disclaimer.
7. Welfare reports.

PART II

ORDERS WITH RESPECT TO CHILDREN IN FAMILY PROCEEDINGS

General

8. Residence, contact and other orders with respect to children.
9. Restrictions on making section 8 orders.
10. Power of court to make section 8 orders.
11. General principles and supplementary provisions.
12. Residence orders and parental responsibility.
13. Change of child's name or removal from jurisdiction.
14. Enforcement of residence orders.

Financial relief

15. Orders for financial relief with respect to children.

Family assistance orders

16. Family assistance orders.

PART III

LOCAL AUTHORITY SUPPORT FOR CHILDREN AND FAMILIES

Provision of services for children and their families

17. Provision of services for children in need, their families and others.
18. Day care for pre-school and other children.
19. Review of provision for day care, child minding etc.

Provision of accommodation for children

20. Provision of accommodation for children: general.
21. Provision of accommodation for children in police protection or detention or on remand, etc.

Duties of local authorities in relation to children looked after by them

22. General duty of local authority in relation to children looked after by them.
23. Provision of accommodation and maintenance by local authority for children whom they are looking after.

---

* Annotations by Judith Masson, M.A. (Cantab.), Ph.D. (Leicester), Lecturer in Law, University of Leicester.

Advice and assistance for certain children

SECT.
24. Advice and assistance for certain children.

Secure accommodation

25. Use of accommodation for restricting liberty.

Supplemental

26. Review of cases and inquiries into representations.
27. Co-operation between authorities.
28. Consultation with local education authorities.
29. Recoupment of cost of providing services etc.
30. Miscellaneous.

PART IV

CARE AND SUPERVISION

General

31. Care and supervision orders.
32. Period within which application for order under this Part must be disposed of.

Care orders

33. Effect of care order.
34. Parental contact etc. with children in care.

Supervision orders

35. Supervision orders.
36. Education supervision orders.

Powers of court

37. Powers of court in certain family proceedings.
38. Interim orders.
39. Discharge and variation etc. of care orders and supervision orders.
40. Orders pending appeals in cases about care or supervision orders.

Guardians ad litem

41. Representation of child and of his interests in certain proceedings.
42. Right of guardian ad litem to have access to local authority records.

PART V

PROTECTION OF CHILDREN

43. Child assessment orders.
44. Orders for emergency protection of children.
45. Duration of emergency protection orders and other supplemental provisions.
46. Removal and accommodation of children by police in cases of emergency.
47. Local authority's duty to investigate.
48. Powers to assist in discovery of children who may be in need of emergency protection.
49. Abduction of children in care etc.
50. Recovery of abducted children etc.
51. Refuges for children at risk.
52. Rules and regulations.

PART VI

COMMUNITY HOMES

SECT.
53. Provision of community homes by local authorities.
54. Directions that premises be no longer used for community home.
55. Determination of disputes relating to controlled and assisted community homes.
56. Discontinuance by voluntary organisation of controlled or assisted community home.
57. Closure by local authority of controlled or assisted community home.
58. Financial provisions applicable on cessation of controlled or assisted community home or disposal etc. of premises.

PART VII

VOLUNTARY HOMES AND VOLUNTARY ORGANISATIONS

59. Provision of accommodation by voluntary organisations.
60. Registration and regulation of voluntary homes.
61. Duties of voluntary organisations.
62. Duties of local authorities.

PART VIII

REGISTERED CHILDREN'S HOMES

63. Children not to be cared for and accommodated in unregistered children's homes.
64. Welfare of children in children's homes.
65. Persons disqualified from carrying on, or being employed in, children's homes.

PART IX

PRIVATE ARRANGEMENTS FOR FOSTERING CHILDREN

66. Privately fostered children.
67. Welfare of privately fostered children.
68. Persons disqualified from being private foster parents.
69. Power to prohibit private fostering.
70. Offences.

PART X

CHILD MINDING AND DAY CARE FOR YOUNG CHILDREN

71. Registration.
72. Requirements to be complied with by child minders.
73. Requirements to be complied with by persons providing day care for young children.
74. Cancellation of registration.
75. Protection of children in an emergency.
76. Inspection.
77. Appeals.
78. Offences.
79. Application of this Part to Scotland.

PART XI

SECRETARY OF STATE'S SUPERVISORY FUNCTIONS AND RESPONSIBILITIES

80. Inspection of children's homes etc. by persons authorised by Secretary of State.
81. Inquiries.

SECT.
82. Financial support by Secretary of State.
83. Research and returns of information.
84. Local authority failure to comply with statutory duty: default power of Secretary of State.

PART XII

MISCELLANEOUS AND GENERAL

Notification of children accommodated in certain establishments

85. Children accommodated by health authorities and local education authorities.
86. Children accommodated in residential care, nursing or mental nursing homes.
87. Welfare of children accommodated in independent schools.

Adoption

88. Amendments of adoption legislation.

Paternity tests

89. Tests to establish paternity.

Criminal care and supervision orders

90. Care and supervision orders in criminal proceedings.

Effect and duration of orders etc.

91. Effect and duration of orders etc.

Jurisdiction and procedure etc.

92. Jurisdiction of courts.
93. Rules of court.
94. Appeals.
95. Attendance of child at hearing under Part IV or V.
96. Evidence given by, or with respect to, children.
97. Privacy for children involved in certain proceedings.
98. Self-incrimination.
99. Legal aid.
100. Restrictions on use of wardship jurisdiction.
101. Effect of orders as between England and Wales and Northern Ireland, the Channel Islands or the Isle of Man.

Search warrants

102. Power of constable to assist in exercise of certain powers to search for children or inspect premises.

General

103. Offences by bodies corporate.
104. Regulations and orders.
105. Interpretation.
106. Financial provisions.
107. Application to Channel Islands.
108. Short title, commencement, extent, etc.

SCHEDULES:
Schedule 1 —Financial Provision for Children.
Schedule 2 —Local Authority Support for Children and Families.
    Part I —Provision of Services for Families.
    Part II —Children Looked After by Local Authorities.
    Part III —Contributions Towards Maintenance of Children.
Schedule 3 —Supervision Orders.
    Part I —General.
    Part II —Miscellaneous.
    Part III —Education Supervision Orders.

Schedule 4 —Management and Conduct of Community Homes.
    Part I —Instruments of Management.
    Part II —Management of Controlled and Assisted Community Homes.
    Part III —Regulations.
Schedule 5 —Voluntary Homes.
    Part I —Registration of Voluntary Homes.
    Part II —Regulations as to Voluntary Homes.
Schedule 6 —Registered Children's Homes.
    Part I —Registration.
    Part II —Regulations.
Schedule 7 —Foster Parents: Limits on Number of Foster Children.
Schedule 8 —Privately Fostered Children.
Schedule 9 —Child Minding and Day Care for Young Children.
Schedule 10 —Amendments of Adoption Legislation.
    Part I —Amendments of Adoption 1976.
    Part II —Amendments of Adoption (Scotland) Act 1978.
Schedule 11 —Jurisdiction.
    Part I —General.
    Part II —Consequential Amendments.
Schedule 12 —Minor Amendments.
Schedule 13 —Consequential Amendments.
Schedule 14 —Transitionals and Savings.
Schedule 15 —Repeals.

An Act to reform the law relating to children; to provide for local authority services for children in need and others; to amend the law with respect to children's homes, community homes, voluntary homes and voluntary organisations; to make provision with respect to fostering, child minding and day care for young children and adoption; and for connected purposes. [16th November 1989]

PARLIAMENTARY DEBATES

Hansard, H.L. Vol. 502, cols. 21, 487, 1130, 1147, 1225, 1252, 1341; Vol. 503, cols. 113, 209, 333, 496, 549, 1318, 1409, 1438, 1533; Vol. 504, col. 294; Vol. 505, col. 341; Vol. 512, col. 717; H.C. Vol. 151, col. 1107; Vol. 158, cols. 474, 619, 1288.

The Bill was considered in Standing Committee B from May 9 to June 13, 1989.

INTRODUCTION AND GENERAL NOTE

Introduction

"The most comprehensive and far reaching reform of child law which has come before Parliament in living memory". *Per* Lord Mackay (*Hansard*, H.L. Vol. 502, col. 488).

This Act reforms and brings together the public and private law relating to children. The reforms to private law are those recommended by the Law Commission in their report "Review of Child Law: Guardianship and Custody", Law Com. No. 172. It substantially recasts child care law following many of the recommendations in the Department of Health and Social Security (D.H.S.S.) *Review of Child Care Law* and the White Paper *The Law on Child Care and Family Services* (1987) Cm. 62. It repeals and replaces the Guardianship of Minors Act 1971, the Guardianship Act 1973, much of the Children and Young Persons Act 1969 and all of the Nurseries and Childminders Regulations Act 1948, the Children Act 1975, the Child Care Act 1980, the Foster Child Act 1980, the Children's Homes Act 1982 and the Children and Young Persons (Amendment) Act 1986. The only area of child law to which there are few changes is child support.

The Act is divided into 12 parts, each one relating to a different aspect of child law, but, as the Lord Chancellor repeatedly stated during its passage through Parliament, it must be read as a whole. It is important to note that the provisions of Pt. I inform the interpretation of the Act generally by stating the principle which the courts must apply in considering certain cases concerning children—the welfare principle—and defining the rights of parents and guardians. The Schedules contain important details of the private law of child support; local authorities' duties to children in the community and to children they are looking after and the duties of other people and organisations caring for children. Many of the detailed rules which are necessary to bring this law into operation relating to, for example, party status and the jurisdiction of the courts have been left to regulations. In other areas there is provision for the Secretary of State to make regulations but these are not essential. Drafting errors in the Act are being corrected in the Courts and Legal Services Bill, s.79 and Sched. 10 which is currently before Parliament.

Background

Concern about the state of child care law expressed by the Short Committee led to the setting up of the D.H.S.S. Review of Child Care Law in 1984. The law was seen as providing an inadequate framework for child protection and preventive work and failing to facilitate parental involvement in the lives of children accommodated by local authorities. It was also far too complex with a collection of sometimes contradictory provisions in different statutes. *The Review of Child Care Law* (R.C.C.L.) recommended major changes to child care law, many of which were accepted by the Government in the White Paper which followed (Cm. 62). The reports of three child death inquiries concerning Jasmine Beckford, Kimberley Carlile and Tyra Henry strengthened views that the law should be clarified and the powers of social workers increased. The Cleveland crisis and the subsequent inquiry turned attention to control of social work decision-making particularly by strengthening the position of the courts. However, despite the many recommendations in these reports, the Children Act 1989 is largely based on the proposals in the White Paper and the R.C.C.L.

In 1984 the Law Commission started a wide ranging review of private law as part of its family law programme. This provided the opportunity not only to reform the law but also to ensure harmonisation between the public and private law relating to children. Report No. 172, containing the Law Commission's recommendations, was published in 1988.

Major Changes

The aim of the legislation is to provide a clear and consistent code for the whole of child law which is comprehensible to all who deal with this area; to avoid problems caused by conflicting powers in public and private law and the confusion engendered by conflicting jurisdiction over children's cases. It realigns the balance between families and the State so as:– to protect families from unwarranted State interference; to emphasise that local authorities have an important role in supporting families in difficulty; and to indicate that there is a continuing role for parents when their children are looked after by a local authority. Local authorities will not be able to by-pass the statutory code by resorting to wardship. The legislation also adjusts the relative power and responsibilities of local authorities and the courts. It will no longer be possible for a court to commit a child into the care of a local authority without a formal application from either the authority or the N.S.P.C.C. Instead, a court concerned about the care of a child will be able to order the local authority to investigate the situation and report back. The High Court will not be able to commit wards to local authority care. Court orders will be needed to retain a child in compulsory care in all cases but local authority decision-making about children in care will not be subject to court direction or review even from the High Court, except in relation to access and emigration. The Lord Chancellor is empowered to make orders concerning admissibility of children's evidence reversing *Re H. Re K.* [1989] Fam.Law 388.

Private Law

(1) Parents and guardians (ss.2–6).

Parenthood replaces guardianship as the key concept from which rights are derived and defined. The "bundle of rights" held by married parents, guardians and those with court orders is labelled "parental responsibility" but not defined in detail in the statute. Unmarried fathers may acquire parental responsibility by a formal agreement under s.4. Parental responsibility can be held by a number of people; parents and guardians do not lose it when others acquire it (except if there is an adoption order), nor when a care order is made, but their freedom to exercise it is restricted.

(2) Court orders (ss.8 and 16).

Orders for custody, care and control and access are abolished and replaced by new orders: "contact orders" replace "access orders"; "residence orders" replace orders for "legal custody", "actual custody" and "custodianship".

There are also three new orders: "prohibited steps orders", a type of injunction; "specific issue orders", where the court decides a particular question about care; "family assistance orders", which replace supervision orders in family proceedings.

(3) The right to apply (ss.9 and 10)

Limitations on applications for court orders are lifted. People who could apply for custody outside wardship—parents, step-parents, guardians and those qualified for custodianship—will be able to apply for "residence" or "contact orders" without leave. Other people, grandparents, foster parents and the child must seek leave for any section 8 order.

Public law: Care

(1) Children in care (ss.20 and 22).

The "voluntary" care system is retained but children under such care are called "children accommodated by the local authority". There is no notice requirement for removing such a child from accommodation; children over 16 years cannot be removed against their will. "Parental rights resolutions" are abolished—a child can only be retained in care compulsorily if a care order is obtained (s.31). Only children who are committed to care under a care order are referred to as "in care". Children cared for by a local authority in exercise of its functions under the Act are referred to as children "looked after by the local authority" (s.22).

(2) Local authority duties.

There is a duty to "safeguard and promote" the welfare of all "children in need" and promote their upbringing by their families (s.17). The duty to give "first consideration" to the welfare of a child in care in s.18 of the Child Care Act 1980 is replaced by a duty to "safeguard and promote" the welfare of any child "looked after" by the authority (s.22). There are new duties to prepare children to leave care and to advise, etc., people under 21 who have been in care (s.24). There is a new power in the Secretary of State to deal with local authorities who are in default (s.84).

(3) Grounds for care proceedings (s.31).

These are completely recast. Truancy cases will be dealt with by "education supervision orders" (s.36), although prosecution of parents (and in some cases care orders) will continue to be available. Local authorities will be able to appeal against refusal of a care order and the order may be continued pending the appeal (ss.94, 40).

(4) Interim orders (s.38).

The test for interim care and supervision orders is clarified—the court must be satisfied that there are "reasonable grounds for believing" that the grounds in s.31 exist. New time limits are set—the maximum duration for the first interim order is eight weeks and for subsequent orders four weeks, but there is no limit on the number of subsequent orders.

(5) Investigation and assessment (ss.43 and 47).

The local authority's responsibilities in investigating cases where a child may be harmed are clarified. They have a duty to see the child. Where an assessment is necessary, but the parents refuse to agree, the applicant may seek a "child assessment order" lasting up to seven days (s.43).

(6) Emergency protection (ss.44–46).

"Place of safety orders" are replaced with more restrictive "emergency protection orders", which last for eight days, can be extended for seven days, and are subject to review after 72 hours. The test for an emergency protection order appears more stringent—the court, not the applicant, must have "reasonable cause to believe that the child is likely to suffer significant harm"—but an order may be available where access to the child has been unreasonably refused. Police powers to detain children for their protection are limited to 72 hours.

(7) Use of wardship (s.100).

Children may no longer be committed to care in wardship proceedings. Local authorities are restricted severely in their use of wardship and will require leave to make an application.

(8) Access to children in care (s.34).

Local authorities are under a duty to "endeavour to promote contact" between children looked after by them and a wide range of family members and friends (Sched. 2, para. 15). Care orders will automatically include a provision allowing the child reasonable contact with parents, guardians etc. Disagreements about contact and its termination will be for the court.

(9) Powers of the courts.

Children will only be able to be committed to care after an application by a local authority or the N.S.P.C.C. The court will be able to direct an investigation (s.37). The power to commit to care in matrimonial, etc., proceedings is abolished—no court will be able to make a care order unless the grounds in s.31 are proved.

(10) Juvenile justice.

Care orders in criminal proceedings (s.7(7)) are abolished and replaced with supervision orders with a residence requirement (Sched. 12, para. 23).

Public law: Day Care

(1) Local authority duties.

There is a qualified duty to provide day care for under fives and supervised activities for older children who are in need. There is a power to provide for others (s.17). Local authorities must review the day care provision in their area at least every three years (s.19).

(2) Childminding and nurseries (ss.71–79).

Local authorities' powers and duties to register and inspect day care provision are clarified. Registration is now required in relation to care of children under the age of eight years. A new enforcement notice procedure is created to deal with unregistered childminders.

Public Law: other care

Local authorities are given new responsibilities for the welfare of children cared for by health authorities or local education authorities (s.85) and for children in residential care homes, nursing homes or mental nursing homes (s.86) and for children in independent boarding schools (s.87). After-care must also be provided (s.24). Those providing care must notify the local authority. The Act makes provision for safe houses for runaways (s.51).

Courts Structure, Jurisdiction and Legal Aid

The foundations of a new structure for dealing with cases under this Act and the Adoption Act 1976 are put in place. The "domestic court" is renamed the "family proceedings court" and will be able to handle most cases. Care cases will usually start in that court but the rules will contain a power to transfer cases to specified county courts or the High Court (s.92 and Sched. 11, Pt. I). Appeals in care cases will be heard in the High Court, not the Crown Court (s.94). Care proceedings are brought within the Civil legal aid scheme (s.99).

Transitional Provisions

These are set out in Sched. 14. Existing private law orders will continue to have effect subject to modification—non custodial parents will have parental responsibility. Existing public law orders or resolutions will be deemed to be care orders.

Commencement

The Act will be brought into force on the date or dates to be appointed (s.108(2)), but ss.89, 96(3)–(7) and Sched. 12, para. 35, which relate to tests to establish paternity, children's evidence and the definition of "parent" in the Child Care Act 1980, will come into effect immediately. Sched. 12, para. 36, which empowers local authorities to pay for special education overseas, will come into effect after two months.

Extent (s.108)

The whole Act applies to England and Wales. Pt. X which relates to nurseries and childminders and other provisions listed in s.108(11), applies to Scotland. The Adoption (Scotland) Act is amended by s.88(2) and Sched. 10, Pt. II. The provisions listed in s.108(12) apply to Northern Ireland. Parts of the Act may be extended to the Channel Islands by Order (s.107).

ABBREVIATIONS

C.C.A. 1980	: Child Care Act 1980.
C.Y.P.A. 1933	: Children and Young Persons Act 1933.
C.Y.P.A. 1969	: Children and Young Persons Act 1969.
Cleveland Report	: Report of the Inquiry into child abuse in Cleveland 1987 (Cm. 412 1988).
Cm. 62	: The Law on Child Care and Family Services.
D.H.S.S.	: Department of Health and Social Security.
D.P.M.C.A. 1988	: Domestic Proceedings and Magistrates' Courts Act 1978.
D.V.M.P.A. 1976	: Domestic Violence and Matrimonial Proceedings Act 1976.
F.L.R.A. 1987	: Family Law Reform Act 1987.
G.M.A. 1971	: Guardianship of Minors Act 1971.
Law Com. 172	: Law Commission Report No. 172: Review of Child Law: Guardianship and Custody (1988).
M.C.A. 1973	: Matrimonial Causes Act 1973.
N.S.P.C.C.	: National Society for the Prevention of Cruelty to Children.

R.C.C.L.   D.H.S.S. Review of Child Care Law (1985).
Short Committee : House of Commons Second Report from the Social Services Com-
                   mittee 1983–4: Children in Care H.C.P. 360.
W.P. 91   : Law Commission Working Paper No. 91, Review of Child Law:
                   Guardianship (1985).
W.P. 96   : Law Commission Working Paper No. 96, Review of Child Law:
                   Custody (1986).

PART I

INTRODUCTORY

Welfare of the child

1.—(1) When a court determines any question with respect to—

(a) the upbringing of a child; or

(b) the administration of a child's property or the application of any income arising from it,

the child's welfare shall be the court's paramount consideration.

(2) In any proceedings in which any question with respect to the upbringing of a child arises, the court shall have regard to the general principle that any delay in determining the question is likely to prejudice the welfare of the child.

(3) In the circumstances mentioned in subsection (4), a court shall have regard in particular to—

(a) the ascertainable wishes and feelings of the child concerned (considered in the light of his age and understanding);

(b) his physical, emotional and educational needs;

(c) the likely effect on him of any change in his circumstances,

(d) his age, sex, background and any characteristics of his which the court considers relevant;

(e) any harm which he has suffered or is at risk of suffering;

(f) how capable each of his parents, and any other person in relation to whom the court considers the question to be relevant, is of meeting his needs;

(g) the range of powers available to the court under this Act in the proceedings in question.

(4) The circumstances are that—

(a) the court is considering whether to make, vary or discharge a section 8 order, and the making, variation or discharge of the order is opposed by any party to the proceedings; or

(b) the court is considering whether to make, vary or discharge an order under Part IV.

(5) Where a court is considering whether or not to make one or more orders under this Act with respect to a child, it shall not make the order or any of the orders unless it considers that doing so would be better for the child than making no order at all.

DEFINITIONS
   "child": ss.9(6), 105(1).
   "harm": ss.31(9), 105(1).
   "section 8 order": ss.8, 11(7).
   "the court": s.92(7).
   "upbringing": s.105(1).

GENERAL NOTE
   This section lays down general principles for courts dealing with cases involving children. It warns courts that delay is likely to prejudice the welfare of the child (subs. (2)). It re-

enacts, with modification (removing the word custody—the concept of custody forms no part of the new code), s.1(1) of the G.M.A. 1971 and expands the meaning of welfare by providing a checklist (subs. (3)) to assist the courts in specific contested cases (subs. (4)) as recommended in Law Com. 172, para. 3.17. In all cases the court is expressly required to consider whether or not *any* order should be made (subs. (5)).

Subs. (1)

Any question. It has been suggested that there are some questions relating to children which are not governed by the paramountcy rules: the decision whether or not a book about a child's father should be banned (*Re X* [1975] Fam. 47 *per* Pennycuick J.).

In *Richards* v. *Richards* [1984] A.C. 174 the majority of the House of Lords held that a child's welfare was not paramount in any case concerning an exclusion injunction which fell to be decided under the Matrimonial Homes Act 1983, s.1(3). This was extended in *Lee* v. *Lee* (1983) 127 S.J. 696 to exclusion orders sought by an unmarried person but there have been suggestions in the Court of Appeal that in some ouster cases the child's welfare is paramount (*Wilde* v. *Wilde* (1988) 18 Fam.Law 202). The wide power to make residence orders may again encourage the courts to attempt to side-step *Richards* by including a term that one parent must leave the place where the child is living. Maintenance is excluded from the definition of upbringing in the Act. Orders relating to maintenance after divorce are also not subject to the test in s.1 but to the requirement in s.25(1) of the Matrimonial Causes Act 1973 to give "first consideration" to welfare.

Upbringing: The Lord Chancellor said this is "a word of general scope" which includes "education and social life while being reared" (*Hansard*, H.L. Vol. 502, col. 1168). It does not include maintenance. The word "custody" has been removed because this concept no longer forms part of child law.

The child's welfare: A child is anyone under the age of 18 years, but the court's power to make orders is restricted by s.9(7) to under 16s unless the case is exceptional. This would seem to put an added gloss on the welfare test. Welfare is not defined but the checklist in subs. (4) indicates some of the issues which may be relevant. Case law will continue to suggest what the judiciary consider to be in children's welfare; psychological and other literature will provide a basis for argument.

Paramount: This does not mean "first and paramount", which Lord Scarman described as a pleonism (*Hansard*, H.L. Vol. 502, col. 1165). "First and paramount" was explained by Lord MacDermott in *J* v. *C* [1970] A.C. 668. The Law Commission noted some confusion from the inclusion of "first" (Law Com. 172, para. 3.13) and proposed a statutory version of the modern accepted interpretation found in cases such as *Re K.D.* [1988] A.C. 806. In the debate the Lord Chancellor explained the new wording as follows (*Hansard*, H.L. Vol. 502, col. 1167): "the welfare of the child should come before and above any other consideration in deciding whether to make an order." Thus the new wording should leave welfare determining decisions and not just heading a list of factors to be considered. The Law Commission also recommended a provision which would indicate how the court should approach cases involving more than one child where the welfare of each conflicted. No such provision was included in the Act so each case must be considered individually without regard to the effect on other children.

Subs. (2)

This may be used to justify a refusal to order reports but is intended to promote prompt action.

Subs. (3)

The value of a checklist was explained in Law Com. 172, para. 3.18. It can guide the courts and help achieve consistency across the country, inform legal advisers and encourage those in dispute to concentrate on the issues which affect their children.

Regard in particular: Other aspects may be considered.

Ascertainable: There is greater emphasis in the Act on consulting children and finding out their views. The courts should not merely suggest that a child is too young to be consulted, nor should they rely on what a parent says the child wants. Guardians ad litem in care proceedings attempt to discover the views of children as young as three years old. The power in s.7(1) to ask for a report from a welfare officer will be very useful, and it will also be important for counsel to be well-versed in the methods used by social workers and others to find out what children want.

Needs: The emphasis should be on an objective assessment of the needs of the individual child but there is a danger that subjectivity in the form of preferences for particular lifestyles might be introduced here, as in *May* v. *May* [1986] 1 E.L.R. 325. Again, it will be important to see the reasons given for identifying particular needs.

Likely effect: Again, evidence should be required.

Any change: There was clear evidence from Eekelaar and Clive *Custody after divorce* (1977) that the status quo was an extremely important factor in determining custody in the past. Child psychologists have also stressed the importance of stability and continuity for healthy development.

Any other person: There is a power in s.10(1)(b) to make orders in favour of any person even without a formal application, *e.g.* partners of parents.

The range of powers: Under the Act, the range of powers is wider than in the previous law. The court can grant anyone any section 8 order (s.10(1)(b)), even where there has been no application, and make the new "family assistance orders" (s.16). The orders themselves also allow the court to direct matters to a greater extent. The court also has a power to prevent further applications under Pts. I and II, that is, applications for parental responsibility (s.4), guardianship (s.5) and section 8 orders without leave (s.91(14)).

Subs. (4)

The Law Commission was concerned that the court should not impose its notion of welfare on parties, provided of course, that their proposals were acceptable. This would put too great a burden on the court (Law Com. 172, para. 3.19). The checklist in subs. (3) is only mandated where the court is considering a contested section 8 order, a care order, a supervision or education supervision order, or an order relating to contact with a child in care. However, the Lord Chancellor suggested that the court could refer to it in other cases (*Hansard*, H.L. Vol. 502, col. 1203), but this does not appear clear from the wording. In so far as the checklist contains a definition of welfare, this may be so, but the courts would appear to be free to disregard listed factors or consider others where the checklist is not mandated, *e.g.* in contested applications by unmarried fathers for parental responsibility (s.4) or disputes about guardianship (s.5).

Opposed by any party to the proceedings: Party status is to be left to rules of court to be made under s.93. Although children have greater rights to make applications with leave under s.10(8), it seems likely that they will not automatically be parties in cases involving them, except care proceedings, because the Lord Chancellor indicated that the status quo would prevail (*Hansard*, H.L. Vol. 502, col. 534).

Subs. (5)

This reflects the Law Commission's view that orders were sometimes unnecessary and could discourage parties negotiating arrangements and remaining involved with their children after separation or divorce (see s.10(1)). However, it is important to note that there are some undesirable consequences of not obtaining an order. Non-parents who look after children without a residence order will not have parental responsibility for the child. This affects their rights in relation to the parents, the local authority and the child. Where a parent has a residence order, the other parent's actions are limited generally by s.2(8) and specifically by s.5 (circumstances when an appointment of a guardian takes effect) and s.13 (covers name change and removal from the jurisdiction). If there is a possibility of abduction, the existence of an order will be important for recovery of the child abroad under the Child Abduction and Custody Act 1985. An order is not necessary for removal of the child to be illegal under the Child Abduction Act 1984. Such removal would thus be wrongful under Art. 3 of the Hague Convention on International Child Abduction. However, if there is no order the European Convention on recognition and enforcement of custody decisions will not assist recovery; an order obtained after removal would be sufficient (Art. 12). A court order is not required to operate the port-stop procedure (*per* David Mellor, Minister of Health, Standing Committee B, col. 506).

Parental responsibility for children

2.—(1) Where a child's father and mother were married to each other at the time of his birth, they shall each have parental responsibility for the child.

(2) Where a child's father and mother were not married to each other at the time of his birth—

(a) the mother shall have parental responsibility for the child;

(b) the father shall not have parental responsibility for the child, unless he acquires it in accordance with the provisions of this Act.

(3) References in this Act to a child whose father and mother were, or (as the case may be) were not, married to each other at the time of his birth must be read with section 1 of the Family Law Reform Act 1987 (which extends their meaning).

(4) The rule of law that a father is the natural guardian of his legitimate child is abolished.

(5) More than one person may have parental responsibility for the same child at the same time.

(6) A person who has parental responsibility for a child at any time shall not cease to have that responsibility solely because some other person subsequently acquires parental responsibility for the child.

(7) Where more than one person has parental responsibility for a child, each of them may act alone and without the other (or others) in meeting that responsibility; but nothing in this Part shall be taken to affect the operation of any enactment which requires the consent of more than one person in a matter affecting the child.

(8) The fact that a person has parental responsibility for a child shall not entitle him to act in any way which would be incompatible with any order made with respect to the child under this Act.

(9) A person who has parental responsibility for a child may not surrender or transfer any part of that responsibility to another but may arrange for some or all of it to be met by one or more persons acting on his behalf.

(10) The person with whom any such arrangement is made may himself be a person who already has parental responsibility for the child concerned.

(11) The making of any such arrangement shall not affect any liability of the person making it which may arise from any failure to meet any part of his parental responsibility for the child concerned.

DEFINITIONS
"child": s.105(1).
"married . . . at the time of his birth": s.2(3).
"parental responsibility": ss.2, 3, 12.

GENERAL NOTE
This states the rules relating to the allocation of parental responsibility between parents. It largely re-enacts current law using the term "parental responsibility" in place of "parental rights and duties". If a child's parents were married at the time of his birth (or subsequently if the child is legitimated (see Legitimacy Act 1976, s.2)), both have parental responsibility (subs. (1)), otherwise only the mother has it (subs. (2)). Parental responsibility can be held by several people concurrently (subs. (5)) and is not lost when another person, or the local authority (see s.33(3)), acquires it (subs. (6)). Each person who has parental responsibility may take action alone to meet it unless there is a statutory requirement to the contrary (subs. (7)), but cannot do anything incompatible with any order under this Act (subs. (8)). This section also clarifies the position about agreements between people with parental responsibility and others about the care of children. Parental responsibility cannot be surrendered (subs. (9)) but arrangements can be made for others to meet it, although this does not remove the primary responsibility (subs. (10)).

Subs. (1)
Father and mother: Unmarried fathers are now included within the definition of father, rather than as relatives as they were under the C.C.A. 1980 because of s.1 of the F.L.R.A. 1987. Step-parents are relatives (s.105(1)). The position in relation to children born to a married woman as a result of A.I.D. is settled by s.27(1) of the F.L.R.A. 1987. This provides that the child "shall be treated as a child of the parties to that marriage and not be treated as the child of any other person". It follows that the biological father is not the father in such cases. S.27 does not apply to egg-implant and the corresponding issue of defining the mother. However, it would seem that the egg donor, not the birth mother, is the legal mother because s.23 indicates that parentage is to be proved by biological samples.

This is not what was recommended by the Warnock report, nor was it apparently intended (see *Montgomery* [1987] J.S.W.L. 321).

At the time of the birth: This must be interpreted in accordance with the F.L.R.A. 1987, s.1(2)(3). It thus includes: some children of void marriages treated as legitimate (Legitimacy Act 1976, s.1 as amended by F.L.R.A. 1987, s.28); legitimated children (Legitimacy Act 1976, s.2); adopted children (Adoption Act 1976, s.39); children otherwise treated as legitimate.

Each: This means separately (see subss. (5) and (7)).

Subs. (2)

In accordance with the provisions of this Act: An unmarried father can acquire parental responsibility: by obtaining a residence order s.12(1); by applying to the court under s.4(1)(a); by making an agreement with the mother in the "prescribed form" under s.4(1)(b); by being appointed the child's guardian by the court (s.5(1)); by being appointed the child's guardian by the mother or another guardian under s.5. The appointment as guardian will not take effect while the mother is alive (s.5(8)).

Subs. (3)

See subs. (1) for details of s.1 of the F.L.R.A. 1987.

Natural guardian: The concept of natural guardianship became irrelevant when the Guardianship Act 1973 gave the mother "like powers"; it is now abolished.

Subs. (7)

Consents: The following actions require the consents of more than one person (usually all people with parental responsibility):

(1) Adoption/freeing for adoption: Adoption Act 1976, ss.16 and 18, but note those who acquire parental responsibility by virtue of a residence order (s.12(3)) or a care order (s.33(6)) do not have the right to consent.
(2) Removal from the jurisdiction: Child Abduction Act 1984.
(3) Marriage: Marriage Act 1949, s.3 and Sched. 2, amended by Sched. 13, para. 5 of this Act.
(4) Applications by non-parents for residence orders and contact orders: Children Act 1989, s.10(5).
(5) Name change/removal from the U.K. (where a residence order or care order is in force): Children Act 1989, ss.13, 33(7).
(6) Provision of local authority accommodation or the removal of a child from it (but only where a residence order is in force): Children Act 1989, s.20(10).

Subs. (8)

This provision is crucial to the new structure because parental responsibility will only be lost by a parent if the child is adopted. Under the old law many rights were suspended where the child was subject to a care order and, after *Dipper* v. *Dipper* [1981] Fam. 31, the position following a custody order was unclear. Now parents will retain parental responsibility but their actions will be limited if there is an order. The Law Commission recommended this change so that the law would clearly recognise that the responsibility of being a parent continued although what was required of parents changed with change of circumstances. In para. 2.11 of Law Com. 172 they gave this example:

"If the child has to live with one parent and go to a school near his home, it would be incompatible with that order for the other parent to arrange for him to have his hair done in a way which will exclude him from school".

It seems unlikely that this provision will be enforceable by contempt proceedings unless the order is very specific. Where it was important to have greater clarity a "prohibited steps order" may be necessary (see ss.8, 9(5)).

Subs. (9)

This replaces the provision in s.1(2) of the Guardianship Act 1973 (as amended by the Family Law Reform Act 1987, s.3) which allowed agreements between separated parents about the exercise of their rights but prevented enforcement if the court thought this was not for the benefit of the child. The common law position that there can be no surrender is restored but modified to allow delegation. Delegation does not remove primary responsibility but clarifies that the delegated person, for example a nanny, a boarding school or another substitute carer has authority to act. Some delegation arrangements will give rise to further obligations under Pts. VII–X and XII which cover different types of substitute care. The position of the person to whom responsibility is delegated is clarified in s.3(5).

Subs. (11)

Any liability: For example, either under the criminal law (see C.Y.P.A. 1933), or to ensure an adequate standard of care which is enforceable through care proceedings under s.31 of this Act, or civil liability to the child.

Meaning of "parental responsibility"

3.—(1) In this Act "parental responsibility" means all the rights, duties, powers, responsibilities and authority which by law a parent of a child has in relation to the child and his property.

(2) It also includes the rights, powers and duties which a guardian of the child's estate (appointed, before the commencement of section 5, to act generally) would have had in relation to the child and his property.

(3) The rights referred to in subsection (2) include, in particular, the right of the guardian to receive or recover in his own name, for the benefit of the child, property of whatever description and wherever situated which the child is entitled to receive or recover.

(4) The fact that a person has, or does not have, parental responsibility for a child shall not affect—

(a) any obligation which he may have in relation to the child (such as a statutory duty to maintain the child); or

(b) any rights which, in the event of the child's death, he (or any other person) may have in relation to the child's property.

(5) A person who—

(a) does not have parental responsibility for a particular child; but

(b) has care of the child,

may (subject to the provisions of this Act) do what is reasonable in all the circumstances of the case for the purpose of safeguarding or promoting the child's welfare.

DEFINITIONS

"child": s.105(1).

"guardian": ss.5, 105(1).

"parental responsibility": ss.2, 3, 12.

GENERAL NOTE

This contains the definition, or rather "non-definition" (*per* Lord Meston, *Hansard*, H.L. Vol. 502, col. 1172), of parental responsibility. Apart from specific points, which will be noted when they occur, the change to "parental responsibility" would seem to be merely a cosmetic one. The Law Commission rejected as impractical a proposal that parental rights and duties should be listed. Therefore it is necessary to return to the common law for a full understanding of the legal position of those with parental responsibility over children (see H. Bevan, *Child Law*, Butterworths, 2nd ed. (1989); Hoggett, *Parents and Children*, Sweet & Maxwell, 3rd ed. (1987).

The decision in *Gillick* v. *West Norfolk Area Health Authority* [1986] A.C. 112 limited the power of parents to make decisions for their mature and capable children. Although Lord Mackay said in Committee,

"This Bill does nothing to change the underlying principle of *Gillick* which has to be taken into account by all who exercise parental responsibility over a child mature and intelligent enough to take decisions for himself". (*Hansard*, H.L. Vol. 502, col. 1351) it appears that the Act both removes rights which young people have and fails to establish procedures which will allow them to be fully involved in decision-making where there is a dispute before the courts.

Subs. (2)

The Law Commission noted that the law relating to rights in the child's estate was confused and uncertain (W.P. 91, para. 2.32.). There was authority that a father did not have power to administer the child's property nor to give a valid receipt on the child's behalf (*M'Reight* v. *M'Reight* (1849) 13 I.Eq. 314). Guardians appeared to have these rights. Now anyone with parental responsibility will have them and specific appointments of guardians of the estate of a child will only be permitted in accordance with any rules (s.5(11)).

Subs. (4)

Although the term "parental responsibility" recognises that parents have powers so that they can bring up their children, its use does not remove the liability and rights of those without parental responsibility. Thus, a father without parental responsibility is liable to maintain the child (Sched. 1, para. 1); a step-parent is liable to maintain a child of the family (M.C.A. 1973, s.25(4): D.P.M.C.A. 1978, s.3(4)); anyone with charge of a child may be liable for neglect (C.Y.P.A. 1933, s.1); anyone with care of the child has the liabilities of a parent to see that the child is educated (Education Act 1944 as amended by Sched. 13, para. 10).

All children die intestate except those who make privileged wills under the Wills (Soldiers and Sailors) Act 1918. Devolution of the estate of an intestate minor is covered by the Administration of Estates Act 1925, s.46, and the Family Law Reform Act 1987, s.18(1). If the child is unmarried his parents will be entitled to his estate in equal shares.

Subs. (5)

Since a person with parental responsibility cannot under s.2(8) act incompatibly with an order under this Act it would seem to follow that a person without such responsibility is similarly restricted, except for situations where an order would only be binding on someone on whom it had been served (see s.14).

Subject to the provisions of this Act: There are a number of specific restrictions in the Act, namely:– s.10: starting proceedings without leave; s.13: changing the child's name or removing his from the jurisdiction; s.20(8): refusing to hand over a child (aged under 16 years) to a parent who wishes to remove him from care.

What is reasonable: The Law Commission suggested that it would be reasonable for someone caring for a child while parents were away to arrange emergency medical treatment but not major elective surgery (Law Com. 172, para. 2.16). The issue is likely to be more complex than that suggests. What is reasonable would also turn on the possibility of contacting the parents for permission, whether the parents were known to have particular views on the matter such as a preference for homoeopathy and the consequences for the child of delaying any action. It was also suggested by the Lord Chancellor that this provision would allow a foster parent to refuse to hand over a child to a parent who was drunk or incapable or, late at night, a child who was asleep (*Hansard*, H.L. Vol. 505, col. 370–1). This is questionable, particularly when s.20(7) provides that the local authority has no right to retain a child against the wishes of a person with parental responsibility. The lack of clarity here is unfortunate and will no doubt lead to arguments based on the distinct responsibility of the foster parents and the local authority, even to re-running cases such as *Krishnan* v. *London Borough of Sutton* [1970] Ch. 181. Any retention of the child relying on s.3(5) could only be temporary—further action, probably an emergency protection order (s.44) or a prohibited steps order (s.8), would be necessary. A further issue arises as to what redress would exist where unreasonable action has been taken. Habeas corpus would theoretically be available for the recovery of the child (the Custody of Children Act 1891 is repealed by this Act) but it was held in *Re K.* (1978) 122 S.J. 626 that this was the wrong procedure for custody disputes and that wardship should be used. Tort law no longer gives parents an action for the loss of a child's services and there seems to be no other right to damages for them. The child may have a right of action for trespass where a doctor has operated or examined without valid consent.

Acquisition of parental responsibility by father

4.—(1) Where a child's father and mother were not married to each other at the time of his birth—

    (a) the court may, on the application of the father, order that he shall have parental responsibility for the child; or

    (b) the father and mother may by agreement ("a parental responsibility agreement") provide for the father to have parental responsibility for the child.

(2) No parental responsibility agreement shall have effect for the purposes of this Act unless—

    (a) it is made in the form prescribed by regulations made by the Lord Chancellor; and

    (b) where regulations are made by the Lord Chancellor prescribing the manner in which such agreements must be recorded, it is recorded in the prescribed manner.

(3) Subject to section 12(4), an order under subsection (1)(a), or a parental responsibility agreement, may only be brought to an end by an order of the court made on the application—

(a) of any person who has parental responsibility for the child; or
(b) with leave of the court, of the child himself.

(4) The court may only grant leave under subsection (3)(b) if it is satisfied that the child has sufficient understanding to make the proposed application.

DEFINITIONS
"child": s.105(1).
"parental responsibility": s.2, 3, 12.
"parental responsibility agreement": s.4(1)(b).
"prescribed": ss.4(2), 105(1).
"the court": s.92(7).

GENERAL NOTE
This section enables an unmarried father to acquire parental responsibility by a court order or an agreement with the mother in the prescribed form. An unmarried father may also obtain parental responsibility in other ways (see the note to s.2(2)). This replaces the more limited provision in the F.L.R.A. 1987, s.4, under which an unmarried father could obtain an order to share the parental rights and duties with the mother. The Law Commission clearly favoured agreements ("judicial proceedings may be unduly elaborate, expensive and unnecessary unless the child's mother objects to the order" (Law Com. 172, para. 2.18)) but agreements and orders may have different effects. Only if there have been court proceedings can issues be *res judicata* (*Re J.S.* [1981] Fam. 22); it would apparently be open to either of the parties to an agreement to contest the issue of paternity at a later date. The welfare test in s.1(1) applies in these proceedings but the checklist in s.1(3) does not (s.1(4)).

Unlike the parental responsibility of married parents, the unmarried father's responsibility may be ended on the application of the child or any person with parental responsibility (subs. (3)). It will also end when the child reaches age 18 (s.91(7), (8)) or is adopted.

Unmarried fathers will be able to obtain orders, even though the child is subject to a care order, as they could obtain orders under s.4 of the F.L.R.A. 1987 (*Re H.* [1989] 2 All E.R. 353). Such a father would then qualify as a parent with parental responsibility, but this will not, under the new system, give him automatic rights to remove a child from care, or give him greater rights than the mother of a child in care. It would, however, enable him to remove a child who was only being looked after by the local authority (see s.20(8)). The unmarried father's rights to have contact (access) with his child in care are identical whether or not there is any s.4 order (s.34(1)). An agreement with the mother would seem to have the same consequences.

Regulations are necessary before this section can be brought into force.

Subs. (1)

On application of the father: The mother has rights automatically (s.2(2)). The father does not need the mother's consent to make an application.

May order: The court will have to consider whether it is in the child's best interests for the father to have parental responsibility (s.1(1)). The meaning of welfare in this context is not defined. Now that divorced parents who cannot agree nevertheless retain parental responsibility the fact that the mother objects to the father and will not co-operate with him may not be a strong reason for denying an order under s.4. Rather, it justifies the making of a residence order to clarify and determine the rights of both the parents. On an application under s.4 the court can make any section 8 order because these are "family proceedings" (ss.8(3), 10(1)(b)). Having parental responsibility may make the father more willing to support his child but s.4 orders should not be made on the basis of such promises. A person with parental responsibility has considerable power to influence and control the child's life (see ss.2, 3) and it is unlikely to be in a child's interests to have such power held by someone who will not be involved in the child's care. If in the course of the proceedings the parents are able to reach agreement it would seem that the court could refuse the order on the basis that it would be better for the matter to be decided by agreement (s.1(5)) but this would leave the father in a weak position because he would not have parental responsibility unless an agreement was made in accordance with subs. (2).

Shall have parental responsibility: The mother still retains it and s.2 applies to deal with conflicts between them. Any disputes can be dealt with by the court on application of either parent (s.10(4)(a)) even if no s.4 order has been made.

Subs. (2)
No parental responsibility agreement shall have effect: However, an informal agreement could still operate as a delegation of responsibility under s.2(9) or indicate what is reasonable for s.3(5).

Subs. (3)
S.12(3) provides that an order for parental responsibility under s.4 shall not be brought to an end while a residence order in favour of an unmarried father continues. Where a residence order in favour of an unmarried father ends on the making of a care order the unmarried father retains parental responsibility. The decision to end the order must be made in the child's best interests (s.1(1)).
Any person with parental responsibility: This means the mother, the unmarried father, a guardian, any person who has a residence order or the local authority if there is a care order.
The child: A child can only obtain leave under subs. (4) if he has sufficient understanding to make the proposed application.

Appointment of guardians

5.—(1) Where an application with respect to a child is made to the court by any individual, the court may by order appoint that individual to be the child's guardian if—
(a) the child has no parent with parental responsibility for him; or
(b) a residence order has been made with respect to the child in favour of a parent or guardian of his who has died while the order was in force.

(2) The power conferred by subsection (1) may also be exercised in any family proceedings if the court considers that the order should be made even though no application has been made for it.

(3) A parent who has parental responsibility for his child may appoint another individual to be the child's guardian in the event of his death.

(4) A guardian of a child may appoint another individual to take his place as the child's guardian in the event of his death.

(5) An appointment under subsection (3) or (4) shall not have effect unless it is made in writing, is dated and is signed by the person making the appointment or—
(a) in the case of an appointment made by a will which is not signed by the testator, is signed at the direction of the testator in accordance with the requirements of section 9 of the Wills Act 1837; or
(b) in any other case, is signed at the direction of the person making the appointment, in his presence and in the presence of two witnesses who each attest the signature.

(6) A person appointed as a child's guardian under this section shall have parental responsibility for the child concerned.

(7) Where—
(a) on the death of any person making an appointment under subsection (3) or (4), the child concerned has no parent with parental responsibility for him; or
(b) immediately before the death of any person making such an appointment, a residence order in his favour was in force with respect to the child,
the appointment shall take effect on the death of that person.

(8) Where, on the death of any person making an appointment under subsection (3) or (4)—

  (a) the child concerned has a parent with parental responsibility for
him; and

  (b) subsection (7)(b) does not apply,
the appointment shall take effect when the child no longer has a parent
who has parental responsibility for him.

(9) Subsections (1) and (7) do not apply if the residence order referred
to in paragraph (b) of those subsections was also made in favour of a
surviving parent of the child.

(10) Nothing in this section shall be taken to prevent an appointment
under subsection (3) or (4) being made by two or more persons acting
jointly.

(11) Subject to any provision made by rules of court, no court shall
exercise the High Court's inherent jurisdiction to appoint a guardian of
the estate of any child.

(12) Where rules of court are made under subsection (11) they may
prescribe the circumstances in which, and conditions subject to which, an
appointment of such a guardian may be made.

(13) A guardian of a child may only be appointed in accordance with
the provisions of this section.

DEFINITIONS

  "appoint", "appointment": s.5(5).
  "child": s.105(1).
  "guardian of a child": s.5.
  "family proceedings": s.8(3).
  "parental responsibility": ss.2, 3, 12.
  "residence order": ss.8(1), 105(3).
  "signed": s.105(1).
  "the court": s.92(7).

GENERAL NOTE

  This section and s.6 simplify and clarify the law of guardianship. They replace ss.3–6 of
the Guardianship of Minors Act 1971 with provisions recommended by the Law Commission
in Law Com. 172.

  A guardian of a child can only be appointed by the court in family proceedings, with or
without an application (subss. (1), (2) and (13)), by a parent with parental responsibility
(subs. (3)) or by an existing guardian (subs. (4)). Two such people may make a joint
appointment (subs. (10)).

  Unmarried fathers will be able to make appointments if they have obtained parental
responsibility or been appointed as guardian. An appointment must be made by a signed
and dated document in writing (subs. (5)); deeds and wills will not be required but will be
effective in relation to both existing and new appointments. The child's guardian obtains
parental responsibility over him (subs. (6)). Appointments will only be effective if the child
has no parent with parental responsibility for him or the deceased person and no other
parent had a residence order immediately before death (subss. (7)–(9)). Thus the situation
will no longer arise where a surviving parent caring for a child has to co-operate with a
guardian appointed by the deceased parent. However, if both parents die, even where only
one held a residence order, the guardians they have appointed will both have the power to
act. Also, for example, where the parents are dead, the grandfather is the guardian and the
child is cared for by an aunt who has a residence order, the grandfather (but not the aunt)
may appoint another guardian to act after his death. That guardian will have power alongside
the aunt.

  A guardian of the child's estate may only be appointed in accordance with the rules (subss.
(11) and (12)).

Subs. (1)

  May: S.1(5) applies. The decision and the appointment must be in the child's best interests
but the checklist in s.1(3) does not apply.

  Individual: Two or more individuals may be appointed (see s.6(1)) but organisations may
not be appointed.

No parent with parental responsibility: Married parents always have parental responsibility unless it is removed by an adoption order. Unmarried fathers may acquire parental responsibility (see note on s.2(2)).

Guardian: A guardian for the child can only be appointed under this section (subs. (13)).

Residence order in favour of a parent or guardian: A residence order in favour of anyone else will not preclude an appointment, nor will it prevent an appointment by a parent or guardian being effective immediately the appointor dies (subs. (9)). If there was a residence order in favour of both parents the court can only appoint a guardian following the death of the surviving parent.

Died: Absence overseas, etc., does not permit the appointment of a guardian but it would be possible for a residence order to be made in such circumstances (see s.10(1)(b) and (5)).

Subs. (5)

The document only needs to be witnessed where it is signed at the direction of but not by the appointor; a will which is defective because it is not properly witnessed may be valid for the purpose of appointing a guardian.

Subs. (7)

Take effect: Until the appointment takes effect the guardian has no special powers and will need to seek leave under s.10(9) if he wishes to obtain a section 8 order.

Guardians: revocation and disclaimer

6.—(1) An appointment under section 5(3) or (4) revokes an earlier such appointment (including one made in an unrevoked will or codicil) made by the same person in respect of the same child, unless it is clear (whether as the result of an express provision in the later appointment or by any necessary implication) that the purpose of the later appointment is to appoint an additional guardian.

(2) An appointment under section 5(3) or (4) (including one made in an unrevoked will or codicil) is revoked if the person who made the appointment revokes it by a written and dated instrument which is signed—

(a) by him; or

(b) at his direction, in his presence and in the presence of two witnesses who each attest the signature.

(3) An appointment under section 5(3) or (4) (other than one made in a will or codicil) is revoked if, with the intention of revoking the appointment, the person who made it—

(a) destroys the instrument by which it was made; or

(b) has some other person destroy that instrument in his presence.

(4) For the avoidance of doubt, an appointment under section 5(3) or (4) made in a will or codicil is revoked if the will or codicil is revoked.

(5) A person who is appointed as a guardian under section 5(3) or (4) may disclaim his appointment by an instrument in writing signed by him and made within a reasonable time of his first knowing that the appointment has taken effect.

(6) Where regulations are made by the Lord Chancellor prescribing the manner in which such disclaimers must be recorded, no such disclaimer shall have effect unless it is recorded in the prescribed manner.

(7) Any appointment of a guardian under section 5 may be brought to an end at any time by order of the court—

(a) on the application of any person who has parental responsibility for the child;

(b) on the application of the child concerned, with leave of the court; or

(c) in any family proceedings, if the court considers that it should be brought to an end even though no application has been made.

DEFINITIONS
"appoint", "appointment": s.5(3)–(5).
"child": s.105(1).
"disclaim", "disclaimer": s.6(5), (6).
"family proceedings": s.8(3).
"guardian": s.5.
"person who has parental responsibility": ss.2(1)(2), 4(1), 5(6), 12(1)(2).
"revocation", "revoke": s.6(2)–(4).
"signed": s.105(1).
"the court": s.92(7).

GENERAL NOTE

This section provides for the revocation, disclaimer and termination of appointments as guardian of a child.

Revocation: can be by a further appointment, except appointment of an additional guardian (subs. (1)), or by a written, signed and dated instrument of revocation (subs. (2)), or by destruction with the intention of revocation except in the case of a will or codicil (subs. (3)), or finally by the revocation of the will or codicil (subs. (4)).

Disclaimer: must be by a written and signed instrument recorded in the prescribed manner (subss. (5) and (6)).

Termination: is carried out by the court on application of those listed in subs. (7).

Subs. (3)

Destruction of a will or codicil does not necessarily revoke it.

With the intention: Accidental destruction will have no effect.

Subs. (5)

Reasonable time: There is no indication of what period of time is reasonable but it would appear that a decision has to be taken once and for all so that change of circumstances (or change of heart) some time later could not be within a reasonable time. However, it is arguable that a person who decides to disclaim, having heard, after six months, that he has a fatal illness, would have acted within a reasonable time.

Subs. (7)

At present it appears that anyone can apply to the High Court under s.6 of the G.M.A. 1971 to have a guardian removed. The Law Commission suggested that this general access should continue and also that local authorities should be able to apply for the removal of a guardian (W.P. No. 91, para. 3.24). This is provided in the case of children in care by para. (a). The guardian can apparently apply and avoid the time limit in subs. (5) operating in a way which is contrary to the child's welfare. The court can also end an appointment of its own motion in family proceedings.

Welfare reports

7.—(1) A court considering any question with respect to a child under this Act may—

(a) ask a probation officer; or

(b) ask a local authority to arrange for—

(i) an officer of the authority; or

(ii) such other person (other than a probation officer) as the authority considers appropriate,

to report to the court on such matters relating to the welfare of that child as are required to be dealt with in the report.

(2) The Lord Chancellor may make regulations specifying matters which, unless the court orders otherwise, must be dealt with in any report under this section.

(3) The report may be made in writing, or orally, as the court requires.

(4) Regardless of any enactment or rule of law which would otherwise prevent it from doing so, the court may take account of—

(a) any statement contained in the report; and

(b) any evidence given in respect of the matters referred to in the report, in so far as the statement or evidence is, in the opinion of the court, relevant to the question which it is considering.

(5) It shall be the duty of the authority or probation officer to comply with any request for a report under this section.

DEFINITIONS
  "child": s.105(1).
  "local authority": s.105(1).
  "the court": s.92(7).

GENERAL NOTE

This section enacts the recommendation of the Law Commission (see Law Com. 172, para. 6.14 *et seq.*). It extends the court's power to call for a welfare report so that it can do so when considering *any* question with respect to a child under the Act. It removes anomalies that there were different powers to call for reports from different people under different statutes and in different courts (see Law Com. 172, para. 6.16). The probation service and local authorities will be under a duty to provide reports as requested (subs. (5)), but a local authority may delegate the task to someone who is not a member of its staff (subs. (1)), *e.g.* a guardian ad litem. The content of reports may be specified by the court (subs. (1)) or in regulations (subs. (2)), but this provision can be brought into force before any regulations have been made. The court's right to consider reports and evidence about matters in reports regardless of the hearsay rule is clarified. The court may do so if it thinks that it is relevant (subs. (4)). Further changes are made to the law of evidence which will allow children's evidence to be given indirectly via a report (see s.96). It is intended that these provisions should reverse *Re H., Re K.* [1989] Fam. Law 388. This section does not remove the rights of parties to ask the court to order reports and to question the reporter. These issues will continue to be dealt with in court rules.

Subs. (1)

Any question . . . under this Act: The power to order reports when considering the appointment of guardians (s.5) or granting parental responsibility to an unmarried father (s.4) is new. The provision is also wider than it might seem at first because the court may make the new section 8 orders in any "family proceedings" (s.8(4)). A court may thus call for a report *inter alia* in an injunction case under the Domestic Violence and Matrimonial Proceedings Act 1976 or the Matrimonial Homes Act 1983.

May: There is no duty to request a report even if the case is contested. The Lord Chancellor stated that some sort of report would generally be required in most contested cases and there would be some uncontested cases where a court would think a report necessary (*Hansard*, H.L. Vol. 502, col. 1203). In considering whether to request a report the court must give paramount consideration to the child's welfare and have regard to the problems caused by delay (s.1(2)). This may influence the choice of reporter.

Subs. (3)

This clarifies the position about the presentation of reports. Written reports are generally more useful to the parties and their representatives because they can be discussed prior to the hearing but if the court seeks only limited information an oral report may suffice.

Subs. (4)

The High Court and the county court already have some power to consider reports regardless of hearsay as did the magistrates' court in some proceedings, but the effect of this was put in doubt by *Re H., Re K.*

The court may: Guidance for guardians ad litem has urged caution when using hearsay in relation to very controversial matters. In *Thompson* v. *Thompson* (1975) [1986] 1 F.L.R. 212, at 217, Buckley L.J. said, "Where a judge has to arrive at crucial findings of fact he should found them upon sworn evidence rather than unsworn report." If regulations are made under subs. (2) they may require the disclosure of the source of hearsay evidence (*per* Lord Chancellor, *Hansard*, H.L. Vol. 502, col. 1214). See also decision of *Re H., Re K.* (above).

PART II

ORDERS WITH RESPECT TO CHILDREN IN FAMILY PROCEEDINGS

General

Residence, contact and other orders with respect to children

8.—(1) In this Act —
"a contact order" means an order requiring the person with whom a child lives, or is to live, to allow the child to visit or stay with the person named in the order, or for that person and the child otherwise to have contact with each other;
"a prohibited steps order" means an order that no step which could be taken by a parent in meeting his parental responsibility for a child, and which is of a kind specified in the order, shall be taken by any person without the consent of the court;
"a residence order" means an order settling the arrangements to be made as to the person with whom a child is to live; and
"a specific issue order" means an order giving directions for the purpose of determining a specific question which has arisen, or which may arise, in connection with any aspect of parental responsibility for a child.

(2) In this Act "a section 8 order" means any of the orders mentioned in subsection (1) and any order varying or discharging such an order.

(3) For the purposes of this Act "family proceedings" means any proceedings—
(a) under the inherent jurisdiction of the High Court in relation to children; and
(b) under the enactments mentioned in subsection (4),
but does not include proceedings on an application for leave under section 100(3).

(4) The enactments are—
(a) Parts I, II and IV of this Act;
(b) the Matrimonial Causes Act 1973;
(c) the Domestic Violence and Matrimonial Proceedings Act 1976;
(d) the Adoption Act 1976;
(e) the Domestic Proceedings and Magistrates' Courts Act 1978;
(f) sections 1 and 9 of the Matrimonial Homes Act 1983;
(g) Part III of the Matrimonial and Family Proceedings Act 1984.

DEFINITIONS
"child": ss.9(6), 105(1).
"contact order": ss.8(1), 11(7).
"family proceedings": s.8(3)(4).
"parental responsibility": ss.2, 3, 12.
"prohibited steps order": s.8(1).
"residence order": ss.8(1), 105(3).
"section 8 order": ss.8, 11(7).
"single issue order": s.8(1).

GENERAL NOTE
This section, together with ss.9 and 10, forms the heart of the new scheme for the private law relating to children. It enacts the recommendations in Pt. II of Law Com. 172. Section 8 orders replace orders for custody or care and control and related orders. Although it was suggested in Parliament that this merely amounted to "cosmetic renaming" (*per* Lord Meston, *Hansard*, H.L. Vol. 502, col. 503), a close examination indicates that the courts are getting substantially greater powers to direct what happens to children who are the subjects of civil proceedings. Additionally, the making of an order will not remove parental

responsibility, although it will restrict the actions of those in whose favour the order is not made (see s.2(8)).

Subs. (1)

A contact order: This order replaces the access order. It requires the person with whom the child is living to allow the child contact with the named person. There is no compulsion on the person who has the benefit of the order to maintain contact, nor can a mature child be required to do so (*Gillick* v. *West Norfolk Area Health Authority* [1986] A.C. 112). If the child visits or stays with someone with parental responsibility (a parent, guardian or a person with a residence order) that person may exercise parental responsibility so far as that is not incompatible with any order under this Act (see s.2(8)). If the child visits or stays with someone without parental responsibility (*e.g.* grandparents) they can take such action as is reasonable (see s.3(5)). Where visits are impractical or undesirable an order can be made to allow receipt of telephone calls or letters. It is likely that orders will usually be for "reasonable contact" which would allow all types of contact. Contact orders cannot be made in respect of children who are in local authority care under a care order (s.9(1)). Contact with children in care is provided for in s.34. Local authorities may not apply for contact orders nor have them made in their favour (s.9(2)). However, an order may be made where the child is only accommodated by the local authority. Although local authorities have wide discretion over the care of children they are accommodating it would be an unwarranted extension of the *Liverpool* principle (*A.* v. *Liverpool City Council* [1982] A.C. 363) to prevent courts from dealing with disputes over contact with such children. The court may only make contact orders in relation to children over 16 years in exceptional circumstances (s.9(7)). Orders only continue in force after the child reaches age 16 years in exceptional circumstances (ss.9(6), 91(10)(11)). If the order is made in favour of a parent it ceases to have any effect if the parents live together for a continuous period of more than six months (s.11(6)). This is so even though the parents are unmarried and the parent with the order is the father and does not have parental responsibility. The making of a care order discharges the order (s.91(2)).

A prohibited steps order: The Law Commission proposed this as part of its aim "to incorporate the most valuable features of wardship into the statutory jurisdictions" (Law Com. 172, para. 4.20). The order differs from the automatic effect of making a child a ward of court in that the actions prohibited or the areas over which control is lost to the court must be specified in the order. When a child is warded "no important step" may be taken without the consent of the court. The new order is clearer but care will need to be taken to consider exactly what decisions should be left to the court. If there is a residence order, removal from the United Kingdom (except for short periods) and name change will automatically require permission under s.13. A "prohibited steps" order could bar removal where there is no residence order, from a place rather than the jurisdiction, or forbid change of school. The order can only relate to action which is within the power of a parent and does not, unlike orders in wardship, appear to bind the child or give the court control over decisions which the child is entitled to take. Thus an order could stop a person allowing a child to have cosmetic surgery or engage in a dangerous sport but would not be effective to prevent a mature young person making such a decision for himself (see s.9(7) and *Gillick*). There are limitations in s.9(5) on the content of these orders. Prohibited steps orders cannot be made in respect of a child subject to a care order (s.9(1)). They cannot be used to achieve results which could be achieved by a residence order or a contact order. Thus the location of the child's home cannot be the subject of this order but should be specified in detail in a residence order. Nor can they be used to circumvent the restrictions on the wardship jurisdiction in s.100(2), *i.e.* to commit a child to local authority care, to require a child to be accommodated by the local authority or to give the local authority power to make decisions about children. Thus a prohibited steps order cannot be used to prevent a child's removal from care when there is no care order but it could be used to prevent someone visiting the child in the foster home as long as there was no care order (s.9(1)). Prohibited steps orders cannot be made in relation to a child over the age of 16 years unless the circumstances are exceptional s.9(7)). Similarly, orders only continue in force after the child is 16 in exceptional circumstances (ss.9(6), 91(10)(11)). What is exceptional in relation to this order may be different from the case of contact which is very much a matter for the child by age 16. The making of a care order discharges the order (s.91(2)).

A residence order: The Law Commission was concerned that orders for custody or care and control should be replaced with an order "flexible enough to accommodate a much wider range of situations" (Law Com. 172, para. 4.12) including where the child lived with both parents after their separation. The phrase "settling the arrangements" is a broad one and gives the court more scope for including conditions. The Lord Chancellor suggested that this could be used to provide that the child lived with the father only while he remained in a particular neighbourhood (*Hansard*, H.L. Vol. 505, col. 345). A residence order may be made in favour of more than one person (s.11(4)). If these people are not living together it may also specify the periods to be spent in each household. A residence order may be made in favour of an unmarried couple who need not be the child's parents. However, if an order is made in favour of parents, each with parental responsibility, it will cease to have effect if they live together for a continuous period of more than six months (s.11(5)).

The granting of a residence order in favour of any person automatically gives them parental responsibility for the child (s.12(2)). Thus people with residence orders are in the same position as parents or guardians except in relation to matters excluded by the statute. S.12(3) prevents those with residence orders who are not parents or guardians giving consent to adoption, freeing for adoption and appointing a guardian. S.13 prevents anyone changing the surname of or removing from the jurisdiction (except for less than a month (s.13(2))) any child who is the subject of a residence order.

A local authority may not apply for a residence order nor have one "made" in its favour (s.9(2)). However, a residence order may be made in respect of any child, even one subject to a care order (s.9(1)). In this case the residence order discharges the care order (s.9(1)). "Phased return" of a child in care may be achieved by making a residence order which settles arrangements for the child to live temporarily with foster parents with increasing visits to the applicants. There is no provision specifically for "phased return" in the Act. The making of a care order discharges a residence order but the local authority has responsibility in relation to contact with those who held residence orders immediately before a care order was made, *e.g.* s.34(1).

Residence orders end when the child reaches the age of 16 unless the court orders otherwise. Orders in respect of older children or to continue after the child is 16 can only be made in exceptional circumstances (ss.9(6), (7) and 91(10)). Such an order might be appropriate in the case of a handicapped child living with non-parents to ensure that the carers retained parental responsibility for the child until age 18 (s.91(11)).

The enforcement of residence orders is dealt with in s.14.

A specific issue order: Under s.1(3) of the Guardianship Act 1973 parents could refer a dispute on any individual question to the court but it was probably more usual for such cases to be dealt with in wardship where the court had control over all major decisions. This new provision extends (s.1(3)) to disputes involving non-parents, including some involving local authorities. The effect is not to give one person a right to take decisions, or to veto them, but to enable the court to give directions. The court could take the disputed decision itself or, alternatively, direct that it should be determined by others. For example, in a case involving medical treatment it could determine that the child should be treated as a specified doctor thought appropriate.

The restrictions in s.9 which apply to prohibited steps orders also apply to specific issue orders. However, s.9(5) still leaves scope for local authorities who wish to require a parent to do something, for example to take a child to a doctor or to a school, to seek a specific issue order.

Subs. (3)

The new legislation provides a single system so that all courts dealing with "family proceedings" can make any section 8 order. Limitations on applications still continue (see ss.9, 10) but the anomalies which related to the types of orders which could be granted are removed. Under the old law, parents and step-parents could apply for custody orders in divorce proceedings; the court could grant these orders in proceedings under the M.C.A. 1973 or for financial relief in domestic proceedings and some other people could make free-standing applications for certain types of order under other Acts such as the G.M.A. 1971 and the Children Act 1975. Anyone with an interest in the child could ward him, although the court would refuse to exercise its jurisdiction if the child were subject to the control of a local authority (*A. v. Liverpool City Council* [1982] A.C. 363; *W. v. Hertfordshire County Council* [1985] 2 All E.R. 301).

"*Family proceedings*":
(1) Under the *inherent jurisdiction* (s.8(3)(a)), *i.e.* wardship.
(2) *Pt. I of the Children Act 1989* (s.8(4)(a)).
   Proceedings for parental responsibility orders (s.4).
   Guardianship proceedings (ss.5, 6).
(3) *Pt. II of the Children Act 1989* (s.8(4)(a)).
   Free standing applications for order (s.10(1)(2)).
   Applications for leave (s.10(2)(b)).
   By the court on its own motion (s.10(1)(b)).
   Applications for financial relief under Sched. 1.

(4) Pt. IV of the Children Act 1989 (s.8(4)(a)).

Care proceedings (s.31).

Proceedings re contact with children in care (s.34).

Proceedings re education supervision orders (s.36).

N.B.: The court does not have this power when it is considering the emergency protection of a child under Pt. V.

(5) *M.C.A. 1973* (s.8(4)(b)).

Divorce, nullity and judicial separation proceedings.

Applications for financial relief following divorce, etc., or in cases of neglect to maintain (s.27). Section 8 orders may be made even though the child is not "a child of the family" within s.52(1) of the M.C.A. 1973 (s.10(1)).

(6) *D.V.M.P.A. 1976* (s.8(4)(b)).

Applications for non molestation orders.

Applications for exclusion orders, etc., where the parties are unmarried.

The Court will thus be able to determine where a child lives and what contact he is to have with the excluded person even if that person is not a parent.

(7) *Adoption Act 1976* (s.8(4)(d)).

Adoption proceedings, proceedings for freeing orders.

Under the old law the court could refuse to grant an adoption order and refer the matter back to the divorce court for a custody order or, if the child was not a child of the family, make a custodianship order (Adoption Act 1976, ss.14(3), 15(4); Children Act 1975, s.37). It will now be able to make a residence order instead of an adoption order in any case. The decision whether to grant a residence order or an adoption order will be for the court to make applying the Adoption Act 1976, s.6. In *Re S* [1987] Fam. 98, it was held that a custodianship order could only be made as an alternative to adoption where it was better for the child, but this decision turned on the construction of the Children Act 1975, s.37(1), which has been repealed. S.1(5) of this Act will now apply. The court will also be able to make a contact order instead of including access conditions in the adoption order (see: *Re C* [1988] 2 W.L.R. 474).

(8) *D.P.M.C.A. 1978* (s.8(4)(e)).

Proceedings for financial relief.

Proceedings for injunctions in cases of domestic violence.

The Court will thus be able to determine where a child lives and what contact he is allowed to have with the excluded person. Section 8 orders may apparently be made even though the child is not "a child of the family" within s.88(1) of the D.P.M.C.A. 1978.

(9) *Ss.1 and 9 of the M.H.A. 1983* (s.8(4)(f)).

Proceedings for exclusion orders and related orders where the parties are married (see: *Richards* v. *Richards* [1984] A.C. 174).

(10) *Pt. III of the Matrimonial and Family Proceedings Act 1984* (s.8(4)(c)).

Proceedings for financial relief after overseas divorce.

Restrictions on making section 8 orders

9.—(1) No court shall make any section 8 order, other than a residence order, with respect to a child who is in the care of a local authority.

(2) No application may be made by a local authority for a residence order or contact order and no court shall make such an order in favour of a local authority.

(3) A person who is, or was at any time within the last six months, a local authority foster parent of a child may not apply for leave to apply for a section 8 order with respect to the child unless—

(a) he has the consent of the authority;

(b) he is a relative of the child; or

(c) the child has lived with him for at least three years preceding the application.

(4) The period of three years mentioned in subsection (3)(c) need not be continuous but must have begun not more than five years before the making of the application.

(5) No court shall exercise its powers to make a specific issue order or prohibited steps order—

(a) with a view to achieving a result which could be achieved by making a residence or contact order; or

(b) in any way which is denied to the High Court (by section 100(2)) in the exercise of its inherent jurisdiction with respect to children.

(6) No court shall make any section 8 order which is to have effect for a period which will end after the child has reached the age of sixteen unless it is satisfied that the circumstances of the case are exceptional.

(7) No court shall make any section 8 order, other than one varying or discharging such an order, with respect to a child who has reached the age of sixteen unless it is satisfied that the circumstances of the case are exceptional.

DEFINITIONS
"child": ss.9(7), 105(1).
"contact order": s.8(1).
"local authority": s.105(1).
"local authority foster parent": s.23(3)(4).
"prohibited steps order": s.8(1).
"residence order": s.8(1).
"section 8 order": ss.8, 11(7).
"specific issue order": s.8(1).
"three years": s.9(4).

GENERAL NOTE
This section states the main limitations on the court making the various section 8 orders; particularly it restricts the court's power in relation to children in local authority care (subss. (1)–(3)). It also ensures that the differences in the types of orders are not blurred (subs. (5)). It provides that orders should only continue or be made (but not varied or discharged) in relation to children over 16 in exceptional circumstances (subss. (6) and (7)).

Subs. (1)
The making of a residence order discharges a care order (s.9(1)). Where a child is subject to a care order, anyone with parental responsibility may apply for its discharge without applying for any further order (s.39(1)), but other people can only do so by obtaining a residence order. To seek a residence order they may need the consent of the local authority (ss.9(3), 10(5)(c)(ii)). A residence order will also give the applicant parental responsibility for the child. The courts will not be able to make a residence order in respect of a child subject to a care order when his parents divorce but the issue of the child's residence can be dealt with on the discharge of the care order (s.8(4)).

The court will not be able to direct the local authority how it should treat the child or to control further the parents of a child in care by issuing a prohibited steps or a single issue order. However, in such cases the local authority may, with leave, seek the direction or assistance of the High Court in wardship (s.100(3)). This may be particularly useful in relation to sensitive areas like sterilisation or abortion. In contrast, local authorities may, with leave, apply for prohibited steps orders and specific issue orders in relation to children whom they are accommodating, for example, to get a decision about medical treatment. They may also seek specific issue orders to make a parent take a child for a medical treatment in circumstances where an emergency protection order (s.44) would not be available and a child assessment order (s.43) would be inadequate.

Subs. (2)
Local authorities cannot by-pass the need to establish the grounds in s.31 by applying for a residence order rather than a care order. This also applies to the use of contact orders as an alternative to supervision orders.

Subs. (3)
Local authority foster parents and former foster parents who have ceased caring for a child within the last six months are the only group subject to this further restriction on applications for leave to seek section 8 orders. Leave of the court is not required for applications for residence or contact orders by people who have cared for the child for three years (s.10(5)(b)), but is necessary for prohibited steps and single issue orders.

The Law Commission thought that it was inappropriate to allow foster parents the right to apply for orders without restriction because this could undermine the authority's plans (Law Com. 172, para. 4.43). S.9(3) goes beyond the Commission's recommendations and gives the authority a right of veto. Where it does not apply, or consent is given, the court will have to consider the local authority's plans in any application for leave (s.10(9)(d)(i)). Where children are being accommodated by the authority, the protection of the rights of parents is limited, since the authority can always give its consent, although it must comply with its duty to "safeguard and promote" the child's welfare under s.22(3) in so doing. However, applications for custodianship orders were rare and there is nothing in the legislation which will necessarily make residence orders more attractive to foster parents.

Subs. (4)
This is broader than the definition which applied to custodianship, but an application for a residence order will not prevent the child's removal from the applicant's home (see notes to s.10).

Subs. (5)
This provision prevents local authorities using prohibited steps orders or specific issue orders to get round the restrictions in subs. (2). Similarly, s.100(2) provides that wardship powers may not be used to subject a child to local authority care or supervision, nor to give a local authority power to make decisions which are part of parental responsibility.

Subss. (6) and (7)
Previously the court's powers to make custody and access orders endured until the child was 18, although they were rarely exercised against the child's wishes. Section 8 orders are now largely restricted to under 16s. Orders may be necessary where a child, through immaturity or handicap, is unable to make decisions for himself, *e.g. Re S.W.* [1986] 1 FLR 24. Orders in wardship will be available until a child is 18 but the changes in the Act will reduce the need for recourse to wardship and local authority's rights of access to it. The Law Commission suggested that a court considering making an order in relation to a child over 16 years should make the child a party (Law Com. 172, para. 3.25). Where a child lives with a non-parent under a residence order that person's consent is necessary for his marriage under 18. Once the order has expired, the consent of the parents and guardians will be required (Marriage Act 1949, s.3(1A) as amended by Sched. 12, para. 5).

Power of court to make section 8 orders

10.—(1) In any family proceedings in which a question arises with respect to the welfare of any child, the court may make a section 8 order with respect to the child if—
(a) an application for the order has been made by a person who—
  (i) is entitled to apply for a section 8 order with respect to the child; or
  (ii) has obtained the leave of the court to make the application; or
(b) the court considers that the order should be made even though no such application has been made.

(2) The court may also make a section 8 order with respect to any child on the application of a person who—
(a) is entitled to apply for a section 8 order with respect to the child; or
(b) has obtained the leave of the court to make the application.

(3) This section is subject to the restrictions imposed by section 9.

(4) The following persons are entitled to apply to the court for any section 8 order with respect to a child—
(a) any parent or guardian of the child;
(b) any person in whose favour a residence order is in force with respect to the child.

(5) The following persons are entitled to apply for a residence or contact order with respect to a child—
(a) any party to a marriage (whether or not subsisting) in relation to whom the child is a child of the family;
(b) any person with whom the child has lived for a period of at least three years;
(c) any person who—

    (i) in any case where a residence order is in force with respect to the child, has the consent of each of the persons in whose favour the order was made;

    (ii) in any case where the child is in the care of a local authority, has the consent of that authority; or

    (iii) in any other case, has the consent of each of those (if any) who have parental responsibility for the child.

(6) A person who would not otherwise be entitled (under the previous provisions of this section) to apply for the variation or discharge of a section 8 order shall be entitled to do so if—

(a) the order was made on his application; or

(b) in the case of a contact order, he is named in the order.

(7) Any person who falls within a category of person prescribed by rules of court is entitled to apply for any such section 8 order as may be prescribed in relation to that category of person.

(8) Where the person applying for leave to make an application for a section 8 order is the child concerned, the court may only grant leave if it is satisfied that he has sufficient understanding to make the proposed application for the section 8 order.

(9) Where the person applying for leave to make an application for a section 8 order is not the child concerned, the court shall, in deciding whether or not to grant leave, have particular regard to—

(a) the nature of the proposed application for the section 8 order;

(b) the applicant's connection with the child;

(c) any risk there might be of that proposed application disrupting the child's life to such an extent that he would be harmed by it; and

(d) where the child is being looked after by a local authority—

    (i) the authority's plans for the child's future; and

    (ii) the wishes and feelings of the child's parents.

(10) The period of three years mentioned in subsection (5)(b) need not be continuous but must not have begun more than five years before, or ended more than three months before, the making of the application.

DEFINITIONS

"child": ss.9(7), 105(1).
"child in care of the local authority": s.105(1).
"child of the family": s.105(1).
"contact order": s.8(1).
"guardian": s.5.
"local authority": s.105(1).
"parental responsibility": ss.2, 3, 12.
"residence order": ss.8(1), 105(3).
"section 8 order": ss.8, 11(7).
"the court": s.92(7).
"three years": s.10(10).

GENERAL NOTE

This section enacts the Law Commission's proposals for a coherent scheme for determining the circumstances in which section 8 orders may be granted. The court is empowered to grant orders on application or of its own motion in family proceedings. Subss. (4)–(7) list the people who are qualified to apply for the different types of section 8 orders or their variation or discharge without leave. Generally these repeat the previous law relating to applications for custody or access, except that grandparents may no longer make applications for contact (access) without leave or the agreement of the parents, etc. Subs. (8) lays down the conditions for granting leave to child applicants, subs. (9) to others. The purpose of the restrictions on making applications is "to protect families from unwarranted interference" (*per* the Lord Chancellor, *Hansard*, H.L. Vol. 503, col. 49). There is no replacement for Children Act 1975, s.41; a child may be removed while an application for a residence order is pending but this will not prevent the order being made (subs. (10)).

This section must be read with s.1, which indicates how the court should exercise its discretion.

Subss. (1) and (2)

May: The Law Commission took the view that orders should only be granted where they were necessary (Law Com., para. 3.2).

"No doubt in many, possibly most, uncontested cases an order is needed in the children's own interests, so as to confirm and give stability to the existing arrangements, to clarify the respective rôles of the parents, to reassure the parent with whom the child is living and even to reassure the public authorities . . . Where a child has a good relationship with both parents the law should seek to disturb this as little as possible. There is always a risk that orders . . . deciding upon residence and contact will have the effect of polarising parents' rôles . . ."

This view was strongly supported by the Lord Chancellor (*Hansard*, H.L. Vol. 502, col. 1226). There are circumstances where orders are desirable (see notes to s.1(5)).

Entitled: For any section 8 order see s.10(4); for residence and contact order see s.10(5); for variation or discharge see s.10(6).

Subs. (4)

Parent: This means the child's mother or father (see notes to s.2(1)).

Guardian: A guardian whose appointment has not yet taken effect under s.5(7) or (8) will need consent under s.10(5) or have to apply for leave under s.10(9). The fact that he has been chosen to be a guardian must be considered under s.10(9)(b).

Any person in whose favour a residence order: A residence order gives a person parental responsibility and thus puts him in the same position as a married parent except where the statute provides otherwise (see s.12(3)).

In force: Residence orders normally expire when the child reaches 16 years (s.91(10)). Where a non-parent wants a residence order to continue beyond age 16 he should either ensure that the initial order states this or apply for its variation before the child reaches 16. If he does not, the order will lapse and he will need to seek leave under s.10(9).

Subs. (5)

The Law Commission, who proposed this provision (Law Com. 172, para. 4.48), stated that its object was "not to provide a qualification for applying . . . but to dispense with the requirement of leave where it would be a meaningless formality".

(*a*) Applications by step-parents and former step-parents. The definition of "child of the family" is the same as in the M.C.A. 1973, s.52(1). It means that the child need not be a child of the applicant or of his spouse or of his former spouse.

(*b*) These applicants could formerly have applied for a custodianship order without the consent of any person (Children Act 1975, s.33(3)(c)). The definition of the three year period is now more liberal but it cannot start more than five years before the application is made (s.10(10)).

(*c*) Applications by others can only be made with the relevant consent:—

(*i*) all of those with a residence order;

(*ii*) where the child is subject to a care order, of the local authority. If the application is by a foster parent who comes within s.10(5)(b), no consent will be required. All other local authority foster parents (and some former foster parents) will require the consent of the authority under s.9(3) or s.10(5)(c)(ii);

(*iii*) of the child's parents or guardians. If there is a residence order, parental consent is not required unless the order is in favour of a parent (s.10(5)(c)(i)).

Subs. (7)

No rules have yet been made; grandparents are most likely to benefit if rules are made.

Subs. (8)

This requires children who wish to make applications to show that they are competent to do so. The issue of sufficient understanding to make decisions was discussed by the House of Lords in *Gillick* v. *West Norfolk Area Health Authority* [1986] A.C. 112. In relation to contraception, Lord Scarman stated, "It is not enough that she should understand the nature of the advice which is being given: she must also have sufficient maturity to understand what is involved" (at p.424). A child applying for a contact order would thus have to want the court to determine the issue of contact and perhaps even have some understanding that involving the court may disturb relationships with carers and may not necessarily achieve the desired aims.

The test of understanding may be different according to the type of application.

Subs. (9)

It may be advisable for anyone who otherwise needs leave to first seek to obtain agreement to the application from those specified in s.10(5). There may be little to be gained by requiring applicants to go through the leave process if there is a strong possibility that leave will eventually be granted.

Until further restrictions are introduced on the wardship jurisdiction, anyone who has to seek leave for a section 8 application may alternatively consider making an application in wardship. Where a residence order is sought the use of wardship may be inconvenient because of the need to seek the court's directions in relation to major decisions unless the court made a residence order in wardship (s.8(3)(a)). Wardship is not available to challenge *intra vires* decisions of local authorities (*A* v. *Liverpool City Council* [1982] A.C. 363, *W* v. *Hertfordshire County Council* [1985] 2 All E.R. 301) and thus cannot be used to get over the hurdle of local authority consent under ss.9(3) or 10(5)(c) unless this has been withheld in bad faith.

The extent to which an application for leave can disrupt a child's life will depend largely on whether provision is made for considering applications *ex parte*. The Lord Chancellor was adamant that para. (c) was not intended to prejudge the substantive issue (*Hansard*, H.L. Vol. 502, col. 1230), although it seems most unlikely that leave would be granted where there was little chance that the desired order would be granted. The High Court has already faced this difficulty when considering applications to place wards for adoption (see Lowe & White, *Wards of Court* (1986) 14.2.3.).

The Law Commission suggested that the requirement for leave would "scarcely be a hurdle at all to close relatives . . . who wish to care for or visit the child" (Law Com. 172, para. 4.4). Closer attention may be paid to those who merely seek to restrict parental action with a prohibited steps or specific issue order. Where the child is being looked after by a local authority para. (d)(i) provides the opportunity for the courts to extend the decisions in *W*. v. *Hertfordshire County Council* [1985] 2 All E.R. 301 and *M*. v. *H*. [1988] 3 W.L.R. 485, so that non-parents are prevented from making any substantive applications in relation to children accommodated by local authorities (not just those subject to care orders) which are not acceptable to the local authority. If the child is sufficiently mature to obtain leave to make his own application under s.10(8), the need to have the local authority's agreement or acquiescence to an application may be avoided. If the child is subject to a care order he will be able to apply for its discharge at any time without establishing that he has any particular understanding under s.39(1)(b), but will be represented by a guardian ad litem who will, if the current rules are repeated, be under an obligation to represent his welfare rather than his wishes. The courts may be more willing to grant leave to relatives, friends or foster parents who wish to care for the child when a discharge application is pending, even where this is opposed by the local authority. Even if leave were not granted under s.10(9), it would still be open for the court to make a residence order in the discharge proceedings.

The welfare principle (s.1(1)) applies to applications for leave as it applies to substantive applications.

Subs. (10)

There was no time set for the beginning of the three year period under the Children Act 1975, s.33, but it had to include the three months preceding the application. The definition of three years differs from that in s.9(4), thus a former foster parent might need leave to apply for a residence order but not the authority's consent to that application. The court would still have to consider the authority's plans under s.10(9)(d).

General principles and supplementary provisions

11.—(1) In proceedings in which any question of making a section 8 order, or any other question with respect to such an order, arises, the court shall (in the light of any rules made by virtue of subsection (2))—
  (a) draw up a timetable with a view to determining the question without delay; and
  (b) give such directions as it considers appropriate for the purpose of ensuring, so far as is reasonably practicable, that that timetable is adhered to.
  (2) Rules of court may—
       (a) specify periods within which specified steps must be taken in relation to proceedings in which such questions arise; and
       (b) make other provision with respect to such proceedings for the

purpose of ensuring, so far as is reasonably practicable, that such questions are determined without delay.

(3) Where a court has power to make a section 8 order, it may do so at any time during the course of the proceedings in question even though it is not in a position to dispose finally of those proceedings.

(4) Where a residence order is made in favour of two or more persons who do not themselves all live together, the order may specify the periods during which the child is to live in the different households concerned.

(5) Where—

    (a) a residence order has been made with respect to a child; and

    (b) as a result of the order the child lives, or is to live, with one of two parents who each have parental responsibility for him,

the residence order shall cease to have effect if the parents live together for a continuous period of more than six months.

(6) A contact order which requires the parent with whom a child lives to allow the child to visit, or otherwise have contact with, his other parent shall cease to have effect if the parents live together for a continuous period of more than six months.

(7) A section 8 order may—

    (a) contain directions about how it is to be carried into effect;

    (b) impose conditions which must be complied with by any person—

        (i) in whose favour the order is made;

        (ii) who is a parent of the child concerned;

        (iii) who is not a parent of his but who has parental responsibility for him; or

        (iv) with whom the child is living,

    and to whom the conditions are expressed to apply;

    (c) be made to have effect for a specified period, or contain provisions which are to have effect for a specified period;

    (d) make such incidental, supplemental or consequential provision as the court thinks fit.

DEFINITIONS

"child": s.105(3).
"parental responsibility": ss.2, 3, 12.
"residence order": ss.8(1), 105(3).
"section 8 order": ss.8, 11(7).
"the court": s.92(7).

GENERAL NOTE

This section contains provision for timetabling (subs. (1)) and allows the courts to make section 8 orders even though the proceedings are still continuing (subs.(3)). It also gives further rules relating to "split" residence orders (subs. (4)), the operation of residence and contact orders in favour of parents who cohabit (subss. (5) and (6)) and the contents of section 8 orders (subs. (7)).

Subs. (1)

Timetable: In any case concerning a section 8 order the court should direct the parties to take action within specific times. In doing so it will have to "be realistic and take account of the circumstances, otherwise it simply will not be adhered to" *per* the Lord Chancellor (*Hansard*, H.L. Vol. 503, col. 1347).

Although the section does not so state, such directions will be enforceable through the law of contempt provided that they are sufficiently clear. Magistrates may similarly punish those who disobey their orders (Magistrates' Courts Act 1980, s.63). A penalty of costs may also be imposed in cases of delay.

Subs. (3)

The Law Commission envisaged that such a power might be used where a party was continuing to delay proceedings (Law Com. 172, para. 4.58). Where such "interim" orders are made the parties should be aware that it may become difficult to get them changed because of the emphasis on the status quo.

Subs. (4)

This specifically allows the court to make a residence order where the child spends time in two or more homes. It does not show any preference for such orders and the courts are likely to continue to be reluctant to grant them if they will lead to a child moving repeatedly after short periods (*Riley* v. *Riley* (1987) 151 J.P. 650). Where a child is at boarding school and spends alternate holidays in different homes a split residence order may be more appropriate than a residence order to one parent and a contact order to the other. If the people concerned are not parents, only the person with a residence order would have parental responsibility; if they are parents, the order made affects the appointment of guardians (s.5).

Subs. (5)

Under the old law only some custody orders lapsed if the parties cohabited (see Law Com. 172, para. 4.13). A residence order only lapses if it is in favour of parents with parental responsibility who cohabit for more than six months. Cohabitation has no effect on a s.4 order granted to an unmarried father by virtue of s.12(1).

Parent: This means mother or father (see note on s.2(1)).

Subs. (6)

This applies even if the unmarried father has not obtained parental responsibility for the child.

Subs. (7)

The directions or conditions will depend on the circumstances of the case and the order sought. The Law Commission considered that these powers would not need to be used frequently (Law Com. 172, para. 4.21–3). S.13 lists the conditions which apply to all residence orders. Those who do not want to share a residence order or allow contact may be encouraged to do so with conditions relating to their particular anxieties. Conditions can only be imposed on third parties who have parental responsibility or with whom the child is living (para. (b)). Conditions need not last as long as the order (s.11(7)(c)).

Directions: *e.g.* in a residence order there could be directions that the child's introduction to their new home should be phased.

Conditions: *e.g.* where the child is cared for by someone who will not consent to a blood transfusion, a condition could be made that the carer will inform someone who will consent where a need arises.

Residence orders and parental responsibility

12.—(1) Where the court makes a residence order in favour of the father of a child it shall, if the father would not otherwise have parental responsibility for the child, also make an order under section 4 giving him that responsibility.

(2) Where the court makes a residence order in favour of any person who is not the parent or guardian of the child concerned that person shall have parental responsibility for the child while the residence order remains in force.

(3) Where a person has parental responsibility for a child as a result of subsection (2), he shall not have the right—

    (a) to consent, or refuse to consent, to the making of an application with respect to the child under section 18 of the Adoption Act 1976;

    (b) to agree, or refuse to agree, to the making of an adoption order, or an order under section 55 of the Act of 1976, with respect to the child; or

    (c) to appoint a guardian for the child.

(4) Where subsection (1) requires the court to make an order under section 4 in respect of the father of a child, the court shall not bring that order to an end at any time while the residence order concerned remains in force.

DEFINITIONS
"child": s.105(1).
"guardian": s.5.
"parental responsibility": ss.2, 3, 12.
"residence order": ss.8(1), 105(3).
"the court": s.92(7).

GENERAL NOTE

This section provides that an unmarried father and any person who is not a parent or guardian will have parental responsibility while a residence order exists in his favour. It also clarifies the rights included in parental responsibility for non-parents. Non-parents are not given power in relation to adoption and freeing applications. They cannot appoint a guardian.

Change of child's name or removal from jurisdiction

13.—(1) Where a residence order is in force with respect to a child, no person may—

(a) cause the child to be known by a new surname; or

(b) remove him from the United Kingdom;

without either the written consent of every person who has parental responsibility for the child or the leave of the court.

(2) Subsection (1)(b) does not prevent the removal of a child, for a period of less than one month, by the person in whose favour the residence order is made.

(3) In making a residence order with respect to a child the court may grant the leave required by subsection (1)(b), either generally or for specified purposes.

DEFINITIONS

"child": s.105(1).
"person who has parental responsibility": ss.2(1), (2), 4(1), 5(6), 12(1)(2).
"residence order": ss.8(1), 105(3).
"the court": s.92(7).

GENERAL NOTE

S.13 re-enacts with modification the conditions imposed in custody orders under the Matrimonial Causes Rules 1977 relating to name change and removal from the jurisdiction.

Subs. (1)

The child's consent is *not* required. A child who objects to the proposed step must seek leave under s.10(8) to apply for a prohibited steps order. It follows that a child will only be able to object if he is of sufficient maturity to gain leave, knows his rights and has the skills to obtain them.

In force: See notes on s.91.

No person: The restriction applies to everyone, not just the parties.

United Kingdom: Not, as formerly, the jurisdiction. The Family Law Act 1986 makes orders enforceable throughout the U.K.

Subs. (2)

Although short term removal by a person with a residence order is not restricted by s.13, it may still pose a substantial threat where that person has substantial links overseas. Removal without the permission of the other parent or the court will still be an offence under the Child Abduction Act 1984 (see note on s.1(5)). A prohibited steps order or a condition under s.11(7) could be sought to preclude any removal. The court would need to be satisfied that this was in the child's best interests. A real threat of permanent removal ought to be sufficient. S.11 could also be used to ensure that trips were notified in advance with an itinerary and contact addresses.

Enforcement of residence orders

14.—(1) Where—

(a) a residence order is in force with respect to a child in favour of any person; and

(b) any other person (including one in whose favour the order is also in force) is in breach of the arrangements settled by that order,

the person mentioned in paragraph (a) may, as soon as the requirement in subsection (2) is complied with, enforce the order under section 63(3) of the Magistrates' Courts Act 1980 as if it were an order requiring the other person to produce the child to him.

(2) The requirement is that a copy of the residence order has been served on the other person.

(3) Subsection (1) is without prejudice to any other remedy open to the person in whose favour the residence order is in force.

DEFINITIONS
   "child": s.105(1).
   "residence order": ss.8(1), 105(3).

GENERAL NOTE
   This section enables residence orders to be enforced under the Magistrates' Courts Act 1980, s.63(3), *i.e.* by a penalty of £50 for every day of breach up to a maximum of £2,000 or by imprisonment for up to two months. These enforcement provisions previously applied to orders for actual custody or for access under the G.M.A. 1971 and the D.P.M.C.A. 1978 as well as orders for actual custody (custodianship) under the Children Act 1975, s.43(1). The magistrates' court must be satisfied beyond reasonable doubt that the breach has occurred before punishing for disobedience (see: *Dean* v. *Dean* [1987] 1 FLR 517). The failure to obey the court order must be wilful (*Patterson* v. *Walcot* [1984] Fam. 32). Where a financial penalty is imposed it is enforceable as a fine (Magistrates' Courts Act 1980, s.63(4)).
   Under the Contempt of Court Act 1981, s.17, enforcement may be by way of complaint or of the court's own motion. A residence order may be enforced against any person, including a person in whose favour the order is made (subs. (1)), but only after the order has been served on him (subs. (2)). Breach of orders made by the county court or the High Court may be enforced as contempts of court.

Financial relief

Orders for financial relief with respect to children

   15.—(1) Schedule 1 (which consists primarily of the re-enactment, with consequential amendments and minor modifications, of provisions of the Guardianship of Minors Acts 1971 and 1973, the Children Act 1975 and of sections 15 and 16 of the Family Law Reform Act 1987) makes provision in relation to financial relief for children.

   (2) The powers of a magistrates' court under section 60 of the Magistrates' Courts Act 1980 to revoke, revive or vary an order for the periodical payment of money shall not apply in relation to an order made under Schedule 1.

GENERAL NOTE
   This section should be read with Sched. 1. The Law Commission explained the reason for this proposal in Law Com. 172, para. 4.59–69. The aim is to replace the confusing and inconsistent provisions relating to financial relief for children with new provisions with identical rules for making orders regardless of who has a residence order. The new provisions do not replace those in the M.C.A. 1973, nor the D.P.M.C.A. 1978, which the Law Commission could not conveniently assimilate into its scheme. They do not impose the obligation to maintain the child under a court order on any new people—only parents and step-parents (all termed "parents" see Sched. 1, para. 16) can be required to pay. Parents, including unmarried fathers without parental responsibility, guardians and people with a residence order will be able to apply for a whole range of orders for a child but secured orders, settlements and property transfers can only be made in the High Court or county court. Repeated applications for settlements and property transfers by the same person in relation to the same child will still not be possible. Variation, etc., does not come within the

Magistrates' Courts Act 1980 but is provided for in Sched. 1, paras. 6, 7. The powers in Sched. 1 will be exercisable in respect of wards (para. 1(7) added by the Courts and Legal Services Bill, Sched. 10, para. 6).

Family assistance orders

Family assistance orders

16.—(1) Where, in any family proceedings, the court has power to make an order under this Part with respect to any child, it may (whether or not it makes such an order) make an order requiring—
  (a) a probation officer to be made available; or
  (b) a local authority to make an officer of the authority available,
to advise, assist and (where appropriate) befriend any person named in the order.

(2) The persons who may be named in an order under this section ("a family assistance order") are—
  (a) any parent or guardian of the child;
  (b) any person with whom the child is living or in whose favour a contact order is in force with respect to the child;
  (c) the child himself.

(3) No court may make a family assistance order unless—
  (a) it is satisfied that the circumstances of the case are exceptional; and
  (b) it has obtained the consent of every person to be named in the order other than the child.

(4) A family assistance order may direct—
  (a) the person named in the order; or
  (b) such of the persons named in the order as may be specified in the order,
to take such steps as may be so specified with a view to enabling the officer concerned to be kept informed of the address of any person named in the order and to be allowed to visit any such person.

(5) Unless it specifies a shorter period, a family assistance order shall have effect for a period of six months beginning with the day on which it is made.

(6) Where—
  (a) a family assistance order is in force with respect to a child; and
  (b) a section 8 order is also in force with respect to the child,
the officer concerned may refer to the court the question whether the section 8 order should be varied or discharged.

(7) A family assistance order shall not be made so as to require a local authority to make an officer of theirs available unless—
  (a) the authority agree; or
  (b) the child concerned lives or will live within their area.

(8) Where a family assistance order requires a probation officer to be made available, the officer shall be selected in accordance with arrangements made by the probation committee for the area in which the child lives or will live.

(9) If the selected probation officer is unable to carry out his duties, or dies, another probation officer shall be selected in the same manner.

DEFINITIONS
  "child": s.105(1).
  "family assistance order": s.16(1).
  "family proceedings": s.8(3).
  "guardian": s.5.
  "local authority": s.105(1).
  "the court": s.92(7).

GENERAL NOTE

Family assistance orders replace supervision orders in custody proceedings. The Law Commission recommended (Law Com. 172, para. 5.10–5.20) the creation of a new order to remove the need to make the more powerful supervision orders where any social work involvement was intended to be short term, for example to help the family cope with the immediate problems arising out of separation, etc., to promote arrangements for contact or facilitate co-operation between the parties. However, the Law Commission intended that the courts would still be able to make supervision orders in family proceedings but that recommendation was not enacted. Supervision orders are now only available after proof of the grounds in s.31.

Family assistance orders may only be made in exceptional circumstances and with the agreement of all those involved (except the child) (subss. (3) and (7)). There is no need for the court to make a section 8 order (subs. (1)), but the supervisor may refer the matter back to court if there is one (subs. (6)). The order lasts for a maximum of six months and cannot be renewed (subs. (5)). The order requires a probation officer or officer of a local authority to be made available (subss. (1), (7)–(9)) and may direct anyone named to keep the officer informed of their or the child's address and permit visits (subs. (4)). It is fundamental to this type of time-limited social work that all those involved should know of its purposes and agree to them. The Law Commission recommended that courts should state what they hope to achieve by an order (para. 5.20). Although there is no specific provision to this end, in s.16 those whose consent is required will need to be given a clear idea what they are agreeing to.

Subs. (1)

An officer: The officer need not be a social worker; it may be more appropriate for a member of a welfare benefits unit to be appointed in some cases.

Advise, assist, befriend: This was the duty of the supervisor under a supervision order in care proceedings (C.Y.P.A. 1969, s.14).

The Law Commission suggested that where there has been a report to the court the report writer should be appointed. This will not be possible if the local authority "subcontracts" reporting work under s.7(1)(b)(ii).

Subs. (2)

Any person with whom the child is living: This rather curious wording is used because no residence order may have been made. However, it is presumably only intended that adults or carers are named, and not the child's siblings, because named people other than the child must consent (s.16(3)(b)).

Subs. (3)

Exceptional: The order must also be in the child's best interests (s.1(1) and (5)).

Other than the child: It is desirable that the child also supports the making of the order, especially if he will be expected to co-operate with the worker. If the child is adamantly opposed, the order may not be in his best interests.

Subs. (6)

The power of the officer is much less than that which a supervisor had in matrimonial proceedings. He may only refer back issues relating to existing section 8 orders and cannot therefore take steps for the child's committal to care. Where a matter is referred back the court can make any section 8 order (s.10(1)(b)) subject to the restrictions in s.9. The officer would not need to make an application. Where the officer is concerned about the child's well-being he should refer the case to the local authority for investigation under s.47(1)(b).

PART III

LOCAL AUTHORITY SUPPORT FOR CHILDREN AND FAMILIES

Provision of services for children and their families

Provision of services for children in need, their families and others

17.—(1) It shall be the general duty of every local authority (in addition to the other duties imposed on them by this Part)—

(a) to safeguard and promote the welfare of children within their area who are in need; and

(b) so far as is consistent with that duty, to promote the upbringing of such children by their families,

by providing a range and level of services appropriate to those children's needs.

(2) For the purpose principally of facilitating the discharge of their general duty under this section, every local authority shall have the specific duties and powers set out in Part 1 of Schedule 2.

(3) Any service provided by an authority in the exercise of functions conferred on them by this section may be provided for the family of a particular child in need or for any member of his family, if it is provided with a view to safeguarding or promoting the child's welfare.

(4) The Secretary of State may by order amend any provision of Part I of Schedule 2 or add any further duty or power to those for the time being mentioned there.

(5) Every local authority—

(a) shall facilitate the provision by others (including in particular voluntary organisations) of services which the authority have power to provide by virtue of this section, or section 18, 20, 23 or 24; and

(b) may make such arrangements as they see fit for any person to act on their behalf in the provision of any such service.

(6) The services provided by a local authority in the exercise of functions conferred on them by this section may include giving assistance in kind or, in exceptional circumstances, in cash.

(7) Assistance may be unconditional or subject to conditions as to the repayment of the assistance or of its value (in whole or in part).

(8) Before giving any assistance or imposing any conditions, a local authority shall have regard to the means of the child concerned and of each of his parents.

(9) No person shall be liable to make any repayment of assistance or of its value at any time when he is in receipt of income support or family credit under the Social Security Act 1986.

(10) For the purposes of this Part a child shall be taken to be in need if—

(a) he is unlikely to achieve or maintain, or to have the opportunity of achieving or maintaining, a reasonable standard of health or development without the provision for him of services by a local authority under this Part;

(b) his health or development is likely to be significantly impaired, or further impaired, without the provision for him of such services; or

(c) he is disabled,

and "family", in relation to such a child, includes any person who has parental responsibility for the child and any other person with whom he has been living.

(11) For the purposes of this Part, a child is disabled if he is blind, deaf or dumb or suffers from mental disorder of any kind or is substantially and permanently handicapped by illness, injury or congenital deformity or such other disability as may be prescribed; and in this Part—

"development" means physical, intellectual, emotional, social or behavioural development; and

"health" means physical or mental health.

Definitions
   "child": s.105(1).
   "child in need": s.17(10).
   "development": s.17(11).

"disabled": s.17(11).
"family": s.17(10).
"functions": s.105(1).
"health": s.17(11).
"local authority": s.105(1).
"person who has parental responsibility": s.2(1)(2), 4(1), 5(6), 12(1)(2).
"services": s.105, Sched. 2, Pt. I.
"voluntary organisation": s.105(1).

GENERAL NOTE

This section sets out the general preventive duty which each local authority owes to "children in need" in their area. The duty is broader than that in s.1 of the C.C.A. 1980, which was negative—written in terms of keeping children out of care rather than promoting their welfare—but it is owed to a restricted group of children. It also replaces, as far as children are concerned, the duties of local authorities under the health and welfare statutes. Consequently ss. 21 and 29 of the National Assistance Act 1948 are amended by Sched. 13, para. 11 to apply to persons over 18 years only; the Chronically Sick and Disabled Persons Act 1970 is extended to "children in need" by Sched. 13, para. 27 and s.21 and Sched. 8 of the National Health Service Act 1977 are repealed so far as they applied to children.

In order to comply with the general duty, a local authority must provide services to "children in need" and their families which are appropriate to their needs (subs. (1)). Services may not be imposed under this provision. This can occur only if the authority has obtained an order under s.31 (or possibly under ss.16 or 36). The Lord Chancellor stated that "Partnership with parents based on agreement so far as possible will be the guiding principle" for the provision of services (*Hansard*, H.L. Vol. 502, col. 491). Sched. 2, Pt. I, expands the section by specifying the action local authorities must take to identify "children in need" and discharge their general duty. In addition, local authorities are under a duty to facilitate the provision of services by others and may delegate provision to others (subs. (5)). Services may include giving assistance in kind or (exceptionally) in cash (subs. (6)). Assistance may be given subject to conditions (subs. (7)) and must be means-tested (subs. (8)). No repayments may be required from a person in receipt of specified social security benefits (subs. (9)). These provisions relating to repayment must be read in conjunction with s.29, which gives further details about liability and recovery.

Subs. (1)

This provision represents a fundamental shift by providing a statutory framework for all preventive work in child care, not only that designed to help keep children out of care. It recognises both the value of family life and that care may have a positive contribution to make to the welfare of children.

S.1 of the C.C.A. 1980 (introduced by the Children and Young Persons Act 1963) was couched in similarly general terms and was open to two alternative interpretations. It either created a general duty to provide services to keep children out of care or it imposed a specific duty to consider the impact of any decision on individual children who might, in consequence, come into care. In *Att.-Gen. Ex rel Tilley* v. *Wandsworth London Borough Council* [1981] 1 W.L.R. 854 both the High Court and the Court of Appeal held that a specific duty was created. Even so, it was extremely difficult to use court proceedings to enforce the duty in s.1. In *R.* v. *Tower Hamlets London Borough Council, ex p. Monaf* (1988) 20 H.L.R. 529, the Court of Appeal held that the local authority had complete discretion about how the duty should be carried out. Thus s.1 could not impose any greater duty to rehouse an intentionally homeless family than that which existed in the Housing Act 1985. The High Court also refused to find that ss.18 and 21 of the C.C.A. 1980, which specified local authorities' duties to children in care, could found an action in damages (*Guevara* v. *London Borough of Hounslow, The Times*, April 17, 1987).

S.2(3) of the C.C.A. 1980 imposed a duty to rehabilitate children in voluntary care where this was consistent with their welfare. The new duty is broader because it is not limited to such children, but would include children in hospitals, in the care of voluntary organisations or in other forms of substitute care like private fostering arrangements. Local authorities have some responsibility for the welfare of such children under Pts. VII–IX and ss.85 and 86.

General duty: The addition of the word "general" would suggest that the interpretation of s.1 in the *Tilley* case would no longer apply, but this is far from clear, particularly since the appropriateness of services can only be judged by looking at the individuals who are in need of them.

Other duties:
> *s.18(1)(3):* day care for some under fives who are "children in need";
> *s.20(1):* provision of accommodation for some children in need;
> *ss.22, 23 and 24(1):* duties to children looked after by the local authority;
> *s.24:* duties to some people who have been in care and the duties listed in Sched. 2, Pt. I.
> *s.84:* this empowers the Secretary of State to deal with default;
> *ss.85, 86, etc:* duties to children living away from home.

Welfare: There is no definition of Welfare for Pt. III. The intention of the Government was to achieve an appropriate balance between the state's powers and those of individual parents. It was guided in its consideration by a number of principles, including that the prime responsibility for the upbringing of children rests with parents and that the state should be ready to help parents to discharge that responsibility, especially where doing so lessened the risk of family breakdown (Cm. 62, para. 5). However, it is well established that the views of individual social workers (and their managers) differ, particularly in relation to the value of the natural family and the consequences of entering local authority care (see Fox, *Two Value Positions in Recent Child Care Law and Practice* (1982) 12 Brit.J. of Social Work 265–290). Even where there is agreement about children's needs there may be no duty on the local authority to satisfy them. For example, the National Child Development Study provides considerable evidence that poverty is associated with poor health, poor educational attainment, employment problems and reception into care for children. Yet s.17 does not require local authorities to take on an income maintenance rôle, nor is it likely that there would be resources to let local authorities exercise their powers in this way.

So far as is consistent: Where it is not, the authority can offer to accommodate under s.20(1)(c) or take care proceedings under s.31. It could also decide to take no action subject to its duty to prevent neglect and abuse (Sched. 2, para. 4) and its duty to investigate suspected abuse and neglect (s.47).

A range and level of services appropriate: What services are provided and the numbers they can serve would seem largely to be left to the local authority, as under the Court of Appeal decision in *ex p. Monaf*. It will be extremely difficult to show that services are not appropriate. If an authority fails to provide services which are widely accepted as desirable—foster care, residential placements for teenagers or day care for the under fives (see ss.18 and 19)—or provides a level of services considered inadequate by the Social Services Inspectorate it might be in breach. Action could then be taken under s.84. However, in many areas there is sufficient disagreement to make challenge impossible.

Subs. (2)

The duties in Sched. 2, Pt. I, are largely qualified, *i.e.* that the local authority shall take *reasonable* steps or make such provisions as *they consider appropriate*. The duties include to identify the extent to which there are children in need in their area (para. 1); to prevent children suffering neglect or abuse (para. 4); to provide specific services including advice, activities, home helps (para. 8) and family centres (para. 9) and, where the child is not living with his family, to enable him to live with or be in contact with them (para. 10). The duties to disabled children which came from the National Assistance Act 1948 and the Chronically Sick and Disabled Persons Act 1970 are absolute. Local authorities must open and maintain a register of disabled children (para. 2) and provide services for them (para. 6). Local authorities are also required to provide information about children likely to suffer harm (para. 4) and take reasonable steps to reduce the need to bring various proceedings or take other specific steps in relation to children (para. 7). In providing day care or encouraging people to act as foster parents, the authority must have regard to the ethnic mix of their area (para. 11). The local authority is also empowered to assist alleged abusers to obtain alternative accommodation and may recoup assistance given under s.17(7)–(9) (para. 5).

Subs. (3)

Family: This is defined in subs. (10) to include "any person with parental responsibility for the child and any other person with whom he has been living". It is not clear whether this adds to a general understanding of family or not. If it does, then relatives with whom the child has not been living, for example, uncles and aunts, or the child's unmarried father, can also receive assistance with a view to safeguarding, etc., the child's welfare. Thus assistance could be given to enable such a person to take over the child's care. If family is more narrowly construed, then such people would either have to obtain parental responsibility by applying to the court (under s.10) or be accepted as local authority foster parents so that they could be assisted through the local authority's duties to children it accommodates under s.23. A wider interpretation of family would appear to be more in keeping with the aims of the legislation.

A member of his family: The assistance may be provided to individuals. This phrase has been interpreted where it appears in the Rent Acts (now s.39, Housing Act 1988) to include the unmarried partner of a tenant (*Dyson Holdings* v. *Fox* [1976] Q.B. 503). Unmarried step-parents with whom the child has been living are clearly included in the definition.

Subs. (4)

The duties in the Schedule can be kept up to date by secondary legislation. Any statutory instrument made under this subsection is subject to the affirmative resolution procedure (s.104(3)).

Amend: The Bill would have permitted the Secretary of State "to modify or repeal" the Schedule but this was considered a "constitutional outrage" by Lord Simon (*Hansard*, H.L. Vol. 502, col. 1295). However, an amendment can go "right up to the edge of repeal" (*per* Lord Simon (*Hansard*, H.L. Vol. 505, col. 349). He also stated that no court could possibly find any amendment was in excess of the Secretary of State's powers).

Subs. (6)

S.1 of the C.C.A. 1980 permitted local authorities to assist in this way. The Lord Chancellor rejected the notion that there should be a broader power because this "could push local authorities into income maintenance rôle which is the function of the Social Security System" (*Hansard*, H.L. Vol. 502, col. 1297).

S.1 payments are disregarded for the purposes of calculating means-tested social security payments and Housing Benefit (Income Support (General) Regulations 1987, reg. 40(2), Sched. 9, para. 28, Family Credit (General) Regulations 1987, reg. 29(2), Sched. 3, para. 18). The Lord Chancellor indicated that the exception would also apply to the new provision (*Hansard*, H.L. Vol. 502, col. 1298).

Assistance in kind: Both the High Court and the Court of Appeal rejected a narrow interpretation of "assistance in kind" which would have excluded provision of accommodation for a family under s.1 of the C.C.A. 1980 (see *Att.-Gen. ex rel. Tilley* v. *Wandsworth London Borough Council* [1981] 1 W.L.R. 854.)

Exceptional circumstances: There are two possible interpretations: a restrictive one which requires the circumstances to be exceptional in the life of the individual recipient and another which requires them to be exceptional in the community.

Subs. (7)

The Health and Social Services and Social Security Adjudications Act 1983, s.17, introduced a consistent scheme for charging for services provided by local authorities. That section applied (*inter alia*) to s.29 of the National Assistance Act 1948, and Sched. 8 of the National Health Service Act 1977, which have both been subsumed in this Act so far as they apply to children. However, there was no power to levy charges in the C.C.A. 1980 except where the child was in care. Thus the new power is broader.

Only parents are liable at common law to maintain their children, although step-parents can be required to make contributions for their care in domestic and matrimonial proceedings. Only parents have a duty to maintain their children enforceable in public law. However, non-parents may be given assistance and can be required to pay for it under s.29. If a service were provided to a non-parent for a child under 16, a charge could be levied on the parents or on the recipient. If the recipient has a residence order or is the child's guardian he could seek reimbursement from the parent through an order for financial relief under Sched. 1. Where a service is provided to keep a child out of care it would seem inappropriate for the local authority to impose a condition as to repayment on a non-parent, because such a person would not be liable to support the child if he were being looked after by the local authority.

It is not clear that refusal to accept a condition about repayment or outstanding debts would justify refusal to provide assistance. The Lord Chancellor stated, "The Bill does not provide that failure of parents to comply with any conditions as to assistance renders the child ineligible for other services. The authority's general duty to provide services appropriate to the needs of children in need would remain" (*Hansard*, H.L. Vol. 502, col. 1299). That statement leaves in doubt the position of an individual child (see the discussion of subs. (1)). Conditions about repayment must be lifted where the payee's means are insufficient (see s.29(2)).

Charges may be recovered in the Magistrates' Court as civil debts (s.29(5)).

Conditions: This might include, for example, interest. The power to charge interest already exists under the comparable Scottish legislation.

Assistance: This would seem to be sufficiently wide to cover any services provided by the local authority under this section or Sched. 2, Pt. I. However, s.29(1) provides that charges may not be levied for advice, guidance or counselling. It may, however, be difficult to separate this from the provision of some services. For example, a place in a family centre intended to improve parenting skills could be seen as guidance or alternatively training and recreational activities (see Sched. 2, para. 9).

Value: There is no set formula for determining the value of a service which could be the cost to the local authority or the benefit of it to the recipient. If it is the benefit this may be impossible to assess. Charges for accommodating children in care are limited to the amount paid to foster parents as a boarding out allowance (Sched. 2, para. 22(5)). Charges for services are not so limited and could theoretically be higher. If so, this would appear to defeat the general duty in s.17(1)(b). Any dispute about conditions can be referred to the complaints system which must be established under s.26(3).

Subs. (8)

Although non-parents may be charged for services, only parents and children have to be means-tested before assistance is given. Even where the local authority does not wish to impose conditions, it must consider means so that in each case an individual decision is taken. Where the child has funds, his parents, as guardians of his property, (s.3(2)) may have to use them to pay for services. Thus money claimed by child victims from the Criminal Injuries Compensation Scheme may find its way to local authorities assisting them.

Have regard to: Formal means-testing is not required but the authority would need basic information about means.

Subs. (9)

It is not clear whether liability to make repayments is suspended or ended by receipt of benefits. The Department of Health considers that payment is only suspended. Thus when benefit ceases the whole liability resumes. This would create a new benefit trap unless charges were re-assessed. This provision is based on one introduced in relation to charges for accommodation by s.19 of the Health and Social Services and Social Security Adjudications Act 1983. The rationale for not levying charges for accommodation on parents in receipt of benefit is that there is no provision in the parents' benefit for the child in care. Here the exemption of benefit recipients appears to recognise that they are too poor to contribute. If this is so, suspension would be more logical.

In receipt of: A high proportion, up to 65 per cent., of those who qualify for family credit do not claim it. A local authority could decide not to require repayments from such people but they have no right to be exempted. Arguably, when means testing the authority should identify such people and provide advice about benefits under s.17(1).

Subss. (10) and (11)

These contain the definition of "child in need."

Reasonable standard of health or development: It is not clear how reasonable is to be judged: by the standards of the area, by national standards, or by the standards appropriate for a developed nation. There is a danger that some authorities may accept lower standards in relation to certain groups such as travellers' children, but this is not justified by the legislation and may contravene the Race Relations Act 1976.

Without the provision of services: Children in need remain "in need" even where services are provided. Thus children looked after by local authorities or voluntary organisations can still be "in need" and assistance can be given to their families (*per* the Lord Chancellor (*Hansard*, H.L. Vol. 502, col. 1287)).

Significantly impaired: S.31(10) defines "significant harm" and requires a comparison between the child and "that which could be reasonably expected of a similar child". Even slight impairments may be significant for the child's long term development if they affect education or socialisation.

Further impaired: If the child's health development is already impaired, further impairment need not be significant.

Family: See discussion under subs. (3) above.

Disabled: The wording, though different from that in the National Assistance Act 1948, s.29(1), which makes provision for disabled adults, precisely mirrors its content. Thus the same people will qualify for services before and after age 18.

Blind: Although partially sighted children do not clearly fall within the definition of disabled, they are "children in need" by virtue of s.17(10)(a) or (b) (*per* David Mellor, Minister of Health, Standing Committee B, col. 101, May 16, 1989).

Prescribed: This means prescribed by the Secretary of State. No conditions were prescribed under s.29 of the 1948 Act.

Day care for pre-school and other children

18.—(1) Every local authority shall provide such day care for children in need within their area who are—

(a) aged five or under; and

(b) not yet attending schools,

as is appropriate.

(2) A local authority may provide day care for children within their area who satisfy the conditions mentioned in subsection (1)(a) and (b) even though they are not in need.

(3) A local authority may provide facilities (including training, advice, guidance and counselling) for those—

(a) caring for children in day care; or

(b) who at any time accompany such children while they are in day care.

(4) In this section "day care" means any form of care or supervised activity provided for children during the day (whether or not it is provided on a regular basis).

(5) Every local authority shall provide for children in need within their area who are attending any school such care or supervised activities as is appropriate—

(a) outside school hours; or

(b) during school holidays.

(6) A local authority may provide such care or supervised activities for children within their area who are attending any school even though those children are not in need.

(7) In this section "supervised activity" means an activity supervised by a responsible person.

DEFINITIONS
"child": s.105(1).
"child in need": s.17(10).
"day care": s.18(4).
"local authority": s.105(1).
"supervised activity": s.18(7).

GENERAL NOTE

This section imposes a duty on local authorities to provide specified services for children in need, *i.e.* day care for under fives who are not attending school (subs. (1)) and supervised activities after school hours and during the holidays for children attending school (subs. (5)). It also empowers local authorities to provide these services for other children (subss. (2) and (6)) and facilities for carers (subs. (3)). Charges can be levied for these services (s.29(1)).

Subs. (1)

Not yet attending schools: School hours for children of this age may be as short as one and a half hours per day (Education (Schools and Further Education) Regulations 1981, reg. 10). Attendance is not defined but education law distinguishes between registered pupils and school attendance. Arguably, a child who has a half-time place in a nursery school is not attending school during the rest of the school day. Schools must be distinguished from day nurseries. Local authorities have powers and duties in relation to nurseries under Pt. X of this Act.

As is appropriate: This gives the authority considerable latitude, but failure to comply may be referred to the Secretary of State under s.84.

Facilities may be provided for workers such as childminders, nursery nurses, play leaders and also for parents and other people who bring children to playgroups, etc. (Subs. (3)).

The definition of "day care" is broad and, unlike s.71(1), not limited to care not on domestic premises. It also covers children cared for by their own families or in their own homes.

Subs. (7)
Responsible person: This is not defined. Arguably, anyone who has charge of children is responsible for them.

Review of provision for day care, child minding etc.

19.—(1) Every local authority in England and Wales shall review—
    (a) the provision which they make under section 18;
    (b) the extent to which the services of child minders are available within their area with respect to children under the age of eight; and
    (c) the provision for day care within their area made for children under the age of eight by persons other, than the authority, required to register under section 71(1)(b).

(2) A review under subsection (1) shall be conducted—
    (a) together with the appropriate local education authority; and
    (b) at least once in every review period.

(3) Every local authority in Scotland shall, at least once in every review period, review—
    (a) the provision for day care within their area made for children under the age of eight by the local authority and by persons required to register under section 71(1)(b); and
    (b) the extent to which the services of child minders are available within their area with respect to children under the age of eight.

(4) In conducting any such review, the two authorities or, in Scotland, the authority shall have regard to the provision made with respect to children under the age of eight in relevant establishments within their area.

(5) In this section—
    "relevant establishment" means any establishment which is mentioned in paragraphs 3 and 4 of Schedule 9 (hospitals, schools and other establishments exempt from the registration requirements which apply in relation to the provision of day care); and
    "review period" means the period of one year beginning with the commencement of this section and each subsequent period of three years beginning with an anniversary of that commencement.

(6) Where a local authority have conducted a review under this section they shall publish the result of the review—
    (a) as soon as is reasonably practicable;
    (b) in such form as they consider appropriate; and
    (c) together with any proposals they may have with respect to the matters reviewed.

(7) The authorities conducting any review under this section shall have regard to—
    (a) any representations made to any one of them by any relevant health authority or health board; and
    (b) any other representations which they consider to be relevant.

(8) In the application of this section to Scotland, "day care" has the same meaning as in section 79 and "health board" has the same meaning as in the National Health Service (Scotland) Act 1978.

DEFINITIONS
"childminder" s.71(2).
"day care": s.18(4).
"health authority": s.105(1).
"local authority": s.105(1).
"local education authority": s.105(1).
"relevant establishment": s.19(5).
"review period": s.19(5).

GENERAL NOTE

This section imposes a new duty on local authorities in England and Wales to review the day care they provide and that for children under eight years by childminders and in play groups and nurseries which are required to register with the local authority (subs. (1)). The review must be carried out with the local education authority at least every three years (subss. (2) and (5)) and must take account of other provisions for under fives in schools and hospitals (subs. (5)). They must also take account of representations by health authorities and others (subs. (7)). The results of the review must be published (subs. (6)). A comparable duty is imposed on Scottish local authorities by subs. (3). For definitions applying to Scotland, see subs. (4) and s.79.

The purpose of the review is so that public and private facilities for under fives complement each other and to assist planning. There will be general guidance from the Secretary of State on the provision of services.

Subs. (2)

Appropriate local authority: This is not defined for the purposes of this section but presumably means the local education authority operating in the area of the local authority.

Subs. (7)

Other representations: This includes "local voluntary groups, parents and employers" (David Mellor, Minister of Health (Standing Committee B, col. 523, June 13, 1989)). The Minister also suggested that this clause would give local people an opportunity to put pressure on local councillors to give more attention to these services (Standing Committee B, col. 124, May 16, 1989).

Provision of accommodation for children

Provision of accommodation for children: general

20.—(1) Every local authority shall provide accommodation for any child in need within their area who appears to them to require accommodation as a result of—

  (a) there being no person who has parental responsibility for him;

  (b) his being lost or having been abandoned; or

  (c) the person who has been caring for him being prevented (whether or not permanently, and for whatever reason) from providing him with suitable accommodation or care.

(2) Where a local authority provide accommodation under subsection (1) for a child who is ordinarily resident in the area of another local authority, that other local authority may take over the provision of accommodation for the child within—

  (a) three months of being notified in writing that the child is being provided with accommodation; or

  (b) such other longer period as may be prescribed.

(3) Every local authority shall provide accommodation for any child in need within their area who has reached the age of sixteen and whose welfare the authority consider is likely to be seriously prejudiced if they do not provide him with accommodation.

(4) A local authority may provide accommodation for any child within their area (even though a person who has parental responsibility for him

is able to provide him with accommodation) if they consider that to do so would safeguard or promote the child's welfare.

(5) A local authority may provide accommodation for any person who has reached the age of sixteen but is under twenty-one in any community home which takes children who have reached the age of sixteen if they consider that to do so would safeguard or promote his welfare.

(6) Before providing accommodation under this section, a local authority shall, so far as is reasonably practicable and consistent with the child's welfare—

(a) ascertain the child's wishes regarding the provision of accommodation; and

(b) give due consideration (having regard to his age and understanding) to such wishes of the child as they have been able to ascertain.

(7) A local authority may not provide accommodation under this section for any child if any person who—

(a) has parental responsibility for him; and

(b) is willing and able to—

(i) provide accommodation for him; or

(ii) arrange for accommodation to be provided for him,

objects.

(8) Any person who has parental responsibility for a child may at any time remove the child from accommodation provided by or on behalf of the local authority under this section.

(9) Subsections (7) and (8) do not apply while any person—

(a) in whose favour a residence order is in force with respect to the child; or

(b) who has care of the child by virtue of an order made in the exercise of the High Court's inherent jurisdiction with respect to children,

agrees to the child being looked after in accommodation provided by or on behalf of the local authority.

(10) Where there is more than one such person as is mentioned in subsection (9), all of them must agree.

(11) Subsections (7) and (8) do not apply where a child who has reached the age of sixteen agrees to being provided with accommodation under this section.

DEFINITIONS
"child" : s.105(1).
"child in need": ss.17(10), 105(7).
"community home": s.53.
"local authority": s.105(1).
"ordinary residence": ss.30(2), 105(6).
"person with parental responsiblity": ss.2(1)(2), 4(1), 5(6), 12(1)(2).
"prescribed": s.105(1).
"residence order": ss.8(1), 105(3).

GENERAL NOTE
This section replaces s.2 of the C.C.A. 1980 and the related sections which provided the statutory framework for the voluntary care system. The concept of "provision of accommodation" replaces reception into care. Local authorities are under a duty to provide accommodation for children in need who satisfy any of the conditions in subs. (1) or subs. (3). They also have the power to provide accommodation for any child and young adults under the age of 21 years (subss. (4) and (5)). Before accommodation is provided, the local authority must ascertain the child's wishes and feelings about this and give due consideration to them (subs. (6)). The voluntary nature of the provision under this section is clear from subss. (7) and (8). Subs. (7) precludes the local authority from providing accommodation for a child under 16 if any person with parental responsibility who is willing and able to provide accommodation for him objects. Subs. (8) states that a person with parental responsibility may remove a child under 16 years at any time. If there is a residence order or order giving

care and control under the inherent jurisdiction of the High Court, these decisions can only be made by a person in whose favour the order was made (subs. (9)). If there is more than one, all must agree (subs. (10)). Those over 16 may themselves decide about going into or remaining in local authority accommodation (subs. (11)).

There is no provision to replace s.13 of the C.C.A. 1980, so people with parental responsibility cannot be required to give 28 days' notice before removing children from local authority accommodation. The government remained adamantly opposed to amendments which would undermine the voluntary nature of arrangements for children to be accommodated by local authorities; accommodation by a local authority should equate with that provided in the family.

The Law on Child Care and Family Services (Cm. 62 1987, para. 23) proposed that local authorities should enter into agreements with parents about the care offered covering the initial placement, schooling and access. There is no provision in s.20 for such agreements but the Lord Chancellor indicated that there would be in regulations which will replace the Boarding Out of Children (Foster Placement) Regulations 1988 (*Hansard*, H.L. Vol. 503, col. 1412). The statute contains no special powers to deal with breaches of agreement by either side; thus failure to give notice as required by an agreement before removing a child would not of itself justify the local authority keeping the child. Complaints against the local authority can be referred to its procedure under s.26(3).

Subs. (1)

This re-enacts s.2(1) of the C.C.A. 1980 with modifications. The duty is now owed only to children in need but is not limited to those under 17. Over 16s must agree (subs. (11)). The requirement that reception into care must be in the child's welfare in s.2(1)(c) is replaced by the general duty in s.17(1). This duty exists alongside the duties in the Housing Act 1985 to homeless persons. During the Bill's passage through the Lords there were several attempts to restrict the local authority's powers to provide care for children rather than homes for homeless families, but all were unsuccessful.

Subs. (2)

This is a modified form of s.2(4) of the C.C.A. 1980.

Prescribed: This means by the Secretary of State; no period has been prescribed.

Subs. (3)

The law relating to accommodation of 16 year olds and older children is not clear. Parents appear not to be under a duty to accommodate them; they have the right to live independently. The duty of local authorities towards over 16s in need is narrower since it only arises if the authority considers their welfare is likely to be "seriously prejudiced" without provision of accommodation. Local authorities may thus discharge young people from care or refuse to provide them with accommodation even though they are in need. However, they will owe them duties under s.17(1) and also under s.24(2) if they have been accommodated after the age of 16 years.

Subs. (4)

This gives the local authority power to accommodate other children. It provides the authority for respite care schemes which the D.H.S.S. R.C.C.L. Chap. 6 was keen to support.

Subs. (5)

This re-enacts s.72 of the C.C.A. 1980, removing the provisions which required the community home to be near the child's employment or place of education etc.

Subs. (6)

This imposes a qualified duty on the local authority to ascertain a child's wishes and give due consideration to them before providing accommodation. S.22(4) makes similar provision in relation to decisions about other matters. If a child is dissatisfied, he may make a representation or complaint under s.26(3), or, if he is over 16, discharge himself from care (subs. (11)).

Subs. (7)

Where the child's welfare requires him to be looked after by the local authority, and there is an effective objection by someone with parental responsibility, the local authority will have to seek an emergency protection order (s.44) or bring care proceedings under s.31. If there are no grounds for an order the authority cannot seek permission to accommodate the child from the High Court by Wardship (s.100(2)(b)).

A person with parental responsibility for a child can object to the local authority accommodating that child and thus prevent it from so doing, but only if he is able and willing to provide accommodation (or make arrangements for this). Thus, if a mother asks for her child to be accommodated, the father's objection will have no effect unless he has parental responsibility (an unmarried father may not, a divorced father will) and he has alternative arrangements for the child's care. If the mother has a residence order and the father does not, her decision to ask the local authority to accommodate her child is effective despite the father's objections because of subs. (9). The father could not prevent the authority providing accommodation, even if he was able and willing to care for the child. He would need either to persuade the authority to place the child with him by virtue of its duty under ss.17(1) and 23(6) or to obtain a residence order under s.10.

Child: Child under 16—see subs. (11).

Is able and willing: This could be interpreted to invalidate the objection of a homeless or inadequately housed parent. Unless the child was suffering, etc. significant harm and an order was obtained the local authority should not have any rights of compulsion.

Subs. (8)

This provision produced considerable disquiet amongst both statutory and voluntary child care organisations. The repeal of the 28 day notice provision was thought to leave children in care vulnerable to sudden removal and be likely to discourage local authorities from using s.20 rather than compulsory measures. The Lord Chancellor was adamant that provision of accommodation should remain an entirely voluntary matter between the "parents" and local authority as proposed in the White Paper (Cm. 62, para. 22(b)) but suggested two methods of protecting children where removal would be harmful. An emergency protection order could be obtained under s.44. Alternatively, the local authority or the carers might rely on s.3(5), which empowers "persons" without parental responsibility to do "what is reasonable in all the circumstances for the purpose of safeguarding or promoting the child's welfare" (*Hansard*, H.L. Vol. 503, col. 1412; Vol. 505, col. 370). This might justify a refusal to return a child in the middle of the night or to a parent who was incapable, but the relationship between s.3(5) and s.20(8) will need to be clarified by litigation. A foster parent could also make the child a ward of court and seek care and control, although the courts will undoubtedly be concerned that such steps are not taken to avoid the restrictions in ss.9, 10 and 100.

Subs. (9)

See comments on subs. (7) above. Where the parents are divorcing and the child is at risk of coming into care this subsection provides a good justification for making a residence order.

Subs. (11)

This provides that 16 and 17 year olds have rights to admit themselves to care and to remain in care against the wishes of their parents. It does not clearly state that they have a right to discharge themselves from care. However, local authorities have no statutory power to detain such children without a care order. The *Gillick* decision recognises that mature young people may make decisions about their own lives except where Parliament has given power to others, so it seems that such young people may "vote with their feet" although they may have extreme difficulty supporting themselves.

Provision of accommodation for children in police protection or detention or on remand, etc.

21.—(1) Every local authority shall make provision for the reception and accommodation of children who are removed or kept away from home under Part V.

(2) Every local authority shall receive, and provide accommodation for, children—

> (a) in police protection whom they are requested to receive under section 46(3)(f);
> (b) whom they are requested to receive under section 38(6) of the Police and Criminal Evidence Act 1984;
> (c) who are—

(i) on remand under section 23(1) of the Children and Young Persons Act 1969; or

(ii) the subject of a supervision order imposing a residence requirement under section 12AA of that Act,

and with respect to whom they are the designated authority.

(3) Where a child has been—

(a) removed under Part V; or

(b) detained under section 38 of the Police and Criminal Evidence Act 1984,

and he is not being provided with accommodation by a local authority or in a hospital vested in the Secretary of State, any reasonable expenses of accommodating him shall be recoverable from the local authority in whose area he is ordinarily resident.

DEFINITIONS

"designated local authority": Sched. 12, para. 23. (C.Y.P.A. 1969, s.124A(2)).
"local authority": s.105(1).
"police protection": s.46(2).

GENERAL NOTE

This section requires local authorities to receive and provide accommodation for certain specified children. These children are first, under subs. (1), children removed or kept away from home under emergency protection orders (s.44) or children being assessed away from home under a child assessment order (s.43); second, under subs. (2)(a), children who have been taken into police protection (s.46); third, under subs. (2)(b), arrested juveniles, *i.e.* those apparently under the age of 17 arrested with or without warrant (Police and Criminal Evidence Act 1984, s.37(15) as amended by C.A. 1989, Sched. 15). (The obligation to place arrested children in the hands of the local authority has been strengthened by amendments to the Police and Criminal Evidence Act 1984, s.38(6)—see Sched. 13, para. 53); and finally under subs. (2)(c), children remanded to care or children subject to a supervision order with a residence requirement (see Sched. 12, para. 23 for the text of C.Y.P.A. 1969, s.12AA).

While these children are accommodated they are owed the duties in Pt. III and Sched. 2 (see s.105(5)).

Duties of local authorities in relation to children looked after by them

General duty of local authority in relation to children looked after by them

22.—(1) In this Act, any reference to a child who is looked after by a local authority is a reference to a child who is—

(a) in their care; or

(b) provided with accommodation by the authority in the exercise of any functions (in particular those under this Act) which stand referred to their social services committee under the Local Authority Social Services Act 1970.

(2) In subsection (1) "accommodation" means accommodation which is provided for a continuous period of more than 24 hours.

(3) It shall be the duty of a local authority looking after any child—

(a) to safeguard and promote his welfare; and

(b) to make such use of services available for children cared for by their own parents as appears to the authority reasonable in his case.

(4) Before making any decision with respect to a child whom they are looking after, or proposing to look after, a local authority shall, so far as is reasonably practicable, ascertain the wishes and feelings of—

(a) the child;

(b) his parents;

(c) any person who is not a parent of his but who has parental responsibility for him; and

    (d) any other person whose wishes and feelings the authority consider to be relevant,
regarding the matter to be decided.

(5) In making any such decision a local authority shall give due consideration—

    (a) having regard to his age and understanding, to such wishes and feelings of the child as they have been able to ascertain;

    (b) to such wishes and feelings of any person mentioned in subsection (4)(b) to (d) as they have been able to ascertain; and

    (c) to the child's religious persuasion, racial origin and cultural and linguistic background.

(6) If it appears to a local authority that it is necessary, for the purpose of protecting members of the public from serious injury, to exercise their powers with respect to a child whom they are looking after in a manner which may not be consistent with their duties under this section, they may do so.

(7) If the Secretary of State considers it necessary, for the purpose of protecting members of the public from serious injury, to give directions to a local authority with respect to the exercise of their powers with respect to a child whom they are looking after, he may give such directions to the authority.

(8) Where any such directions are given to an authority they shall comply with them even though doing so is inconsistent with their duties under this section.

DEFINITIONS

    "accommodation": s.22(2).
    "child looked after by a local authority": ss.22(1), 105(4).
    "functions": s.105(5).
    "in care": s.105(1).
    "local authority": s.105(1).
    "person who is not a parent but who has parental responsibility": ss.5(6), 12(2).
    "services": s.105(1).

GENERAL NOTE

    This section sets out the general duty owed by local authorities to children they are looking after, that is, children subject to care orders and children accommodated under ss.20 and 21. Specific duties are set out in ss.23, 24, 26 and Sched. 2, Pt. II. The duties owed under this part of the Act are the same whether or not children are subject to a care order, but local authorities have greater control in relation to children in care because they have parental responsibility in respect of them (s.31(3)). The general duties in subss. (3), (4) and (5) have been taken from the C.C.A. 1980, ss.18 and 19, and amended partly in accordance with the recommendations of the R.C.C.L., paras. 2.18 and 9.3–5. The obligation in s.18(1) of the C.C.A. 1980 to give "first consideration" to the child's welfare has been amended; local authorities are now required to "safeguard and promote" it (subs. (3)). The old duty was interpreted by Lord Brandon in *M.* v. *H.* [1988] 3 W.L.R. 485 as being no different from giving first and paramount consideration as required by s.1 of the G.M.A. 1971. However, the R.C.C.L., para. 2.18, drew a distinction between these two provisions, preferring s.18(1) because it took account of the need for the local authority to consider other children it was looking after. The Government rejected both versions. The wording of the duty is crucial because s.18(1) provided one basis for challenging local authority decisions. In *Liddle* v. *Sunderland Borough Council* (1983) 13 Fam. Law 250, Latey J. quashed a decision to close a children's home because the social services committee had taken the decision without considering its impact on the individual children who lived there. Arguably, the outcome would be the same under the new Act because a local authority which has taken a decision which will affect the welfare of an individual child can hardly be found to have safeguarded or promoted that child's welfare if it has acted in total disregard of it. However, there is no longer a requirement to consider welfare in relation to *any* decision so it would be possible to determine that a home had to be closed and only as a consequence see how the children's welfare should be promoted. Also, the removal of the word "first" eliminates the priority which Latey J. determined had to be given to children if there was an even balance between them and another client group at pp.252–3.

Where a local authority has acted so incompetently that the child's welfare has been seriously prejudiced, it is not clear that there would be a remedy. In *Guevara* v. *London Borough of Hounslow, The Times*, April 17, 1987, the High Court, as a preliminary issue, held that the council was not entitled to immunity, that duties under the 1980 Act could found a claim to damages, but that the proper procedure would have been to apply for judicial review because of the decision of the House of Lords in *O'Reilly* v. *Mackman* [1983] 2 A.C. 237 and *Cocks* v. *Thanet District Council* [1983] 2 A.C. 286. However, this reasoning has been criticised on the basis that it is for the respondent to show that the plaintiff's choice of procedure is so improper as to be an abuse of process. If a person sought compensation for the care they received as a child, the use of judicial review with an ancillary claim for damages under Ord. 53, r.7 would seem to be highly artificial, since the decisions taken would be incapable of review (see [1987] J.S.W.L. 374). Where the authority is in default, the Secretary of State may use his powers in s.84 (see below).

The duty in the C.C.A. 1980, s.18(1) to ascertain children's wishes and feelings about decisions and give due consideration to them is extended to parents, people with parental responsibility and other relevant adults (subss. (4) and (5)). There is a new duty to give due consideration to children's race, creed, culture and language (subs. (5)). Local authorities may act inconsistently with their duties where it is necessary to do so to protect members of the public (subs. (6)). The Secretary of State may also issue directions to them in such cases (subs. (7)) with which they must comply (subs. (8)).

The Government plans to issue detailed guidance to local authorities on this section *per* Lord Chancellor (*Hansard*, H.L. Vol. 502, col. 351).

Subs. (1)

Looked after: These children need to be distinguished from those who are "in care", *i.e.* those subject to care orders (s.31(1)) to whom other duties are also owed (see s.33).

Provided with accommodation: See s.20 for the duties and powers to provide accommodation under the Act. The Local Authority Social Services Act 1970, s.2 and Sched. 1 list the relevant functions. They include provision of accommodation under the previous child care, health and welfare and adoption legislation. Children may also be accommodated by the local authority under s.21. The types of accommodation which can be used are listed in s.23(2) and include placement with relatives. Day care is not accommodation (subs. (2)).

Subs. (3)

Welfare: Views of welfare differ (see note on s.17(1)). This was formerly s.18(2) of the C.C.A. 1980. The local authority has a wide discretion in relation to the use of services, which do not need to be services provided by the local authority.

Subs. (4)

This imposes a qualified duty on the local authority to consult before making any decision with respect to a child they are looking after. This duty also applies prior to the child's admission to care in all cases, including those under care proceedings and emergency protection orders. It reflects the view that a child is a "person, not an object of concern" and that the local authority should, where possible, work in partnership with parents (Cm. 62, para. 21).

When there is a guardian ad litem he or she should be consulted and may assist in ascertaining the child's views. In *R.* v. *North Yorkshire County Council*, ex p. *M.* [1989] 1 All E.R. 143, Ewbank J. held that the local authority should not have moved a child to an adoptive placement while care proceedings were pending without consulting the guardian ad litem. However, this decision appears to be restricted to periods when the guardian is currently preparing a case for the court and does not extend to consulting former guardians. There is no intention to widen the guardian's rôle: *per* Lord Chancellor (*Hansard*, H.L. Vol. 502, col. 1348).

Any decision with respect to a child: This would appear narrower than the previous wording "relating to". In *Att.-Gen.* v. *Hammersmith and Fulham London Borough Council, The Times*, December 18, 1979, Dillon J. drew a distinction between a decision "affecting a child" which was not covered by the duty and one "relating to a child", but this was rejected by Latey in *Liddle* v. *Sunderland Borough Council* (1983) 13 Fam. Law 250. Decisions may relate to or affect children without being made in respect of them, for example, a decision to close a library or a park. Decisions relating to the closure of community homes which these cases involved would seem to be made in respect of children because they cannot be made wihout further decisions about what should happen to the children involved.

Reasonably practicable: It will not be possible to ascertain wishes of: babies (although young children aged three up can express wishes to people skilled in communicating with children); unknown fathers; people who refuse to respond and those whose whereabouts are unknown.

Parents: This includes the unmarried father without parental responsibility.

Any other person: The local authority has wide discretion here, but if the child is already accommodated, the decision to consult must safeguard and promote his welfare. A differently defined group also has a right to make representations (see s.26(3)(e)). It would be difficult for the authority to argue that any relative who has looked after the child or offered to provide him with a home should not be consulted.

Subs. (5)

This subsection lists three matters to which the local authority must give due consideration. What is "due consideration" will depend on the circumstances, but the authority must bear in mind the *Gillick* decision which indicates that young people have increasing rights of self-determination as they mature and must also consider the legal status which the person concerned has. Where the child is not in care the local authority does not have parental responsibility and this limits its power to make decisions (see s.3(5)). People consulted under (d) do not have parental responsibility. The local authority must give greater weight to the views of the parent of a mature child or to the views of someone without parental responsibility over those of someone with it where this promotes or safeguards the child's welfare.

Religious persuasion: At common law, parents have the right to choose the child's religion, although following the *Gillick* decision the child acquires this right when he is sufficiently mature. Under s.10(3) of the C.C.A. 1980 a local authority was prohibited from bringing up a child subject to a care order in a religious creed which he would not otherwise have followed. S.4(3) of the same Act provided that a parental rights resolution did not authorise the local authority to change a child's religious creed. Further protection of beliefs was included in the Boarding Out Regulations 1988, r.5(4). There may not be any difference between religious creed and religious persuasion but persuasion may be wider and encompass the beliefs and practices of new religious groups. Matters which are not related to religious persuasion may be considered under cultural background.

Racial origin: This is not defined but "racial group" is defined in s.3(1) of the Race Relations Act 1976 and has been held to include Sikhs, gypsies and Rastafarians. The inclusion of this phrase indicates that a "colour blind" approach to child care by which non-white children were generally placed with white families may no longer be acceptable but it does not require same-race placement. Adoption of black children into white families has been shown to lead to the children being confused about their racial identity (Gill and Jackson *Adoption and Race* (1983) Batsford). However, these issues are highly controversial. Under Sched. 2, para. 11 the local authority has a duty to have regard to ethnic issues when recruiting foster parents.

Cultural and linguistic background: This is not defined.

These issues are as relevant to children in residential care as to children with foster parents.

Subss. (6), (7) and (8)

These provisions were previously found in ss.18(3) and 19 of the C.C.A. 1980. They have been amended in accordance with the recommendation of the R.C.C.L. (para. 9.5) to restrict them to "protection from serious injury". The local authority may have to make an application under s.25 to place the child in secure accommodation.

Members of the public: Arguably, this does not include people like social workers who are at risk because of their work. Other children accommodated by the local authority must be protected under s.22(3)(a).

Serious injury: This excludes minor injury and damage to property.

Provision of accommodation and maintenance by local authority for children whom they are looking after

23.—(1) It shall be the duty of any local authority looking after a child—

   (a) when he is in their care, to provide accommodation for him; and

   (b) to maintain him in other respects apart from providing accommodation for him.

(2) A local authority shall provide accommodation and maintenance for any child whom they are looking after by—
  (a) placing him (subject to subsection (5) and any regulations made by the Secretary of State) with—
      (i) a family;
      (ii) a relative of his; or
      (iii) any other suitable person,
  on such terms as to payment by the authority and otherwise as the authority may determine;
  (b) maintaining him in a community home;
  (c) maintaining him in a voluntary home;
  (d) maintaining him in a registered children's home;
  (e) maintaining him in a home provided by the Secretary of State under section 82(5) on such terms as the Secretary of State may from time to time determine; or
  (f) making such other arrangements as—
      (i) seem appropriate to them; and
      (ii) comply with any regulations made by the Secretary of State.
(3) Any person with whom a child has been placed under subsection (2)(a) is referred to in this Act as a local authority foster parent unless he falls within subsection (4).
(4) A person falls within this subsection if he is—
  (a) a parent of the child;
  (b) a person who is not a parent of the child but who has parental responsibility for him; or
  (c) where the child is in care and there was a residence order in force with respect to him immediately before the care order was made, a person in whose favour the residence order was made.
(5) Where a child is in the care of a local authority, the authority may only allow him to live with a person who falls within subsection (4) in accordance with regulations made by the Secretary of State.
(6) Subject to any regulations made by the Secretary of State for the purposes of this subsection, any local authority looking after a child shall make arrangements to enable him to live with—
  (a) a person falling within subsection (4); or
  (b) a relative, friend or other person connected with him,
unless that would not be reasonably practicable or consistent with his welfare.
(7) Where a local authority provide accommodation for a child whom they are looking after, they shall, subject to the provisions of this Part and so far as is reasonably practicable and consistent with his welfare, secure that—
  (a) the accommodation is near his home; and
  (b) where the authority are also providing accommodation for a sibling of his, they are accommodated together.
(8) Where a local authority provide accommodation for a child whom they are looking after and who is disabled, they shall, so far as is reasonably practicable, secure that the accommodation is not unsuitable to his particular needs.
(9) Part II of Schedule 2 shall have effect for the purposes of making further provision as to children looked after by local authorities and in particular as to the regulations that may be made under subsections (2)(a) and (f) and (5).

DEFINITIONS
  "community home": s.53.
  "disabled": s.17(11).

"local authority": s.105(1).
"local authority foster parent": s.23(3), (4).
"person who is not a parent but who has parental responsibility": ss.5(6), 12(2).
"registered children's home": s.63.
"relative": s.105(1).
"voluntary home": s.60.

GENERAL NOTE

This section imposes a duty on local authorities to provide accommodation and to maintain children they are looking after (subs. (1)). It adds four specific but qualified duties: a duty from s.21(1) of the C.C.A. 1980 to secure that any accommodation is near his home (subs. (7)(a)); a duty similar to that in C.C.A. 1980, s.2(3) to place the child with relatives or friends (subs. (6)); and two new duties: a duty to accommodate siblings together (subs. (7)(b)) and a duty to secure that accommodation for a disabled child is "not unsuitable to his needs" (subs. (8)). The types of accommodation which can be used are listed in subs. (2). Local authorities are also required to comply with Sched. 2, Pt. II and regulations under s.23(2)(a), (f) and (5). The current regulations for foster placement, the Boarding Out of Children (Foster Placement) Regulations 1988 and the Placement (Charge and Control) Regulations 1988 are to be replaced with updated regulations. It will also be possible to make regulations to cover placements in hostels and halfway houses.

Sched. 2, Pt. II empowers the local authority to make payments to allow visits between children they are looking after, their families and friends (para. 16). It requires the local authority to appoint a visitor (and pay their reasonable expenses) for children they are looking after who are not visited and whose welfare demands it. Mature children may object to the appointment or continuation of a visitor (para. 17). The authority may guarantee apprenticeships for children they are looking after (para. 18). If the local authority wishes a child in care to live outside England and Wales it must obtain the approval of the court which can only be granted under stringent conditions (para. 19(1), (3)–(5)). Where approval is granted the child may be adopted (para. 19(6)). If the court gives its approval the order may be stayed pending an appeal (para. 19(7), (8)). Arrangements may be made for a child who is looked after by the authority but not in care to live outside England and Wales with the consent of everyone with parental responsibility (para. 19(2)). Para. 20 sets out the local authority's functions where a child in care dies.

For a discussion of possible legal action to enforce these duties, see notes to s.22.

Subs. (1)

This duty was formerly found in s.21(1) of the C.C.A. 1980.

Maintain: The local authority's duty is arguably no less than that of a parent with adequate, but not unlimited, resources. See also s.22(3)(b).

Subs. (2)

The local authority retains complete discretion over placement but must comply with the duty to safeguard and promote the child's welfare in s.22(3)(a), the provisions in Sched. 2, Pt. II, and any regulations. Accommodation must be "suitable" because of the duty in s.22(3) (*per* Lord Chancellor (*Hansard*, H.L. Vol. 505, col. 378)).

The local authority also has discretion about whether to pay for the child's care and how much to pay, as under the present law. Disputes can be dealt with under the procedure established under s.26(3).

Placing: Where a voluntary organisation arranges the placement the child is still placed by the local authority, and thus the carer is a local authority foster parent. Placements by voluntary organisations are also subject to the Boarding Out Regulations.

Other arrangements: These include an assortment of placements which are increasingly used for teenagers such as hostels and halfway houses. At present there are no regulations relating to such placements and thus no clear rules about supervision of such placements or medical examination of the children.

Subs. (3)

The term "foster parent" is controversial because it suggests replacement of the natural parent. Although the Government accepts that fostering encompasses a variety of forms, it was not willing to have the phrase "foster carer" enshrined in statute.

Subss. (4) and (5)

The Accommodation of Children (Charge and Control) Regulations 1988 made under the C.C.A. 1980, s.22A, currently cover such "home on trial" placements. These regulations will be replaced under the new Act.

In the care of: The current regulations do not apply to children in voluntary care (*i.e.* under s.2 of the C.C.A. 1980) but do apply to children committed to care in domestic, matrimonial and care proceedings. The new regulations will be limited to children under care orders (see s.105(1)) including children compulsorily in care under the old provisions (see Sched. 14, paras. 15–17 and 21). There is no authority to restrict the return home of children who are merely accommodated by the local authority.

Subs. (6)
If this person lives outside England and Wales, Sched. II, para. 19 must be complied with.

Subs. (7)
The local authority has wide discretion but must carry out its duties in accordance with s.22.

Near his home: This provision was originally introduced into s.21(1) of the C.C.A. 1980 by the Health and Social Services and Social Security Adjudication Act 1983. The D.H.S.S. circular issued to local authorities in relation to it (LAC (83)13) stated "Local authorities . . . should bear in mind the importance of maintaining links between the child and his family and his home area. Maintenance of these links will be easier if the child lives nearby." A child's home may be where his parents live or where he used to live; links with both are important and most children return to their home area when they leave care, even if they do not live with their families. There are specific duties about maintaining contact in Sched. 2, para. 15.

The notes of guidance on the Boarding Out (Foster Care) Regulations 1988 state:
> "the needs of each child should be considered and assessed separately before efforts are made to reconcile the needs of both or all. One sibling should not be denied opportunities in order to satisfy the needs of another. If placement together is not in the best interests of each sibling, or cannot be achieved, separation with careful and carefully monitored arrangements for continuing contact may have to be considered" (para. 143(f)).

There would seem to be no reason why this guidance should not be repeated when this provision is in force.

Subs. (8)
This merely underlines that special care needs to be taken with the placement of disabled children.

Subs. (9)
Paras. 12–14 of Sched. 2 give an indication of the matters which may be covered by regulations; they are not mandatory. The Boarding Out Regulations 1988 and the Charge and Control Regulations 1988 were finalised after the Children Bill had been drafted, so it is likely that many of their features will be retained in new regulations.

Advice and assistance for certain children

Advice and assistance for certain children

24.—(1) Where a child is being looked after by a local authority, it shall be the duty of the authority to advise, assist and befriend him with a view to promoting his welfare when he ceases to be looked after by them.

(2) In this Part "a person qualifying for advice and assistance" means a person within the area of the authority who is under twenty-one and who was, at any time after reaching the age of sixteen but while still a child—

(a) looked after by a local authority;
(b) accommodated by or on behalf of a voluntary organisation;
(c) accommodated in a registered children's home;
(d) accommodated—
    (i) by any health authority or local education authority; or
    (ii) in any residential care home, nursing home or mental nursing home,

for a consecutive period of at least three months; or

(e) privately fostered,

but who is no longer so looked after, accommodated or fostered.

(3) Subsection (2)(d) applies even if the period of three months mentioned there began before the child reached the age of sixteen.

(4) Where—

(a) a local authority know that there is within their area a person qualifying for advice and assistance;

(b) the conditions in subsection (5) are satisfied; and

(c) that person has asked them for help of a kind which they can give under this section,

they shall (if he was being looked after by a local authority or was accommodated by or on behalf of a voluntary organisation) and may (in any other case) advise and befriend him.

(5) The conditions are that—

(a) it appears to the authority that the person concerned is in need of advice and being befriended;

(b) where that person was not being looked after by the authority, they are satisfied that the person by whom he was being looked after does not have the necessary facilities for advising or befriending him.

(6) Where as a result of this section a local authority are under a duty, or are empowered, to advise and befriend a person, they may also give him assistance.

(7) Assistance given under subsections (1) to (6) may be in kind or, in exceptional circumstances, in cash.

(8) A local authority may give assistance to any person who qualifies for advice and assistance by virtue of subsection (2)(a) by—

(a) contributing to expenses incurred by him in living near the place where he is, or will be—

(i) employed or seeking employment; or

(ii) receiving education or training; or

(b) making a grant to enable him to meet expenses connected with his education or training.

(9) Where a local authority are assisting the person under subsection (8) by making a contribution or grant with respect to a course of education or training, they may—

(a) continue to do so even though he reaches the age of twenty-one before completing the course; and

(b) disregard any interruption in his attendance on the course if he resumes it as soon as is reasonably practicable.

(10) Subsections (7) to (9) of section 17 shall apply in relation to assistance given under this section (otherwise than under subsection (8)) as they apply in relation to assistance given under that section.

(11) Where it appears to a local authority that a person whom they have been advising and befriending under this section, as a person qualifying for advice and assistance, proposes to live, or is living, in the area of another local authority, they shall inform that other local authority.

(12) Where a child who is accommodated—

(a) by a voluntary organisation or in a registered children's home;

(b) by any health authority or local education authority; or

(c) in any residential care home, nursing home or mental nursing home,

ceases to be so accommodated, after reaching the age of sixteen, the organisation, authority or (as the case may be) person carrying on the home shall inform the local authority within whose area the child proposes to live.

(13) Subsection (12) only applies, by virtue of paragraph (b) or (c), if the accommodation has been provided for a consecutive period of at least three months.

Definitions
"assistance": s.24(7).
"child looked after by a local authority": ss.22(1), 105(4).
"health authority": s.105(1).
"local authority": s.105(1).
"local education authority": s.105(1).
"mental nursing home": s.105(1).
"nursing home": s.105(1).
"person qualifying for advice and assistance": s.24(2).
"privately fostered": s.66.
"registered children's home": s.63.
"voluntary organisation": s.105(1).

General Note
This section implements many of the recommendations in Chapter 10 of the R.C.C.L. which were intended to remove anomalies and to strengthen local authorities' functions in relation to the preparation for leaving care and the after-care of children cared for away from their families. It replaces ss.27–29 and 69 of the C.C.A. 1980 and removes the anomalies in those provisions. Local authorities now have a duty to advise, assist and befriend all children they are looking after with a view to providing their long-term welfare, not just their welfare during childhood (subs. (1)). They have a duty to advise and befriend people under 21 (not under 18 as previously under C.C.A. 1980, s.28) who, after the age of 16, were looked after by a local authority or accommodated by or on behalf of a voluntary organisation, who request help and satisfy the conditions in subs. (5) (subss. (2) and (4)). There is also a power to advise and befriend such young people who were cared for in the other establishments listed in subs. (2). All people qualifying for advice can be given assistance (subs. (6)), which may, exceptionally, be in cash (subs. (7)). Financial assistance may also be given to enable a person who was looked after by the local authority after age 16 (not 17 as previously) to be accommodated near their place of work or training, etc., and to meet the costs of training, etc. (subs. (8)). Grants for education or training may continue beyond age 21 (subs. (9)). Subs. (10) imports the provisions about repayment from s.17(7)–(9). In order to facilitate the performance of these duties, local authorities are under a duty to pass information to other local authorities about people they have been advising and befriending (subs. (1)); voluntary organisations, health authorities, local education authorities and those who carry on registered homes have a duty to inform local authorities about children who leave their care (subs. (12)). Where care is by a health authority or local education authority or in a residential care home, nursing home or mental nursing home, the powers and duties only arise if the child was accommodated for more than three consecutive months, which may start before the child reached age 16 (subss. (3) and (13)). Local authorities have other responsibilities to children in such establishments under ss.85 and 86.

Subs. (1)
This duty applies to all children, including those who return to their families after brief periods. It imposes an obligation to prepare children for leaving care and for living independently when they grow up, and is thus broader than the duty under the old law which referred to welfare throughout childhood.

Subss. (2)–(5)
These four subsections set out a further duty (only a power if subs. (2)(c)–(e) applies) to provide after-care to certain people under 21 who have been in care after the age of 16 years. This duty replaces the provisions in ss.27–29 of the C.C.A. 1980, which imposed different duties in relation to children committed to care and children received into care, and linked some assistance to employment, education or training. This duty should be considered alongside the duty in s.20(3) to provide accommodation for certain 16 to 18-year-olds who are in need and the power to provide accommodation to under 21s in s.20(5).

Person qualifying for advice and assistance: As well as the conditions in subss. (2) and (3), the person will have to meet the conditions in subss. (4) and (5), *i.e.* the local authority will have to know about the person (subs. (4)(a)); he must have asked for help of a kind which they can give (subs. (4)(c)); he must satisfy the local authority that he needs advice and befriending (subs. (5)(a)) and, if he was not looked after by the local authority, that the person who looked after him does not have the necessary facilities (subs. (5)(b)).

A local authority: This does not necessarily mean the one in whose area the child now lives. However, a person who requests help from an authority different from the one which looked after him will also have to satisfy the condition in subs. (5)(b). This could mean that authority A would refuse help because authority B 100 miles away could provide it, but this should only be so where authority B has facilities for advising and befriending people outside its area.

Accommodated in a registered children's home: This does not include children placed in such homes by local authorities; they are included in (a) (see s.23(2)(a) for local authority's power to place in such homes).

Privately fostered: Local authorities have a further duty relating to the welfare of such children in s.67 of the Act.

Know: The authority will know if a request is made by or on behalf of the child or if it is informed by another authority under subs. (11), or by another organisation under subs. (12).

Conditions: See "a person qualifying" (above).

Help of a kind . . . : This means help they are able to give. This includes assistance under subs. (7), but the local authority is only under a duty to advise and befriend. Arguably, a request for housing to the Housing Department should trigger this section since accommodation could be provided under subs. (7) as "assistance in kind" (see *Att.-Gen.* v. *Wandsworth London Borough Council*, ex p. *Tilley* [1981] 1 W.L.R. 854, where the Court of Appeal rejected the view that assistance under s.1 of the C.C.A. 1980 did not include accommodation).

They shall: The authority has no power to help where the conditions are not satisfied, except for those under 18 who are in need (s.17(1)) and all children under s.20(4).

They may: The authority can impose other additional conditions, but must act in accordance with its other duties, particularly under ss.17(1) and 20(3). These duties only apply to under 18s who are in need.

It appears to the authority: The authority has wide discretion.

Subss. (6) and (7)

The local authority only has a power to provide assistance in cash or in kind. It was not intended that they should acquire any income maintenance function for young people ex-care, even though the Social Security Act 1986 appeared to expect that all young people had families to support them. Under the 1986 Act young people faced severe financial problems:— under 18s could not generally apply for Income Support; Housing Benefit was paid to them as a reduced rate, and lower benefit rates for single people under 25 presumed that they had a family to rely on (Income Support (General) Regulations 1987, reg. 13A). Attempts were made in the Lords, and during Committee Stage in the Commons, to include amendments to the 1986 Act in the Children Bill but all were unsuccessful. However, a small concession was made which allows some children living away from their families to obtain Income Support at the rate for 18–24 year-olds (see *Hansard*, Commons written answers, March 13, 1989; col. 27–8). Where an authority makes a capital grant to a young person leaving care it will not affect entitlement to benefit, provided that it is under £3,000 (Income Support (General) Regulations 1987, reg. 53(1)).

Exceptional circumstances: See note on s.17(6).

Subss. (8)–(10)

S.17(7)–(9) allows assistance (but not advice, befriending and grants under subs. (8)) to be subject to conditions about repayment. They require assistance to be means-tested, but provide that there is no liability to repay while the person is in receipt of certain benefits. See the discussion of s.17(7)–(9).

Subs. (12)

There are other duties to notify the local authority about such children in ss.85 and 86.

Secure accommodation

Use of accommodation for restricting liberty

25.—(1) Subject to the following provisions of this section, a child who is being looked after by a local authority may not be placed, and, if placed, may not be kept, in accommodation provided for the purpose of restricting liberty ("secure accommodation") unless it appears—

    (a) that—

        (i) he has a history of absconding and is likely to abscond from any other description of accommodation; and

        (ii) if he absconds, he is likely to suffer significant harm; or

    (b) that if he is kept in any other description of accommodation he is likely to injure himself or other persons.

  (2) The Secretary of State may by regulations—

    (a) specify a maximum period—

        (i) beyond which a child may not be kept in secure accommodation without the authority of the court; and

        (ii) for which the court may authorise a child to be kept in secure accommodation;

    (b) empower the court from time to time to authorise a child to be kept in secure accommodation for such further period as the regulations may specify; and

    (c) provide that applications to the court under this section shall be made only by local authorities.

  (3) It shall be the duty of a court hearing an application under this section to determine whether any relevant criteria for keeping a child in secure accommodation are satisfied in his case.

  (4) If a court determines that any such criteria are satisfied, it shall make an order authorising the child to be kept in secure accommodation and specifying the maximum period for which he may be so kept.

  (5) On any adjournment of the hearing of an application under this section, a court may make an interim order permitting the child to be kept during the period of the adjournment in secure accommodation.

  (6) No court shall exercise the powers conferred by this section in respect of a child who is not legally represented in that court unless, having been informed of his right to apply for legal aid and having had the opportunity to do so, he refused or failed to apply.

  (7) The Secretary of State may by regulations provide that—

    (a) this section shall or shall not apply to any description of children specified in the regulations;

    (b) this section shall have effect in relation to children of a description specified in the regulations subject to such modifications as may be so specified;

    (c) such other provisions as may be so specified shall have effect for the purpose of determining whether a child of a description specified in the regulations may be placed or kept in secure accommodation.

  (8) The giving of an authorisation under this section shall not prejudice any power of any court in England and Wales or Scotland to give directions relating to the child to whom the authorisation relates.

  (9) This section is subject to section 20(8).

DEFINITIONS

"child": s.105(1).

"child looked after by a local authority": ss.22(1), 105(4).

"secure accommodation": s.25(1).

"significant harm": ss.31(9)(10), 105(1).

"the court": s.92(7).

GENERAL NOTE

This section re-enacts with minor modifications noted below s.21A of the C.C.A. 1980 and sets the restrictions on the use of secure accommodation. Further rules concerning the use of secure accommodation are contained in the Secure Accommodation (No. 2) Regulations 1983. The power to make regulations is retained in subs. (2) and there is no suggestion that any new regulations will be markedly different from the current ones. The operation of s.21A was criticised in (unpublished) research commissioned by the Department of Health (Harris and Timms *Between Hospital and Prison or thereabouts*). Courts did not operate effectively to check the use of secure accommodation and children were not well represented. However, no substantive changes have been made to the system, although local authorities are now under a specific duty to avoid the need for children in their area to be placed in secure accommodation (Sched. 2, para. 7(c)). The Government does, however, realise the importance of "strong gate-keeping" to prevent the misuse of secure accommodation, and further guidance about this is likely to be issued (David Mellor, Minister of Health (Standing Committee B, col. 196; May 18, 1989)). Secure accommodation has been held to include a behaviour modification unit at a hospital where the regime was intended to restrict liberty (*R.* v. *Northampton Juvenile Court,* ex p. *London Borough of Hammersmith* [1985] 15 Fam. Law 25). At present, secure accommodation is not provided in private children's homes; there is provision under Sched. 5, para. 7 and Sched. 6, para. 10 for regulations to prohibit its use in voluntary homes and registered children's homes.

These cases will probably continue to be heard by magistrates (but see s.92, Sched. 11 and any rules). An appeal against the granting or refusal of a secure accommodation order will go to the High Court under s.94.

Subs. (1)

The conditions for a secure accommodation placement or order (except for a child remanded to care (see reg. 7)) are unchanged except as noted below, as are the groups of children to which the provisions apply. Subs. (7) permits the Secretary of State to exclude classes of children by regulation but no indication has been given that this would be done to take any new class out. Children under place of safety orders cannot be placed in secure accommodation, nor can those accommodated under what is now s.20(5).

Significant harm: C.C.A. 1980, s.21A(1) required that the child's "physical, mental or moral welfare" be at risk and it should be compared with what can reasonably be expected of a similar child. The new provision would seem to embrace the same concepts as before in less specific language, but the addition of "significant" may suggest greater harm than "at risk".

Subs. (2)

The period under the present regulations is 72 hours (reg. 10). Courts may authorise detention for three months with renewals of six months.

Subs. (6)

Right to apply for legal aid: See s.99. Civil legal aid will be available without either a means or a merits test under the new provision.

Subs. (9)

This makes it clear that a person with parental responsibility can remove a child who is accommodated by the local authority from secure accommodation. Children over 16 who are not in care may also be able to leave (see notes to s.20(11)).

Supplemental

Review of cases and inquiries into representations

26.—(1) The Secretary of State may make regulations requiring the case of each child who is being looked after by a local authority to be reviewed in accordance with the provisions of the regulations.

(2) The regulations may, in particular, make provision—
    (a) as to the manner in which each case is to be reviewed;
    (b) as to the considerations to which the local authority are to have regard in reviewing each case;
    (c) as to the time when each case is first to be reviewed and the frequency of subsequent reviews;
    (d) requiring the authority, before conducting any review, to seek the views of—
        (i) the child;

         (ii) his parents;

         (iii) any person who is not a parent of his but who has parental responsibility for him; and

         (iv) any other person whose views the authority consider to be relevant,

including, in particular, the views of those persons in relation to any particular matter which is to be considered in the course of the review;

(e) requiring the authority to consider, in the case of a child who is in their care, whether an application should be made to discharge the care order;

(f) requiring the authority to consider, in the case of a child in accommodation provided by the authority, whether the accommodation accords with the requirements of this Part;

(g) requiring the authority to inform the child, so far as is reasonably practicable, of any steps he may take under this Act;

(h) requiring the authority to make arrangements, including arrangements with such other bodies providing services as it considers appropriate, to implement any decision which they propose to make in the course, or as a result, of the review;

(i) requiring the authority to notify details of the result of the review and of any decision taken by them in consequence of the review to—

         (i) the child;

         (ii) his parents;

         (iii) any person who is not a parent of his but who has parental responsibility for him; and

         (iv) any other person whom they consider ought to be notified;

(j) requiring the authority to monitor the arrangements which they have made with a view to ensuring that they comply with the regulations.

(3) Every local authority shall establish a procedure for considering any representations (including any complaint) made to them by—

(a) any child who is being looked after by them or who is not being looked after by them but is in need;

(b) a parent of his;

(c) any person who is not a parent of his but who has parental responsibility for him;

(d) any local authority foster parent;

(e) such other person as the authority consider has a sufficient interest in the child's welfare to warrant his representations being considered by them,

about the discharge by the authority of any of their functions under this Part in relation to the child.

(4) The procedure shall ensure that at least one person who is not a member or officer of the authority takes part in—

(a) the consideration; and

(b) any discussions which are held by the authority about the action (if any) to be taken in relation to the child in the light of the consideration.

(5) In carrying out any consideration of representations under this section a local authority shall comply with any regulations made by the Secretary of State for the purpose of regulating the procedure to be followed.

(6) The Secretary of State may make regulations requiring local authorities to monitor the arrangements that they have made with a view to

ensuring that they comply with any regulations made for the purposes of subsection (5).

(7) Where any representation has been considered under the procedure established by a local authority under this section, the authority shall—

    (a) have due regard to the findings of those considering the representation; and

    (b) take such steps as are reasonably practicable to notify (in writing)—

        (i) the person making the representation;

        (ii) the child (if the authority consider that he has sufficient understanding); and

        (iii) such other persons (if any) as appear to the authority to be likely to be affected,

of the authority's decision in the matter and their reasons for taking that decision and of any action which they have taken, or propose to take.

(8) Every local authority shall give such publicity to their procedure for considering representations under this section as they consider appropriate.

DEFINITIONS

"accommodation provided by the local authority": ss.22(2), 105(5).
"child": s.105(1).
"child looked after by the local authority": ss.22(1), 105(4).
"functions": s.105(1).
"in care": s.105(1).
"local authority": s.105(1).
"local authority foster parent": s.23(3)(4).
"person who is not a parent but who has parental responsibility": ss.5(6), 12(2).

GENERAL NOTE

This section provides for two distinct matters. Subss. (1) and (2) deal with "Statutory Reviews"; the remainder of the section provides for local authority systems for handling complaints and representations about the discharge of their functions under Pt. III.

Each local authority is required to monitor the progress of every child it is looking after by holding reviews (known as "Statutory Reviews"). Subss. (1) and (2) replace s.27(4) of the C.Y.P.A. 1969, which was itself due to be amended by the Children Act 1975 and s.20 of the C.C.A. 1980. Neither of these provisions were brought into force, so the power to make regulations has not yet been exercised. S.27(4) required six-monthly reviews but there is considerable evidence that reviews were often missed or carried out in a desultory manner (see Sinclair, *Decision-making in Statutory Reviews on Children in Care* (1984), Gower). Local authorities must also comply with the provisions about decision-making in s.22 when holding reviews.

Subs. (2)

This is only a suggested list of contents. It is far broader than that in s.20 of the C.C.A. 1980 and the wording allows the inclusion of matters which are not mentioned. Detailed regulations can be expected. The Lord Chancellor said:

"I believe that the total review ought, at any rate in many cases, to include more than just a meeting . . . for example getting a report in relation to the child . . ." (*Hansard,* H.L. Vol. 503, col. 166–7).

Subss. (3)–(8)

This requires each local authority to set up its own scheme for dealing with representations and complaints, as proposed in Cm. 62, para. 31. Such procedures were said to have three functions: they enable standards to be maintained, problems to be defused and children to be protected (*per* Lord Meston, (*Hansard,* H.L. Vol. 503, col. 175)). Subs. (3) determines whose representations must be considered within the system. It is clear that complaints may be made about action and at least by children in need and their parents about failure to make provision. Subs. (4) requires that the procedure contains an independent element and subs. (5) obliges the local authority to comply with any regulations made under subs. (6). The regulations are likely to control quite closely the way complaints are handled. Subs. (7)

provides that the local authority shall give due consideration to the findings of its complaints panel and notify the complainant, the child and any other person of its decision and its action. It does *not* have to follow the recommendation of the panel. Subs. (8) requires the local authority to publicise its complaints procedure. Sched. 7, para. 6 requires the local authority to provide a complaints system in relation to fostering limits and exemptions.

Subs. (3)

A procedure: The procedure will have to comply with the rules of natural justice. It will be important that the people involved in hearing complaints have not taken the decisions or action complained about.

Representations (including any complaint): The term representation was chosen by the Government, but they agreed that "complaint" should be added. It is now "clear that there is a statutory right to make a complaint" (*per* Lord Prys-Davies (*Hansard*, H.L. Vol. 503, col. 172)).

Such other persons: The local authority has a similarly wide duty in relation to their wishes and feelings under s.22(4)(d); it could include a guardian ad litem, a teacher, or a grandparent.

Under this part: This means not under Pts. IV and V in relation to child protection. There is no provision in the Act for complaints about such action. The care provided to a child and the services (or their refusal) to a family in a case of child abuse would come within Pt. III. Complaints of maladministration can be referred to the relevant Local Government Ombudsman.

Subs. (4)

Takes part in: The independent person need not have any particular power.

Who is not: Former councillors and former employees can be included, although this would reduce the independence and thus the usefulness of the system.

Subss. (5) and (6)

This provision may be brought into force without regulations being made, but local authorities will have to comply with any that are made.

Subs. (7)

This sets out the action which local authorities must take in relation to representations and complaints made under this procedure.

Due regard: The local authority is not required to follow the findings of the panel, but it would seem that they might be vulnerable to judicial review under the *Wednesbury* rule if any subsequent decision totally disregarded a finding and there had been no change of circumstances.

Such other persons: The local authority has broad discretion but should take care not to generate further complaints.

Subs. (8)

There is a duty to publish details about services under this part in Sched. 2, para. 1(2). Although there are differences of opinion about the provision of information to young children in care, it is difficult to see how it might be appropriate not to inform all parents of children looked after and all foster parents.

Co-operation between authorities

27.—(1) Where it appears to a local authority that any authority or other person mentioned in subsection (3) could, by taking any specified action, help in the exercise of any of their functions under this Part, they may request the help of that other authority or person, specifying the action in question.

(2) An authority whose help is so requested shall comply with the request if it is compatible with their own statutory or other duties and obligations and does not unduly prejudice the discharge of any of their functions.

(3) The persons are—

    (a) any local authority;

    (b) any local education authority;

    (c) any local housing authority;

(d) any health authority; and
(e) any person authorised by the Secretary of State for the purposes of this section.

(4) Every local authority shall assist any local education authority with the provision of services for any child within the local authority's area who has special educational needs.

DEFINITIONS
"functions": s.105(1).
"health authority": s.105(1).
"local authority": s.105(1).
"local education authority": s.105(1).
"local housing authority": s.105(1).
"special education needs": s.105(1).

GENERAL NOTE
This section provides for co-operation between local authorities and other bodies to facilitate the exercise of any local authority powers or duties under Pt. III. Consultation with the local education authority is provided for in s.28. Consultation in child protection work is provided for in s.47(9)–(11).

Consultation with local education authorities

28.—(1) Where—
(a) a child is being looked after by a local authority; and
(b) the authority propose to provide accommodation for him in an establishment at which education is provided for children who are accommodated there,
they shall, so far as is reasonably practicable, consult the appropriate local education authority before doing so.

(2) Where any such proposal is carried out, the local authority shall, as soon as is reasonably practicable, inform the appropriate local education authority of the arrangements that have been made for the child's accommodation.

(3) Where the child ceases to be accommodated as mentioned in subsection (1)(b), the local authority shall inform the appropriate local education authority.

(4) In this section "the appropriate local education authority" means—
(a) the local education authority within whose area the local authority's area falls; or,
(b) where the child has special educational needs and a statement of his needs is maintained under the Education Act 1981, the local education authority who maintain the statement.

DEFINITIONS
"appropriate local education authority": s.28(4).
"child looked after by . . .": ss.22(1) and 105(4).
"local authority": s.105(1).

GENERAL NOTE
This section imposes new duties on local authorities to consult the appropriate local education authority before they accommodate a child at an establishment which provides education (subs. (1)) and to inform them of the placement (subs. (2)) and when it ends (subs. (3)). It will apply to placements in boarding schools and homes which are also schools. The local education authority is required to consult the social services before applying for an education supervision order by s.36(8).

Recoupment of cost of providing services etc.

29.—(1) Where a local authority provide any service under section 17 or 18, other than advice, guidance or counselling, they may recover from a person specified in subsection (4) such charge for the service as they consider reasonable.

(2) Where the authority are satisfied that that person's means are insufficient for it to be reasonably practicable for him to pay the charge, they shall not require him to pay more than he can reasonably be expected to pay.

(3) No person shall be liable to pay any charge under subsection (1) at any time when he is in receipt of income support or family credit under the Social Security Act 1986.

(4) The persons are—

    (a) where the service is provided for a child under sixteen, each of his parents;

    (b) where it is provided for a child who has reached the age of sixteen, the child himself; and

    (c) where it is provided for a member of the child's family, that member.

(5) Any charge under subsection (1) may, without prejudice to any other method of recovery, be recovered summarily as a civil debt.

(6) Part III of Schedule 2 makes provision in connection with contributions towards the maintenance of children who are being looked after by local authorities and consists of the re-enactment with modifications of provisions in Part V of the Child Care Act 1980.

(7) Where a local authority provide any accommodation under section 20(1) for a child who was (immediately before they began to look after him) ordinarily resident within the area of another local authority, they may recover from that other authority any reasonable expenses incurred by them in providing the accommodation and maintaining him.

(8) Where a local authority provide accommodation under section 21(1) or (2)(a) or (b) for a child who is ordinarily resident within the area of another local authority and they are not maintaining him in—

    (a) a community home provided by them;

    (b) a controlled community home; or

    (c) a hospital vested in the Secretary of State,

they may recover from that other authority any reasonable expenses incurred by them in providing the accommodation and maintaining him.

(9) Where a local authority comply with any request under section 27(2) in relation to a child or other person who is not ordinarily resident within their area, they may recover from the local authority in whose area the child or person is ordinarily resident any expenses reasonably incurred by them in respect of that person.

DEFINITIONS

    "child looked after by a local authority": ss.22(1), 105(4).

    "community home": s.53.

    "controlled community home": s.53(4).

    "hospital": s.105(1).

    "local authority": s.105(1).

    "ordinary residence": ss.30(2), 105(6).

    "service": s.105(1).

GENERAL NOTE

This section enables local authorities to charge for services (other than advice, guidance or counselling) provided under ss.17 or 18 (subss. (1)–(5)). It should be read with those relating to conditional provisions of assistance in ss.17(7)–(9) and 24(10). The rules relating to charging for accommodation formerly in Pt. V of the C.C.A. 1980, are in Sched. 2, Pt. III; there have been no substantial amendments (subs. (6)). Subs. (7)–(9) provide for recoupment of costs between authorities.

Subs. (1)

Any service: This includes assistance in cash or kind, under ss.17(6) and 24(7), but not advice or contributions under s.24(8), etc. Day centre, family centre or nursery placements can be charged for, as can family aides, laundry, etc. Where the service includes advice, there will need to be a discount to ensure that no charge is levied for that.

Subss. (2)–(3)

This requires the local authority to take account of means when levying charges so those of insufficient means are not required to pay more than they can reasonably be expected to. Even though a charge is levied, there is no liability to pay while a person is in receipt of income support or family credit.

Reasonably expected to pay: As well as the person's resources it will be necessary to consider his expenditure and other debts. It must be unreasonable to expect someone to pay for a service if he risks losing his house and must devote all "spare" resources to arrears on his mortgage or rent.

No person shall be liable: See note to s.17(9).

In receipt of: See note to s.17(9).

Subs. (4)

The only people who are liable for children at common law are parents, and their liability ends when the children reach 16 years.

Provided for a member of the child's family: Some services which are provided for more than one person may present problems. A day nursery placement may appear to be a placement for the child but if it provides a break for the carer, it could be said to be a service for them as well. No problems are created if the child is under 16 and living with parents, since parents will be liable for a service to them and to the child. This is not so if a child is living with relatives, because they have no liability for services for the child.

Member of the child's family: See notes on s.17(3).

Subs. (5)

It will be recovered in the magistrates' court under s.58 of the Magistrates' Courts Act 1980.

Subs. (6)

The new provisions for charges for children in care are largely a rewritten revision of those in Pt. V of the C.C.A. 1980 "putting more emphasis on reasonableness" (*per* Lord Chancellor (*Hansard*, H.L. Vol. 503, col. 1497)). An authority may only seek contributions if it is reasonable to do so (para. 21(2)). The high cost of collecting contributions may lead to authorities deciding not to try to recover contributions, but para. 21(1) appears to require an individual decision in each case. Local authorities may not specify a sum greater than it is reasonably practicable for the contributor to pay (para. 22(5)(b)) and a court making a contribution order must give due regard to the contributor's means (para. 23(3)(b)). The same people—parents and children over 16—can be charged for accommodation provided under s.20 or to children on care orders. The categories of exempt care are the same (para. 21(5) and (7)) and contributors are not liable for any period while they are on Income Support or Family Credit (para. 21(4)). The two stage process is retained: the local authority must serve a contribution notice under para. 22, to which the contributor may agree. If he does, contributions are now recovered as a civil debt (Magistrates' Courts Act 1980, s.58). Where no agreement is reached, the local authority may apply to the court for an order (para. 23). No order may be made for a sum greater than that specified in the notice (para. 23(3)(a)). Contribution orders made in the magistrates' court are enforceable like magistrates' courts maintenance orders under s.150 of the Magistrates' Courts Act 1980 (para. 24). The Lord Chancellor undertook in Parliament to review the provision of legal aid in these proceedings "because I believe it appropriate that it should be available" (*Hansard*, H.L. Vol. 503, col. 1498). The powers of local authorities to obtain affiliation orders and have existing orders varied in their favour was abolished with affiliation orders by the F.L.R.A. 1987. There are no corresponding powers for local authorities to seek financial relief under Sched. 1 and Sched. 2, para, 21(6).

There is a new power in the Secretary of State to make regulations about the assessment of contributions, agreements and arrangements for payment (para. 25). There was no indication to Parliament that this power would be exercised.

Subss. (7)–(9).

Where accommodation is provided under s.20(1) (but not where it is provided under s.20(3) to a child in need over the age of 16), or under s.21(2)(a) or (b) but not in any of the facilities listed in subs. (8), the local authority may charge the authority where the child is ordinarily resident. Alternatively, the paying authority may take over the child's care. A decision to move a child can only be made in accordance with s.22(3). Disputes about ordinary residence are determined by the Secretary of State (s.30(2)).

Expenses reasonably incurred: The fact that the "home authority" would not have provided the service does not make it unreasonable.

Miscellaneous

30.—(1) Nothing in this Part shall affect any duty imposed on a local authority by or under any other enactment.

(2) Any question arising under section 20(2), 21(3) or 29(7) to (9) as to the ordinary residence of a child shall be determined by agreement between the local authorities concerned or, in default of agreement, by the Secretary of State.

(3) Where the functions conferred on a local authority by this Part and the functions of a local education authority are concurrent, the Secretary of State may by regulations provide by which authority the functions are to be exercised.

(4) The Secretary of State may make regulations for determining, as respects any local education authority functions specified in the regulations, whether a child who is being looked after by a local authority is to be treated, for purposes so specified, as a child of parents of sufficient resources or as a child of parents without resources.

DEFINITIONS

"functions": s.105(1).
"local authority": s.105(1).
"local education authority": s.105(1).
"ordinary residence": s.105(6).

GENERAL NOTE

Subs. (3)

This re-enacts s.30 of the C.C.A. 1980. Regulations already exist (see Local Authorities and Local Education Authorities (Allocation of Funding) Regulations 1951 (S.I. 1951, No. 1472).

Subs. (4)

This re-enacts s.30 of the C.C.A. 1980.

A child of parents of sufficient resources . . .: This is not defined in any of the Education Acts 1944–1988. Under s.111 of the Education Act 1988, a local authority may levy charges for board and lodging in certain circumstances. If full charges would involve "financial hardship" to the parent, charges may be remitted (s.111(5)). A parent who would suffer financial hardship is presumably one with insufficient resources. There is no comparable provision in relation to charges for "optional extras" under s.110; schools and education authorities have to formulate and keep under review charging and remission policies.

PART IV

CARE AND SUPERVISION

General

Care and supervision orders

31.—(1) On the application of any local authority or authorised person, the court may make an order—

(a) placing the child with respect to whom the application is made in the care of a designated local authority; or

(b) putting him under the supervision of a designated local authority or of a probation officer.

(2) A court may only make a care order or supervision order if it is satisfied—

(a) that the child concerned is suffering, or is likely to suffer, significant harm; and

(b) that the harm, or likelihood of harm, is attributable to—

(i) the care given to the child, or likely to be given to him if the order were not made, not being what it would be reasonable to expect a parent to give to him; or

(ii) the child's being beyond parental control.

(3) No care order or supervision order may be made with respect to a child who has reached the age of seventeen (or sixteen, in the case of a child who is married).

(4) An application under this section may be made on its own or in any other family proceedings.

(5) The court may—

(a) on an application for a care order, make a supervision order;

(b) on an application for a supervision order, make a care order.

(6) Where an authorised person proposes to make an application under this section he shall—

(a) if it is reasonably practicable to do so; and

(b) before making the application,

consult the local authority appearing to him to be the authority in whose area the child concerned is ordinarily resident.

(7) An application made by an authorised person shall not be entertained by the court if, at the time when it is made, the child concerned is—

(a) the subject of an earlier application for a care order, or supervision order, which has not been disposed of; or

(b) subject to—

(i) a care order or supervision order;

(ii) an order under section 7(7)(b) of the Children and Young Persons Act 1969; or

(iii) a supervision requirement within the meaning of the Social Work (Scotland) Act 1968.

(8) The local authority designated in a care order must be—

(a) the authority within whose area the child is ordinarily resident; or

(b) where the child does not reside in the area of a local authority, the authority within whose area any circumstances arose in consequence of which the order is being made.

(9) In this section—

"authorised person" means—

(a) the National Society for the Prevention of Cruelty to Children and any of its officers; and

(b) any person authorised by order of the Secretary of State to bring proceedings under this section and any officer of a body which is so authorised;

"harm" means ill-treatment or the impairment of health or development;

"development" means physical, intellectual, emotional, social or behavioural development;

"health" means physical or mental health; and

"ill-treatment" includes sexual abuse and forms of ill-treatment which are not physical.

(10) Where the question of whether harm suffered by a child is significant turns on the child's health or development, his health or development shall be compared with that which could reasonably be expected of a similar child.

(11) In this Act—

"a care order" means (subject to section 105(1)) an order under subsection (1)(a) and (except where express provision to the contrary is made) includes an interim care order made under section 38; and

"a supervision order" means an order under subsection (1)(b) and (except where express provision to the contrary is made) includes an interim supervision order made under section 38.

DEFINITIONS

"authorised person": s.31(9).
"care order": ss.31(11), 105(1).
"child": ss.31(3), 105(1).
"designated local authority": s.31(8).
"development": s.31(9).
"family proceedings": s.8(3).
"harm": s.31(9).
"health": s.31(9).
"ill-treatment": s.31(9).
"local authority": s.105(1).
"ordinary residence": s.105(6).
"significant": s.31(10).
"supervision order": s.31(11).
"the court": s.92(7).

GENERAL NOTE

This section sets out the conditions which must be satisfied before a court grants a care or supervision order. It largely follows the recommendations of the R.C.C.L. Ch. 15 and Cm. 62, paras. 59–60. Compulsory measures of care can only be imposed through care proceedings. Parental rights resolutions and committal to care in matrimonial and other proceedings are abolished; local authorities cannot obtain care orders or any equivalent powers in wardship (s.100) or by section 8 orders (s.9). Thus there is no "safety net" and children can only be protected by an order if the conditions in subs. (2) are satisfied. If the order is refused, the local authority may appeal to the High Court (s.94). If an interim order has been made the child can be kept in care during the appeal period (s.40). Local authorities may apply by commencing care proceedings or in any family proceedings (subs. (4)). The lack of alternatives may affect the way the courts interpret their powers under s.31.

The existing grounds for orders in s.1(2) of the C.Y.P.A. 1969 and s.3 of the C.C.A. 1980 are replaced by the conditions in subs. (2) and the requirement to satisfy s.1(3)–(5). The court must give paramount consideration to the child's welfare (as defined in the checklist) and may only make an order if it is better than not to do so. The Lord Chancellor stated in his Joseph Jackson memorial lecture [1989] N.L.J. 505 that these conditions should not be regarded as grounds for a care order but the "minimum circumstances" which would justify state intervention in family life.

In general, cases which come within s.1(2) of the C.Y.P.A. 1969 or s.3 of the C.C.A. 1980 are covered, *i.e.* it will be possible to obtain an order to require a child's placement in care or to prevent the parents from removing him from care as before. However, the administrative procedure is abolished so it will be necessary to satisfy a court in all cases. Moreover, the circumstances listed below pose particular problems:—

(1) Orders can only be obtained in respect of people under 17 (or under 16 if they have married). The only interventions to protect a wayward older teenager such as occurred in *Re SW* [1986] 1 F.L.R. 24 would be through criminal proceedings or, if the person was suffering from mental disorder, under the Mental Health Act 1983.

(2) Cases involving "Schedule 1 offenders" (C.Y.P.A. 1933) or previous findings under C.Y.P.A. 1969, s.1(2)(a) no longer receive special consideration although these factors will be relevant to the "likelihood of harm" and "care" in s.31(2)(b).

(3) Truancy is no longer a ground for an order but where non-attendance at school satisfies s.31(2) a care order may be made. S.36 provides educational supervision orders as the main intervention to deal with truants; it will still be possible to

prosecute parents under the Education Act 1944, s.37, but not to imprison them (s.40 as amended by Sched. 15).

(4) The imposition of the tests in s.1 may, in some cases (particularly cases of moral danger concerning either teenage girls with unsuitable associates or younger children involved in petty crime), lead to courts refusing an order on the ground that it would only exacerbate problems.

(5) Cases under s.3 of the C.C.A. 1980, where there was no finding of parental unfitness, may not be covered by the new legislation. These include some cases of abandonment under s.3(1)(b)(i) and cases under s.3(1)(d). There is no equivalent provision to that of "statutory abandonment" which occurred if parents did not notify their address to the local authority for 12 months (C.C.A. 1980, s.3(8)). It will not be possible to get an order where the parent can provide appropriate care. Where the child is "bonded" with a foster parent it is possible that the parent's care might fall within subs. 2(b) even though it would be adequate for another child. If a care order is not available the foster carers may be able to apply for a residence order under s.10(5) if they have cared for the child for three years or have the necessary consents. The local authority's consent will be required where the child has not lived with the applicants for three years (s.9(3)).

(6) Cases where care orders are sought but it is intended that the child should remain in the family home. In *R.* v. *G and Surrey County Council* [1984] Fam. 100 the Court of Appeal upheld the making of an order under s.43(1) of the M.C.A. 1973 in such a case. The divorced parents were continuing their quarrel over access and the children repeatedly moved from one parent to the other. The court was prepared to find that the exceptional circumstances test in s.43 was satisfied. However, the addition of the requirement in s.1(5), together with the fact that parents retain parental responsibility under a care order, and the wide powers of the supervisor under a supervision order, would suggest that a supervision order would generally be more appropriate in such cases.

The statute also clearly allows for the protection of some children who were usually dealt with in wardship because of doubts about the scope of the old provisions.

(1) Children at risk: first born, new born babies of mentally ill or severely subnormal parents, drug addicts and other people who seem unable to care; children whose parents are no longer coping (because of mental illness or other problems) but who have not yet been harmed. The decision in *Re D* [1987] A.C. 317, H.L., which allowed the removal under s.1(2)(a) of the C.Y.P.A. 1969 of a baby born with foetal drug syndrome did not permit orders in relation to all children local authorities sought to protect.

(2) Children who entered voluntary care after incidents of abuse and neglect who could not be brought before the court under the C.Y.P.A. 1969 because of the lapse of time but against whose parents there was insufficient evidence to ground a parental rights resolution.

Apart from the changes to the grounds, the section largely repeats the provisions of the C.Y.P.A. 1969. Proceedings can only be brought by local authorities and the N.S.P.C.C. (no other people have been authorised by the Secretary of State). Subs. (7) contains new restrictions on applications by authorised persons. There is no procedure equivalent to that in s.3 of the Children and Young Persons Act 1963 which enabled parents to force a local authority to take action in relation to a child who is beyond control. A parent who is unable to control his child can only request assistance from the local authority and make a complaint under s.26(3)(b) if it is refused. A child who is beyond parental control arguably comes within the definition of "in need" in s.17(10)(a).

Subs. (1)

On application: this may be in care proceedings or by intervening in any "family proceedings" as defined in s.8(3) (subs. (4)).

The court: see notes to s.92 and Sched. 11.

Subs. (2)

There is no distinction between the grounds for a care or supervision order although the court may continue to be willing to make supervision orders rather than care orders in weaker cases.

In addition to the test here, the court must be satisfied that the order is in the child's welfare as defined in the checklist (s.1(3)) and that it is better to make the order than not (s.1(5)). If the court is not satisfied it may still make a section 8 order because these are family proceedings (ss.8(3) and (4), 10(1)).

This provision will doubtless be the subject of considerable judicial interpretation. Two separate elements which are both contentious have to be established:—

(a) that the child is suffering significant harm, and

(b) that this is attributable either to the care given to the child or the child being beyond parental control.

Significant: The R.C.C.L. which proposed the new grounds stated at para. 15.15:—

("having set an acceptable standard of upbringing for the child, it should be necessary to show some substantial deficit in that standard. Minor shortcomings in the health and care provided or minor deficits in physical, psychological or social developments should not give rise to any compulsory intervention unless they are having, or are likely to have, serious and lasting effects upon the child").

What is "significant harm" is explained in subs. (10) by reference to what "could reasonably be expected" of a "similar child" (see below). The R.C.C.L. noted that a child who has been non-accidentally injured or an older sexually abused child "may not have suffered any lasting impairment in his health and development and the resulting emotional damage may be difficult to prove" (para. 15.16). It suggested a form of wording to cover these cases but this has not been included in the Act. It is likely that there will be increased emphasis on medical and psychological evidence to establish significant harm, particularly the emotional damage which may follow from abuse. Evidence or further evidence may be obtained during a child assessment order (s.43), an emergency protection order (s.44) or under an interim order (s.38). Also reliance may be placed on the likelihood of further significant injuries when there have been a series of insignificant ones.

Is suffering: The fact that there has been harm in the past will not be sufficient unless it is likely that it will be repeated. A local authority which suspects harm and offers to accommodate a child will not necessarily be able to use care proceedings to prevent the child's removal from care after a prolonged period. However, the words "his development is being avoidably prevented" in the C.Y.P.A. 1969, s.1(2), were held not to require that the state persisted at the time of the hearing; *M* v. *Westminster City Council* [1985] F.L.R. 325.

Is likely to suffer: The R.C.C.L. stated in para. 15.18:—

"In our view . . . 'likely' will place a burden of proof upon local authorities which will be sufficiently difficult for them to discharge, especially in relation to mental or emotional harm and this will prevent unwarranted intervention."

The standard of proof is the civil standard. In the past the courts have balanced the size of the risk against the severity of harm if the event occurs. However, unless the risk establishes that the harm is "likely" the test is not satisfied.

Attributable to: There has to be a link but not direct causation. For example, harm could be attributable to parental care where the parent failed to ensure that his child did not have contact with someone who was a known child abuser.

Care: Where the child has been accommodated by the local authority for a long time and the parents are not caring for another child it may be difficult to show what their current standard of care is. Reliance on a previously observed care may be sufficient unless the parents are able to point to changes which suggest that they would now care differently.

Reasonable to expect: The need for some children such as those with asthma or brittle bones to receive a higher standard of care is provided for. There was concern during the debate in the House of Lords that this provision might by thought to indicate that different standards of care could be expected from different classes or communities but this was not accepted as a correct interpretation by the Lord Chancellor (*Hansard*, H.L. Vol. 503, col. 354).

Beyond parental control: This was formerly a ground for an order under C.Y.P.A. 1969, s.1(2)(d). Under the new provision it is only a ground where it produces significant harm or the likelihood of such harm. The word "parental" should include the care of whoever has been entrusted by the parents with the child's care if the parents are not able or willing to exercise effective control themselves.

Subs. (6)

This contains the additional procedural conditions imposed on action by the N.S.P.C.C. (there are no other authorised persons). If it is reasonably practicable the N.S.P.C.C. must consult the local authority before starting proceedings. There was no requirement to consult under the old law but consultation was regarded as good practice and the local authority had to be notified of the proceedings. Consultation under subs. (6) will automatically bring the local authority's duty to investigate under s.47(1) into play. The local authority may then decide to start care proceedings. If the N.S.P.C.C. has obtained an emergency protection order under s.44, s.52(3) allows for rules to be made which would give the authority the right to take over the proceedings.

Subs. (7)
Restricts applications by the N.S.P.C.C. where:
    (a) there is a local authority application pending, or
    (b) the child is subject to an existing care or supervision order, including a supervision order made in criminal proceedings.

These limitations reflect the view of the R.C.C.L. in para. 12.15 that proceedings should usually be brought by the local authority and also current practice. However, there is nothing in the Act to stop the N.S.P.C.C. bringing proceedings where the local authority has agreed to provide accommodation on a voluntary basis following, *e.g.* suspected abuse. It is important that professional rivalries do not interfere with planning for children.

Subs. (8)
If the wrong authority is designated it would need to appeal against the order.
Does not reside: For example a child visiting from outside England and Wales.

Subss. (9) and (10)
The definition of significant harm is constructed like a Russian doll! It also applies to child assessment orders under s.43, emergency protection orders under s.44, the police power to remove a child under s.46, the local authority's duty to investigate under s.47 and detention in secure accommodation, s.25.
Impairment of health or development: This seems wide enough to cover any case of neglect—poor nutrition, low standards of hygiene, poor emotional care or through failure to seek treatment for an illness or condition.
Ill-treatment: The Lord Chancellor explained what was meant (*Hansard*, H.L. Vol. 503, col. 342): "Ill-treatment is not a precise term and would include, for example, instances of verbal abuse or unfairness falling a long way short of significant harm". This could not form the basis of an application but such ill-treatment might produce significant harm in a vulnerable child and thus justify intervention.
Reasonably be expected: This may pose problems if the child already has a handicap and either there is little information about what is normal for such children or the range of development is extremely broad.
A similar child: According to the Lord Chancellor a child with the same physical attributes as the child concerned, not a child of the same background (see *Hansard*, H.L. Vol. 503, col. 354). However, this ignores the fact that social and environmental factors contribute very significantly to what can be achieved.

Period within which application for order under this Part must be disposed of

32.—(1) A court hearing an application for an order under this Part shall (in the light of any rules made by virtue of subsection (2))—
    (a) draw up a timetable with a view to disposing of the application without delay; and
    (b) give such directions as it considers appropriate for the purpose of ensuring, so far as is reasonably practicable, that that timetable is adhered to.
(2) Rules of court may—
    (a) specify periods within which specified steps must be taken in relation to such proceedings; and
    (b) make other provision with respect to such proceedings for the purpose of ensuring, so far as is reasonably practicable, that they are disposed of without delay.

DEFINITIONS
    "care order": ss.31(11), 105(1).
    "supervision order": s.31(11).
    "the court": s.92(7).

GENERAL NOTE
This section should be read with s.1(2) which warns of the dangers of delay. "Ensuring proper timetabling arrangements is one of the Bill's better reforms" *per* David Mellor,

Minister of Health (Standing Committee B, col. 231, May 23, 1989). The courts have recognised that delay is particularly damaging to children and can lead to a denial of justice. The length of time taken to complete care and related proceedings in the magistrates' courts was studied as part of the D.H.S.S. project on representation of children in care proceedings; Murch and Mills in *The Length of Care Proceedings* (1987), commented that in some places a "culture of 'acceptable delay' " had developed. This provision and any rules made under it may help move cases through the system but it is likely, at least initially, that care proceedings will take even longer. The inclusion of some more complex cases previously dealt with in wardship and the possibility of transfer are likely to slow matters down. The change in the time limits for interim orders may exacerbate this. Clerks to the Justices will need to be very firm with parties and their lawyers. Delay in proceedings under s.34 may be less damaging to the parents than it was under s.12A–F of the C.C.A. 1980, because contact between parent and child will not have been terminated by the authority.

Subs. (1)

The minister would not commit himself to ensure that time-tabling would be required at the first court hearing, (Standing Committee B, col. 231, May 23, 1989). Guardians ad litem may be given responsibilities to take action to prevent delay at pre-hearing reviews under s.41(10)(c) and may be able to apply for discharge of an interim order. A penalty of costs may be imposed on a party who is responsible for delay.

Care orders

Effect of care order

33.—(1) Where a care order is made with respect to a child it shall be the duty of the local authority designated by the order to receive the child into their care and to keep him in their care while the order remains in force.

(2) Where—

(a) a care order has been made with respect to a child on the application of an authorised person; but

(b) the local authority designated by the order was not informed that that person proposed to make the application,

the child may be kept in the care of that person until received into the care of the authority.

(3) While a care order is in force with respect to a child, the local authority designated by the order shall—

(a) have parental responsibility for the child; and

(b) have the power (subject to the following provisions of this section) to determine the extent to which a parent or guardian of the child may meet his parental responsibility for him.

(4) The authority may not exercise the power in subsection (3)(b) unless they are satisfied that it is necessary to do so in order to safeguard or promote the child's welfare.

(5) Nothing in subsection (3)(b) shall prevent a parent or guardian of the child who has care of him from doing what is reasonable in all the circumstances of the case for the purpose of safeguarding or promoting his welfare.

(6) While a care order is in force with respect to a child, the local authority designated by the order shall not—

(a) cause the child to be brought up in any religious persuasion other than that in which he would have been brought up if the order had not been made; or

(b) have the right—

(i) to consent or refuse to consent to the making of an application with respect to the child under section 18 of the Adoption Act 1976;

(ii) to agree or refuse to agree to the making of an adoption order, or an order under section 55 of the Act of 1976, with respect to the child; or

(iii) to appoint a guardian for the child.

(7) While a care order is in force with respect to a child, no person may—
(a) cause the child to be known by a new surname; or
(b) remove him from the United Kingdom,
without either the written consent of every person who has parental responsibility for the child or the leave of the court.
(8) Subsection (7)(b) does not—
(a) prevent the removal of such a child, for a period of less than one month, by the authority in whose care he is; or
(b) apply to arrangements for such a child to live outside England and Wales (which are governed by paragraph 19 of Schedule 2).
(9) The power in subsection (3)(b) is subject (in addition to being subject to the provisions of this section) to any right, duty, power, responsibility or authority which a parent or guardian of the child has in relation to the child and his property by virtue of any other enactment.

DEFINITIONS
    "authorised person": s.31(9).
    "care order": ss.31(11), 105(1).
    "designated local authority": s.31(8).
    "guardian": s.5.
    "parental responsibility": ss.2, 3.
    "person who has parental responsibility": ss.2(1)(2), 4(1), 5(6), 12(1), 33(3).

GENERAL NOTE
    This section sets out the powers and responsibilities of the various parties when a care order is made. The comparable provisions relating to supervision orders are in s.35 and Sched. 3, Pts. I and II.
    The N.S.P.C.C. are an authorised person (see s.31(9)) and may keep the child in their care until he is received by the local authority but only if the authority was not informed of the application under s.31(6) (subs. (3)).
    The parents: retain parental responsibility for the child but can only exercise it in accordance with:– s.2(8), which precludes action incompatible with a court order; subss. (3) and (4) which give the local authority the power to determine, in accordance with the child's welfare, the extent to which the parents may exercise their responsibility; and subs. (5). John Eekelaar strongly criticised the notion that both the parents and the authority should have parental responsibility ([1989] New L.J. 760). He noted that there was no statutory provision allowing the courts to deal with disputes (except over contact) in such cases because specific issue orders are not available (s.9(1)). He suggested that the courts might not follow the decisions in *A* v. *Liverpool City Council* [1982] A.C. 363 and *Re W* [1985] 2 All E.R. 301, which prevented the use of wardship to review the exercise of local authority discretion over children in care because the Act expressly gives the parents parental responsibility alongside the authority. He further suggested that a refusal to exercise wardship in such circumstances could be a breach of Art. 6 of the European Convention on Human Rights because parental responsibility is a "civil right" which should be determined through a fair hearing by an independent tribunal. He argued that care orders are made because of parental failure and this should justify the removal of parental responsibility. However, the Government does not seem to have heeded this advice. S.33 was redrafted to make it clear that "the local authority must be in the driving seat" (*per* David Mellor, Minister of Health, Standing Committee B, col. 232, May 23, 1989), but parents retain their status. It seems that this has been done to encourage maintenance of links with the family, rehabilitation and perhaps also to justify charging for the child's care. Whatever limits this provision puts on day-to-day decisions by parents it is clear that they still have the right to give or withhold agreement to adoption or freeing for adoption and to appoint a guardian. The parents apparently retain their rights to determine the (immature) child's religion (subs. (6)). They cannot change his name or remove him from the U.K. without consent. Parents retain their right to inherit on the child's intestacy.
    The Local Authority: This has a duty to receive the child into care and keep him in care while the order is in force. The child can only be accommodated in accordance with s.23. He can only live with a parent, a person with parental responsibility, or someone who had a

residence order before the care order was made in accordance with regulations made under s.23(5). New regulations will replace the current Accommodation of Children (Charge and Control) Placements Regulations 1988. The local authority is also under the duties prescribed in ss.17, 22, 24, 26 and Sched. 2, Pt. II.

The local authority has parental responsibility (subs. (3)) but cannot change the child's religion, agree to his adoption or freeing for adoption, or appoint a guardian. If the child is mature he may make his own decision about religion and the local authority may support it (David Mellor, Standing Committee B, col. 234, May 23, 1989). The local authority does have the right to consent to his marriage (see Marriage Act 1949, s.3(1) as amended by Sched. 12, para. 5). It cannot change a child's name (nor allow a foster parent to do so) without the consent of all persons with parental responsibility or the court. A court could only allow name change if it was in the child's welfare. In cases involving remarried parents the courts have been quite unwilling to allow name change without cogent reasons (see *Re W.G.* (1976) 6 Fam.L. 210, *W* v. *A* [1981] Fam. 14) although the Court of Appeal has not always maintained opposition (*R (B.M.)* v. *R (D.N.)* [1978] 2 All E.R. 33). The local authority may remove the child from the U.K. without consent for a period of less than one month. Longer periods require the consent of every person with parental responsibility or the court. If the child is to live outside England and Wales, then Sched. 2, para. 19, applies and the approval of the court is required.

Parental contact etc. with children in care

34.—(1) Where a child is in the care of a local authority, the authority shall (subject to the provisions of this section) allow the child reasonable contact with—

   (a) his parents;

   (b) any guardian of his;

   (c) where there was a residence order in force with respect to the child immediately before the care order was made, the person in whose favour the order was made; and

   (d) where, immediately before the care order was made, a person had care of the child by virtue of an order made in the exercise of the High Court's inherent jurisdiction with respect to children, that person.

(2) On an application made by the authority or the child, the court may make such order as it considers appropriate with respect to the contact which is to be allowed between the child and any named person.

(3) On an application made by—

   (a) any person mentioned in paragraphs (a) to (d) of subsection (1); or

   (b) any person who has obtained the leave of the court to make the application,

the court may make such order as it considers appropriate with respect to the contact which is to be allowed between the child and that person.

(4) On an application made by the authority or the child, the court may make an order authorising the authority to refuse to allow contact between the child and any person who is mentioned in paragraphs (a) to (d) of subsection (1) and named in the order.

(5) When making a care order with respect to a child, or in any family proceedings in connection with a child who is in the care of a local authority, the court may make an order under this section, even though no application for such an order has been made with respect to the child, if it considers that the order should be made.

(6) An authority may refuse to allow the contact that would otherwise be required by virtue of subsection (1) or an order under this section if—

   (a) they are satisfied that it is necessary to do so in order to safeguard or promote the child's welfare; and

   (b) the refusal—

      (i) is decided upon as a matter of urgency; and

      (ii) does not last for more than seven days.

(7) An order under this section may impose such conditions as the court considers appropriate.

(8) The Secretary of State may by regulations make provision as to—

    (a) the steps to be taken by a local authority who have exercised their powers under subsection (6);

    (b) the circumstances in which, and conditions subject to which, the terms of any order under this section may be departed from by agreement between the local authority and the person in relation to whom the order is made;

    (c) notification by a local authority of any variation or suspension of arrangements made (otherwise than under an order under this section) with a view to affording any person contact with a child to whom this section applies.

(9) The court may vary or discharge any order made under this section on the application of the authority, the child concerned or the person named in the order.

(10) An order under this section may be made either at the same time as the care order itself or later.

(11) Before making a care order with respect to any child the court shall—

    (a) consider the arrangements which the authority have made, or propose to make, for affording any person contact with a child to whom this section applies; and

    (b) invite the parties to the proceedings to comment on those arrangements.

DEFINITIONS
"care order" ss.31(11), 105(1).
"guardian": s.5.
"local authority": s.105(3).
"residence order": ss.8(1), 105(3).
"the court": s.92(7).

GENERAL NOTE
This provides for contact (access) between children in care and their families and the only judicial means for dealing with disputes about contact for such children. Disputes may also be referred to the complaints system, established under s.26(3). This section should be read with Sched. 2, para. 15, which imposes on the local authority a qualified duty "to endeavour to promote contact" between children who are looked after by the authority, their families and their friends. It replaces s. 12A–12G of the C.C.A. 1980; there is no provision for the replacement of the D.H.S.S. Code of Practice on Access which consequently ceases to have effect. Local authorities are no longer empowered to terminate access between children in care and their parents. Decisions about the refusal of contact, its frequency and duration are all to be made by the court (subss. (2) to (5)).

The legislation reflects the view that contact is "a right of the child" (*per* Wrangham J. in *M.* v. *M.* [1973] 2 All E.R. 81) both in its wording and the fact that children may apply for orders (subss. (2) and (4)).

Local authorities are under a duty to allow a child in care reasonable contact with his parents, guardians or anyone who held a residence order in respect of the child or care under the inherent jurisdiction before the care order was made (sub. (1)) except where subs. (6) applies. The local authority, the child, those listed in subs. (1) and anyone with leave may apply for orders (subs. (3)) allowing contact between the child and a named person and variation or discharge of an order concerning them (subs. (9)). Only the local authority and the child may apply for an order for contact to be refused (subs. (4)). The local authority may refuse to comply with an order for contact under subs. (6) for up to seven days if this is necessary to safeguard the child's welfare as a matter of urgency. Any order may be made, or conditions attached (subs. (7)) by the court of its own motion (subs. (5)). Orders can be made when a care order is made (this includes when an interim order is made (s. 31(11)) or later (including in family proceedings) (subss. (5) and (10)). The court must consider the local authority's arrangements for contact when a care order (or interim care order) is made (subs. (11)). When exercising its powers under the section, the court must apply the welfare principle in s.1, including the checklist in s.1(3) (s.1(4)). Thus the approach to applications may not be very different from that under the previous law, where access was only ordered following a termination by the local authority where there was a substantial chance of rehabilitation (see Millham *et al., Access disputes in Child Care,* Gower (1989)' and *Re KD* [1987] 2 F.L.R. 365).

Limitations on repeated applications are provided in s. 91(17) but are less restrictive than under the previous law, which allowed only one bite at the cherry (see *T.* v. *West Glamorgan County Council, The Times,* October 12, 1989).

Subs. (1)

This lists the people (other than the local authority or the child) who may apply for contact to a child in care without the leave of the court.

In care: If the child is only accommodated, a dispute can be dealt with by a section 8 contact order. The duty in Sched. 2, para. 15 applies to all children looked after by the authority. There is also a power in para. 16 to contribute towards travel costs, etc.

Subject to the provisions of this section: Contact may be refused under a court order or under subs. (6). A condition could be imposed (under subs. (7)) in an order refusing contact to require the local authority to re-instate it if refusal was no longer necessary for the child's welfare. A provision specifically to this effect was originally included in the Bill but was removed because of drafting difficulties. There is power under subs. (8)(b) to make regulations about reinstatement of contact.

Reasonable contact: This phraseology has applied to contact between divorced or separated parents and their children for many years. In those cases the parties are left to work out what is reasonable but can return to the court to have contact defined if they cannot agree. The local authority's view of what is reasonable must safeguard and promote the child's welfare because of the duty in s. 22(3). It should reflect not only the child's needs determined by reference to his or her current development but also the importance of maintaining contact in the long term. Unless the contact is satisfying for the adult and the child, arrangements are unlikely to be kept. This will affect the child's chances of returning to his family and the support available to him when he leaves care (see Millham *et al. Lost in Care* Gower (1986)). If the local authority thinks it is necessary to refuse contact, it may do so but only for seven days in accordance with subs. (6). A court order refusing contact must then be obtained. If the order is refused, contact must be permitted pending any appeal, as s. 40 does not apply.

Parents: This includes the unmarried father who has not acquired parental responsibility and thus sidesteps the complications caused by *M. and H. (Minors)* [1988] 3 W.L.R. 485 and the error in the drafting of the F.L.R.A. 1987. This error is remedied by Sched. 12, para. 35 which came into effect on Royal Assent.

Contact: This is not defined for the purposes of this section, but would seem to include all methods of sustaining links between people. It would thus include access visits as well as telephone calls and letters. Any order made would thus be directly comparable with a contact order in s.8. Overnight stays will have to comply with the regulations made under s.23(5).

Where there was a residence order: These orders are discharged automatically by the making of a care order (s.91(2)).

Subs. (2)

The child: There is no statutory test of maturity as under s.10(8), but it is difficult to see how a child who does not understand something of the issues can be said to have made an application. A child does not need to have full grasp of the matter because he will probably be represented by a guardian ad litem and a solicitor. The parents could only make an application on the child's behalf if the authority permitted them to under s.33(3)(b).

The court: These cases are likely to be dealt with in the magistrates' court (see notes to s.92 and Sched. 11 on the allocation of cases).

May make: S.1(5) applies. The policy that orders should not be made unless they are necessary applies here also (see s.10(1)). Orders will help clarify the situation of the child, the family and the local authority.

Such order as it considers appropriate: An order for reasonable contact will only be appropriate if it appears that the agreement can be reached by the parties. If contact is defined in terms of time, place, duration and frequency a condition can be included under subs. (7) to allow variation in some or all of these matters by agreement. Refusals of contact can only be made in accordance with subs. (4).

That person: A cannot seek orders which will affect B's contact, only A's.

Subs. (3)

There are no conditions for these applications for leave. Rules will presumably require applicants for leave to indicate their relationship to the child and the extent to which they have had contact with him in the past. Where the child wishes to maintain the relationship the need for leave may be avoided by the child applying for the order. There may also be advantages in this course of action under the legal aid scheme and because of the attitude of the courts.

To be allowed: Parents and others who want to restrict contact between the child and other people (friends, relatives, etc.), will have to request the authority (or child) to seek such an order. If the authority does not agree, they may make a complaint under s.26(3).

Subs. (4)

If the local authority wishes to refuse contact between the child and a person listed in subs. (1) and that person wants contact, it will need to obtain an order. No such order is required to end contact by others, *e.g.* grandparents, because the authority has no duty to allow reasonable contact with them. However, such a person refused contact can seek leave to obtain an order. A child may refuse to see a person and need not obtain an order unless there is no other way to resist contact.

Subs. (5)

The court may make these orders for contact of its own motion in care proceedings or in any family proceedings relating to the child. No order may be made until there is a care order or an interim care order (subs. (10)).

Subs. (6)

A comparable provision existed under the C.C.A. 1980, s.12E, but the test here seems easier to satisfy, which reflects the fact that it applies to excuse the local authority from complying with an order or its duty under subs. (1). It is no longer necessary to show that a child's welfare is seriously at risk, only that the refusal of contact is necessary "to safeguard or promote the child's welfare". It must be decided upon as a matter of urgency. Regulations under subs. (8) may direct the local authority to take further steps in these cases.

Matter of urgency: Where contact has been continuing, it would seem that this test should only be satisfied if an incident has occurred or information has been obtained suggesting that the child is substantially at risk. The decision to place a child for adoption would not justify an emergency refusal, nor would any other change of placement. Although the child's need to settle down has often been given as a reason for refusing contact, there is no evidence that contact with the family damages the child's ability to settle; in fact the most recent evidence is to the contrary (Berridge & Cleaver, *Foster Home Breakdown,* Blackwell (1987)). Where there has been no recent contact with the person it may be easier to justify refusal, at least if there are good reasons for believing that the court would not grant an order. Local authorities will need to take care, however, if lack of past contact is due to a breach of duties they owe under Sched. 2, para. 15.

Subs. (10)

Orders may be made at any time after the care order has been made and can thus be made when the child is freed for adoption (Adoption Act 1978, s.18), avoiding the difficulties caused because freeing orders, unlike adoption orders, could not be made subject to conditions.

Subs. (11)

The duty to consider and invite comment does not apply to family proceedings relating to a child in care, *e.g.* where the court considers contact during an (unsuccessful) application for a residence order in respect of a child in care.

Parties: Party status will be determined by rules made under s.93. It is quite possible that someone other than a party to the care proceedings will be granted contact. Only if that person has actually applied for an order will they be a party. Views of all interested persons should be canvassed by the guardian ad litem and there may be further possibilities of making representations under the rules.

Supervision orders

Supervision orders

35.—(1) While a supervision order is in force it shall be the duty of the supervisor—

(a) to advise, assist and befriend the supervised child;
(b) to take such steps as are reasonably necessary to give effect to the order; and
(c) where—
    (i) the order is not wholly complied with; or
    (ii) the supervisor considers that the order may no longer be necessary,
to consider whether or not to apply to the court for its variation or discharge.

(2) Parts I and II of Schedule 3 make further provision with respect to supervision orders.

DEFINITIONS
"supervised child", "supervisor": s.105(1).
"supervision order": s.31(11).
"the court": s.92(7).

GENERAL NOTE
This section sets out the primary duty of the supervisor where the court makes a supervision order (subs. (1)). Details of the terms of supervision orders are found in Sched. 3, Pts. I and II. The Act incorporates provisions relating to supervision previously found in the Magistrates' Courts (Children and Young Persons) Rules 1970; it replaces some, but not all, of the provisions in the C.Y.P.A. 1969 dealing with supervision and further amends and clarifies the law. It is particularly important to note that supervision orders will only last for one year from the date on which they were made, unless they are extended (Sched. 3, para. 6). The supervisor may apply to extend it (para. 6(2)) and may seek its variation or discharge (subs. (1)(c) and s.39(2)). The maximum duration for a supervision order is three years. A supervision order cannot continue after the child has reached age 18 (s.91(13)) and is brought to an end if the child's return is ordered or a decision registered under the Child Abduction and Custody Act 1985, ss.16, 25(1)(a)(b) as amended by Sched. 13, para. 57.

The Short Committee were concerned that very few supervision orders were made in care cases and suggested that this reflected their perceived ineffectiveness (para. 150). The R.C.C.L. proposed that requirements should be imposed on the parent or any person with whom the child is living. This has been done in Sched. 3, paras. 1, 3 and 8. Such people are termed *responsible persons* and are defined in Sched. 3, para. 1. They must provide information to the supervisor and comply with requirements imposed under para. 3. These may not be imposed without their consent and can only last 90 days (para. 7). Requirements cover taking reasonable steps to ensure that the child complies with the directions of the supervisor or attends for medical examination or treatment. They may also require the responsible person to meet the supervisor and keep him informed of his address.

Requirements may be imposed on the supervised child as under the present law (para. 2), but no requirements may be imposed for more than 90 days (para. 7). Requirements can cover where the child lives, meetings with specified people and participation in specified activities. These do not require the child's consent. Under C.Y.P.A. 1969, s.14A, refusal to allow visits or medical examinations were grounds for an order under C.Y.P.A. 1933, s.40. There is no similar provision here and the supervisor would have to satisfy the grounds for an emergency protection order in s.44. Para. 4 provides detailed provisions relating to medical and psychiatric examination; para. 5 provides for treatment. The court may include a direction requiring the child to submit to examination or treatment. Children who have sufficient understanding cannot be made subject to such conditions without their consent, (paras. 4(4) and 5(5)). This gives effect to the *Gillick* decision which gives mature minors decision-making authority over medical matters (see notes to s.43).

Para. 9 replaces C.Y.P.A. 1969, s.13, without any substantial amendment. Children will continue to be supervised by local authority social workers unless para. 9(2) applies. Para. 11 provides for regulations. A supervision order ends existing care or supervision orders (para. 10).

There is provision for interim supervision orders, for discharge and for appeals in ss.38 to 40 and s.94.

Education supervision orders

36.—(1) On the application of any local education authority, the court may make an order putting the child with respect to whom the application is made under the supervision of a designated local education authority.

(2) In this Act "an education supervision order" means an order under subsection (1).

(3) A court may only make an education supervision order if it is satisfied that the child concerned is of compulsory school age and is not being properly educated.

(4) For the purposes of this section, a child is being properly educated only if he is receiving efficient full-time education suitable to his age, ability and aptitude and any special educational needs he may have.

(5) Where a child is—

    (a) the subject of a school attendance order which is in force under section 37 of the Education Act 1944 and which has not been complied with; or

    (b) a registered pupil at a school which he is not attending regularly within the meaning of section 39 of that Act,

then, unless it is proved that he is being properly educated, it shall be assumed that he is not.

(6) An education supervision order may not be made with respect to a child who is in the care of a local authority.

(7) The local education authority designated in an education supervision order must be—

    (a) the authority within whose area the child concerned is living or will live; or

    (b) where—

        (i) the child is a registered pupil at a school; and

        (ii) the authority mentioned in paragraph (a) and the authority within whose area the school is situated agree,

the latter authority.

(8) Where a local education authority propose to make an application for an education supervision order they shall, before making the application, consult the social services committee (within the meaning of the Local Authority Social Services Act 1970) of the appropriate local authority.

(9) The appropriate local authority is—

    (a) in the case of a child who is being provided with accommodation by, or on behalf of, a local authority, that authority; and

    (b) in any other case, the local authority within whose area the child concerned lives, or will live.

(10) Part III of Schedule 3 makes further provision with respect to education supervision orders.

DEFINITIONS

"appropriate local authority": s.36(9).
"child": ss.36(3), 105(1).
"designated local education authority": s.36(7).
"education supervision order": s.36(2), Sched. 3, Pt. III.
"local authority": s.105(1).
"local education authority": s.105(1).
"properly educated": s.36(4)(5).
"registered pupil": s.105(1).
"social services committee": s.36(8).
"the court": s.92(7).

GENERAL NOTE

This provides for a new type of order, the "education supervision order" which will be the usual order for dealing with non-attendance at school. Education supervision orders can only be made on application by a local education authority (subs. (1)) in respect of children of compulsory school age (subs. (3)) who are not receiving suitable, efficient full-time education (subs. (4)). A child is deemed to satisfy the conditions for making an education supervision order if either of the conditions in subs. (5) exists. The education supervision order will place the child under the supervision of the designated authority, which will be the authority where the child lives, unless he goes to school elsewhere and the two authorities agree (subs. (7)). The education authority must consult the social services committee of the appropriate authority, *i.e.* the authority accommodating the child or the one for the area where the child lives (subs. (9)), before making the application (subs. (8)). Education supervision orders are not available for children in local authority care (subs. (6)).

The details of education supervision orders are contained in Sched. 3, Pt. III (see subs. (10)).

It seems likely that this order will replace the "Leeds System" for dealing with truants. Under the "Leeds system" care proceedings were started but repeatedly adjourned. During the periods of adjournment attendance was monitored. Orders were not made provided that attendance did not fall below a specified level. The removal of non-attendance as a free standing ground for a care order, the timetabling provisions in s.32 and the general doubts about the legality of such repeated adjournments may end that way of dealing with truants. Whether education supervision orders will be successful remains to be seen.

Subss. (3) and (4)
Compulsory school age: This is defined in the Education Act 1944, s.35. A child must attend school from the beginning of the term immediately following his fifth birthday until the age of 16. The upper age limit is affected by the Education Act 1962, s.9, which sets leaving dates and deems a pupil not having attained the age of 16 until the leaving date. S.95 of the Education Act 1944 permits the court to presume that a pupil is under or over a specific age where the person bringing the proceedings under the Education Act has been unable, despite reasonable diligence, to find out a child's age. However, that provision does not apply here, so it will be necessary to show, on the balance of probabilities, that the child is of school age.

Properly educated: This is further explained in subs. (4). S.36 of the Education Act 1944 imposes a duty on the parent of every child "to cause him to receive efficient full-time education suitable to his age, ability and aptitude and to any special education needs he may have." A parent who fails in this duty can be served with a school attendance order or prosecuted under Education Act 1944, s.39. Failure to comply with a school attendance order is an offence (s.37(5)), but the parents may no longer be imprisoned (Education Act 1944, s.40 as amended by Sched. 15). It is not necessary for a school attendance order to be in force before the education supervision order procedure is used. However, the court with the criminal case may direct the local authority to institute proceedings for an education supervision order. The authority need not comply but must give reasons for the decision to the court within eight weeks (Education Act 1944, s.40(3)(4)). The court may also end the school attendance order when it makes an education supervision order (Education Act 1944, s.40(4), as amended by Sched. 13, para. 8). When there is a dispute about the quality of the education, because the child is being educated otherwise than at school, subs. (5) requires proof of proper education.

Subs. (5)
A school attendance order which has not been complied with: Compliance with a school attendance order requires the parent to cause the child to become a registered pupil at a school named in the order (Education Act 1944, s.37(2)) and to attend that school.

Registered pupil: This is defined in the Education Act 1944, s.114(1). The child's name must appear on the school register.

Attending regularly: The Education Act 1944, s.39, imposes a duty on the parents to secure their child's regular attendance at school, but permits absence with leave or for any of the reasons set out in s.39(2):— illness, any unavoidable cause, religious observance on day exclusively set aside for such observance by the parent's religious body, lack of suitable arrangements for transport in certain cases where the school is not within walking distance. All these excuses have been the subject of litigation (see *The Law of Education*, Butterworths, 9th Edition).

Subs. (6)
Local authorities are expected to have sufficient skills and resources to ensure that children in care are properly educated. An education supervision order should be otiose.

Subs. (7)
The local education authority must consult the social services committee but does not require its consent to an application for an education supervision order. However, this duty provides a basis to require co-operation and should help to ensure that the local education

authority is more fully aware of the child's circumstances. If education problems are evident when the local authority investigates a case it must consult the L.E.A. under s.47(5).

Subs. (10)

The details of education supervision orders are found in Sched. 3, Pt. III. The supervisor has a duty to advise, assist and befriend the supervised child and his parents (as defined in the Education Act 1944, s.114(1D) amended by Sched. 13, para. 10). This definition includes anyone with parental responsibility and anyone caring for the child. He may also give them directions. Failure to comply with a direction is an offence (level 3) (para. 18). Where failure is persistent, the appropriate local authority must be notified and must investigate (para. 19). Before giving directions the supervisor should consult the parents and child particularly to find out their wishes as to the place of the child's education and give due consideration to their wishes (para. 12). Where an education supervision order is in force, the parents' duties under ss.36 and 39 of the Education Act 1944 are replaced by their duty to comply with any directions under the order. The parent and child can be required to keep the supervisor notified of the child's address and allow visits (para. 16). Also, any school attendance order under s.37 ceases to have any effect and ss.37 and 76 of the 1944 Act and ss.6 and 7 of the Education Act 1980 cease to apply to the child (para. 13). An education supervision order can exist alongside a supervision order in criminal proceedings but there can be no educational requirement under s.12C of the C.Y.P.A. 1969 in the criminal supervision order. Failure to comply with a direction under the education supervision order is excluded if compliance would breach the criminal supervision order (paras. 13 and 14). Education supervision orders last for one year but can be extended on one occasion only for up to three years (para. 15). There is no restriction on the number of education supervision orders for any child, but, unless circumstances have changed, the fact that a child is still not being properly educated after the expiry of the education supervision order may suggest that alternative methods of securing attendance are required. Care proceedings will only rarely be available because of the tests in s.31(2). The parents may be prosecuted but the child may not apparently be made a ward of court (*Re Baker* [1962] Ch. 201), at least until the statutory powers have been fully pursued and leave has been obtained (s.100(3)).

Education supervision orders are discharged automatically when the child ceases to be of compulsory school age or by the making of a care order (para. 15(6)). Applications for discharge can be made by the child, a parent, or the local authority (para. 17). Procedure will be dealt within the rules made under s.93. The Secretary of State also has a power to make regulations relating to education supervision orders (para. 20).

Powers of court

Powers of court in certain family proceedings

37.—(1) Where, in any family proceedings in which a question arises with respect to the welfare of any child, it appears to the court that it may be appropriate for a care or supervision order to be made with respect to him, the court may direct the appropriate authority to undertake an investigation of the child's circumstances.

(2) Where the court gives a direction under this section the local authority concerned shall, when undertaking the investigation, consider whether they should—

(a) apply for a care order or for a supervision order with respect to the child;

(b) provide services or assistance for the child or his family; or

(c) take any other action with respect to the child.

(3) Where a local authority undertake an investigation under this section, and decide not to apply for a care order or supervision order with respect to the child concerned, they shall inform the court of—

(a) their reasons for so deciding;

(b) any service or assistance which they have provided, or intend to provide, for the child and his family; and

(c) any other action which they have taken, or propose to take, with respect to the child.

(4) The information shall be given to the court before the end of the period of eight weeks beginning with the date of the direction, unless the court otherwise directs.

(5) The local authority named in a direction under subsection (1) must be—

(a) the authority in whose area the child is ordinarily resident; or

(b) where the child does not reside in the area of a local authority, the authority within whose area any circumstances arose in consequence of which the direction is being given.

(6) If, on the conclusion of any investigation or review under this section, the authority decide not to apply for a care order or supervision order with respect to the child—

(a) they shall consider whether it would be appropriate to review the case at a later date; and

(b) if they decide that it would be, they shall determine the date on which that review is to begin.

DEFINITIONS

"appropriate authority": s.37(5).
"care order": s.31(11).
"child": s.105(1).
"family proceedings": s.8(3).
"local authority": s.105(1).
"ordinary residence": s.105(6).
"supervision order": s.31(11).
"the court": s.92(7).

GENERAL NOTE

The court's powers in this section replace the powers to commit children to care in matrimonial, guardianship and domestic proceedings. Such committals, made on the grounds of "exceptional circumstances", did not fit with the Government's wish to create a single standard for care orders based on substantial harm, as recommended by the R.C.C.L. paras. 8.20–22 and 15.35–37, Cm.62 1987 and Law Com. 172, para. 5.1. Nor did it fit with their proposed division of responsibility between local authorities and courts, which was intended to give local authorities greater control over the use of major resources like care. Now the court may only direct a local authority to undertake an investigation of the child's circumstances; it can do so in a wider range of proceedings, *family proceedings*, which include applications for injunctions in cases of domestic violence (subs. (1)). It is not limited to "children of the family".

Where the court makes a direction, it may make an interim order if there are reasonable grounds for believing that s.31(2) is satisfied (s.38(1)). The court's power to direct investigation exists alongside the local authority's duty to initiate investigation in cases of suspected harm under s.47 and its duty to take reasonable steps to identify children in need under Sched. 2, para. 1. A direction under subs. (1) imposes a duty on the authority to consider whether to apply for a care or supervision order, to provide services to the child or his family or take any other action (subs. (2)). There is no statutory duty to obtain access to the child as under s.47(4), but it is difficult to see that a proper investigation could be done without seeing him. If the local authority decides not to take action, it must inform the court, within eight weeks (unless otherwise directed (subs. (4))) of the reasons for so doing and any action they have taken (or proposed to take) with respect to the child (subs. (3)). The local authority must also consider whether to review a decision not to take proceedings at a later date and decide when this should be (subs. (6)).

Subs. (1)

It appears to the court: This is most likely to occur as a result of a welfare officer's report.

May be appropriate: The standard is low. It is not necessary for the court to think that a care order should be made. It may want to ensure that the authority gives full consideration to the child's needs. However, where the court has identified a problem within the family, which may be remedied by social work support, a family assistance order under s.16 may be more appropriate. Family assistance orders cannot be imposed without the consent of the adults concerned. Where this is not forthcoming, and the court considers further action is desirable, this is the only course open to it.

May direct: In making its decision the court must apply s.1(1).

Subs. (2)

The local authority must investigate, but need only consider the action outlined here. It does not have to take it, but under subs. (3) it will have to explain why it has not applied for a care or supervision order, and the action it has taken.

Services: These may be provided under ss.17, 18, 20 and 24.

Assistance: This may be in cash or in kind (s.17(6)).

Subs. (3)

There appears to be no duty to report back if the local authority has decided to take care proceedings but has not yet done so. Even if an application has been made, it would not necessarily come to the court's attention if it were made to a different court. A decision to apply for a care order in an unspecified time in the future without further action could be unreasonable.

Any other action: Consultations with other bodies, *e.g.* the local education authority about an application for an education supervision order.

Subs. (4)

The court's power would seem to allow it to demand quicker action. Eight weeks would appear to be a reasonable time to complete such an investigation, but no doubt some hard-pressed authorities will seek longer.

Subs. (5)

Does not reside: These words are replaced by "is not ordinary resident" (Courts and Legal Services Bill, Sched. 10, para. 7).

Circumstances: This will need to be interpreted widely because the direction may not have been made because of any specific occurrence but just general unease. In such a case the appropriate authority would be the one where the relevant adults are living.

Subs. (6)

Again, the local authority has wide discretion, but, having made a decision, must comply with it. The regulations concerning reviews under s.26(1) do not apply to these reviews because the child is not being looked after by the authority.

Interim orders

38.—(1) Where—

(a) in any proceedings on an application for a care order or supervision order, the proceedings are adjourned; or

(b) the court gives a direction under section 37(1),

the court may make an interim care order or an interim supervision order with respect to the child concerned.

(2) A court shall not make an interim care order or interim supervision order under this section unless it is satisfied that there are reasonable grounds for believing that the circumstances with respect to the child are as mentioned in section 31(2).

(3) Where, in any proceedings on an application for a care order or supervision order, a court makes a residence order with respect to the child concerned, it shall also make an interim supervision order with respect to him unless satisfied that his welfare will be satisfactorily safeguarded without an interim order being made.

(4) An interim order made under or by virtue of this section shall have effect for such period as may be specified in the order, but shall in any event cease to have effect on whichever of the following events first occurs—

(a) the expiry of the period of eight weeks beginning with the date on which the order is made;

(b) if the order is the second or subsequent such order made with respect to the same child in the same proceedings, the expiry of the relevant period;

(c) in a case which falls within subsection (1)(a), the disposal of the application;

(d) in a case which falls within subsection (1)(b), the disposal of an application for a care order or supervision order made by the authority with respect to the child;

(e) in a case which falls within subsection (1)(b) and in which—
    (i) the court has given a direction under section 37(4), but
    (ii) no application for a care order or supervision order has been made with respect to the child,

the expiry of the period fixed by that direction.

(5) In subsection (4)(b) "the relevant period" means—

(a) the period of four weeks beginning with the date on which the order in question is made; or

(b) the period of eight weeks beginning with the date on which the first order was made if that period ends later than the period mentioned in paragraph (a).

(6) Where the court makes an interim care order, or interim supervision order, it may give such directions (if any) as it considers appropriate with regard to the medical or psychiatric examination or other assessment of the child; but if the child is of sufficient understanding to make an informed decision he may refuse to submit to the examination or other assessment.

(7) A direction under subsection (6) may be to the effect that there is to be—

(a) no such examination or assessment; or

(b) no such examination or assessment unless the court directs otherwise.

(8) A direction under subsection (6) may be—

(a) given when the interim order is made or at any time while it is in force; and

(b) varied at any time on the application of any person falling within any class of person prescribed by rules of court for the purposes of this subsection.

(9) Paragraphs 4 and 5 of Schedule 3 shall not apply in relation to an interim supervision order.

(10) Where a court makes an order under or by virtue of this section it shall, in determining the period for which the order is to be in force, consider whether any party who was, or might have been, opposed to the making of the order was in a position to argue his case against the order in full.

DEFINITIONS
    "care order": s.31(11).
    "interim care order": s.38.
    "interim supervision order": s.38.
    "relevant period": s.38(5).
    "residence order": s.8(1).
    "supervision order": s.31(11).
    "the court": s.92(7).

GENERAL NOTE
    The R.C.C.L. identified three problems with interim orders. First, s.2(10) of the C.Y.P.A. 1969 did not clearly state a ground for making an interim order and the standards applied by courts differed widely. This was remedied by the decision in *R.* v. *Croydon Juvenile Court,* ex p. *N.* [1987] 151 J.P. 523, which held that there must be a prima facie case for a care order and the court must exercise its discretion in a judicial manner, giving paramount consideration to the welfare of the child. Second, even though it was rarely possible to process a case within four weeks, the duration of interim orders meant that repeated hearings occurred. Third, there was no power to make an interim supervision order. This section remedies those problems and also clarifies the law relating to medical examinations while an

interim order is in force. It departs from the proposals in the R.C.C.L. and Cm. 62 1987 (para. 61) quite markedly in relation to the duration of orders, and it is not clear how easily these generous provisions sit with s.1(2) which aims to minimise delays. This section does not apply to interim orders in other types of family proceedings.

Interim care orders: These can now be made in two situations:—

    (1) When an application for a care or supervision order is adjourned;

    (2) When the court orders an investigation under s.37(1).

In both these cases the court must be satisfied that there are reasonable grounds for believing that the conditions of substantial harm in s.31(2) are satisfied and that it is better to make an order than not. (s.1(5), subs. (1) and (2)).

Interim supervision orders: These can be made as in (1) and (2) above or (3) where the court makes a *residence order* in care proceedings, unless the child's welfare will be satisfactorily safeguarded without one (subs. (3)).

The maximum duration for orders made under s.38 is set out in subss. (4) and (5). Orders can be made for eight weeks with extensions of four weeks (or longer if the original order was for less than four weeks). There is no limit to the number of interim orders which can be made, but the court will need to comply with the timetabling provisions in s.32. Regardless of the length of the order it will automatically end when the application for the order is disposed of or the period fixed by the court under s.37(4) expires without an application for a care or supervision order being made. When fixing the duration of an interim order, the court is required to consider whether any person who was or might have been opposed to the order could argue his case fully (subs. (10)).

When the court makes an interim order it may make directions about medical or psychiatric examination or an assessment of the child (subs. (6)). Directions may bar such examination or permit it only subject to specific conditions (subs. (7)). Such a direction may be made or varied at any time while the interim order is in force on the application of anyone permitted to apply by the rules made under s.93 (subs. (8)). Where a direction is given, the child may not be examined without his permission if he has sufficient understanding to make decisions about medical matters, as under the *Gillick* test (see notes to s.43(8)).

Interim care orders are care orders for the purposes of the Act (s.31(11)). The local authority thus acquires all the powers of parental responsibility except those matters excluded under s.33. It owes duties to the child, who is by virtue of the order in care and who must therefore be accommodated in accordance with s.23. Such a child could only be returned home during the order if the placement complied with regulations under s.23(5). Similarly, an interim supervision order is a supervision order and the supervisor has functions under s.35 and Sched. 3, Pt. III, but may not require the child to submit to medical examination or treatment (subs.(9)).

Subs. (1)

Any proceedings: This includes applications for care orders in "family proceedings".

Subs. (2)

Reasonable grounds for believing: The wording is slightly different from that for an emergency protection order under s.44(1)(a), but there appears to be no substantial difference. In *R.* v. *Birmingham City Council* ex p. *Birmingham Juvenile Court* [1988] 1 W.L.R. 337, the Court of Appeal held that the rules which allow a parent to rebut an allegation made against him apply to proceedings for an interim order. The new provision would suggest that there may need to be a fairly full hearing of the issue even when the making of the order is not contested.

Subs. (3)

It may be more appropriate to make a family assistance order under s.16. The test in subs. (2) does not have to be satisfied in such cases.

Subss. (6)–(9)

There is no need for directions. Where an interim care order is made, the local authority has parental responsibility and may make decisions about the child's medical treatment accordingly. Neither the authority's decision nor a court order can bind a mature person because of the *Gillick* ruling and subs. (6). A parent who objects to the child's examination or assessment should seek a direction under subs. (7). However, the court will no doubt be mindful that it may have difficulty reaching its decision, particularly in cases of neglect, physical or sexual abuse if medical evidence is lacking.

Subs. (10)

If a party were not in a position to argue fully, a short order with substantial court time for a hearing on the return date is appropriate. It does not appear that any restrictions have been imposed to prevent a full airing of the issues for each successive interim order as under *R.* v. *Birmingham Juvenile Court* ex p. *P and S* [1984] F.L.R. 343.

Discharge and variation etc. of care orders and supervision orders

39.—(1) A care order may be discharged by the court on the application of—

(a) any person who has parental responsibility for the child;
(b) the child himself; or
(c) the local authority designated by the order.

(2) A supervision order may be varied or discharged by the court on the application of—

(a) any person who has parental responsibility for the child;
(b) the child himself; or
(c) the supervisor.

(3) On the application of a person who is not entitled to apply for the order to be discharged, but who is a person with whom the child is living, a supervision order may be varied by the court in so far as it imposes a requirement which affects that person.

(4) Where a care order is in force with respect to a child the court may, on the application of any person entitled to apply for the order to be discharged, substitute a supervision order for the care order.

(5) When a court is considering whether to substitute one order for another under subsection (4) any provision of this Act which would otherwise require section 31(2) to be satisfied at the time when the proposed order is substituted or made shall be disregarded.

DEFINITIONS

"care order": s.31(11).
"person who has parental responsibility": ss.2(1)(2), 4(1), 5(6), 12(1).
"person entitled to apply for a care order to be discharged": s.39(1).
"person entitled to apply for a supervision order to be discharged": s.39(2).
"supervision order": s.31(11).
"supervisor": s.105(1).
"the court": s.92(7).

GENERAL NOTE

This provision clarifies the law relating to discharge of care or supervision orders and largely implements the recommendations of the R.C.C.L., Ch. 20, about the powers of the court and the grounds for discharge. A care order can also be discharged by the making of a residence order (see s.91(1)). For a full discussion of residence orders, see ss. 8 and 10.

Those who may apply for the discharge of a care order are listed in subs. (1); for the variation or discharge of a supervision order in subss. (2) and (3). A person with whom the child is living, *i.e.* "a responsible person" who can be required to comply with the directions of the supervisor under Sched. 3, Pts. I and II may seek variation of the order in so far as it affects himself. The test to be applied in discharge proceedings is the welfare test in s.1; the checklist in s.1(3) applies. Thus it is clear that the court must consider not parental fitness but the child's welfare. Despite the virtual abolition of wardship for local authorities and the defects recognised in the old law, there is no specific power in the court to order a phased return of the child, but this may be achieved by a residence order (see s.8), or possibly using s.40.

There is no longer any power to vary a care order. However, when an application to discharge a care order is made, the court may substitute a supervision order (subs. (4)); the grounds in s.31(2) do not have to be re-proved (subs. (6)), but the tests in s.1 will have to be applied. Thus the Act is no more onerous than the C.Y.P.A. 1969 in this respect. In contrast, it will now be necessary for the grounds in s.31(2) to be re-proved before a care order can be made.

S.91(15) restricts a repeated application for the discharge of an order within six months without the leave of the court.

Subs. (1)

An unmarried father without parental responsibility, a person in whose favour a residence order was in force prior to the care order or anyone else without parental responsibility who wishes to end the local authority's care of the child cannot apply for the discharge of the care order under this section but must apply for a residence order under s.10 instead. The local authority considering whether to apply for discharge must comply with its other duties, particularly those in s.22.

The child: There is no statutory restriction on applications by immature minors but the child will be represented by a guardian ad litem under s.41, who may be able to decide not to pursue the application depending on the exact wording of the new court rules.

Subs. (3)

A person with whom the child is living: This means "a responsible person" under Sched. 3, para. 1. For the obligations of a responsible person see Sched. 3, paras. 3, 7 and 8 and notes to s.35.

Subs. (4)

A supervision order cannot apparently be substituted under this section where someone else seeks to have the care order discharged by applying for a residence order. Nor can an interim supervision order be made under s.38(3). A family assistance order under s.16 could be made.

Orders pending appeals in cases about care or supervision orders

40.—(1) Where—

    (a) a court dismisses an application for a care order; and

    (b) at the time when the court dismisses the application, the child concerned is the subject of an interim care order,

the court may make a care order with respect to the child to have effect subject to such directions (if any) as the court may see fit to include in the order.

(2) Where—

    (a) a court dismisses an application for a care order, or an application for a supervision order; and

    (b) at the time when the court dismisses the application, the child concerned is the subject of an interim supervision order,

the court may make a supervision order with respect to the child to have effect subject to such directions (if any) as the court may see fit to include in the order.

(3) Where a court grants an application to discharge a care order or supervision order, it may order that—

    (a) its decision is not to have effect; or

    (b) the care order, or supervision order, is to continue to have effect but subject to such directions as the court sees fit to include in the order.

(4) An order made under this section shall only have effect for such period, not exceeding the appeal period, as may be specified in the order.

(5) Where—

    (a) an appeal is made against any decision of a court under this section; or

    (b) any application is made to the appellate court in connection with a proposed appeal against that decision,

the appellate court may extend the period for which the order in question is to have effect, but not so as to extend it beyond the end of the appeal period.

(6) In this section "the appeal period" means—

    (a) where an appeal is made against the decision in question, the period between the making of that decision and the determination of the appeal; and

(b) otherwise, the period during which an appeal may be made against the decision.

Definitions
"appeal period": s.40(6).
"appellate court": s.94(1).
"care order": s.31(11).
"child": s.105(1).
"interim care order": s.38(1).
"interim supervision order": s.38(1).
"the court": s.92(7).

General Note
This section enables the court to order that a child who is subject to an interim care order remains in care until the determination of any appeal against refusal to make a care order (subs. (1)). Similar powers apply in relation to supervision orders (subs. (2)) and orders for discharge (subs. (3)). The court may include directions as it sees fit, *e.g.* in relation to contact with the parents, or even where the child should reside (subss. (1) to (3)) and may specify a shorter period (subs. (4)). It would appear that this provision could be used to achieve phased return of the child on the discharge of a care order. The court could, under subs. (3), continue the care order but direct increasing contact with a view to home placement and grant leave to the parents to reapply for discharge after three months.
This section enables the child to be protected while the local authority decides whether to appeal and, if it does, until the appeal is determined. However, its operation is not automatic; the court has the discretion, which it must exercise, giving first consideration to the child's welfare. Where the court refuses to continue a care order, it will not be possible to ward the child. The appellate court will be able to extend an order but not, apparently, revive one which has lapsed pending the appeal. The local authority would have to start fresh proceedings.
A similar power to stay a decision approving the arrangements for a child in care to live abroad is included in Sched. 2, para. 19.

Subs. (6)
The time limit for appeals against refusal to grant care orders, etc., will be set out in the court rules made under s.93.

Guardians ad litem

Representation of child and of his interests in certain proceedings

41.—(1) For the purpose of any specified proceedings, the court shall appoint a guardian ad litem for the child concerned unless satisfied that it is not necessary to do so in order to safeguard his interests.
(2) The guardian ad litem shall—
    (a) be appointed in accordance with rules of court; and
    (b) be under a duty to safeguard the interests of the child in the manner prescribed by such rules.
(3) Where—
    (a) the child concerned is not represented by a solicitor; and
    (b) any of the conditions mentioned in subsection (4) is satisfied,
the court may appoint a solicitor to represent him.
(4) The conditions are that—
    (a) no guardian ad litem has been appointed for the child;
    (b) the child has sufficient understanding to instruct a solicitor and wishes to do so;
    (c) it appears to the court that it would be in the child's best interests for him to be represented by a solicitor.
(5) Any solicitor appointed under or by virtue of this section shall be appointed, and shall represent the child, in accordance with rules of court.
(6) In this section "specified proceedings" means any proceedings—
    (a) on an application for a care order or supervision order;

(b) in which the court has given a direction under section 37(1) and has made, or is considering whether to make, an interim care order;

(c) on an application for the discharge of a care order or the variation or discharge of a supervision order;

(d) on an application under section 39(4);

(e) in which the court is considering whether to make a residence order with respect to a child who is the subject of a care order;

(f) with respect to contact between a child who is the subject of a care order and any other person;

(g) under Part V;

(h) on an appeal against—

    (i) the making of, or refusal to make, a care order, supervision order or any order under section 34;

    (ii) the making of, or refusal to make, a residence order with respect to a child who is the subject of a care order; or

    (iii) the variation or discharge, or refusal of an application to vary or discharge, an order of a kind mentioned in sub-paragraph (i) or (ii);

    (iv) the refusal of an application under section 39(4); or

    (v) the making of, or refusal to make, an order under Part V; or

(i) which are specified for the time being, for the purposes of this section, by rules of court.

(7) The Secretary of State may by regulations provide for the establishment of panels of persons from whom guardians ad litem appointed under this section must be selected.

(8) Subsection (7) shall not be taken to prejudice the power of the Lord Chancellor to confer or impose duties on the Official Solicitor under section 90(3) of the Supreme Court Act 1981.

(9) The regulations may, in particular, make provision—

(a) as to the constitution, administration and procedures of panels;

(b) requiring two or more specified local authorities to make arrangements for the joint management of a panel;

(c) for the defrayment by local authorities of expenses incurred by members of panels;

(d) for the payment by local authorities of fees and allowances for members of panels;

(e) as to the qualifications for membership of a panel;

(f) as to the training to be given to members of panels;

(g) as to the co-operation required of specified local authorities in the provision of panels in specified areas; and

(h) for monitoring the work of guardians ad litem.

(10) Rules of court may make provision as to—

(a) the assistance which any guardian ad litem may be required by the court to give to it;

(b) the consideration to be given by any guardian ad litem, where an order of a specified kind has been made in the proceedings in question, as to whether to apply for the variation or discharge of the order;

(c) the participation of guardians ad litem in reviews, of a kind specified in the rules, which are conducted by the court.

(11) Regardless of any enactment or rule of law which would otherwise prevent it from doing so, the court may take account of—

(a) any statement contained in a report made by a guardian ad litem who is appointed under this section for the purpose of the proceedings in question; and

(b) any evidence given in respect of the matters referred to in the report,

in so far as the statement or evidence is, in the opinion of the court, relevant to the question which the court is considering.

DEFINITIONS

"care order": s.31(11).
"guardian ad litem", "guardian ad litem panel": s.41(2), (7).
"residence order": s.8(1).
"specified proceedings": s.41(6).
"supervision order": s.31(11).
"the court": s.92(7).

GENERAL NOTE

This section provides the new statutory basis for the guardian ad litem service originally introduced by the Children Act 1975 and found in C.Y.P.A. 1969, ss. 32A and 32B. It should be read with s.42, which sets out the powers of the guardian ad litem to examine local authority records. The existing framework is retained, although there is scope for change. The Government indicated during the Bill's passage that the status quo in relation to party status and representation of children would largely continue. Most of the detailed provisions are currently found in regulations, particularly the Magistrates' Courts (Children and Young Persons) Rules 1988. These will need to be amended; subss. (10) and (11) contain wide powers to make regulations. The Lord Chancellor indicated that the new rules would impose similar duties on guardians (*Hansard*, H.L. Vol. 503, col. 409).

There is no longer any need for the court to order separate representation before it appoints a guardian ad litem. The wording of subs. (1) is more positive than that in s.32A(1) of the C.Y.P.A. 1969. The Lord Chancellor indicated that he expected that a guardian would be appointed in almost every case:— "We accept that the courts are unlikely to find many cases in which it would be inappropriate to appoint a guardian ad litem" (*Hansard*, H.L. Vol. 503, col. 408). There will clearly be a demand for many more guardians ad litem in some areas. The range of proceedings in which a guardian can be appointed is wider than under the present law—guardians will have a role in proceedings under Pt. V for child assessment orders (s.43), emergency protection orders (s.44) and possibly recovery orders (s.50) and relevant appeals (subs. (6)). This will bring a marked increase in involvement of guardians (and will require the setting up of a system of duty guardians). There has been no suggestion that guardians should be appointed in other types of "family proceedings". Where no guardian is appointed the court may still obtain a welfare report under s.7.

Guardians will continue to operate with solicitors. Rules of court will provide for the guardian to appoint a solicitor (*Hansard*, H.L. Vol. 503, col. 409). If no solicitor has been appointed, the court will be able to do so if any of the conditions in subs. (4) are satisfied (subs. (3)). Thus if the guardian is appointed sufficiently early he will be able to choose the solicitor for the child but the court will have a power to ensure representation. Where a solicitor is appointed he will have to comply with the court rules when representing the child (subs. (5)).

Guardians ad litem will continue to be appointed to panels managed by local authorities (subs. (7)). The Government did not pursue its heavily criticised scheme for an Office of Child Protection outlined in the Green Paper, *Improvements in Care Proceedings*. However, it is aware of criticism that the existing system lacks independence and hopes to improve this aspect of the service. "We are preparing to develop panels which will take in larger groupings of local authorities than is the case at present in most areas, and to appoint panel managers who are clearly responsible for running them. When the panel manager is more distanced from any one local authority, the possibility of conflict of interest should be substantially reduced or removed" (*per* Sir Nicholas Lyell, Solicitor General (Standing Committee B, col. 464, June 8, 1989)). The position of the Official Solicitor is not affected by these changes, but the decrease in wardships, and the fact that guardians will be able to be appointed for proceedings in the county court and the High Court, is likely to have an impact. If a case is started in the magistrates' court and transferred to a higher court the original guardian will be able to continue (*Hansard*, H.L. Vol. 503, col. 422, *cf. Re B (A Minor) (Wardship: Guardian ad litem*) [1989] 1 F.L.R. 268).

Subs. (11) clarifies the position of evidence and reports by the guardian ad litem. It disapplies the hearsay rule and allows the court to take account of any relevant statement. However, after *Bradford City Metropolitan Borough Council* v. *K, The Times,* August 18, 1989, it may be that the statement is only admissible as evidence that it was made and not of its content. See also s.96, which makes further provision for children's evidence.

New rules and regulations will have to be made before the Act can be brought into operation, but these may be very similar to the existing ones.

Right of guardian ad litem to have access to local authority records

42.—(1) Where a person has been appointed as a guardian ad litem under this Act he shall have the right at all reasonable times to examine and take copies of—

(a) any records of, or held by, a local authority which were compiled in connection with the making, or proposed making, by any person of any application under this Act with respect to the child concerned; or

(b) any other records of, or held by, a local authority which were compiled in connection with any functions which stand referred to their social services committee under the Local Authority Social Services Act 1970, so far as those records relate to that child.

(2) Where a guardian ad litem takes a copy of any record which he is entitled to examine under this section, that copy or any part of it shall be admissible as evidence of any matter referred to in any—

(a) report which he makes to the court in the proceedings in question; or

(b) evidence which he gives in those proceedings.

(3) Subsection (2) has effect regardless of any enactment or rule of law which would otherwise prevent the record in question being admissible in evidence.

DEFINITIONS
"child": s.105(1).
"functions": s.105(1).
"guardian ad litem": s.41(2), (7).
"local authority": s.105(1).

GENERAL NOTE
This section gives a guardian ad litem a right of access to (and to take copies of) the local authority's records relating to the application before the court, or to social work functions performed in relation to the child (subs. (1)). Any copy will be admissible as evidence of any matter referred to in the guardian's evidence or report (subss. (2) and (3)). It should not be evidence of its veracity, only of the fact that the authority had the information. This should end the difficulties experienced by some guardians with their investigations of local authority records. However, the section does not apply to records held by other bodies such as the health authority or the N.S.P.C.C. Where the local authority has liaised closely with another body it may hold copies of their records, which could then be seen; rules of court made under s.93 could require disclosure of such records. If the proceedings take place in the magistrates' court, the Magistrates' Court Act 1980, s.97, could be used to secure the attendance of a witness with a document but there is currently no legal machinery to obtain disclosure there. However, it has been held that the local authority must inform the applicants of the evidence which is to be used against them (and any which is not) before the hearing (*R.* v. *Hampshire County Council* ex p. *K, The Independent,* November 15, 1989). The Solicitor-General gave two reasons for this provision: (1) that the guardian must have all the relevant information and it was not sufficient to rely on the local authority's duty to disclose it; and (2) that local authority records could not be open to all the parties because they may be protected by privilege and wide disclosure could interfere with social work on a case (*Hansard*, H.C. Vol. 158, col. 626).

PART V

PROTECTION OF CHILDREN

Child assessment orders

43.—(1) On the application of a local authority or authorised person for an order to be made under this section with respect to a child, the court may make the order if, but only if, it is satisfied that—

   (a) the applicant has reasonable cause to suspect that the child is suffering, or is likely to suffer, significant harm;

   (b) an assessment of the state of the child's health or development, or of the way in which he has been treated, is required to enable the applicant to determine whether or not the child is suffering, or is likely to suffer, significant harm; and

   (c) it is unlikely that such an assessment will be made, or be satisfactory, in the absence of an order under this section.

(2) In this Act "a child assessment order" means an order under this section.

(3) A court may treat an application under this section as an application for an emergency protection order.

(4) No court shall make a child assessment order if it is satisfied—

   (a) that there are grounds for making an emergency protection order with respect to the child; and

   (b) that it ought to make such an order rather than a child assessment order.

(5) A child assessment order shall—

   (a) specify the date by which the assessment is to begin; and

   (b) have effect for such period, not exceeding 7 days beginning with that date, as may be specified in the order.

(6) Where a child assessment order is in force with respect to a child it shall be the duty of any person who is in a position to produce the child—

   (a) to produce him to such person as may be named in the order; and

   (b) to comply with such directions relating to the assessment of the child as the court thinks fit to specify in the order.

(7) A child assessment order authorises any person carrying out the assessment, or any part of the assessment, to do so in accordance with the terms of the order.

(8) Regardless of subsection (7), if the child is of sufficient understanding to make an informed decision he may refuse to submit to a medical or psychiatric examination or other assessment.

(9) The child may only be kept away from home—

   (a) in accordance with directions specified in the order;

   (b) if it is necessary for the purposes of the assessment; and

   (c) for such period or periods as may be specified in the order.

(10) Where the child is to be kept away from home, the order shall contain such directions as the court thinks fit with regard to the contact that he must be allowed to have with other persons while away from home.

(11) Any person making an application for a child assessment order shall take such steps as are reasonably practicable to ensure that notice of the application is given to—

   (a) the child's parents;

   (b) any person who is not a parent of his but who has parental responsibility for him;

   (c) any other person caring for the child;

   (d) any person in whose favour a contact order is in force with respect to the child;

   (e) any person who is allowed to have contact with the child by virtue of an order under section 34; and

   (f) the child,

before the hearing of the application.

(12) Rules of court may make provision as to the circumstances in which—

   (a) any of the persons mentioned in subsection (11); or

   (b) such other person as may be specified in the rules,

may apply to the court for a child assessment order to be varied or discharged.

(13) In this section "authorised person" means a person who is an authorised person for the purposes of section 31.

DEFINITIONS
"authorised person": ss.31(9), 43(13).
"child": s.105(1).
"child assessment order": s.43(2).
"contact order": s.8(1).
"emergency protection order": s.44(4).
"local authority": s.105(1).
"person . . . who has parental responsibility": ss.2(1), (2), 4(1), 5(6), 12(1)(2).
"significant harm": s.31(9)(10).
"the court": s.92(7).

GENERAL NOTE
This section, which was the subject of considerable controversy during the Bill's passage through Parliament, provides for child assessment orders. This provision was added because of concern that the more rigorous requirements for an emergency protection order could mean that it was impossible to get an emergency protection order where there was fear for the child's safety but no hard evidence. For example, where a child had suddenly ceased to attend a day nursery or family centre in suspicious circumstances, or where neighbours reported repeated screaming. In such cases the first action of the social worker or health visitor should be to attempt to see the child (under s.47(4) there is a duty to do so). If access is refused or the parent refuses or fails to take the child for a medical or other examination which would indicate the child's condition, an application may be made for a child assessment order. However, refusal may provide grounds for an emergency protection order under s.44(1)(b) or (c). That being the case, it is not clear when a child assessment order will be used. Rather, the child assessment order is something which must be considered by the case conference planning intervention.

Only the local authority or N.S.P.C.C. (subss. (1) and (13)) may apply for a child assessment order. The court may only grant the order if:

(1) the *applicant* (not the court as for an emergency protection order) has reasonable cause to believe that the child is suffering (or likely to suffer) significant harm;

(2) an assessment is required to determine whether the child is suffering (or likely to suffer) significant harm;

(3) it is unlikely that there would be an assessment without a court order (subs. (1)); and

(4) the grounds for an emergency protection order are not satisfied or it would not be appropriate to make an emergency protection order (subs. (4)).

The court may make an emergency protection order on an application for a child assessment order (subs. (3)). Applications will be made on notice (subs. (11)) and the child will usually be represented by a guardian ad litem.

A child assessment order requires any person who can do so to produce the child for an assessment and comply with the terms of order (subs. (6)); it authorises the child's assessment in accordance with the order (subs. (7)) but does not permit any examination or assessment of a mature child without his permission (subs. (8)). The child may be kept away from home for assessment (but not for protection) in accordance with the court's directions (subs. (1)). The parents retain parental responsibility and the applicant will only be able to take such steps as are permitted by the court without parental consent. Those seeking a child assessment order will need to explain to the court the types of assessment required and how they should be carried out. The order lasts for only seven days but need not begin immediately (subs. (5)). It could be postponed until, *e.g.* a hospital bed became available. If the child is kept away from home, the court must consider contact (subs. (10)). S.1(1), the welfare principle, applies to these decisions. A child assessment order can be made on any child under 18.

Provision for variation and discharge will be made in rules (subs. (12)).

Four advantages have been identified for the child assessment order by Jim Harding, Child Care Director of the N.S.P.C.C.:—

(1) *Parental responsibility is retained by parents*: This is so although the court may order the child's removal from home, his assessment and even contact with third parties without the parents' consent and against the parents' wishes.

(2) *The child may be seen by the family doctor in a familiar environment*: This is possible but not mandated by the section. The applicant will want to be satisfied that the

assessment is thorough and may wish the child to be examined by a specialist paediatrician, etc. It is essential that the assessment is thorough because there can be no further application for a child assessment order within six months (s.91(15)).

(3) *Parents are more likely to co-operate with this type of order and the social work relationship with the family will not be damaged*: Lack of co-operation is a precondition for the order. The order is an "evidence-seeking" order and will be used where there is suspicion, often as a precursor to further proceedings. It will take great social work skill to establish a good relationship with the family in such circumstances.

(4) *The child can be protected in serious but not emergency situations*: This order does not protect the child, it permits assessment. Where protection is required and evidence exists, care proceedings should be started. If there is insufficient evidence and no co-operation in allowing the child to be assessed it may be possible to get an emergency protection order under s.44. Both a child assessment order and an emergency protection order require *at least* that the applicant has a reasonable cause to suspect that the child is suffering or likely to suffer significant harm.

Subs. (1)

Reasonable cause to suspect: See s.47(1)(b)).

An assessment: This is not a term of art and is used loosely to cover medical and psychiatric testing as well as developmental screening or an opinion formed following observation and discussion by a child care social worker. It may be difficult for any assessment to be carried out where the applicant lacks base line data *i.e.* data about the child at an earlier period. The type of assessment which can be carried out will be limited by the duration of the order. It was originally proposed that these orders should last for three months to allow for thorough inter-disciplinary assessment, but the duration was restricted because the grounds for an order are broad. The order does not permit an assessment of the family, only the individual child who is subject to the order. Where a medical or social history forms an essential part of the assessment, the order can require the person who produced the child to answer questions concerning the child. For further details on assessment see D.H. *Protecting Children: A guide to social workers undertaking comprehensive assessment* (1988).

In the absence of an order: Courts will need to be careful not to accept, without inquiry, a statement that the parents will agree to the assessment. If the order is refused and the parents fail to co-operate, no further application for a child assessment order (but not an emergency protection order) may be made within six months. Rules of court will require the applicant to explain what steps have been taken to obtain co-operation (*per* David Mellor, Minister of Health (*Hansard*, H.C. Vol. 158, col. 549).

Subs. (4)

There are grounds for making an emergency protection order: See s.44(1).

Subs. (6)

The duty of any person . . . to produce the child: Failure to comply with a child assessment order may be dealt with under the Magistrates' Courts Act 1980, s.63. However, a simpler (but more Draconian) power of enforcement is found in s.44(1)(b). Refusal to allow access where there was a child assessment order would be unreasonable and thus justify the court making an emergency protection order.

Any person who is in a position to produce the child: A person who is looking after the child but who does not have parental responsibility for him might argue that he is not in such a position. However, he must comply with s.3(5) and a parent cannot lawfully veto the child's production because he cannot exercise parental responsibility in conflict with a court order (s.2(8)). It would thus seem that anyone with the child, including a childminder or teacher, would have to produce him.

Subs. (8)

Comparable provisions apply in relation to emergency protection orders, interim orders and supervision orders. Children who are under 16 but are capable of understanding the nature of medical examination or treatment can only be examined or treated with their agreement. This sub-section implements the decision of the House of Lords in *Gillick* v. *West Norfolk Area Health Authority* [1986] A.C. 112. However, it is not exactly clear what a young person must understand in order to establish that he has the maturity to refuse an assessment. Lord Scarman said of the decision to seek contraceptive services, "It is not enough that she should understand the nature of the advice which is being given: she must have sufficient maturity to understand what is involved. There are moral and family questions, especially her relationships with her parents; long term problems associated with the emotional impact of pregnancy and its termination and there are risks to health of sexual intercourse at her age, risks which contraception may diminish but cannot eliminate. It follows that a doctor will have to satisfy himself that she is able to appraise these factors before he can safely proceed on the basis that she has at law capacity to consent to contraceptive treatment" (at p.189).

Where an assessment is necessary to establish whether or not the child has been physically, sexually or emotionally abused, there is a further complication. The abuse may have so traumatised a child that although he is mature generally, he is incapable of mature decisions in this aspect of his life. However, doctors must also avoid the view that a child who disagrees is *ipso facto* immature. The doctor will have to explain the need for the assessment and the consequences of its refusal. Where possible, other avenues of evidence should be explored.

It is doubtful that a mature child's refusal can be overcome by an order of the High Court in wardship (see J. Eekelaar, *The emergence of children's rights* 6 Ox J.L.S. 161, 181).

Subs. (10)

As the court thinks fit: As well as considering the child's welfare, the court will have to consider the effect of contact on the assessment process.

Orders for emergency protection of children

44.—(1) Where any person ("the applicant") applies to the court for an order to be made under this section with respect to a child, the court may make the order if, but only if, it is satisfied that—

  (a) there is reasonable cause to believe that the child is likely to suffer significant harm if—

    (i) he is not removed to accommodation provided by or on behalf of the applicant; or

    (ii) he does not remain in the place in which he is then being accommodated;

  (b) in the case of an application made by a local authority—

    (i) enquiries are being made with respect to the child under section 47(1)(b); and

    (ii) those enquiries are being frustrated by access to the child being unreasonably refused to a person authorised to seek access and that the applicant has reasonable cause to believe that access to the child is required as a matter of urgency; or

  (c) in the case of an application made by an authorised person—

    (i) the applicant has reasonable cause to suspect that a child is suffering, or is likely to suffer, significant harm;

    (ii) the applicant is making enquiries with respect to the child's welfare; and

    (iii) those enquiries are being frustrated by access to the child being unreasonably refused to a person authorised to seek access and the applicant has reasonable cause to believe that access to the child is required as a matter of urgency.

(2) In this section—

  (a) "authorised person" means a person who is an authorised person for the purposes of section 31; and

  (b) "a person authorised to seek access', means—

    (i) in the case of an application by a local authority, an officer of the local authority or a person authorised by the authority to act on their behalf in connection with the enquiries; or

    (ii) in the case of an application by an authorised person, that person.

(3) Any person—

  (a) seeking access to a child in connection with enquiries of a kind mentioned in subsection (1); and

  (b) purporting to be a person authorised to do so,

shall, on being asked to do so, produce some duly authenticated document as evidence that he is such a person.

(4) While an order under this section ("an emergency protection order") is in force it—

(a) operates as a direction to any person who is in a position to do so to comply with any request to produce the child to the applicant;

(b) authorises—

(i) the removal of the child at any time to accommodation provided by or on behalf of the applicant and his being kept there; or

(ii) the prevention of the child's removal from any hospital, or other place, in which he was being accommodated immediately before the making of the order; and

(c) gives the applicant parental responsibility for the child.

(5) Where an emergency protection order is in force with respect to a child, the applicant—

(a) shall only exercise the power given by virtue of subsection (4)(b) in order to safeguard the welfare of the child;

(b) shall take, and shall only take, such action in meeting his parental responsibility for the child as is reasonably required to safeguard or promote the welfare of the child (having regard in particular to the duration of the order); and

(c) shall comply with the requirements of any regulations made by the Secretary of State for the purposes of this subsection.

(6) Where the court makes an emergency protection order, it may give such directions (if any) as it considers appropriate with respect to—

(a) the contact which is, or is not, to be allowed between the child and any named person;

(b) the medical or psychiatric examination or other assessment of the child.

(7) Where any direction is given under subsection (6)(b), the child may, if he is of sufficient understanding to make an informed decision, refuse to submit to the examination or other assessment.

(8) A direction under subsection (6)(a) may impose conditions and one under subsection (6)(b) may be to the effect that there is to be—

(a) no such examination or assessment; or

(b) no such examination or assessment unless the court directs otherwise.

(9) A direction under subsection (6) may be—

(a) given when the emergency protection order is made or at any time while it is in force; and

(b) varied at any time on the application of any person falling within any class of person prescribed by rules of court for the purposes of this subsection.

(10) Where an emergency protection order is in force with respect to a child and—

(a) the applicant has exercised the power given by subsection (4)(b)(i) but it appears to him that it is safe for the child to be returned; or

(b) the applicant has exercised the power given by subsection (4)(b)(ii) but it appears to him that it is safe for the child to be allowed to be removed from the place in question,

he shall return the child or (as the case may be) allow him to be removed.

(11) Where he is required by subsection (10) to return the child the applicant shall—

(a) return him to the care of the person from whose care he was removed; or

(b) if that is not reasonably practicable, return him to the care of—

(i) a parent of his;

(ii) any person who is not a parent of his but who has parental responsibility for him; or

(iii) such other person as the applicant (with the agreement of the court) considers appropriate.

(12) Where the applicant has been required by subsection (10) to return the child, or to allow him to be removed, he may again exercise his powers with respect to the child (at any time while the emergency protection order remains in force) if it appears to him that a change in the circumstances of the case makes it necessary for him to do so.

(13) Where an emergency protection order has been made with respect to a child, the applicant shall, subject to any direction given under subsection (6), allow the child reasonable contact with—

(a) his parents;

(b) any person who is not a parent of his but who has parental responsibility for him;

(c) any person with whom he was living immediately before the making of the order;

(d) any person in whose favour a contact order is in force with respect to him;

(e) any person who is allowed to have contact with the child by virtue of an order under section 34; and

(f) any person acting on behalf of any of those persons.

(14) Wherever it is reasonably practicable to do so, an emergency protection order shall name the child; and where it does not name him it shall describe him as clearly as possible.

(15) A person shall be guilty of an offence if he intentionally obstructs any person exercising the power under subsection (4)(b) to remove, or prevent the removal of, a child.

(16) A person guilty of an offence under subsection (15) shall be liable on summary conviction to a fine not exceeding level 3 on the standard scale.

DEFINITIONS
"applicant": s.44(1).
"authorised person": ss.31(9), 44(2).
"child": s.105(1).
"contact order": s.8(1).
"emergency protection order": ss.44(4), 45(1).
"hospital": s.105(1).
"parental responsibility": ss.2, 3, 44(5).
"person authorised to seek access": s.44(2).
"person who has parental responsibility": ss.2(1)(2), 4(1), 5(6), 12(1)(2).
"significant harm": ss.31(9)(10), 105(1).
"the court": s.92(7).

GENERAL NOTE
This section sets out the grounds for and effect of an emergency protection order, the new order which replaces the place of safety order. Although under subs. (1)(a) the court (not the applicant as before) must be satisfied of the ground, this does not apply to subs. (1)(b) or subs. (1)(c). It appears that these grounds for an emergency protection order will be easier to satisfy than the grounds for a place of safety order in the C.Y.P.A. 1969, s.28(1).
There are effectively three grounds for the order:—

(1) reasonable cause to believe that the child is likely to suffer significant harm if not removed (subs. (1)(a)(i));

(2) reasonable cause, etc., if not kept at current place of accommodation (subs. (1)(a)(ii));

(3) *the applicant* has reasonable cause to suspect that a child is suffering or likely to suffer significant harm, is making enquiries (subs. (1)(b)(i) and (1)(c)(i) and (ii)), and the enquiries are being frustrated by access being unreasonably refused and the applicant has reasonable cause to believe that access is required as a matter of urgency.

The order operates as a direction to anyone who is in a position to do so, to produce the child (subs. (4)(a); see note on s.43(6)). It can be granted in respect of any child under 18. It requires the applicant to comply with regulations (subs. (5)(c)). It gives the applicant the power to remove the child, or prevent his removal, but only where it is necessary to safeguard the child's welfare (subss. (4)(b) and (5)(a)). However, where the child is removed or detained, the applicant is under a duty to return or release him if it is safe to do so (subs. (10)), if possible to the person from whose care he was removed (subs. (11)). The applicant may remove the child once more if this appears necessary (subs. (12)). Thus, a child who is subject to an emergency protection order need not be removed from his home and may be returned during the period of the order. The order enables the applicant to decide whether to remove the child. There is no power under an emergency protection order to order the removal of any adult from the home, but the local authority has a power to assist the perpetrator to obtain alternative accommodation under Sched. 2, para. 5.

The order grants the applicant parental responsibility for the child but only permits him to take such action as is reasonably required to safeguard the welfare of the child (subss. (5)(c) and (5)(b)).

The law concerning medical examination and assessment of children under emergency orders is clarified. The applicant's parental responsibility will allow him to authorise what is reasonably required to safeguard the child's welfare. This should include examinations made to obtain evidence for care proceedings. However, the court may direct or bar examinations (subss. (6)(b), (8) and (9)). Even where an examination or assessment is permitted by the court, it cannot be made if a child with sufficient understanding to make an informed decision objects (subs. (7); see s.43(8)). The agreement of anyone with parental responsibility other than the applicant is not required.

The applicant is required to allow the child reasonable contact with the persons listed in subs. (13). The court may make directions about contact (subss. (6)(a) and (8)).

Where possible, the child should be named (subs. (14)). It is an offence (summary conviction: fine level 3) intentionally to obstruct the child's removal or detention under subs. (4)(b) (subss. (15) and (16)).

The local authority has a duty to provide accommodation for children subject to emergency protection order under s.21.

This section should be read with ss. 43, 45, 46, and 48. An emergency protection order can be made by a single magistrate under regulations made under Sched. 11, para. 4.

Subs. (1)

there is . . . . : It is no longer sufficient for *the applicant* alone to have a reasonable belief of significant harm, etc., unless subs. (1)(b) applies. He must convince the court. The civil standard of proof applies, but the courts are likely to wish to match the degree of evidence with the seriousness of the order. Where only *the applicant* has a reasonable belief, a child assessment order may be available (see s.43).

Access: The authorised person has a duty to obtain access under s.47(4), but access is not defined. Being able to see the child, fully clothed, may not be sufficient, since it will not enable any conclusion to be drawn from the enquiries. Social workers have been criticised for not demanding sufficient access to the child (see, *e.g.* Kimberley Carlile Inquiry 1987) and therefore it may be necessary to undress the child. However, refusal to have a child medically examined would not appear to be within this subsection because it is not refusal of access to a person authorised. Where this was the problem the applicant would need to rely on subs. (1)(a) or seek a child assessment order under s.43.

A matter of urgency: This will depend on the nature of the suspicion, the age of the child and the existence of opportunities to see the child, for example at school. The fact that the alleged conduct has occurred for a period already does not prevent access being a matter of urgency.

Being unreasonably refused: The person seeking access may be required to produce evidence of his authority (subs. (3)). It is not clear where it would be reasonable to refuse access to someone who produces such evidence. The excuse that the child was asleep or unwell would probably not be sufficient and access at night may be reasonable in some cases. However, a parent who requires the person to wait or to return at a later time may not have refused access.

Subs. (5)

Only such action as . . . . : The applicant's parental responsibility is strictly limited; consents given would not be valid if they were not reasonably required but there appears to be no liability on the applicant or redress for the parents if the provision is not complied with. A child who was harmed following permission unlawfully given might have an action in negligence.

Subs. (7)
See note on s. 43(8).

Subs. (11)
The applicant appears to have free choice between subs. (11)(b)(i) and subs. (11)(b)(ii), but must act in accordance with the child's welfare and should consult the child, etc. (see s.22(4) and (5)). If neither placement seems appropriate, the applicant must seek the court's agreement to another placement.

Subs. (13)
The applicant is likely to need to seek directions to establish priorities for contact. Although contact may help the child cope with the crisis of being returned, there is a danger, particularly in sexual abuse cases, that pressure will be put on the child by relatives (not just the perpetrator) to withdraw the allegations.

Solicitors acting for the parents may need to see the child to obtain information about the case. Such interviews are likely to be stressful and it may be appropriate for a social worker or supportive friend to be with the child during visits.

Reasonable contact: It may be reasonable to allow contact only by telephone with some people.

Duration of emergency protection orders and other supplemental provisions

45.—(1) An emergency protection order shall have effect for such period, not exceeding eight days, as may be specified in the order.

(2) Where—

    (a) the court making an emergency protection order would, but for this subsection, specify a period of eight days as the period for which the order is to have effect; but

    (b) the last of those eight days is a public holiday (that is to say, Christmas Day, Good Friday, a bank holiday or a Sunday),

the court may specify a period which ends at noon on the first later day which is not such a holiday.

(3) Where an emergency protection order is made on an application under section 46(7), the period of eight days mentioned in subsection (1) shall begin with the first day on which the child was taken into police protection under section 46.

(4) Any person who—

    (a) has parental responsibility for a child as the result of an emergency protection order; and

    (b) is entitled to apply for a care order with respect to the child,

may apply to the court for the period during which the emergency protection order is to have effect to be extended.

(5) On an application under subsection (4) the court may extend the period during which the order is to have effect by such period, not exceeding seven days, as it thinks fit, but may do so only if it has reasonable cause to believe that the child concerned is likely to suffer significant harm if the order is not extended.

(6) An emergency protection order may only be extended once.

(7) Regardless of any enactment or rule of law which would otherwise prevent it from doing so, a court hearing an application for, or with respect to, an emergency protection order may take account of—

    (a) any statement contained in any report made to the court in the course of, or in connection with, the hearing; or

    (b) any evidence given during the hearing,

which is, in the opinion of the court, relevant to the application.

(8) Any of the following may apply to the court for an emergency protection order to be discharged—

(a) the child;

(b) a parent of his;

(c) any person who is not a parent of his but who has parental responsibility for him; or

(d) any person with whom he was living immediately before the making of the order.

(9) No application for the discharge of an emergency protection order shall be heard by the court before the expiry of the period of 72 hours beginning with the making of the order.

(10) No appeal may be made against the making of, or refusal to make, an emergency protection order or against any direction given by the court in connection with such an order.

(11) Subsection (8) does not apply—

　　(a) where the person who would otherwise be entitled to apply for the emergency protection order to be discharged—

　　　　(i) was given notice (in accordance with rules of court) of the hearing at which the order was made; and

　　　　(ii) was present at that hearing; or

　　(b) to any emergency protection order the effective period of which has been extended under subsection (5).

(12) A court making an emergency protection order may direct that the applicant may, in exercising any powers which he has by virtue of the order, be accompanied by a registered medical practitioner, registered nurse or registered health visitor, if he so chooses.

DEFINITIONS

"bank holiday": s.105(1).

"care order": s.31(11).

"emergency protection order": s.44(4).

"person who has parental responsibility as a result of an emergency protection order": s.44(1)(4).

"person who is not a parent but has parental responsibility": ss.5(6), 12(2), 33(3).

"significant harm": s.31(9), (10).

"the court": s.92(7).

GENERAL NOTE

This section makes further provision in respect of emergency protection orders, particularly about their duration. Rules will permit applications for an emergency protection order to be made *Ex parte* (*per* David Mellor, Minister of Health (Standing Committee B, col. 329, May 25, 1989)).

Emergency protection orders last for a maximum of eight days, (subs. (1)), except where the last day is a public holiday as defined in subs. (2), when they can extend to the next day which is not a holiday. While the order is in force, a local authority or the N.S.P.C.C. can apply for it to be extended once for up to seven days (subss. (4)–(6)). The court may also grant an extension if it is satisfied that there are reasonable grounds to believe that the child is likely to suffer significant harm if the order is not extended (subs. (5)). An order which has not been extended may be discharged after 72 hours on application of anyone listed in subs. (8) except a person who was given notice and was present at the original hearing (subs. (11)).

There is no appeal against the granting or refusal of an emergency protection order or a direction contained in one (subs. (10)). However, it will also be possible to challenge the court by judicial review (*per* the Lord Chancellor (*Hansard,* H.L. Vol. 503, col. 440)). Subs. (12) enables the court to direct that when the applicant exercises any of the powers under the order he may be accompanied by a registered medical practitioner, nurse or health visitor. S.41(6)(g) makes provision for guardians ad litem in these proceedings.

Subs. (1)

Very short orders (orders for less than 72 hours) will preclude applications for discharge under subs. (9) but will impose a heavy burden on the authority to prepare for an extension hearing and care proceedings. A local authority might use judicial review to challenge an unreasonably short order. It could not seek instead to protect the child by wardship because of the restriction in s.100.

Subs. (4)

A successful applicant for an emergency protection order gets parental responsibility by virtue of s.44(4)(c). S.31(1) and (9) states who may apply for a care order (a local authority or the N.S.P.C.C.). Other applicants, the police and ordinary citizens, cannot apply for an extension, but regulations made under s.52(3) may allow the local authority to take over responsibility for such a case and apply for an extension.

Subs. (5)

The test for an extension is the same as that for the original order, but the applicant may need to be prepared to justify intervention more explicitly if the original order was made *ex parte,* because applications for extensions are likely to be heard *inter partes.* Where there is an extension hearing this will provide the only opportunity to challenge the order (subs. (11)).

Subs. (7)

This disapplies the hearsay rule. A comparable but narrower protection exists in relation to reports to the court under s.7 and guardians ad litem's evidence under s.41(11). The matter in question will have to be proved properly when the care order is made but hearsay in a report will still be allowed (see also notes to s.96).

Subs. (11)

Where notice of the original application is given, but the person notified is unable to obtain full legal advice and representation, he may be best advised to stay away from the court and preserve his ability to apply for discharge after 72 hours.

Removal and accommodation of children by police in cases of emergency

46.—(1) Where a constable has reasonable cause to believe that a child would otherwise be likely to suffer significant harm, he may—

(a) remove the child to suitable accommodation and keep him there; or

(b) take such steps as are reasonable to ensure that the child's removal from any hospital, or other place, in which he is then being accommodated is prevented.

(2) For the purposes of this Act, a child with respect to whom a constable has exercised his powers under this section is referred to as having been taken into police protection.

(3) As soon as is reasonably practicable after taking a child into police protection, the constable concerned shall—

(a) inform the local authority within whose area the child was found of the steps that have been, and are proposed to be, taken with respect to the child under this section and the reasons for taking them;

(b) give details to the authority within whose area the child is ordinarily resident ("the appropriate authority") of the place at which the child is being accommodated;

(c) inform the child (if he appears capable of understanding)—

(i) of the steps that have been taken with respect to him under this section and of the reasons for taking them; and

(ii) of the further steps that may be taken with respect to him under this section;

(d) take such steps as are reasonably practicable to discover the wishes and feelings of the child;

(e) secure that the case is inquired into by an officer designated for the purposes of this section by the chief officer of the police area concerned; and

(f) where the child was taken into police protection by being removed to accommodation which is not provided—

(i) by or on behalf of a local authority; or

(ii) as a refuge, in compliance with the requirements of section 51,

secure that he is moved to accommodation which is so provided.

(4) As soon as is reasonably practicable after taking a child into police protection, the constable concerned shall take such steps as are reasonably practicable to inform—

(a) the child's parents;

(b) every person who is not a parent of his but who has parental responsibility for him; and

(c) any other person with whom the child was living immediately before being taken into police protection,

of the steps that he has taken under this section with respect to the child, the reasons for taking them and the further steps that may be taken with respect to him under this section.

(5) On completing any inquiry under subsection (3)(e), the officer conducting it shall release the child from police protection unless he considers that there is still reasonable cause for believing that the child would be likely to suffer significant harm if released.

(6) No child may be kept in police protection for more than 72 hours.

(7) While a child is being kept in police protection, the designated officer may apply on behalf of the appropriate authority for an emergency protection order to be made under section 44 with respect to the child.

(8) An application may be made under subsection (7) whether or not the authority know of it or agree to its being made.

(9) While a child is being kept in police protection—

(a) neither the constable concerned nor the designated officer shall have parental responsibility for him; but

(b) the designated officer shall do what is reasonable in all the circumstances of the case for the purpose of safeguarding or promoting the child's welfare (having regard in particular to the length of the period during which the child will be so protected).

(10) Where a child has been taken into police protection, the designated officer shall allow—

(a) the child's parents;

(b) any person who is not a parent of the child but who has parental responsibility for him;

(c) any person with whom the child was living immediately before he was taken into police protection;

(d) any person in whose favour a contact order is in force with respect to the child;

(e) any person who is allowed to have contact with the child by virtue of an order under section 34; and

(f) any person acting on behalf of any of those persons,

to have such contact (if any) with the child as, in the opinion of the designated officer, is both reasonable and in the child's best interests.

(11) Where a child who has been taken into police protection is in accommodation provided by, or on behalf of, the appropriate authority, subsection (10) shall have effect as if it referred to the authority rather than to the designated officer.

DEFINITIONS

"appropriate authority": s.46(3)(b).

"child": s.105(1).

"contact order": s.8(1).

"designated officer": s.46(3)(e).

"local authority": s.105(1).

"ordinary residence": s.105(6).

"person who is not a parent but has parental responsibility": ss.5(6), 12(2), 33(3), 44(4).

"police protection": s.46(2).
"refuge": s.51.
"significant harm": s.31(9)(10).

GENERAL NOTE

This section replaces the power of a constable to detain a child at risk under s.28(2) of the C.Y.P.A. 1969 and reduces the maximum period for police protection from eight days to 72 hours (subs. (6)). The ground for such detention in subs. (1) is comparable to that for an emergency protection order under s.44(1)(a), but the constable, not the court, must have reasonable cause to believe that the child is likely to suffer significant harm. Police action under s.46 may be either removing a child to suitable accommodation (accommodation provided by or on behalf of the local authority or a refuge under s.51 (subs. (3)(f))) or taking reasonable steps to prevent his removal from a hospital or elsewhere (subs. (1)).

The duties owed by a constable taking action under this section are more onerous than under s.28(3) and (4) of the C.Y.P.A. 1969. These additional duties are intended to provide "safeguards which should reduce the stress that may accompany the removal of a child and ensure both that the child does not remain away from home unnecessarily and that contact with the family is maintained" (*per* David Mellor, Minister of Health (Standing Committee B, col. 337, June 6, 1989)). The constable must inform the child and the parent figures listed in subs. (4) of the steps taken, the reasons for them, and what else may be done (subss. (2) and (4)). He must inform the local authority of the reasons for the action and the child's whereabouts and secure that the child is moved to suitable accommodation (subs. (3)). He must inform the child of the action taken and to be taken and discover his wishes and feelings (subs. (3)(c) and (d)). The constable must also ensure that the case is investigated by a designated officer (subs. (3)(c)). The powers and responsibilities of the designated officer are also strengthened; he does not have parental responsibility for the child but may take reasonable action to safeguard the child's welfare (subs. (9)). He must allow the people specified in subs. (10) to have contact with the child. He must release the child when his investigation is completed, unless he considers that the child would be likely to suffer significant harm (subs. (5)). In such a case he may apply for an emergency protection order (subs. (7)).

Although a child who appears capable of understanding must be informed, etc., there is no duty on the police to consult the child or take account of his wishes either in relation to contact under subs. (10) or any other course of action. The police use their current powers in s.28 to detain a child whose parents have been arrested, to remove children at risk in cases of abuse, etc., or when they find children in unsuitable places, *e.g.* hitch-hiking on the motorway. Police standing orders tell them to return young people under the age of 18 to their parents (*per* Lord Elwyn Jones (*Hansard*, H.L. Vol. 503, col. 444)). The Act requires the local authority to be informed once the child has been taken into police protection. However, it does not apply where a constable is merely returning a missing child home.

There is no statutory provision for review, but judicial review would theoretically be available where duties in the Act were not complied with. There is also the possibility of an action for false imprisonment.

Subs. (1)

Suitable accommodation: This no longer has to be "a place of safety" but it must be accommodation within subs. (3)(f). If the child needs medical attention he can presumably be taken to hospital, but an emergency protection order may be necessary because the police do not obtain parental responsibility (see subs. (9)) and cannot consent to treatment except where it is reasonable to safeguard the child, *e.g.* in an emergency.

Subs. (4)

If the parents are informed that the designated officer intends to apply for an emergency protection order, it may be possible for these proceedings to be *inter partes*. This could be the best way of resolving conflicts at an early stage, but the period of 72 hours gives the parents little time to obtain proper representation. See also s.45(11).

Subs. (5)

There is a duty to release unless the condition is satisfied. If it is satisfied, there is no duty on the designated officer to seek an emergency protection order, but notification of the local authority brings its duty to investigate under s.47 into play. The authority must consider whether it should ask the designated officer to apply for an emergency protection order (s.47(3)(c)).

Subs. (7)

The duration of any emergency protection order applied for will be limited by s.45(3); the period of police protection and the emergency protection order cannot together exceed eight days. The local authority may also apply for an emergency protection order while the child is in police protection. It should not be possible for anyone to apply for an emergency protection order to end police protection. In *Nottinghamshire County Council* v. *Q.* [1982] 2 W.L.R. 954, the Divisional Court held that a parent's application for an interim order under C.Y.P.A. 1969, s.28(6) was an abuse of the process.

On behalf of: Any police officer may seek an order on his own behalf under s.44.

Subs. (9)

The wording of para. (b) parallels that in s.3(5) which defines the power of a person who is *in loco parentis*, but the designated officer has a duty to act. This further clouds the effect of parental responsibility because it would seem unrealistic for the officer to be under a duty to obtain medical treatment if his position did not also enable him to consent to it. Although there may be little difficulty over emergency treatment for serious injuries, where investigations are necessary to determine whether the child has been physically or sexually abused an emergency protection order or child assessment order should be sought.

Subs. (10)

Contact may reassure the child or the parents about the situation, but could be used by the parents or someone acting on their behalf to silence the child. It may thus be necessary to find out the child's views before allowing contact and to arrange supervision. The designated officer has to balance the parents' wishes and the child's needs.

Reasonable: What is reasonable must take into account the length of police protection, the circumstances in which the child entered police protection, the child's age, health (emotional and physical) and wishes. Attention should be given to the timing, duration and frequency of visits from parents (or anyone investigating the case), the location and the general arrangements for visits. Where a number of different people wish to visit the child it may be necessary to prioritise claims. Here again the child's wishes will be crucial to his welfare.

Subs. (11)

The officer's duties under subs. (10) fall to the authority if the child is being accommodated by or on behalf of them, but not if he is in a refuge. Where a local authority is accommodating the child it will also be under the duties in Pt. III and have to consider the wishes and feelings of the child and his parents in accordance with s.22.

Local authority's duty to investigate

47.—(1) Where a local authority—

    (a) are informed that a child who lives, or is found, in their area—

        (i) is the subject of an emergency protection order; or

        (ii) is in police protection; or

    (b) have reasonable cause to suspect that a child who lives, or is found, in their area is suffering, or is likely to suffer, significant harm,

the authority shall make, or cause to be made, such enquiries as they consider necessary to enable them to decide whether they should take any action to safeguard or promote the child's welfare.

(2) Where a local authority have obtained an emergency protection order with respect to a child, they shall make, or cause to be made, such enquiries as they consider necessary to enable them to decide what action they should take to safeguard or promote the child's welfare.

(3) The enquiries shall, in particular, be directed towards establishing—

    (a) whether the authority should make any application to the court, or exercise any of their other powers under this Act, with respect to the child;

    (b) whether, in the case of a child—

(i) with respect to whom an emergency protection order has been made; and

(ii) who is not in accommodation provided by or on behalf of the authority,

it would be in the child's best interests (while an emergency protection order remains in force) for him to be in such accommodation; and

(c) whether, in the case of a child who has been taken into police protection, it would be in the child's best interests for the authority to ask for an application to be made under section 46(7).

(4) Where enquiries are being made under subsection (1) with respect to a child, the local authority concerned shall (with a view to enabling them to determine what action, if any, to take with respect to him) take such steps as are reasonably practicable—

(a) to obtain access to him; or

(b) to ensure that access to him is obtained, on their behalf, by a person authorised by them for the purpose,

unless they are satisfied that they already have sufficient information with respect to him.

(5) Where, as a result of any such enquiries, it appears to the authority that there are matters connected with the child's education which should be investigated, they shall consult the relevant local education authority.

(6) Where, in the course of enquiries made under this section—

(a) any officer of the local authority concerned; or

(b) any person authorised by the authority to act on their behalf in connection with those enquiries—

(i) is refused access to the child concerned; or

(ii) is denied information as to his whereabouts,

the authority shall apply for an emergency protection order, a child assessment order, a care order or a supervision order with respect to the child unless they are satisfied that his welfare can be satisfactorily safeguarded without their doing so.

(7) If, on the conclusion of any enquiries or review made under this section, the authority decide not to apply for an emergency protection order, a child assessment order, a care order or a supervision order they shall—

(a) consider whether it would be appropriate to review the case at a later date; and

(b) if they decide that it would be, determine the date on which that review is to begin.

(8) Where, as a result of complying with this section, a local authority conclude that they should take action to safeguard or promote the child's welfare they shall take that action (so far as it is both within their power and reasonably practicable for them to do so).

(9) Where a local authority are conducting enquiries under this section, it shall be the duty of any person mentioned in subsection (11) to assist them with those enquiries (in particular by providing relevant information and advice) if called upon by the authority to do so.

(10) Subsection (9) does not oblige any person to assist a local authority where doing so would be unreasonable in all the circumstances of the case.

(11) The persons are—

(a) any local authority;

(b) any local education authority;

(c) any local housing authority;

(d) any health authority; and

(e) any person authorised by the Secretary of State for the purposes of this section.

(12) Where a local authority are making enquiries under this section with respect to a child who appears to them to be ordinarily resident within the area of another authority, they shall consult that other authority, who may undertake the necessary enquiries in their place.

DEFINITIONS
"care order": s.31(11).
"child": s.105(1).
"child assessment order": s.43(2).
"emergency protection order": s.44(4).
"health authority": s.105(1).
"local authority": s.105(1).
"local education authority": s.105(1).
"local housing authority": s.105(1).
"ordinary residence": s.105(6).
"police protection": s.46(2).
"significant harm": s.31(9)(10).
"supervision order": s.31(11).

GENERAL NOTE
This section imposes duties on local authorities to investigate certain cases of suspected harm. These exist alongside the duty to investigate under s.37 where a court order has been made. It is both wider and more specific than the duty in s.2 of the C.Y.P.A. 1969, which it replaces. The duty to make (or cause to be made) the enquiries which they consider necessary applies where the authority is informed or suspects that there is a child in their area who is subject to an emergency protection order, under police protection or at risk (subs. (1)), or they have obtained an emergency protection order (subs. (2)). Subs. (3) directs the local authority to consider specific courses of action; subs. (4) imposes a qualified duty to see (or have seen) the child concerned. Where investigations are frustrated by unreasonable refusal of access to the child there may be grounds for an emergency protection order under s.44(1)(b). The authority is left with some discretion on how to act but must, of course, act reasonably and without negligence. Once the authority has decided to take action it is under a qualified duty to act (subs. (8)). Where access to the child is denied to the person carrying out the enquiries, the authority *must* apply for an emergency protection order, a child assessment order, a care order or a supervision order unless it is satisfied that the child's welfare does not require it (subs. (6)).

Ignorance of and failure to use the powers in C.Y.P.A. 1933, s.40 to gain access to Kimberley Carlile which contributed to her death, were heavily criticised by the Inquiry *A Child in Mind* Greenwich London Borough Council (1987). The importance of a duty on social workers to take action makes clear what they should do and provides a lever for gaining access to the child. Where the authority decides not to act, it must also decide whether and when to review that decision (subs. (7)).

When carrying out its enquiries under this section the local authority must consult the local education authority where education issues arise. If the child appears to be resident elsewhere the local authority must consult the other authorities who may undertake these enquiries (subs. (2)). There is a qualified duty (subs. (10)) on the organisations mentioned in subs. (11) to assist the local authority if requested to do so (subs. (9)). This puts on a statutory footing the co-operation already stated to be good practice in the D.H.S.S. guidance booklet *Working Together* (1988).

Subss. (1) and (2)
Reasonable cause to suspect: It would appear that there is a duty to investigate every allegation unless it is thought to be unfounded, or the harm suggested is not significant.
Cause to be made: The primary responsibility is on the local authority but it may "delegate" it. In some areas many initial allegations are dealt with by the N.S.P.C.C. The enquiries will necessarily involve other agencies. See subss. (9) to (11).
Such enquiries: Although the local authority has discretion, it must consider the points in subs. (3), obtain access unless it has sufficient information (subs. (4)) and consult the L.E.A. in relation to education matters (subs. (5)).

Subs. (3)
Other powers under this Act: This includes their powers (and duties) to children under Pt. III (particularly in relation to children in need) and powers under Pts. VII–X and ss.85–87.

It would be in the child's best interests . . . to be in such accommodation: The Act does not give the local authority the right to take over the child's accommodation but under s.52(3)(b) rules may require the applicant to hand over the child. The N.S.P.C.C. may still bring proceedings even though the child is accommodated by the local authority (s.31(7)).

Subs. (4)
Person authorised: This is not the same as an authorised person under s.31(9). If the local authority delegates enquiries to other agencies it will also have to authorise their personnel to gain access. Only if access is denied to a person who has been authorised does the duty in subs. (6) apply. Refusal of access to an unauthorised person would also appear entirely reasonable (see s.44(1)(b)).

Subs. (6)
Under this section: The power does not apparently apply to investigations under s.37. However, court-ordered investigation may bring s.47(1)(b) into play; there will then be a duty to gain access and take action if this is denied.

Subs. (7)
A comparable duty to consider reviewing a decision exists in s.37(6).

Subs. (8)
This appears to change a local authority power into a qualified duty to determine that the child is in need. For example, if a local authority finds that a six-year-old is being left alone after school, it has a power to provide after-school care under s.18(6). It would not be reasonably practicable for the authority to provide such care if they had already determined not to have such facilities, if there were no vacancies, or if the parents refused to allow the child to attend. In this last case the authority could force attendance through a condition in a supervision order if they could satisfy the test in s.31(2). Where the local authority had no facilities of its own it could still provide advice and guidance to the parents about private facilities. For further details of the local authority's powers see Pt. III and Sched. 2, Pt. I. (see also notes to s.17).

Subss. (9)–(11)
The list in subs. (11) does not include the police or the probation service. David Mellor explained these omissions on the basis that "police refusal to co-operate on any matter would be indefensible" and that probation officers, as officers of the court "are already under a duty to assist in these matters" (Standing Committee B, col. 342, June 6, 1989). Even if guidance is issued this is not a satisfactory solution.
Where doing so would be unreasonable: A problem clearly arises with confidentiality owed by a professional to his client. In *Working Together* D.H.S.S. (1988), the following guidance was given: "Ethical and statutory codes concerned with confidentiality and data protection are not intended to prevent the exchange of information between different professional staff who have a responsibility for ensuring the protection of children" (para. 5.4). Both the B.M.A. and medical defence societies have expressed the view that a doctor may not only respond to requests for information, he may initiate action by passing on his concerns. The United Kingdom Central Council for Nursing, Midwifery and Health Visiting advises that practitioners should consult with others and be prepared to justify decisions to pass on or withhold confidential information. Local authorities have primary responsibility for child protection and cannot expect other agencies (except the N.S.P.C.C.) to put the same emphasis on child protection work as they do.

Subs. (12)
The duty is on the authority which starts the enquiries; the home authority is empowered but not required to take over the enquiries.

Powers to assist in discovery of children who may be in need of emergency protection

48.—(1) Where it appears to a court making an emergency protection order that adequate information as to the child's whereabouts—
    (a) is not available to the applicant for the order; but
    (b) is available to another person,

it may include in the order a provision requiring that other person to disclose, if asked to do so by the applicant, any information that he may have as to the child's whereabouts.

(2) No person shall be excused from complying with such a requirement on the ground that complying might incriminate him or his spouse of an offence; but a statement or admission made in complying shall not be admissible in evidence against either of them in proceedings for any offence other than perjury.

(3) An emergency protection order may authorise the applicant to enter premises specified by the order and search for the child with respect to whom the order is made.

(4) Where the court is satisfied that there is reasonable cause to believe that there may be another child on those premises with respect to whom an emergency protection order ought to be made, it may make an order authorising the applicant to search for that other child on those premises.

(5) Where—

    (a) an order has been made under subsection (4);
    (b) the child concerned has been found on the premises; and
    (c) the applicant is satisfied that the grounds for making an emergency protection order exist with respect to him,

the order shall have effect as if it were an emergency protection order.

(6) Where an order has been made under subsection (4), the applicant shall notify the court of its effect.

(7) A person shall be guilty of an offence if he intentionally obstructs any person exercising the power of entry and search under subsection (3) or (4).

(8) A person guilty of an offence under subsection (7) shall be liable on summary conviction to a fine not exceeding level 3 on the standard scale.

(9) Where, on an application made by any person for a warrant under this section, it appears to the court—

    (a) that a person attempting to exercise powers under an emergency protection order has been prevented from doing so by being refused entry to the premises concerned or access to the child concerned; or
    (b) that any such person is likely to be so prevented from exercising any such powers,

it may issue a warrant authorising any constable to assist the person mentioned in paragraph (a) or (b) in the exercise of those powers, using reasonable force if necessary.

(10) Every warrant issued under this section shall be addressed to, and executed by, a constable who shall be accompanied by the person applying for the warrant if—

    (a) that person so desires; and
    (b) the court by whom the warrant is issued does not direct otherwise.

(11) A court granting an application for a warrant under this section may direct that the constable concerned may, in executing the warrant, be accompanied by a registered medical practitioner, registered nurse or registered health visitor if he so chooses.

(12) An application for a warrant under this section shall be made in the manner and form prescribed by rules of court.

(13) Wherever it is reasonably practicable to do so, an order under subsection (4), an application for a warrant under this section and any such warrant shall name the child; and where it does not name him it shall describe him as clearly as possible.

DEFINITIONS
    "applicant": s.44(1).
    "child": s.105(1).

"emergency protection order": s.44(4).
"the court": s.92(7).

GENERAL NOTE

This section empowers the court to strengthen the force of an emergency protection order by including an order requiring a person to disclose the child's whereabouts to the applicant (subs. (1)), permitting the applicant to enter premises to search for the child or another child (subss. (3) and (4)) or attaching a warrant to it (subss. (9) and (10)).

Subss. (1) and (2)

Disclosure: A comparable provision exists in s.33 of the Family Law Act 1986, which applies to orders under Pt. I of that Act which includes section 8 orders. The Cleveland Inquiry Report, p.228, recommended that such a power should exist in child protection cases. It must appear to the court that the person ordered to supply information has it. Failure to comply with the order is contempt of court and may amount to an offence under s.44(15). Self incrimination does not justify refusal to comply, but a person who had abducted a child from care contrary to s.49 could not be prosecuted for that offence relying solely on his statement. This immunity does not apply to an offence of perjury.

Subss. (3)–(8)

Entry and search: There is no automatic power of entry under an emergency protection order but the court may add a power. The police have a right to enter without warrant to save life or limb under s.17(1)(e) of the Police and Criminal Evidence Act 1984, which is unaffected by this Act. Where a child is found by the police in these circumstances he may be taken into police protection if s.46(1) is satisfied. No additional test has to be satisfied for an entry power under subs. (3), so this may become a standard form of emergency protection order. However, in cases where there is likely to be resistance, the applicant may be advised either to obtain a warrant under subs. (9) or at least have police assistance available. If there is reasonable cause to believe that another child is on the premises, an emergency protection order can include a power to search for that child (subs. (4)). The second child should be named, if reasonably practicable (subs. (13)). If the second child is found on the premises and *the applicant* is satisfied of the significant harm test, the power operates as an emergency protection order in respect of him and the applicant may remove him (subs. (5)) but must notify the court (subs. (6)). Obstruction of this power of entry and search is an offence (summary conviction: level 3 fine) (subs. (7)). These powers replace those in C.Y.P.A. 1933, s.40.

Subss. (9)–(13)

Warrants: The applicant for an emergency protection order may apply for a warrant when he applies for the emergency protection order or afterwards, but will have to show that one is needed because he has been prevented from exercising the order by refusal of entry or access to the child or is likely to be so prevented (subs. (9)). A warrant under subs. (9) can only be exercised by the police, but the applicant may accompany the constable unless the court directs otherwise (subs. (10)). There is no longer a duty on the applicant to accompany the constable. If the applicant goes with the constable he may be able to determine whether the child should be removed from the home. However, since there will already be an emergency protection order there is no need for any special form of warrant to authorise removal as there was under the C.Y.P.A. 1933. The court may also direct that the constable be accompanied by a doctor, nurse or health visitor if he wishes.

Applications for warrants are currently heard by single magistrates. This is likely to continue, subject to Sched. 11, para. 3.

Abduction of children in care etc.

49.—(1) A person shall be guilty of an offence if, knowingly and without lawful authority or reasonable excuse, he—

(a) takes a child to whom this section applies away from the responsible person;

(b) keeps such a child away from the responsible person; or

(c) induces, assists or incites such a child to run away or stay away from the responsible person.

(2) This section applies in relation to a child who is—

(a) in care;

(b) the subject of an emergency protection order; or

(c) in police protection,

and in this section "the responsible person" means any person who for the time being has care of him by virtue of the care order, the emergency protection order, or section 46, as the case may be.

(3) A person guilty of an offence under this section shall be liable on summary conviction to imprisonment for a term not exceeding six months, or to a fine not exceeding level 5 on the standard scale, or to both.

DEFINITIONS

"child": s.105(1).

"emergency protection order": s.44(4).

"in care": s.105(1).

"in police protection": s.46(2).

"responsible person": s.49(2).

GENERAL NOTE

This section re-enacts with modifications the C.C.A. 1980 ss.13, 14, and 16. It makes it an offence (summary conviction: level 5 fine and/or six months' imprisonment) to remove from a responsible person, keep away, or induce to leave, a child who is subject to a care order, an emergency protection order or in police protection (subs. (1)). It does not apply to children who are merely accommodated under s.20 or being assessed under a child assessment order.

Subs. (1)

Without lawful authority or reasonable excuse: This exception is extended to all the offences in subs. (1).

Recovery of abducted children etc.

50.—(1) Where it appears to the court that there is reason to believe that a child to whom this section applies—

(a) has been unlawfully taken away or is being unlawfully kept away from the responsible person;

(b) has run away or is staying away from the responsible person; or

(c) is missing,

the court may make an order under this section ("a recovery order").

(2) This section applies to the same children to whom section 49 applies and in this section "the responsible person" has the same meaning as in section 49.

(3) A recovery order—

(a) operates as a direction to any person who is in a position to do so to produce the child on request to any authorised person;

(b) authorises the removal of the child by any authorised person;

(c) requires any person who has information as to the child's whereabouts to disclose that information, if asked to do so, to a constable or an officer of the court;

(d) authorises a constable to enter any premises specified in the order and search for the child, using reasonable force if necessary.

(4) The court may make a recovery order only on the application of—

(a) any person who has parental responsibility for the child by virtue of a care order or emergency protection order; or

(b) where the child is in police protection, the designated officer.

(5) A recovery order shall name the child and—

(a) any person who has parental responsibility for the child by virtue of a care order or emergency protection order; or

(b) where the child is in police protection, the designated officer.

(6) Premises may only be specified under subsection (3)(d) if it appears to the court that there are reasonable grounds for believing the child to be on them.

(7) In this section—
  "an authorised person" means—
    (a) any person specified by the court;
    (b) any constable;
    (c) any person who is authorised—
        (i) after the recovery order is made; and
        (ii) by a person who has parental responsibility for the child by virtue of a care order or an emergency protection order,
      to exercise any power under a recovery order; and
  "the designated officer" means the officer designated for the purposes of section 46.
(8) Where a person is authorised as mentioned in subsection (7)(c)—
    (a) the authorisation shall identify the recovery order; and
    (b) any person claiming to be so authorised shall, if asked to do so, produce some duly authenticated document showing that he is so authorised.
(9) A person shall be guilty of an offence if he intentionally obstructs an authorised person exercising the power under subsection (3)(b) to remove a child.
(10) A person guilty of an offence under this section shall be liable on summary conviction to a fine not exceeding level 3 on the standard scale.
(11) No person shall be excused from complying with any request made under subsection (3)(c) on the ground that complying with it might incriminate him or his spouse of an offence; but a statement or admission made in complying shall not be admissible in evidence against either of them in proceedings for an offence other than perjury.
(12) Where a child is made the subject of a recovery order whilst being looked after by a local authority, any reasonable expenses incurred by an authorised person in giving effect to the order shall be recoverable from the authority.
(13) A recovery order shall have effect in Scotland as if it had been made by the Court of Session and as if that court had had jurisdiction to make it.
(14) In this section "the court", in relation to Northern Ireland, means a magistrates' court within the meaning of the Magistrates' Courts (Northern Ireland) Order 1981.

DEFINITIONS
  "authorised person": s.50(7).
  "care order": s.31(11).
  "child": ss.49(2), 105(1).
  "emergency protection order": s.44(4).
  "local authority": s.105(1).
  "looked after by a local authority": s.22(1).
  "person who has parental responsibility by virtue of a care order": s.33(3).
  "person who has parental responsibility by virtue of an emergency protection order": s.44(1)(4).
  "police protection": s.46(2).
  "recovery order": s.50.
  "responsible person": s.49(2).
  "the court": ss.50(14), 92(7).
  "the designated officer": ss.46(3)(e), 50(7).

GENERAL NOTE
  This section amends and clarifies the law relating to recovery of children absent from care which is found in C.Y.P.A. 1969, s.32, as amended by Sched. 12, para. 27 and C.C.A. 1980, ss.15 and 16. It only applies to children subject to care orders (including interim orders), emergency protection orders or in police protection (subs. (2)). In other cases the inherent jurisdiction of the High Court and the powers under the Family Law Act 1986, ss.33 and 34,

apply. The power to arrest a child absent from care without warrant is supplemented by the power to make a recovery order (subs. (1)), on the application of the person with parental responsibility by virtue of the emergency protection order or care order or the designated officer (subs. (4)). A recovery order directs any person who can to produce the child; it authorises removal of the child by an authorised person; it requires any person who has information to disclose it to a constable and authorises a constable to search specified premises (subss. (3) and (6)). It is an offence (summary conviction: level 3 fine) intentionally to obstruct an authorised person removing the child (subs. (9)). A person required to provide information cannot refuse on the grounds of self-incrimination but his statement is only admissible in proceedings against him for perjury (subs. (11)). Recovery orders have effect throughout the U.K. (subss. (13) and (14)).

Guidance will be issued to local authorities about the recovery of children. There is no exemption from the recovery provisions for children in "safe houses" but the Government expects that recovery orders will not be needed. If an order is sought, the organisation running the "safe house" will have to be informed so that they can attend and argue against recovery. If an order is made, it must be obeyed (subs. (9)). If those running the "safe house" wish to take steps to prevent harm to the child, they will be able to seek an emergency protection order, but a child will not be able to be held compulsorily in a "safe house" (*per* David Mellor, Minister of Health (Standing Committee B, col. 542, June 13, 1989)).

Subs. (1)

This is wider than s.49(1) in that a recovery order may be made where no offence has been committed.

Unlawfully: This applies if an offence under s.49 of this Act or s.2 of the Child Abduction Act 1984 has been committed.

May make an order: S.1(1) applies. If the child is in a safe house and satisfactory arrangements can be made between the organisation and the local authority, an order would not be necessary. Where a child repeatedly returns home and is not in danger then an order may be counter-productive.

Refuges for children at risk

51.—(1) Where it is proposed to use a voluntary home or registered children's home to provide a refuge for children who appear to be at risk of harm, the Secretary of State may issue a certificate under this section with respect to that home.

(2) Where a local authority or voluntary organisation arrange for a foster parent to provide such a refuge, the Secretary of State may issue a certificate under this section with respect to that foster parent.

(3) In subsection (2) "foster parent" means a person who is, or who from time to time is, a local authority foster parent or a foster parent with whom children are placed by a voluntary organisation.

(4) The Secretary of State may by regulations—

    (a) make provision as to the manner in which certificates may be issued;

    (b) impose requirements which must be complied with while any certificate is in force; and

    (c) provide for the withdrawal of certificates in prescribed circumstances.

(5) Where a certificate is in force with respect to a home, none of the provisions mentioned in subsection (7) shall apply in relation to any person providing a refuge for any child in that home.

(6) Where a certificate is in force with respect to a foster parent, none of those provisions shall apply in relation to the provision by him of a refuge for any child in accordance with arrangements made by the local authority or voluntary organisation.

(7) The provisions are—

    (a) section 49;

    (b) section 71 of the Social Work (Scotland) Act 1968 (harbouring children who have absconded from residential establishments etc.), so far as it applies in relation to anything done in England and Wales;

(c) section 32(3) of the Children and Young Persons Act 1969 (compelling, persuading, inciting or assisting any person to be absent from detention, etc.), so far as it applies in relation to anything done in England and Wales;

(d) section 2 of the Child Abduction Act 1984.

DEFINITIONS
"foster parent": s.51(3).
"local authority": s.105(1).
"local authority foster parent": s.23(3), (4).
"registered children's home": s.63.
"voluntary home": s.60.
"voluntary organisation": s.105(1).

GENERAL NOTE
This section empowers the Secretary of State to issue certificates to voluntary homes, registered homes (subs. (1)) and foster parents (subs. (2)) which will exempt them from the offences, listed in subs. (7), of harbouring, etc., children for whom they are providing a refuge. The Secretary of State is also empowered to make regulations about the granting and withdrawal of certificates and imposing requirements while the certificate is in force. "The regulations will impose vigorous requirements on those running refuges . . . Bona fide organisations will have no difficulty complying with those requirements" (*per* David Mellor, Minister of Health (*Hansard,* H.C. Vol. 158, col. 609).

This section is intended to enable "safe houses" legally to provide care for children who are absent from local authority accommodation or from home without permission. There was concern that those running such facilities, notably the Children's Society, could be liable for prosecution, and that criminal liability would lead to children being removed from the refuge, or their whereabouts being discovered. Also, that lack of regulations could lead to inadequate assistance or abuse of this group of vulnerable children.

It will still be possible to obtain a recovery order to remove a child who has run away to a safe house under s.50.

Rules and regulations

52.—(1) Without prejudice to section 93 or any other power to make such rules, rules of court may be made with respect to the procedure to be followed in connection with proceedings under this Part.

(2) The rules may, in particular make provision—

(a) as to the form in which any application is to be made or direction is to be given;

(b) prescribing the persons who are to be notified of—
(i) the making, or extension, of an emergency protection order; or
(ii) the making of an application under section 45(4) or (8) or 46(7); and

(c) as to the content of any such notification and the manner in which, and person by whom, it is to be given.

(3) The Secretary of State may by regulations provide that, where—

(a) an emergency protection order has been made with respect to a child;

(b) the applicant for the order was not the local authority within whose area the child is ordinarily resident; and

(c) that local authority are of the opinion that it would be in the child's best interests for the applicant's responsibilities under the order to be transferred to them,

that authority shall (subject to their having complied with any requirements imposed by the regulations) be treated, for the purposes of this Act, as though they and not the original applicant had applied for, and been granted, the order.

(4) Regulations made under subsection (3) may, in particular, make provision as to—

(a) the considerations to which the local authority shall have regard in forming an opinion as mentioned in subsection (3)(c); and

(b) the time at which responsibility under any emergency protection order is to be treated as having been transferred to a local authority.

DEFINITIONS

"emergency protection order": s.44(4).

"local authority": s.105(1).

GENERAL NOTE

This provides for rules to be made in relation to the emergency protection of children. S.28(3) of the C.Y.P.A. 1969 required parents and guardians to be notified of place of safety orders. It is likely that the notification requirements in relation to emergency protection orders will be much broader because of the rights to challenge orders under s.45(8) and the provisions about contact in s.44(13).

Regulations may provide for the transfer of responsibility to local authorities from others with an emergency protection order. The N.S.P.C.C. is most likely to be affected by transfers since it is the only body authorised to apply for a care order. The N.S.P.C.C. was keen to ensure that transfer was ordered by the court but this was rejected by the Government (David Mellor (Standing Committee B, col. 346, June 6, 1989)).

PART VI

COMMUNITY HOMES

Provision of community homes by local authorities

53.—(1) Every local authority shall make such arrangements as they consider appropriate for securing that homes ("community homes") are available—

(a) for the care and accommodation of children looked after by them; and

(b) for purposes connected with the welfare of children (whether or not looked after by them),

and may do so jointly with one or more other local authorities.

(2) In making such arrangements, a local authority shall have regard to the need for ensuring the availability of accommodation—

(a) of different descriptions; and

(b) which is suitable for different purposes and the requirements of different descriptions of children.

(3) A community home may be a home—

(a) provided, managed, equipped and maintained by a local authority; or

(b) provided by a voluntary organisation but in respect of which a local authority and the organisation—

(i) propose that, in accordance with an instrument of management, the management, equipment and maintenance of the home shall be the responsibility of the local authority; or

(ii) so propose that the management, equipment and maintenance of the home shall be the responsibility of the voluntary organisation.

(4) Where a local authority are to be responsible for the management of a community home provided by a voluntary organisation, the authority shall designate the home as a controlled community home.

(5) Where a voluntary organisation are to be responsible for the management of a community home provided by the organisation, the local authority shall designate the home as an assisted community home.

(6) Schedule 4 shall have effect for the purpose of supplementing the provisions of this Part.

DEFINITIONS
   "assisted community home": s.53(5).
   "child looked after by the local authority": s.22(1).
   "community home": s.53.
   "controlled community home": s.53(4).
   "instrument of management": Sched. 4.
   "local authority": s.105(1).
   "voluntary organisation": s.105(1).

GENERAL NOTE
   This section imposes a duty on local authorities to ensure that community homes are available for the care and accommodation of children they are looking after and for purposes connected with the welfare of children. Subss. (1) to (5) re-enact with minor drafting amendments C.C.A.1980, s.31. These provisions are supplemented by Sched. 4 which replaces ss.35–39 of the C.C.A. 1980. Paras. 1 and 2 permit the Secretary of State to make instruments of management for homes which are assisted or controlled community homes. Para. 3 makes further rules about the management, equipment and maintenance of such homes. Para. 4 gives the Secretary of State wide powers to make regulations about the placement and welfare of children in community homes and the conduct of such homes. New regulations will replace the Community Homes Regulations 1972 (S.I. No. 319). Drafting errors in this Schedule are corrected in the Courts and Legal Services Bill, Sched. 10, para. 9. The word "voluntary" should be omitted from paras. 1(1), (2), (4), (5), (6)(b)(i), (8) and (9).

Directions that premises be no longer used for community home

   54.—(1) Where it appears to the Secretary of State that—
       (a) any premises used for the purposes of a community home are unsuitable for those purposes; or
       (b) the conduct of a community home—
           (i) is not in accordance with regulations made by him under paragraph 4 of Schedule 4; or
           (ii) is otherwise unsatisfactory,
   he may, by notice in writing served on the responsible body, direct that as from such date as may be specified in the notice the premises shall not be used for the purposes of a community home.

   (2) Where—
       (a) the Secretary of State has given a direction under subsection (1); and
       (b) the direction has not been revoked,
   he may at any time by order revoke the instrument of management for the home concerned.

   (3) For the purposes of subsection (1), the responsible body—
       (a) in relation to a community home provided by a local authority, is that local authority;
       (b) in relation to a controlled community home, is the local authority specified in the home's instrument of management; and
       (c) in relation to an assisted community home, is the voluntary organisation by which the home is provided.

DEFINITIONS
   "assisted community home": s.53(5).
   "community home": s.53(1).
   "controlled community home": s.53(4).

"instrument of management": Sched. 4, Pt. I.
"responsible body": s.48(3), Sched. 4, para. 3(3).
"voluntary organisation": s.105(1).

GENERAL NOTE
This re-enacts, with minor drafting amendments, C.C.A. 1980, s.40. It permits the Secretary of State to direct that premises cease to be used as a community home.

Determination of disputes relating to controlled and assisted community homes

55.—(1) Where any dispute relating to a controlled community home arises between the local authority specified in the home's instrument of management and—

(a) the voluntary organisation by which the home is provided; or

(b) any other local authority who have placed, or desire or are required to place, in the home a child who is looked after by them,

the dispute may be referred by either party to the Secretary of State for his determination.

(2) Where any dispute relating to an assisted community home arises between the voluntary organisation by which the home is provided and any local authority who have placed, or desire to place, in the home a child who is looked after by them, the dispute may be referred by either party to the Secretary of State for his determination.

(3) Where a dispute is referred to the Secretary of State under this section he may, in order to give effect to his determination of the dispute, give such directions as he thinks fit to the local authority or voluntary organisation concerned.

(4) This section applies even though the matter in dispute may be one which, under or by virtue of Part II of Schedule 4, is reserved for the decision, or is the responsibility, of—

(a) the local authority specified in the home's instrument of management; or

(b) (as the case may be) the voluntary organisation by which the home is provided.

(5) Where any trust deed relating to a controlled or assisted community home contains provision whereby a bishop or any other ecclesiastical or denominational authority has power to decide questions relating to religious instruction given in the home, no dispute which is capable of being dealt with in accordance with that provision shall be referred to the Secretary of State under this section.

(6) In this Part "trust deed", in relation to a voluntary home, means any instrument (other than an instrument of management) regulating—

(a) the maintenance, management or conduct of the home; or

(b) the constitution of a body of managers or trustees of the home.

DEFINITIONS
"assisted community home": s.53(5).
"child looked after by a local authority": s.22(1).
"controlled community home": s.53(4).
"home": Sched. 4, para. 3(3).
"instrument of management": Sched. 4, Pt. I.
"local authority": s.105(1).
"managers": Sched. 4, para. 3(3).
"trust deed": s.55(6).
"voluntary home": s.60(3).
"voluntary organisation": s.105(1).

GENERAL NOTE
Subss. (1)–(5) re-enact with minor drafting amendments C.C.A. 1980, s.42. They provide for certain disputes relating to controlled or assisted community homes to be determined by the Secretary of State. Subs. (6) re-enacts C.C.A. 1980, s.36(5).

Discontinuance of voluntary organisation of controlled or assisted community home

56.—(1) The voluntary organisation by which a controlled or assisted community home is provided shall not cease to provide the home except after giving to the Secretary of State and the local authority specified in the home's instrument of management not less than two years' notice in writing of their intention to do so.

(2) A notice under subsection (1) shall specify the date from which the voluntary organisation intend to cease to provide the home as a community home.

(3) Where such a notice is given and is not withdrawn before the date specified in it, the home's instrument of management shall cease to have effect on that date and the home shall then cease to be a controlled or assisted community home.

(4) Where a notice is given under subsection (1) and the home's managers give notice in writing to the Secretary of State that they are unable or unwilling to continue as its managers until the date specified in the subsection (1) notice, the Secretary of State may by order—

(a) revoke the home's instrument of management; and
(b) require the local authority who were specified in that instrument to conduct the home until—

(i) the date specified in the subsection (1) notice; or
(ii) such earlier date (if any) as may be specified for the purposes of this paragraph in the order,

as if it were a community home provided by the local authority.

(5) Where the Secretary of State imposes a requirement under subsection (4)(b)—

(a) nothing in the trust deed for the home shall affect the conduct of the home by the local authority;
(b) the Secretary of State may by order direct that for the purposes of any provision specified in the direction and made by or under any enactment relating to community homes (other than this section) the home shall, until the date or earlier date specified as mentioned in subsection (4)(b), be treated as a controlled or assisted community home;
(c) except in so far as the Secretary of State so directs, the home shall until that date be treated for the purposes of any such enactment as a community home provided by the local authority; and
(d) on the date or earlier date specified as mentioned in subsection (4)(b) the home shall cease to be a community home.

DEFINITIONS
"assisted community home": s.53(5).
"community home": s.53(1).
"controlled community home": s.53(4).
"home": Sched. 4, para. 3(3).
"instrument of management": Sched. 4, Pt. I.
"local authority": s.105(1).
"managers": Sched. 4, para. 3(3).
"trust deed": s.55(6).
"voluntary organisation" s.105(1).

GENERAL NOTE
This re-enacts with minor drafting amendments C.C.A. 1980, s.43. It requires voluntary organisations providing controlled or assisted community homes to give two years' notice before they stop providing a home.

Closure by local authority of controlled or assisted community home

57.—(1) The local authority specified in the instrument of management for a controlled or assisted community home may give—

(a) the Secretary of State; and

(b) the voluntary organisation by which the home is provided,

not less than two years' notice in writing of their intention to withdraw their designation of the home as a controlled or assisted community home.

(2) A notice under subsection (1) shall specify the date ("the specified date") on which the designation is to be withdrawn.

(3) Where—

(a) a notice is given under subsection (1) in respect of a controlled or assisted community home;

(b) the home's managers give notice in writing to the Secretary of State that they are unable or unwilling to continue as managers until the specified date; and

(c) the managers' notice is not withdrawn,

the Secretary of State may by order revoke the home's instrument of management from such date earlier than the specified date as may be specified in the order.

(4) Before making an order under subsection (3), the Secretary of State shall consult the local authority and the voluntary organisation.

(5) Where a notice has been given under subsection (1) and is not withdrawn, the home's instrument of management shall cease to have effect on—

(a) the specified date; or

(b) where an earlier date has been specified under subsection (3), that earlier date,

and the home shall then cease to be a community home.

DEFINITIONS
"assisted community home": s.53(5).
"controlled community home": s.53(4).
"community home": s.53(1).
"home": Sched. 4, para. 3(3).
"instrument of management": Sched. 4, Pt. I.
"local authority": s.105(1).
"managers": Sched. 4, para. 3(3).
"the specified date": s.57(2).
"voluntary organisation": s.105(1).

GENERAL NOTE
This re-enacts with minor drafting amendments C.C.A. 1980, s.43A. It permits local authorities to withdraw the designation of a community as controlled or assisted and requires them to give two years' notice of their intention to do so.

Financial provisions applicable on cessation of controlled or assisted community home or disposal etc. of premises

58.—(1) Where—

(a) the instrument of management for a controlled or assisted community home is revoked or otherwise ceases to have effect under section 54(2), 56(3) or (4)(a) or 57(3) or (5); or

(b) any premises used for the purposes of such a home are (at any time after 13th January 1987) disposed of, or put to use otherwise than for those purposes,

the proprietor shall become liable to pay compensation ("the appropriate compensation") in accordance with this section.

(2) Where the instrument of management in force at the relevant time relates—

(a) to a controlled community home; or

(b) to an assisted community home which, at any time before the instrument came into force, was a controlled community home,

the appropriate compensation is a sum equal to that part of the value of any premises which is attributable to expenditure incurred in relation to the premises, while the home was a controlled community home, by the authority who were then the responsible authority.

(3) Where the instrument of management in force at the relevant time relates—

(a) to an assisted community home; or

(b) to a controlled community home which, at any time before the instrument came into force, was an assisted community home,

the appropriate compensation is a sum equal to that part of the value of the premises which is attributable to the expenditure of money provided by way of grant under section 82, section 65 of the Children and Young Persons Act 1969 or section 82 of the Child Care Act 1980.

(4) Where the home is, at the relevant time, conducted in premises which formerly were used as an approved school or were an approved probation hostel or home, the appropriate compensation is a sum equal to that part of the value of the premises which is attributable to the expenditure—

(a) of sums paid towards the expenses of the managers of an approved school under section 104 of the Children and Young Persons Act 1933; or

(b) of sums paid under section 51(3)(c) of the Powers of Criminal Courts Act 1973 in relation to expenditure on approved probation hostels or homes.

(5) The appropriate compensation shall be paid—

(a) in the case of compensation payable under subsection (2), to the authority who were the responsible authority at the relevant time; and

(b) in any other case, to the Secretary of State.

(6) In this section—

"disposal" includes the grant of a tenancy and any other conveyance, assignment, transfer, grant, variation or extinguishment of an interest in or right over land, whether made by instrument or otherwise;

"premises" means any premises or part of premises (including land) used for the purposes of the home and belonging to the proprietor;

"the proprietor" means—

(a) the voluntary organisation by which the home is, at the relevant time, provided; or

(b) if the premises are not, at the relevant time, vested in that organisation, the persons in whom they are vested;

"the relevant time" means the time immediately before the liability to pay arises under subsection (1); and

"the responsible authority" means the local authority specified in the instrument of management in question.

(7) For the purposes of this section an event of a kind mentioned in subsection (1)(b) shall be taken to have occurred—

(a) in the case of a disposal, on the date on which the disposal was completed or, in the case of a disposal which is effected by a series of transactions, the date on which the last of those transactions was completed;

(b) in the case of premises which are put to different use, on the date on which they first begin to be put to their new use.

(8) The amount of any sum payable under this section shall be determined in accordance with such arrangements—

(a) as may be agreed between the voluntary organisation by which the home is, at the relevant time, provided and the responsible authority or (as the case may be) the Secretary of State; or

(b) in default of agreement, as may be determined by the Secretary of State.

(9) With the agreement of the responsible authority or (as the case may be) the Secretary of State, the liability to pay any sum under this section may be discharged, in whole or in part, by the transfer of any premises.

(10) This section has effect regardless of—

(a) anything in any trust deed for a controlled or assisted community home;

(b) the provisions of any enactment or instrument governing the disposition of the property of a voluntary organisation.

DEFINITIONS

"appropriate compensation": s.58(1)–(4).
"assisted community home": s.53(5).
"controlled community home": s.53(4).
"community home": s.53(1).
"disposal": s.58(6).
"instrument of management": Sched. 4, Pt. I.
"local authority": s.105(1).
"premises": s.58(6).
"proprietor": s.58(6).
"relevant time": s.58(6).
"responsible authority": s.58(6).
"trust deed": s.55(6).
"voluntary organisation": s.105(1).

GENERAL NOTE

This re-enacts with substantial re-drafting C.C.A. 1980, s.44. It requires proprietors of controlled or assisted community homes which close, to repay any increase in the value of the premises which is attributable to the expenditure of public money ("the appropriate compensation") to the responsible authority or the Secretary of State. As under the 1980 Act, sums repaid to the Secretary of State under this section have to be paid to the Consolidated Fund s.106(2). Where a local authority receives a grant to provide secure accommodation somewhere other than in an assisted community home and the secure accommodation ceases to be used, the local authority must repay the grant (s. 82(3)). Voluntary organisations can receive grants from the Secretary of State for the establishment, maintenance or improvement of assisted community homes under s.82(4). There is a further power for the Secretary of State to provide special facilities in s.82(5).

PART VII

VOLUNTARY HOMES AND VOLUNTARY ORGANISATIONS

Provision of accommodation by voluntary organisations

59.—(1) Where a voluntary organisation provide accommodation for a child, they shall do so by—

(a) placing him (subject to subsection (2)) with—

(i) a family;

(ii) a relative of his; or

(iii) any other suitable person,

on such terms as to payment by the organisation and otherwise as the organisation may determine;

(b) maintaining him in a voluntary home;

(c) maintaining him in a community home;

(d) maintaining him in a registered children's home;

(e) maintaining him in a home provided by the Secretary of State under section 82(5) on such terms as the Secretary of State may from time to time determine; or

(f) making such other arrangements (subject to subsection (3)) as seem appropriate to them.

(2) The Secretary of State may make regulations as to the placing of children with foster parents by voluntary organisations and the regulations may, in particular, make provision which (with any necessary modifications) is similar to the provision that may be made under section 23(2)(a).

(3) The Secretary of State may make regulations as to the arrangements which may be made under subsection (1)(f) and the regulations may in particular make provision which (with any necessary modifications) is similar to the provision that may be made under section 23(2)(f).

(4) The Secretary of State may make regulations requiring any voluntary organisation who are providing accommodation for a child—

(a) to review his case;

(b) to consider any representations (including any complaint) made to them by any person falling within a prescribed class of person,

in accordance with the provisions of the regulations.

(5) Regulations under subsection (4) may in particular make provision which (with any necessary modifications) is similar to the provision that may be made under section 26.

(6) Regulations under subsection (2) to (4) may provide that any person who, without reasonable excuse, contravenes or fails to comply with a regulation shall be guilty of an offence and liable on summary conviction to a fine not exceeding level 4 on the standard scale.

DEFINITIONS

"child": 105(1).

"community home": s.53(1).

"registered children's home": s.63.

"relative": s.105(1).

"voluntary home": s.60(3).

"voluntary organisation": s.105(1).

GENERAL NOTE

This section sets out the powers of voluntary organisations to provide accommodation for children. It imposes equivalent duties on voluntary organisations as are imposed on local authorities by s.23. It empowers the Secretary of State to make regulations about boarding out (subs. (2)), placements generally (subs. (3)) and about reviews and complaints (subs. (4)). Voluntary organisations are likely to be required to set up complaints systems like those in s.26 for all their cases. Regulations may provide criminal penalties for their breach (subs. (6)).

The current Boarding Out of Children (Foster Care) Regulations 1988 apply to voluntary organisations, as do the Administr‚ation of Children's Homes Regulations 1951. Both these sets of regulations will be replaced; replacement regulations are likely to apply similarly to local authorities and voluntary organisations, so that neither the children nor their parents receive a lesser standard of consideration than children looked after by local authorities. Where a placement is arranged by a voluntary organisation for a child looked after by the local authority, the local authority will continue to be responsible for the placement (see ss.23 and 62(1)).

Registration and regulation of voluntary homes

60.—(1) No voluntary home shall be carried on unless it is registered in a register to be kept for the purposes of this section by the Secretary of State.

(2) The register may be kept by means of a computer.

(3) In this Act "voluntary home" means any home or other institution providing care and accommodation for children which is carried on by a voluntary organisation but does not include—
  (a) a nursing home, mental nursing home or residential care home;
  (b) a school;
  (c) any health service hospital;
  (d) any community home;
  (e) any home or other institution provided, equipped and maintained by the Secretary of State; or
  (f) any home which is exempted by regulations made for the purposes of this section by the Secretary of State.

(4) Schedule 5 shall have effect for the purposes of supplementing the provisions of this Part.

DEFINITIONS
"child": s.105(1).
"community home": s.53(1).
"health service hospital": s.105(1).
"mental nursing home": s.105(1).
"nursing home": s.105(1).
"residential care home": s.105(1).
"school": s.105(1).
"voluntary home": s.60(3).
"voluntary organisation": s.105(1).

GENERAL NOTE
This section requires voluntary homes, defined in subs. (3), to be registered by the Secretary of State, as previously under C.C.A. 1980, s.57(1). Provisions as to registration are included in Sched. 5.

The Secretary of State has a power to inspect premises where children are being accommodated by or on behalf of a voluntary organisation under s.80(1)(c) and the children under s.80(6). There are also powers in relation to other premises (see s.80 below). He may also direct a voluntary organisation to provide information under s.80(4) and (5).

The definition of voluntary home previously found in C.C.A. 1980, s.56, has been clarified. The intention is to provide a coherent code relating to all establishments and private homes (except those provided by the child's family or close relatives) and the care and welfare of all children living there. Where an establishment is a voluntary home the Secretary of State will be responsible for registration and inspection. Local authorities will be responsible for registration and inspection of registered children's homes (Pt. VIII of the Act), private foster homes (Pt. IX of the Act), nursing homes, mental nursing homes and residential care homes (all under the Registered Homes Act 1984). Local authorities will also have responsibilities for safeguarding the welfare of all children in such homes (ss.62, 64(4), 67 and 86) and also the welfare of children in independent schools (s.87) and children accommodated for a consecutive period of at least three months by a local education authority or health authority (s.85). Provision is made for community homes in Pt. VI and Sched. 4.

Pt. I of Sched. 5 contains the provisions relating to registration of voluntary homes previously found in C.C.A. 1980, ss.57(1)–(6), 57A–57D and 59. There are minor drafting amendments and the penalty for failure to notify the Secretary of State of the particulars required is raised from a level 1 to a level 2 offence (Sched. 5 para. 6(6)). Para. 7 empowers the Secretary of State to make regulations about voluntary homes and voluntary organisations. This expands on the powers under C.C.A. 1980, s.60, which applied the Administration of Children's Homes Regulations 1951 (S.I. No.1217) to such homes. The new power enables the Secretary of State to make regulations relating to discipline (para. 7(2)(c)). It is likely that corporal punishment will be banned in such establishments. It also enables the Secretary of State to prohibit voluntary organisations from providing secure accommodation (para. 7(2)(f)). There is no intention to allow such homes to provide this (*per* Baroness David (*Hansard,* H.L. Vol. 503, col. 499)). Para. 8 permits the Secretary of State to make regulations disqualifying people from involvement with voluntary homes. Such provision is made in relation to children's homes by s.65. The provisions relating to service of notices in C.C.A. 1980, s.57(8)–(11), are now found in s.105(8)–(10).

Duties of voluntary organisations

61.—(1) Where a child is accommodated by or on behalf of a voluntary organisation, it shall be the duty of the organisation—

(a) to safeguard and promote his welfare;

(b) to make such use of the services and facilities available for children cared for by their own parents as appears to the organisation reasonable in his case; and

(c) to advise, assist and befriend him with a view to promoting his welfare when he ceases to be so accommodated.

(2) Before making any decision with respect to any such child the organisation shall, so far as is reasonaly practicable, ascertain the wishes and feelings of—

(a) the child;

(b) his parents;

(c) any person who is not a parent of his but who has parental responsibility for him; and

(d) any other person whose wishes and feelings the organisation consider to be relevant,

regarding the matter to be decided.

(3) In making any such decision the organisation shall give due consideration—

(a) having regard to the child's age and understanding, to such wishes and feelings of his as they have been able to ascertain;

(b) to such other wishes and feelings mentioned in subsection (2) as they have been able to ascertain; and

(c) to the child's religious persuasion, racial origin and cultural and linguistic background.

DEFINITIONS

"child": s.105(1).

"person who is not a parent but has parental responsibility": ss.5(6), 12(2), 33(3), 44(4).

"voluntary organisation": s.105(1).

GENERAL NOTE

This section imposes comparable duties on voluntary organisations accommodating children to those required of local authorities under s.22(3)–(5) and s.24(1). This is broader and more specific than the duty in C.C.A. 1980, s.64A, which it replaces. Further duties may be imposed by regulations made under Sched. 5, para. 7.

Duties of local authorities

62.—(1) Every local authority shall satisfy themselves that any voluntary organisation providing accommodation—

(a) within the authority's area for any child; or

(b) outside that area for any child on behalf of the authority, are satisfactorily safeguarding and promoting the welfare of the children so provided with accommodation.

(2) Every local authority shall arrange for children who are accommodated within their area by or on behalf of voluntary organisations to be visited, from time to time, in the interests of their welfare.

(3) The Secretary of State may make regulations—

(a) requiring every child who is accommodated within a local authority's area, by or on behalf of a voluntary organisation, to be visited by an officer of the authority—

(i) in prescribed circumstances; and

(ii) on specified occasions or within specified periods; and

(b) imposing requirements which must be met by any local authority, or officer of a local authority, carrying out functions under this section.

(4) Subsection (2) does not apply in relation to community homes.

(5) Where a local authority are not satisfied that the welfare of any child who is accommodated by or on behalf of a voluntary organisation is being satisfactorily safeguarded or promoted they shall—

  (a) unless they consider that it would not be in the best interests of the child, take such steps as are reasonably practicable to secure that the care and accommodation of the child is undertaken by—

      (i) a parent of his;

      (ii) any person who is not a parent of his but who has parental responsibility for him; or

      (iii) a relative of his; and

  (b) consider the extent to which (if at all) they should exercise any of their functions with respect to the child.

(6) Any person authorised by a local authority may, for the purpose of enabling the authority to discharge their duties under this section—

  (a) enter, at any reasonable time, and inspect any premises in which children are being accommodated as mentioned in subsection (1) or (2);

  (b) inspect any children there;

  (c) require any person to furnish him with such records of a kind required to be kept by regulations made under paragraph 7 of Schedule 5 (in whatever form they are held), or allow him to inspect such records, as he may at any time direct.

(7) Any person exercising the power conferred by subsection (6) shall, if asked to do so, produce some duly authenticated document showing his authority to do so.

(8) Any person authorised to exercise the power to inspect records conferred by subsection (6)—

  (a) shall be entitled at any reasonable time to have access to, and inspect and check the operation of, any computer and any associated apparatus or material which is or has been in use in connection with the records in question; and

  (b) may require—

      (i) the person by whom or on whose behalf the computer is or has been so used; or

      (ii) any person having charge of, or otherwise concerned with the operation of, the computer, apparatus or material, to afford him such assistance as he may reasonably require.

(9) Any person who intentionally obstructs another in the exercise of any power conferred by subsection (6) or (8) shall be guilty of an offence and liable on summary conviction to a fine not exceeding level 3 on the standard scale.

DEFINITIONS

  "child": s.105(1).

  "community home": s.53(1).

  "functions": s.105(1).

  "local authority": s.105(1).

  "person who is not a parent but has parental responsibility": ss.5(6), 12(2), 33(3), 44(4).

  "relative": s.105(1).

  "voluntary organisation": s.105(1).

GENERAL NOTE

  This section specifies the duties of local authorities with respect to voluntary homes. It also applies, with the exception of subs. (3), to children's homes (see s.64(4)). It re-drafts and expands C.C.A. 1980, s.68.

  Local authorities have a duty to satisfy themselves that voluntary organisations providing accommodation within their area are satisfactorily safeguarding and promoting the welfare of the children (subs. (1)). They also have a duty to arrange for such children (except those in community homes (subs. (4)) to be visited in accordance with regulations made under subs. (3) (subs. (2)). (The welfare of children in community homes is catered for by the Community Homes Regulations 1972 and replacement regulations made under Sched. 4, para. 4.) These duties are additional to any they may owe under s.17 and Sched. 2, Pt. I, to children in need and under s.22 and Sched. 2, Pt. II to children accommodated in a voluntary home by or on behalf of a local authority. Subs. (5) imposes a qualified duty on the local authority to take action if a child's welfare is not being satisfactorily safeguarded. Where compulsory measures are necessary, the relevant powers are provided by Pts. IV and V of this Act. Subs. (6) gives the local authority a power to inspect premises, the children themselves and records in order to carry out its duties. Subs. (8) extends this to having access to computer facilities. Subs. (9) provides that it is an offence (summary conviction level 3 fine) intentionally to obstruct the exercise of the powers in subss. (6) or (8). A similar offence with a lower penalty existed in C.C.A. 1980, s.68(5). Local authorities are also under a duty to provide after-care for children accommodated by voluntary organisations under s.24(4). The voluntary organisation must notify the authority when a child over 16 leaves (s.24(12)).

Subs. (1)
   On behalf of the authority: Such a child would be a child looked after by the authority under s.22. The power to accommodate such a child by placing him in a voluntary home is provided in s.23(2)(c). Where the voluntary organisation arranges a foster placement for a child looked after by the local authority, the foster parent is a local authority foster parent under s.23(3), and the local authority has powers under the Boarding-Out Regulations 1988 (and their replacement).

Subs. (2)
   Visited: Unless the contrary is provided by regulations made under subs. (3), the visits need not be by an officer of the local authority. They may be by an employee of the voluntary organisation or a volunteer. The duties of the visitor may be specified in regulations.
   From time to time: These words were previously found in C.C.A. 1980, s.68(1). Local authority discretion will be curtailed by regulations made under subs. (3).

Subs. (5)
   This limited duty does not apply where the child is being accommodated on behalf of a local authority. In such cases the local authority owes more onerous duties under Pt. III, particularly s.22. If the child is in need the local authority will have other duties under Sched. 2.
   Not satisfied . . . being satisfactorily safeguarded: This is a lower threshold than the "significant harm" test in Pts. IV and V.
   Unless it would not be in the best interests of the child: This could cover situations where a mature child did not want to leave, where the parents or others were unwilling to provide a home or where any other home would be even less satisfactory. It would also allow a local authority to delay action until a convenient time, *e.g.* the end of the school year.
   Such steps as are reasonably practicable: This could include searching for the child's family.
   Consider the extent . . .: Once the local authority is aware that the child is suffering or is likely to suffer "significant harm" its duty under s.47 arises and it must, under s.47(4), obtain access to the child. It may then seek orders under Pts. IV or V.

Subs. (6)
   The comparable provision in C.C.A. 1980, s.68(2), was interpreted in Clarke Hall and Morrison 10th Edition, para. A 463, as not providing a right of entry without warrant. A warrant could be obtained under s.102 or attached to an emergency protection order under s.48(9).
   At any reasonable time: This is not defined. Any time when the children are up could be reasonable. Entry at other times would require an emergency protection order under s.44 and, if entry were refused, a warrant.

Subs. (9)
   Intentionally obstructs: The word "intentionally" has been added to the offence in C.C.A. 1980, s.68(5). Anything which makes it more difficult for a person to carry out his duty may amount to obstruction. (*Rice* v. *Connolly* [1966] 2 Q.B. 414).

PART VIII

REGISTERED CHILDREN'S HOMES

Children not to be cared for and accommodated in unregistered children's homes

63.—(1) No child shall be cared for and provided with accommodation in a children's home unless the home is registered under this Part.

(2) The register may be kept by means of a computer.

(3) For the purposes of this Part, "a children's home"—

    (a) means a home which provides (or usually provides or is intended to provide) care and accommodation wholly or mainly for more than three children at any one time; but

    (b) does not include a home which is exempted by or under any of the following provisions of this section or by regulations made for the purposes of this subsection by the Secretary of State.

(4) A child is not cared for and accommodated in a children's home when he is cared for and accommodated by—

    (a) a parent of his;

    (b) a person who is not a parent of his but who has parental responsibility for him; or

    (c) any relative of his.

(5) A home is not a children's home for the purposes of this Part if it is—

    (a) a community home;

    (b) a voluntary home;

    (c) a residential care home, nursing home or mental nursing home;

    (d) a health service hospital;

    (e) a home provided, equipped and maintained by the Secretary of State; or

    (f) a school (but subject to subsection (6)).

(6) An independent school is a children's home if—

    (a) it provides accommodation for not more than fifty children; and

    (b) it is not approved by the Secretary of State under section 11(3)(a) of the Education Act 1981.

(7) A child shall not be treated as cared for and accommodated in a children's home when—

    (a) any person mentioned in subsection (4)(a) or (b) is living at the home; or

    (b) the person caring for him is doing so in his personal capacity and not in the course of carrying out his duties in relation to the home.

(8) In this Act "a registered children's home" means a children's home registered under this Part.

(9) In this section "home" includes any institution.

(10) Where any child is at any time cared for and accommodated in a children's home which is not a registered children's home, the person carrying on the home shall be—

    (a) guilty of an offence; and

    (b) liable to a fine not exceeding level 5 on the standard scale,

unless he has a reasonable excuse.

(11) Schedule 6 shall have effect with respect to children's homes.

(12) Schedule 7 shall have effect for the purpose of setting out the circumstances in which a person may foster more than three children without being treated as carrying on a children's home.

DEFINITIONS
"child": s.105(1).
"children's home": s.63(3)–(9).
"community home": s.53(1).
"health service hospital": s.105(1).
"home": s.63(9).
"independent school": s.105(1).
"mental nursing home": s.105(1).
"nursing home": s.105(1).
"privately fostered child": s.66(1).
"registered children's home": s.63(8).
"residential care home": s.105(1).
"school": s.105(1).
"voluntary home": s.60(3).
"voluntary organisation": s.105(1).

GENERAL NOTE
All children's homes as defined in s.63(3)–(7) must now be registered with the local authority.

Subs. (4)–(7)
The definition of children's home is basically the same as that in the Children's Homes Act 1982, although there is some re-drafting, particularly in relation to schools. Under the 1982 Act there was no lower figure for the number of children and no power in the Secretary of State to exempt homes from registration (subs. (3)). Children cared for and accommodated by their own families (*i.e.* those listed in subs. (4)) are not cared for or accommodated in children's homes. Where the home is a children's home but a child lives there with a parent or person with parental responsibility, or is cared for by someone in a personal capacity, he is not treated as cared for, etc., in a children's home (subs. (7)) and thus the local authority's functions do not affect him.
More than three children: This should be read with Sched. 7 (see note on s.63(12) below). A home with less than three children is dealt with under Pt. IX, which provides for private foster homes.
An independent school: This is defined in the Education Act 1944 as "a school for five or more pupils which is not maintained by a local education authority or a school in respect of which grants are made . . .". Subs. (6) requires independent schools which are not approved to take children who have been statemented under the Education Act 1981, s.7, to register as children's homes if they accommodate not more than 50 children. A school which is required to register must continue to register even if the number of pupils changes (Sched. 6, para. 1(10)). Independent boarding schools which are exempted from registering as children's homes are subject to local authority inspection under s.87.

Subs. (10)
This offence (maximum penalty level 5 fine) is wider than that in Children's Homes Act 1982, s.2(2), because of the duty to register all children's homes. Also, foster homes which exceed the usual fostering limit are treated as children's homes (see note to Sched. 7).
Reasonable excuse: A person who fails to register and who has exceeded the usual fostering limit temporarily may have an excuse.

Subs. (11)
Sched. 6, Pt. I contains provisions about registration previously found in the Children's Homes Act 1982, ss.4–8. Children's homes must be registered by the person carrying on the home with the local authority in whose area the home is situated (para. 1(1)). Applications must be made in the prescribed manner (para. 1(2)). The local authority must comply with the requirements of any regulations concerning applications and be satisfied that the home complies with requirements in para. 2 and any regulations made under Sched. 6, Pt. II. Para. 3 makes provision for annual review of registration, Para. 4 for cancellation of registration. Paras. 5–7 deal with procedure and para. 8 provides for appeals to the Registered Homes Tribunal. If an application is refused or cancelled, no further application may be made for six months (para. 9). Pt. II empowers the Secretary of State to make regulations about the placement of children, their welfare and the conduct of children's homes. The power is identical to that in Sched. 5, para. 7(1), but the topics listed in para. 10(2) are slightly different. There is power to make regulations about discipline, to require information about visiting facilities to be provided, to prohibit the use of secure accommo-

dation and to require procedures for reviews and complaints. The Lord Chancellor indicated that there was no intention to let these private homes use secure accommodation (*Hansard*, H.L. Vol. 504, col. 336). Failure to comply with regulations without reasonable excuse may be made an offence (para. 10(3)).

Subs. (12)
Sched. 7 limits the number of children who may be fostered by any foster parent (including a private foster parent) to three, "the usual fostering limit" (para. 2), but does not prevent fostering a greater number who are all siblings (para. 3), or where the local authority for the foster parent's home area has given a written exemption (para. 4). "Siblings" is not defined and could include half brothers and sisters, step-brothers and sisters or even children brought up as brother and sister, *e.g.* cousins. Exemptions will apply to named children (para. 4(3)) but regulations may be made to provide for cases of urgency (para. 4(5)). If the number is exceeded, except where permitted, the person is treated as carrying on a children's home (para. 5) and must comply with Pt. VIII. Local authorities are required to establish procedures for the consideration of exemptions and must comply with any regulations about this. Regulations made under s.26 will apply to complaints by parents, children and local authority foster parents; local authorities must also provide for complaints by anyone seeking exemption (para. 6(1)). Private foster parents may appeal to the court under Sched. 7, para. 8(1)(e), against a refusal to grant an exemption.

Welfare of children in children's homes

64.—(1) Where a child is accommodated in a children's home, it shall be the duty of the person carrying on the home to—
(a) safeguard and promote the child's welfare;
(b) make such use of the services and facilities available for children cared for by their own parents as appears to that person reasonable in the case of the child; and
(c) advise, assist and befriend him with a view to promoting his welfare when he ceases to be so accommodated.
(2) Before making any decision with respect to any such child the person carrying on the home shall, so far as is reasonably practicable, ascertain the wishes and feelings of—
(a) the child;
(b) his parents;
(c) any other person who is not a parent of his but who has parental responsibility for him; and
(d) any person whose wishes and feelings the person carrying on the home considers to be relevant,
regarding the matter to be decided.
(3) In making any such decision the person concerned shall give due consideration—
(a) having regard to the child's age and understanding, to such wishes and feelings of his as he has been able to ascertain;
(b) to such other wishes and feelings mentioned in subsection (2) as he has been able to ascertain; and
(c) to the child's religious persuasion, racial origin and cultural and linguistic background.
(4) Section 62, except subsection (4), shall apply in relation to any person who is carrying on a children's home as it applies in relation to any voluntary organisation.

DEFINITIONS
"children's home": s.63.
"child": s.105(1).
"person who is not a parent but has parental responsibility": ss.5(6), 12(2), 33(3), 44(4).

GENERAL NOTE
This section imposes a duty on the person carrying on a children's home (even one which is not registered) to promote the child's welfare, etc. An identical duty exists for voluntary

organisations under s.61 and there are comparable duties on local authorities under Pt. III (see notes on those provisions, especially s.22). Subs. (4) applies s.62 (except s.62(4)) to children's homes. Thus local authorities have duties to satisfy themselves that the children's welfare is being safeguarded and to arrange for children to be visited. (See note to s.62). There was no comparable provision under the Children's Homes Act 1982, only a duty to inspect. Where the home is unregistered, it may be impossible for the local authority to carry out its duties. The local authority also has power to provide after-care for children who were accommodated in registered children's homes (s.24). The person carrying on the home must notify the local authority when a child over 16 leaves (s.24(12)).

Persons disqualified from carrying on, or being employed in, children's homes

65.—(1) A person who is disqualified (under section 68) from fostering a child privately shall not carry on, or be otherwise concerned in the management of, or have any financial interest in, a children's home unless he has—

(a) disclosed to the responsible authority the fact that he is so disqualified; and

(b) obtained their written consent.

(2) No person shall employ a person who is so disqualified in a children's home unless he has—

(a) disclosed to the responsible authority the fact that that person is so disqualified; and

(b) obtained their written consent.

(3) Where an authority refuse to give their consent under this section, they shall inform the applicant by a written notice which states—

(a) the reason for the refusal;

(b) the applicant's right to appeal against the refusal to a Registered Homes Tribunal under paragraph 8 of Schedule 6; and

(c) the time within which he may do so.

(4) Any person who contravenes subsection (1) or (2) shall be guilty of an offence and liable on summary conviction to imprisonment for a term not exceeding six months or to a fine not exceeding level 5 on the standard scale or to both.

(5) Where a person contravenes subsection (2) he shall not be guilty of an offence if he proves that he did not know, and had no reasonable grounds for believing, that the person whom he was employing was disqualified under section 68.

DEFINITIONS
"children's home": s.63.
"responsible authority": Sched. 6, para. 3(1).

GENERAL NOTE
This re-enacts with minor amendments the power to disqualify a person from carrying on, being employed or having a financial interest in a children's home, previously found in the Children's Homes Act 1982, s.10. The grounds for disqualification are found in regulations made under s.68 of this Act and also apply to disqualification from private fostering. The grounds for disqualification under the Foster Children Act 1980, s.7, were wider than those under s.10; it is likely that the new regulations applying to those involved in registered children's homes will also be wider. Where a person is disqualified, it is always open to him to seek the local authority's written consent. If consent is refused, an appeal may be made to the Registered Homes Tribunal (subs. (3)). The offence under subs. (4) is slightly different from that under s.10(4) in that where a person did not know that his employee had committed an offence, he will only be guilty if he could reasonably have known. At present local authorities can check the credentials of their employees and of people whose homes they register under the Act by arrangement with the police. There is no such provision for private individuals to check.

Subs. (3)

The time within which he may do so: No appeal may be brought more than 28 days after service of the notice (Sched. 6, para. 8(3)).

PART IX

PRIVATE ARRANGEMENTS FOR FOSTERING CHILDREN

Privately fostered children

66.—(1) In this Part—
  (a) "a privately fostered child" means a child who is under the age of sixteen and who is cared for, and provided with accommodation by, someone other than—
      (i) a parent of his;
      (ii) a person who is not a parent of his but who has parental responsibility for him; or
      (iii) a relative of his; and
  (b) "to foster a child privately" means to look after the child in circumstances in which he is a privately fostered child as defined by this section.

(2) A child is not a privately fostered child if the person caring for and accommodating him—
  (a) has done so for a period of less than 28 days; and
  (b) does not intend to do so for any longer period.

(3) Subsection (1) is subject to—
  (a) the provisions of section 63; and
  (b) the exceptions made by paragraphs 1 to 5 of Schedule 8.

(4) In the case of a child who is disabled, subsection (1)(a) shall have effect as if for "sixteen" there were substituted "eighteen".

(5) Schedule 8 shall have effect for the purposes of supplementing the provision made by this Part.

DEFINITIONS
  "disabled": ss.17(11), 105(1).
  "person who is not a parent . . . but has parental responsibility": ss.5(6), 12(2), 33(3), 44(1)(4).
  "privately fostered child": s.66(1).
  "relative": s.105(1).
  "to foster a child privately": s.66(1).

GENERAL NOTE
  This section contains the definition of a "privately fostered" child. It must be read with Sched. 7, paras. 2 and 5 and also with Sched. 8, paras. 1 and 2, which contain the exemptions. Children under 16, and those under 18 who are disabled (subs. (4)) come within the definition and the protection it entails. The definition seeks to exclude children living with their families (subs. (1)(a) and Sched. 8, para. 2(a)); children looked after by a local authority (Sched. 8, para. 1) and children whose welfare is secured because of the requirement to register the establishment in which they live and/or the duty of local authorities in respect of children in such establishments (Sched. 8, para. 2). These exceptions do not apply where a child is being cared for in such an establishment by someone living there in a personal capacity who does come within para. 1(a) (Sched. 8, para. 2(2)). Children are also exempted from the definition where the local authority has responsibility for their welfare under a supervision order, the Mental Health Act 1983 or the Adoption Act 1976 (Sched. 8, paras. 3–5). Some children accommodated in boarding schools are protected under *these* provisions rather than s.87. Where independent schools accommodate children in the holidays, Sched. 8, para. 9 applies most of the provisions relating to private fostering to them.

Subs. (2) sets down the time condition which excludes arrangements which are planned to and which actually do last for less than 28 days. Subs. (3) specifies that any child who falls outside both s.63 and Sched. 8, paras. 1–5, is a privately fostered child.

Sched. 8, para. 6, allows the appropriate local authority to impose requirements in circumstances where a person fosters privately or proposes to do so. These requirements are additional to the limit set by Sched. 7 (see s.63(12)). This is a redrafted version of s.9 of the Foster Children Act 1980 and the local authority must now give reasons for imposing a requirement (Sched. 8, para. 6(4)). Where a requirement is imposed, the local authority may also prohibit private fostering in accordance with s.69(3) and (5) if the requirement is not complied with in the specified period (s.69(6)). Sched. 8, para. 7 replaces ss. 4 to 6 of the Foster Children Act 1980. All the duties to notify depend on the Secretary of State making the necessary regulations. The Lord Chancellor indicated that regulations would be made (*Hansard,* H.L. Vol. 504, col. 339). No regulations were made under the previous Act. Regulations may require notification to the local authority by parents and people with parental responsibility who know of a proposed placement, private foster parents and third parties involved in the arrangements. At present, only private foster parents must notify their local authority. The regulations may also require parents, etc., to keep the local authority informed of their address, and private foster parents to disclose information about themselves, including any convictions and the names of people in their household. Sched. 8, para. 8, provides for appeals. It is wider than s.11 of the Foster Children Act 1980, which it replaces, and allows appeals against requirements imposed under Sched. 8, para. 6; appeal against the refusal of the local authority to consent to fostering by persons disqualified under s.68 or refusal to grant, etc., an exemption from the fostering limit in Sched. 7; and finally allows appeal against a refusal to cancel a prohibition under s.69. While an appeal is pending, the requirement condition or cancellation of an exemption is not effective (Sched. 8, para. 6(3)). Appeals must still be lodged within 14 days. They are currently heard by the juvenile court and will now be heard by the new "family proceedings court". The court may make or vary an exemption or impose a condition (para. 8(6)). Only private foster parents may appeal under this provision (para. 8(8)). Para. 10 contains the prohibition against advertising (currently provided for by s.15 of the Foster Children Act 1980) but there is no longer a power to make regulations in respect of such advertisements. Para. 11 precludes a private foster parent from insuring the life of a privately fostered child; it repeats s.19 of the Foster Children Act 1980.

Welfare of privately fostered children

67.—(1) It shall be the duty of every local authority to satisfy themselves that the welfare of children who are privately fostered within their area is being satisfactorily safeguarded and promoted and to secure that such advice is given to those caring for them as appears to the authority to be needed.

(2) The Secretary of State may make regulations—

(a) requiring every child who is privately fostered within a local authority's area to be visited by an officer of the authority—

(i) in prescribed circumstances; and

(ii) on specified occasions or within specified periods; and

(b) imposing requirements which are to be met by any local authority, or officer of a local authority, in carrying out functions under this section.

(3) Where any person who is authorised by a local authority to visit privately fostered children has reasonable cause to believe that—

(a) any privately fostered child is being accommodated in premises within the authority's area; or

(b) it is proposed to accommodate any such child in any such premises, he may at any reasonable time inspect those premises and any children there.

(4) Any person exercising the power under subsection (3) shall, if so required, produce some duly authenticated document showing his authority to do so.

(5) Where a local authority are not satisfied that the welfare of any child who is privately fostered within their area is being satisfactorily safeguarded or promoted they shall—

(a) unless they consider that it would not be in the best interests of the child, take such steps as are reasonably practicable to secure that the care and accommodation of the child is undertaken by—
(i) a parent of his;
(ii) any person who is not a parent of his but who has parental responsibility for him; or
(iii) a relative of his; and
(b) consider the extent to which (if at all) they should exercise any of their functions under this Act with respect to the child.

DEFINITIONS
"functions": s.105(1).
"local authority": s.105(1).
"person who is not a parent . . . but has parental responsibility": ss.5(6), 12(2).
"privately fostered child": s.66(1).
"relative": s.105(1).

GENERAL NOTE
This section states the duty of the local authority in respect of private fostering arrangements. There is a general duty for the local authority to satisfy itself of the welfare of privately fostered children and a new duty to secure that necessary advice is given to all carers (subs. (1)). There is no longer a duty to visit, but regulations may provide for this (subs. (2)). S.3(3) of the Foster Children Act 1980 provided a statutory duty to visit until regulations were made. Subss. (3) and (4) of this section contain the power to inspect previously in s.8 of the Foster Children Act 1980. Subs. (5) states the duty of the local authority in cases where they are not satisfied about the child's welfare. It is identical to s.62(5), which applies to care by voluntary organisations and in children's homes. The duty to notify in Sched. 8, para. 7, should ensure that the local authority is aware of many (but probably not all) children to whom it owes these duties. The local authority has power to provide after-care for privately fostered children (see notes to s.24).

Subs. (1)
Satisfactorily safeguarded: The standards and care in private foster homes are often markedly below what would be acceptable from a local authority foster parent. The local authority can do a number of things in these situations depending on the standard of care and the availability of alternatives. It must exercise its powers under subs. (5), but this could mean leaving the child in the foster home. In such cases, providing or arranging for advice may be appropriate. Only if the child is suffering or likely to suffer significant harm can the local authority take compulsory measures of care (ss.31 and 44). If the child is "in need" the authority will have further duties under Pt. III and Sched. 2, para. 10 and could offer to accommodate the child under s.20, or offer other services.

Subs. (3)
This does not give a right of entry without warrant (see note to s.62(6)). A warrant may be obtained under s.102 or if an emergency protection order is obtained under s.48(9).

Persons disqualified from being private foster parents

68.—(1) Unless he has disclosed the fact to the appropriate local authority and obtained their written consent, a person shall not foster a child privately if he is disqualified from doing so by regulations made by the Secretary of State for the purposes of this section.

(2) The regulations may, in particular, provide for a person to be so disqualified where—
(a) an order of a kind specified in the regulations has been made at any time with respect to him;
(b) an order of a kind so specified has been made at any time with respect to any child who has been in his care;
(c) a requirement of a kind so specified has been imposed at any time with respect to any such child, under or by virtue of any enactment;
(d) he has been convicted of any offence of a kind so specified, or has

been placed on probation or discharged absolutely or conditionally
for any such offence;
(e) a prohibition has been imposed on him at any time under section
69 or under any other specified enactment;
(f) his rights and powers with respect to a child have at any time been
vested in a specified authority under a specified enactment.
(3) Unless he has disclosed the fact to the appropriate local authority
and obtained their written consent, a person shall not foster a child
privately if—
(a) he lives in the same household as a person who is himself prevented
from fostering a child by subsection (1); or
(b) he lives in a household at which any such person is employed.
(4) Where an authority refuse to give their consent under this section,
they shall inform the applicant by a written notice which states—
(a) the reason for the refusal;
(b) the applicant's right under paragraph 8 of Schedule 8 to appeal
against the refusal; and
(c) the time within which he may do so.
(5) In this section—
"the appropriate authority" means the local authority within whose
area it is proposed to foster the child in question; and
"enactment" means any enactment having effect, at any time, in any
part of the United Kingdom.

DEFINITIONS
"appropriate authority": s.68(5).
"child": s.105(1).
"enactment": s.68(5).
"local authority": s.105(1).
"to foster a child privately": s.66(1).

GENERAL NOTE
This section disqualifies people in circumstances prescribed in regulations from involvement in private fostering without the consent of the appropriate local authority (subs. (1)).
The reasons for disqualification were formerly set out in s.7 of the Foster Children Act 1980
and covered people who had had children removed from them by a court order, those who
had lost parental rights by a local authority resolution, those who had had any children
removed by a local authority in exercise of powers under the adoption legislation, and
scheduled offenders (C.Y.P.A. 1933, Sched. 1). It is likely that similar provisions will appear
in regulations. The disqualification also applies where another person in the same household,
or an employee, comes within the regulations (subs. (3)). Where a local authority refuses its
consent under subss. (1) or (3) it must give reasons (subs. (4)). Sched. 8, para. 8 provides
a right of appeal against such a refusal. Fostering in contravention of this provision is an
offence (s.70(1)(d)), but if the disqualification does not relate to the foster parent, he has a
defence if he did not know and had no reasonable grounds for believing that the other
person was disqualified (s.70(2)).

Subs. (3)
Household: S.7(2) of the Foster Children Act 1980 used the word "premises", which
would seem to be wider than "household". A lodger who cooked and ate separately would
probably not be a member of the same household. In divorce law, household has been
explained in an abstract sense; it essentially refers to people held together by a particular
kind of tie (*Santos* v. *Santos* [1972] Fam. 247 at 262). Thus a married couple have been held
to be living in separate households where there has been an end of any life in common
(*Hopes* v. *Hopes* [1949] P.227). The explanation of the term household in s.1(2)(a) of the
C.Y.P.A. 1969 by Arnold P. in *R.* v. *Birmingham Juvenile Court* ex p. *S.* [1984] Fam. 93 is
not helpful here since it was concerned with whether three people could be considered to be
in the same household as another three people when there was only one person in common.
Employed: A non resident person who helped out for a share of fees might not be an
employee, only an independent contractor (see *Ready Mixed Concrete* v. *Minister of Pensions*
[1969] 2 Q.B. 497). A wide interpretation of employment would protect children but may
be considered inappropriate because of the penal liability in s.70.

Power to prohibit private fostering

69.—(1) This section applies where a person—
    (a) proposes to foster a child privately, or
    (b) is fostering a child privately.

(2) Where the local authority for the area within which the child is proposed to be, or is being, fostered are of the opinion that—
    (a) he is not a suitable person to foster a child;
    (b) the premises in which the child will be, or is being, accommodated are not suitable; or
    (c) it would be prejudicial to the welfare of the child for him to be, or continue to be, accommodated by that person in those premises,
the authority may impose a prohibition on him under subsection (3).

(3) A prohibition imposed on any person under this subsection may prohibit him from fostering privately—
    (a) any child in any premises within the area of the local authority; or
    (b) any child in premises specified in the prohibition;
    (c) a child identified in the prohibition, in premises specified in the prohibition.

(4) A local authority who have imposed a prohibition on any person under subsection (3) may, if they think fit, cancel the prohibition—
    (a) of their own motion; or
    (b) on an application made by that person,
if they are satisfied that the prohibition is no longer justified.

(5) Where a local authority impose a requirement on any person under paragraph 6 of Schedule 8, they may also impose a prohibition on him under subsection (3).

(6) Any prohibition imposed by virtue of subsection (5) shall not have effect unless—
    (a) the time specified for compliance with the requirement has expired; and
    (b) the requirement has not been complied with.

(7) A prohibition imposed under this section shall be imposed by notice in writing addressed to the person on whom it is imposed and informing him of—
    (a) the reason for imposing the prohibition;
    (b) his right under paragraph 8 of Schedule 8 to appeal against the prohibition; and
    (c) the time within which he may do so.

DEFINITIONS
    "child": s.66(4).
    "local authority": s. 105(1)
    "to foster a child privately": s.66(1).

GENERAL NOTE
    This section redrafts with some minor amendments the provisions of the Foster Children Act 1980, s.10. It permits the local authority to prohibit an individual from fostering a child privately on any of the grounds in subs. (2). The prohibition may be general (subs. (3)(a)), relate to specific premises (subs. (3)(b)) or apply only to a particular child at a particular place (subs. (3)(c)). Where a prohibition is applied, the local authority may cancel it if it is no longer justified (subs. (4)). A change in circumstances (required by s.10(3) of the Foster Children Act 1980) is no longer necessary. Where a prohibition is imposed, the local authority must give reasons. Sched. 8, para. 8 provides a right of appeal to be exercised within 14 days. Where a requirement is imposed under Sched. 8, para. 6, but not complied with, a prohibition may be added (subss. (5) and (6)). All prohibitions must be notified in writing with reasons (subs. (7)).

Offences

70.—(1) A person shall be guilty of an offence if—

(a) being required, under any provision made by or under this Part, to give any notice or information—

(i) he fails without reasonable excuse to give the notice within the time specified in that provision; or

(ii) he fails without reasonable excuse to give the information within a reasonable time; or

(iii) he makes, or causes or procures another person to make, any statement in the notice or information which he knows to be false or misleading in a material particular;

(b) he refuses to allow a privately fostered child to be visited by a duly authorised officer of a local authority;

(c) he intentionally obstructs another in the exercise of the power conferred by section 67(3);

(d) he contravenes section 68;

(e) he fails without reasonable excuse to comply with any requirement imposed by a local authority under this Part;

(f) he accommodates a privately fostered child in any premises in contravention of a prohibition imposed by a local authority under this Part;

(g) he knowingly causes to be published, or publishes, an advertisement which he knows contravenes paragraph 10 of Schedule 8.

(2) Where a person contravenes section 68(3), he shall not be guilty of an offence under this section if he proves that he did not know, and had no reasonable ground for believing, that any person to whom section 68(1) applied was living or employed in the premises in question.

(3) A person guilty of an offence under subsection (1)(a) shall be liable on summary conviction to a fine not exceeding level 5 on the standard scale.

(4) A person guilty of an offence under subsection (1)(b), (c) or (g) shall be liable on summary conviction to a fine not exceeding level 3 on the standard scale.

(5) A person guilty of an offence under subsection (1)(d) or (f) shall be liable on summary conviction to imprisonment for a term not exceeding six months, or to a fine not exceeding level 5 on the standard scale, or to both.

(6) A person guilty of an offence under subsection (1)(e) shall be liable on summary conviction to a fine not exceeding level 4 on the standard scale.

(7) If any person who is required, under any provision of this Part, to give a notice fails to give the notice within the time specified in that provision, proceedings for the offence may be brought at any time within six months from the date when evidence of the offence came to the knowledge of the local authority.

(8) Subsection (7) is not affected by anything in section 127(1) of the Magistrates' Courts Act 1980 (time limit for proceedings).

DEFINITIONS

"duly authorised officer": s.67(3), (4).

"local authority": s. 105(1).

"privately fostered child", "to foster a child privately": s. 66(1), (4).

GENERAL NOTE

This section lists the offences for breach of the provisions relating to private fostering. No new offences are created but the level of penalties is different from those in s.16 of the Foster Children Act 1980, and there are two new defences. First there is a defence of

"reasonable excuse" for the offence of failing to notify or provide information under
s.70(1)(a) and (e). Secondly there is a defence that the person "did not know and had no
reasonable ground for believing" for the offence in s.68(3) of failing to disclose the offences
of a disqualified person who is not the foster parent (subs. (2)).

PART X

CHILD MINDING AND DAY CARE FOR YOUNG CHILDREN

Registration

71.—(1) Every local authority shall keep a register of—
    (a) persons who act as child minders on domestic premises within
        the authority's area; and
    (b) persons who provide day care for children under the age of
        eight on premises (other than domestic premises) within that
        area.
(2) For the purposes of this Part—
    (a) a person acts as a child minder if—
        (i) he looks after one or more children under the age of
        eight, for reward; and
        (ii) the period, or the total of the periods, which he spends
        so looking after children in any day exceeds two hours; and
    (b) a person does not provide day care for children unless the
        period, or the total of the periods, during which children are
        looked after exceeds two hours in any day.
(3) Where a person provides day care for children under the age of
eight on different premises situated within the area of the same local
authority, that person shall be separately registered with respect to each
of those premises.
(4) A person who—
    (a) is the parent, or a relative, of a child;
    (b) has parental responsibility for a child; or
    (c) is a foster parent of a child,
does not act as a child minder for the purposes of this Part when looking
after that child.
(5) Where a person is employed as a nanny for a child, she does not act
as a child minder when looking after that child wholly or mainly in the
home of the person so employing her.
(6) Where a person is so employed by two different employers, she
does not act as a child minder when looking after any of the children
concerned wholly or mainly in the home of either of her employers.
(7) A local authority may refuse to register an applicant for registration
under subsection (1)(a) if they are satisfied that—
    (a) the applicant; or
    (b) any person looking after, or likely to be looking after, any children
        on any premises on which the applicant is, or is likely to be, child
        minding,
is not fit to look after children under the age of eight.
(8) A local authority may refuse to register an applicant for registration
under subsection (1)(a) if they are satisfied that—
    (a) any person living, or likely to be living, at any premises on which
        the applicant is, or is likely to be, child minding; or
    (b) any person employed, or likely to be employed, on those premises,
is not fit to be in the proximity of children under the age of eight.
(9) A local authority may refuse to register an applicant for registration
under subsection (1)(b) if they are satisfied that any person looking after,

or likely to be looking after, any children on the premises to which the application relates is not fit to look after children under the age of eight.

(10) A local authority may refuse to register an applicant for registration under subsection (1)(b) if they are satisfied that—

(a) any person living, or likely to be living, at the premises to which the application relates; or

(b) any person employed, or likely to be employed, on those premises,

is not fit to be in the proximity of children under the age of eight.

(11) A local authority may refuse to register an applicant for registration under this section if they are satisfied—

(a) in the case of an application under subsection (1)(a), that any premises on which the applicant is, or is likely to be, child minding; or

(b) in the case of an application under subsection (1)(b), that the premises to which the application relates,

are not fit to be used for looking after children under the age of eight, whether because of their condition or the condition of any equipment used on the premises or for any reason connected with their situation, construction or size.

(12) In this section—

"domestic premises" means any premises which are wholly or mainly used as a private dwelling;

"premises" includes any vehicle.

(13) For the purposes of this Part a person acts as a nanny for a child if she is employed to look after the child by—

(a) a parent of the child;

(b) a person who is not a parent of the child but who has parental responsibility for him; or

(c) a person who is a relative of the child and who has assumed responsibility for his care.

(14) For the purposes of this section, a person fosters a child if—

(a) he is a local authority foster parent in relation to the child;

(b) he is a foster parent with whom the child has been placed by a voluntary organisation; or

(c) he fosters the child privately.

(15) Any register kept under this section—

(a) shall be open to inspection by members of the public at all reasonable times; and

(b) may be kept by means of a computer.

(16) Schedule 9 shall have effect for the purpose of making further provision with respect to registration under this section including, in particular, further provision for exemption from the requirement to be registered and provision for disqualification.

DEFINITIONS

"child": s.71(2), (3).
"childminder": s.71(2)(a).
"day care": ss.18, 71(2)(b).
"domestic premises": s.71(12).
"fosters": s.71(14).
"local authority": s.105(1).
"nanny": s.71(13).
"parental responsibility": ss.2(1), (2), 5(6), 12(1), (2), 44(1), (4).
"premises": s.71(12).
"relative": s.105(1).

GENERAL NOTE

This section should be read with Sched. 9. Subs. (1) requires local authorities to keep two registers:— one of childminders (defined in subss. (2) and (4)–(6)) and the other of people providing day care (defined in subss. (2) and (3)). People need only register if they care for children under the age of eight, for more than two hours a day and, in the case of childminders, for reward (subs. (2)). Sched. 9, paras. 3–5 exempt most schools, residential homes which are covered by other registration provisions in the Act, N.H.S. hospitals, and occasional facilities, *i.e.* those available for less than six days in any year. Parents, relatives, people with parental responsibility, foster parents (subs. (4)) and nannies (including those shared between two families) (subss. (5) and (6)) are not required to register. Registrations must be made in accordance with Sched. 9, para. 1, and comply with any regulations made by the Secretary of State. A guidance circular will also be issued (*Hansard*, H.C. Vol. 158, col. 801). When a person is registered, he must be issued with a certificate stating his name, address and any requirements imposed on the registration (Sched. 9, para. 6). The local authority is required to register anyone who makes a proper application and pays the prescribed fee (para. 1(4)) unless the provisions of subss. (8) to (11) or Sched. 9, para. 2, apply. The authority may refuse to register the applicant if the applicant or any person looking after children on the same premises is not a fit person to look after children under the age of eight years (subss. (7) and (9)), or if any person living or employed at those premises is not a fit person to be in close proximity to such children (subss. (9) and (10)). A person who is disqualified by virtue of regulations made under Sched. 9, para. 2 may not be registered. Registration may also be refused where the premises or any equipment is unfit (subs. (11)). Local authorities must inspect registered premises at least once a year (s.76(4)) and charge a prescribed fee for this (Sched. 9, para. 7). The charging of fees for registration was a matter of considerable controversy during the debate at Report Stage in the Commons. The Minister undertook to set a low fee, no more than £10, for non profit-making organisations (*Hansard*, H.C. Vol. 158, col. 803). Sched. 9, para. 8, requires any local education authority who could help the local authority with its functions under Part X to do so, if requested.

Subs. (1)

This must be read in conjunction with subss. (4) to (6), (13), (14) and Sched. 9, paras. 3–5, which list the exceptions.

Subs. (2)

For reward: This is not defined but arguably requires an element of profit. If so, neighbours who care for each other's children on an exchange basis, even if they do so for over two hours, would not need to register, nor would those in baby-sitting schemes. There is no "reward" requirement for day care providers, thus all playgroups taking place outside the home must register.

Subs. (4)

Foster parent: This includes all types of foster parent and children placed with them for fostering (subs. (14)). If a foster parent also acts as a childminder for other children, a second registration will be required (David Mellor, Minister of Health (Standing Committee B, col. 393, June 6, 1989)).

Subss. (5) and (6)

The distinction between a nanny in a nanny-share arrangement and a childminder would seem to be a very fine one, turning on the nature of the contract between the parent and the carer. If A and B jointly employ C, sharing costs and having the control employers have, C will be a nanny. If A employs C and arranges for B's children to be cared for by C, C will be a nanny for A's children and a childminder for B's. If A and B enter into a contract with C to look after their children but do not employ her, she will be a childminder, even if she works in one of their houses.

Subss. (7)–(10)

Not fit to look after children: Sched. 9, para. 2, enables the Secretary of State to make regulations disqualifying people from registration under s.71, but the wording and the promise to issue guidance (David Mellor, Minister of Health (Standing Committee B, col. 393, June 6, 1989)) indicate that the local authority has a discretion to refuse to register others. It will need to be able to justify refusals (s.77(2)) and must act fairly (see *R.* v. *Norfolk County Council*, ex p. *M, The Times*, February 27, 1989). The fact that someone's name appears on the "at risk" register will not be sufficient to grant a refusal if it results from an unfair and one-sided procedure.

Not fit to be in the proximity of children under the age of eight: Where the person is not involved in the care of the children, the conduct or circumstances justifying refusal to register a childminder or day care provider should be more serious. However, the behaviour need not be culpable, *e.g.* very disturbing or violent behaviour resulting from mental illness or infirmity may be sufficient.

Living at premises: This does not mean household. Where a lodger lived on the premises, *i.e.* not in a separate self-contained flat, his presence could justify refusal to register (*cf.* registration to foster children privately (s.68(3))). A person living in the same household as a disqualified person is automatically disqualified unless they disclose the fact to the local authority and obtain their consent (Sched. 9, para. 2(3)).

Employed: See note to s.68(2).

Subs. (11)

The premises . . . are not fit: This requirement covers aspects of safety—fire guards, stair gates, window locks, etc., as well as the size and situation of the premises. Registration could be refused where planning permission had not been obtained or a restrictive covenant precluded use.

Subs. (13)

Assumed responsibility for his care: This concept does not appear elsewhere in the Act. It would seem to require the parent giving up responsibility in practice but not in law. (See s.3).

Requirements to be complied with by child minders

72.—(1) Where a local authority register a person under section 71(1)(a), they shall impose such reasonable requirements on him as they consider appropriate in his case.

(2) In imposing requirements on him, the authority shall—

    (a) specify the maximum number of children, or the maximum number of children within specified age groups, whom he may look after when acting as a child minder;

    (b) require him to secure that any premises on which he so looks after any child, and the equipment used in those premises, are adequately maintained and kept safe;

    (c) require him to keep a record of the name and address of—

        (i) any child so looked after by him on any premises within the authority's area;

        (ii) any person who assists in looking after any such child; and

        (iii) any person living, or likely at any time to be living, at those premises;

    (d) require him to notify the authority in writing of any change in the persons mentioned in paragraph (c)(ii) and (iii).

(3) The Secretary of State may by regulations make provision as to—

    (a) requirements which must be imposed by local authorities under this section in prescribed circumstances;

    (b) requirements of such descriptions as may be prescribed which must not be imposed by local authorities under this section.

(4) In determining the maximum number of children to be specified under subsection (2)(a), the authority shall take account of the number of other children who may at any time be on any premises on which the person concerned acts, or is likely to act, as a child minder.

(5) Where, in addition to the requirements mentioned in subsection (2), a local authority impose other requirements, those other requirements must not be incompatible with any of the subsection (2) requirements.

(6) A local authority may at any time vary any requirement imposed under this section, impose any additional requirement or remove any requirement.

DEFINITIONS
  "child": ss.71(2), 105(1).
  "childminder": s.71(2)(a).
  "local authority": s.105(1).
  "premises": s.71(12).

GENERAL NOTE

This section requires local authorities to impose reasonable requirements on registrations of childminders under s.71(1)(a), relating to first, the maximum number of children within specified age groups, second, the safety of premises and equipment, third, the keeping of records of the children, any assistants and anyone living at the premises and fourth, notification of any changes in the assistants or the occupants of the premises (subss. (1) and (2)). It empowers the Secretary of State to make regulations imposing or banning specific requirements. Other requirements may be imposed so long as they are not incompatible with those in subs. (2) or contrary to regulations made under subs. (3). Requirements may be varied or removed (subs. (6)). When specifying the number of children, the authority must take account of other children at the premises, *i.e.* the minder's own children and those of others living there (subs. (4)).

The important difference between these clauses and the present law is that local authorities will now have to impose requirements with which the registered person will have to comply, but the local authorities will also have the scope to add other conditions. At present there is no obligation to impose conditions at all, but if the local authority decides to do so, it may only apply those listed in the Act (David Mellor, Minister of Health (Standing Committee B col. 394, June 6, 1989)). The authority must give reasons for imposing its requirements (s.77(2)) and must act reasonably (subs. 1) and the *Wednesbury* principle applies. Appeals may be made to the court against requirements (s.77(6)).

Requirements to be complied with by persons providing day care for young children

73.—(1) Where a local authority register a person under section 71(1)(b) they shall impose such reasonable requirements on him as they consider appropriate in his case.

(2) Where a person is registered under section 71(1)(b) with respect to different premises within the area of the same authority, this section applies separately in relation to each registration.

(3) In imposing requirements on him, the authority shall—

  (a) specify the maximum number of children, or the maximum number of children within specified age groups, who may be looked after on the premises;

  (b) require him to secure that the premises, and the equipment used in them, are adequately maintained and kept safe;

  (c) require him to notify the authority of any change in the facilities which he provides or in the period during which he provides them;

  (d) specify the number of persons required to assist in looking after children on the premises;

  (e) require him to keep a record of the name and address of—

    (i) any child looked after on the registered premises;

    (ii) any person who assists in looking after any such child; and

    (iii) any person who lives, or is likely at any time to be living, at those premises;

  (f) require him to notify the authority of any change in the persons mentioned in paragraph (e)(ii) and (iii).

(4) The Secretary of State may by regulations make provision as to—

  (a) requirements which must be imposed by local authorities under this section in prescribed circumstances;

  (b) requirements of such descriptions as may be prescribed which must not be imposed by local authorities under this section.

(5) In subsection (3), references to children looked after are to children looked after in accordance with the provision of day care made by the registered person.

(6) In determining the maximum number of children to be specified under subsection (3)(a), the authority shall take account of the number of other children who may at any time be on the premises.

(7) Where, in addition to the requirements mentioned in subsection (3), a local authority impose other requirements, those other requirements must not be incompatible with any of the subsection (3) requirements.

(8) A local authority may at any time vary any requirement imposed under this section, impose any additional requirement or remove any requirement.

DEFINITIONS
"child": ss.71(2)(3), 105(1).
"children looked after": s.73(5).
"day care": ss.18, 71(2)(b).
"local authority": s.105(1).
"premises": s.71(12).

GENERAL NOTE
This section requires local authorities to impose conditions on the registration of day care providers under s.71(1)(b). It provides comparable power to s.72. The same types of requirement must be imposed as under s.72(2), but additionally the local authority must require the registered person to notify the authority of changes in the facilities offered and specify the number of assistants (subs. (3)). The Secretary of State may make regulations about requirements (subs. (4)). The local authority also has a power to vary and to impose other requirements (subss. (7) and (8)). Where a day care provider is registered in respect of more than one set of premises under s.71(3), these provisions apply separately to each set of premises (subs. (2)). An appeal may be made against the imposition of a requirement under s.77.

Cancellation of registration

74.—(1) A local authority may at any time cancel the registration of any person under section 71(1)(a) if—
(a) it appears to them that the circumstances of the case are such that they would be justified in refusing to register that person as a child minder;
(b) the care provided by that person when looking after any child as a child minder is, in the opinion of the authority, seriously inadequate having regard to the needs of that child; or
(c) that person has—
(i) contravened, or failed to comply with, any requirement imposed on him under section 72; or
(ii) failed to pay any annual fee under paragraph 7 of Schedule 9 within the prescribed time.

(2) A local authority may at any time cancel the registration of any person under section 71(1)(b) with respect to particular premises if—
(a) it appears to them that the circumstances of the case are such that they would be justified in refusing to register that person with respect to those premises;
(b) the day care provided by that person on those premises is, in the opinion of the authority, seriously inadequate having regard to the needs of the children concerned; or
(c) that person has—
(i) contravened, or failed to comply with, any requirement imposed on him under section 73; or
(ii) failed to pay any annual fee under paragraph 7 of Schedule 9 within the prescribed time.

(3) A local authority may at any time cancel all registrations of any person under section 71(1)(b) if it appears to them that the circumstances of the case are such that they would be justified in refusing to register that person with respect to any premises.

(4) Where a requirement to carry out repairs or make alterations or additions has been imposed on a registered person under section 72 or 73, his registration shall not be cancelled on the ground that the premises are not fit to be used for looking after children if—

(a) the time set for complying with the requirements has not expired, and

(b) it is shown that the condition of the premises is due to the repairs not having been carried out or the alterations or additions not having been made.

(5) Any cancellation under this section must be in writing.

(6) In considering the needs of any child for the purposes of subsection (1)(b) or (2)(b), a local authority shall, in particular, have regard to the child's religious persuasion, racial origin and cultural and linguistic background.

DEFINITIONS

"child": ss.71(2), (3), 105(1).
"child minder": s.71(2)(a).
"day care": ss.18, 71(2)(b).
"local authority": s.105(1).
"premises": s.71(12).

GENERAL NOTE

This section empowers local authorities to cancel the registration of childminders and day care providers (subss. (1) and (2)). Cancellations must be notified in writing (subs. (5)) with reasons (s.77(2)) and can be appealed to the court (s.77(6)). S.75 provides a separate power to obtain a court order cancelling a registration in an emergency. A childminder's registration may be cancelled if, first, circumstances justify refusing to register that person (s.71(7) and (8)), second, the care provided is "seriously inadequate" or third, the childminder has contravened or failed to comply with a requirement imposed under s.72, or failed to pay the annual fee. Comparable grounds justify the cancellation of the registration of a day care provider (subss. (2) and (3)). Registrations may not be cancelled on the grounds that the premises are not fit where repairs, alterations or adaptations to the premises have been required, if the time set for complying has not expired and the condition of the premises is due to this (subs. (4)).

Subss. (1) and (2)

Seriously inadequate: It is not clear how far down the scale care has to be before it becomes seriously inadequate. Arguably, higher quality care should be required of people registered under s.71, than is required of parents, before a child can be removed under s.31 because, unlike parents, there is no overpowering reason to recognise and protect the status of the childminder or day-care provider. Also, a further intervention is provided for in cases of significant harm under s.75. Poor supervision which leads or might lead to minor injuries to the children concerned, poor hygiene, insufficient heat or light, may all produce inadequate care, which could be serious for the children if it continued. Local authorities may find it easier to cancel registrations if they seek to rely on other grounds in addition to that in subs. (4)(b), for example failure to comply with a requirement. Where there is a concern about the quality of care, voluntary assistance could be provided, or even a requirement imposed under ss.72 or 73 in an attempt to raise the standard of care.

Having regard to the needs of that child: Care may not be seriously inadequate for all children on the premises. Regard must be had to the child's religious persuasion, racial origin and cultural and linguistic background in determining his needs (subs. (6)). Although care may not be considered seriously inadequate because it is by a member of a different ethnic group, if the carer is unable to communicate with the child, fails to provide food acceptable to the diet followed by the child, or denigrates the child's cultural heritage, it could be so.

Protection of children in an emergency

75.—(1) If—
  (a) a local authority apply to the court for an order—
      (i) cancelling a registered person's registration;
      (ii) varying any requirement imposed on a registered person under section 72 or 73; or
      (iii) removing a requirement or imposing an additional requirement on such a person; and
  (b) it appears to the court that a child who is being, or may be, looked after by that person, or (as the case may be) in accordance with the provision for day care made by that person, is suffering, or is likely to suffer, significant harm,
the court may make the order.

(2) Any such cancellation, variation, removal or imposition shall have effect from the date on which the order is made.

(3) An application under subsection (1) may be made *ex parte* and shall be supported by a written statement of the authority's reasons for making it.

(4) Where an order is made under this section, the authority shall serve on the registered person, as soon as is reasonably practicable after the making of the order—
  (a) notice of the order and of its terms; and
  (b) a copy of the statement of the authority's reasons which supported their application for the order.

(5) Where the court imposes or varies any requirement under subsection (1), the requirement, or the requirement as varied, shall be treated for all purposes, other than those of section 77, as if it had been imposed under section 72 or (as the case may be) 73 by the authority concerned.

DEFINITIONS
  "child": ss.71(2), (3), 105(1).
  "court": s.92(7).
  "day care": ss.18, 71(2)(b).
  "significant harm": s.31(9), (10).

GENERAL NOTE
  This section enables local authorities to apply to the court for orders cancelling a registration or changing the requirements imposed on a registered person (subs. (1)). The court may make the order if it appears that a child who is being looked after by a registered person is suffering, etc., significant harm. Orders may be made *ex parte* and must be supported by a written statement of the authority's reasons (subs. (3)). Orders have effect from the day when they are made (subs. (2)) and must be served on the registered person with the written reasons as soon as reasonably practicable (subs. (4)). There is no further appeal against a requirement, varied or imposed by the court, under this section (subs. (5)). The order does not give the authority any rights over the child, but they could accommodate him under s.20(1)(c). This power is additional to those under Pts. IV and V which might be necessary to protect the carer's own children.

Subs. (1)
  Appears to the court: *i.e.* on the balance of probabilities. The wording may suggest a lower standard of proof than that for an emergency protection order under s.44 where the court must "be satisfied".

Inspection

76.—(1) Any person authorised to do so by a local authority may at any reasonable time enter—
  (a) any domestic premises within the authority's area on which child minding is at any time carried on; or

(b) any premises within their area on which day care for children under the age of eight is at any time provided.

(2) Where a local authority have reasonable cause to believe that a child is being looked after on any premises within their area in contravention of this Part, any person authorised to do so by the authority may enter those premises at any reasonable time.

(3) Any person entering premises under this section may inspect—
    (a) the premises;
    (b) any children being looked after on the premises;
    (c) the arrangements made for their welfare; and
    (d) any records relating to them which are kept as a result of this Part.

(4) Every local authority shall exercise their power to inspect the premises mentioned in subsection (1) at least once every year.

(5) Any person inspecting any records under this section—
    (a) shall be entitled at any reasonable time to have access to, and inspect and check the operation of, any computer and any associated apparatus or material which is, or has been, in use in connection with the records in question; and
    (b) may require—
        (i) the person by whom or on whose behalf the computer is or has been so used; or
        (ii) any person having charge of, or otherwise concerned with the operation of, the computer, apparatus or material,
    to afford him such reasonable assistance as he may require.

(6) A person exercising any power conferred by this section shall, if so required, produce some duly authenticated document showing his authority to do so.

(7) Any person who intentionally obstructs another in the exercise of any such power shall be guilty of an offence and liable on summary conviction to a fine not exceeding level 3 on the standard scale.

DEFINITIONS
    "child": ss.71(2), (3), 105(1).
    "childminder": s.71(2)(a).
    "court": s.92(7).
    "day care": ss.18, 71(2)(a).
    "domestic premises": s.71(12).
    "local authority": s.105(1).
    "premises": s.71(12).

GENERAL NOTE
This section gives the local authority comparable powers of entry and inspection of premises used for childminding or day care as it has under ss.62 to 67 in relation to voluntary homes, children's homes and premises used for private fostering. It also requires the authority to inspect such premises at least once a year (subs. (4)). Authorised officers of the local authority are empowered to enter premises to inspect the premises (subss. (1) and (2)), any children being looked after there, the arrangements for the welfare of those children and the required records (sub. (3)). Where records are computerised, the assistance of the computer's operator can be required (sub. (5)). An offence is committed by anyone who intentionally obstructs the exercise of the power. Where entry is refused, a warrant can be obtained under s.102(6) or if an emergency protection order is obtained, under s.44 or s.48(9).

Subss. (1) and (2)
Any premises may be entered where the local authority has reasonable cause to believe there has been a breach of the registration requirement or any of its terms.

Reasonable time: It would be reasonable to enter at any time when minding or day care was being carried out.

May enter: See discussion of s.62(6).

Subs. (3)

Any child looked after: There is no power to inspect other children, but a social worker could request permission from the person with parental responsibility. If permission were refused, information about the state of the minded children might help convince the court of the need to make a child assessment order or an emergency protection order.

Subs. (4)

This is intended to be a minimum requirement. "Guidance . . . will make it clear that annual inspection is a minimum" (David Mellor, Minister of Health (Standing Committee B, col. 394, June 6, 1989)).

Appeals

77.—(1) Not less than 14 days before—

    (a) refusing an application for registration under section 71;

    (b) cancelling any such registration;

    (c) refusing consent under paragraph 2 of Schedule 9;

    (d) imposing, removing or varying any requirement under section 72 or 73; or

    (e) refusing to grant any application for the variation or removal of any such requirement,

the authority concerned shall send to the applicant, or (as the case may be) registered person, notice in writing of their intention to take the step in question ("the step").

(2) Every such notice shall—

    (a) give the authority's reasons for proposing to take the step; and

    (b) inform the person concerned of his rights under this section.

(3) Where the recipient of such a notice informs the authority in writing of his desire to object to the step being taken, the authority shall afford him an opportunity to do so.

(4) Any objection made under subsection (3) may be made in person or by a representative.

(5) If the authority, after giving the person concerned an opportunity to object to the step being taken, decide nevertheless to take it they shall send him written notice of their decision.

(6) A person aggrieved by the taking of any step mentioned in subsection (1) may appeal against it to the court.

(7) Where the court imposes or varies any requirement under subsection (8) or (9) the requirement, or the requirement as varied, shall be treated for all purposes (other than this section) as if it had been imposed by the authority concerned.

(8) Where the court allows an appeal against the refusal or cancellation of any registration under section 71 it may impose requirements under section 72 or (as the case may be) 73.

(9) Where the court allows an appeal against such a requirement it may, instead of cancelling the requirement, vary it.

(10) In Scotland, an appeal under subsection (6) shall be by summary application to the sheriff and shall be brought within 21 days from the date of the step to which the appeal relates.

(11) A step of a kind mentioned in subsection (1)(b) or (d) shall not take effect until the expiry of the time within which an appeal may be brought under this section or, where such an appeal is brought, before its determination.

DEFINITIONS

    "notice": ss.77(2), 105(8)–(10).

    "the step": s.77(1).

GENERAL NOTE

This section provides appeal rights to those whose application has been refused or cancelled and also rights of appeal against requirements in registrations (subs. (1)). 14 days before taking the proposed action ("the step") the local authority must notify the applicant in writing of their intentions, the reasons for them and the applicant's rights of appeal (subs. (2)). Where the applicant informs the authority that he objects to the proposed action, the authority must give him an opportunity to do so (subss. (3) and (4)) and may still decide afterwards to take the action (subs. (5)). A person aggrieved may appeal to the court (subs. (6)). The court may impose or vary requirements when granting an appeal (subss. (7) and (8)). A requirement imposed by the court may not be subject to further appeal (subs. (9)). Where the authority is proposing (or refusing) to change the requirements the status quo is maintained until the expiry of the time limit for appealing or the hearing of the appeal (subs. (11)). In Scotland, cases under the Nurseries and Childminders Regulation Act 1948 were heard by the Sheriff. This will continue under subs. (10). In England, cases will be heard in the family proceedings court (s.92). In addition, if the local authority has acted improperly, a case could be made for Judicial Review.

Offences

78.—(1) No person shall provide day care for children under the age of eight on any premises within the area of a local authority unless he is registered by the authority under section 71(1)(b) with respect to those premises.

(2) If any person contravenes subsection (1) without reasonable excuse, he shall be guilty of an offence.

(3) No person shall act as a child minder on domestic premises within the area of a local authority unless he is registered by the authority under section 71(1)(a).

(4) Where it appears to a local authority that a person has contravened subsection (3), they may serve a notice ("an enforcement notice") on him.

(5) An enforcement notice shall have effect for a period of one year beginning with the date on which it is served.

(6) If a person with respect to whom an enforcement notice is in force contravenes subsection (3) without reasonable excuse he shall be guilty of an offence.

(7) Subsection (6) applies whether or not the subsequent contravention occurs within the area of the authority who served the enforcement notice.

(8) Any person who without reasonable excuse contravenes, or otherwise fails to comply with, any requirement imposed on him under section 72 or 73 shall be guilty of an offence.

(9) If any person—

    (a) acts as a child minder on domestic premises at any time when he is disqualified by regulations made under paragraph 2 of Schedule 9; or

    (b) contravenes any of sub-paragraphs (3) to (5) of paragraph 2,

he shall be guilty of an offence.

(10) Where a person contravenes sub-paragraph (3) of paragraph 2 he shall not be guilty of an offence under this section if he proves that he did not know, and had no reasonable grounds for believing, that the person in question was living or employed in the household.

(11) Where a person contravenes sub-paragraph (5) of paragraph 2 he shall not be guilty of an offence under this section if he proves that he did not know, and had no reasonable grounds for believing, that the person whom he was employing was disqualified.

(12) A person guilty of an offence under this section shall be liable on summary conviction—

    (a) in the case of an offence under subsection (8), to a fine not exceeding level 4 on the standard scale;

    (b) in the case of an offence under subsection (9), to imprisonment for a term not exceeding six months, or to a fine not exceeding level 5 on the standard scale, or to both; and

    (c) in the case of any other offence, to a fine not exceeding level 5 on the standard scale.

DEFINITIONS

"child": ss.71(2), (3), 105(1).
"childminder": s.71(2)(a).
"day care": ss.18, 71(2)(b).
"domestic premises": s.71(12).
"enforcement notice": s.78(4).
"local authority": s.105(1).
"premises": s.71(12)

GENERAL NOTE

This section lists the offences for failure to comply with this Part and provides a simple enforcement notice procedure where a childminder fails to register. The offences are as follows:—

(1) Providing, without reasonable excuse, day care at premises for children under the age of eight without registering with the local authority (subs. (2)). Penalty: fine level 5 (subs. (12)(c)).

(2) Childminding anywhere in breach of an enforcement notice (subs. (6)). Penalty: fine level 5 (subs. (12)(c)).

(3) Failing, without reasonable excuse, to comply with requirements imposed under ss.12 and 13 (subs. (8)). Penalty: fine level 4 (subs. (12)(a)).

(4) Childminding when disqualified (subs. (9)). Penalty: fine level 5 and/or six months' imprisonment (subs. (12)(b)).

All offences are triable summarily (subs. (12)). The defences of lack of knowledge, etc. (subs. (10) and (11)) are new and also apply to the comparable offences under s.70(1)(d), which applies to private fostering.

Enforcement notices can be served on anyone who acts as a childminder without registering (subs. (4)) and are effective for one year (subs. (5)). It is only an offence to carry on unregistered childminding if an enforcement notice has been served, but the offence is committed even if the minding occurs in another area (subs. (7)). Once a notice has been served, a person can only lawfully carry out childminding by registering in accordance with s.71(1)(a). The fact of previous unregistered minding should not mean that the person is necessarily unfit to mind within s.71(7) but may do so. Unregistered minding has in the past been very common, but the standard in such homes has given cause for concern (see B & S Jackson *Child minder—A Study in Action Research* (1979) Routledge).

Application of this Part to Scotland

79. In the application to Scotland of this Part—

(a) "the court" means the sheriff;

(b) "day care" means any form of care or of activity supervised by a responsible person provided for children during the day (whether or not it is provided on a regular basis);

(c) "education authority" has the same meaning as in the Education (Scotland) Act 1980;

(d) "local authority foster parent" means a foster parent with whom a child is placed by a local authority;

(e) for references to a person having parental responsibility for a child there shall be substituted references to a person in whom parental rights and duties relating to the child are vested; and

(f) for references to fostering a child privately there shall be substituted references to maintaining a foster child within the meaning of the Foster Children (Scotland) Act 1984.

GENERAL NOTE

This section amends definitions in Part X so that it may apply to Scotland.

PART XI

SECRETARY OF STATE'S SUPERVISORY FUNCTIONS AND RESPONSIBILITIES

Inspection of children's homes etc. by persons authorised by Secretary of State.

80.—(1) The Secretary of State may cause to be inspected from time to time any—

(a) children's home;

(b) premises in which a child who is being looked after by a local authority is living;

(c) premises in which a child who is being accommodated by or on behalf of a local education authority or voluntary organisation is living;

(d) premises in which a child who is being accommodated by or on behalf of a health authority is living;

(e) premises in which a child is living with a person with whom he has been placed by an adoption agency;

(f) premises in which a child who is a protected child is, or will be, living;

(g) premises in which a privately fostered child, or child who is treated as a foster child by virtue of paragraph 9 of Schedule 8, is living or in which it is proposed that he will live;

(h) premises on which any person is acting as a child minder;

(i) premises with respect to which a person is registered under section 71(1)(b);

(j) residential care home, nursing home or mental nursing home required to be registered under the Registered Homes Act 1984 and used to accommodate children;

(k) premises which are provided by a local authority and in which any service is provided by that authority under Part III;

(l) independent school providing accommodation for any child;

(2) An inspection under this section shall be conducted by a person authorised to do so by the Secretary of State.

(3) An officer of a local authority shall not be so authorised except with the consent of that authority.

(4) The Secretary of State may require any person of a kind mentioned in subsection (5) to furnish him with such information, or allow him to inspect such records (in whatever form they are held), relating to—

(a) any premises to which subsection (1) or, in relation to Scotland, subsection (1)(h) or (i) applies;

(b) any child who is living in any such premises;

(c) the discharge by the Secretary of State of any of his functions under this Act; or

(d) the discharge by any local authority of any of their functions under this Act,

as the Secretary of State may at any time direct.

(5) The persons are any—

(a) local authority;

(b) voluntary organisation;

(c) person carrying on a children's home;

(d) proprietor of an independent school;

(e) person fostering any privately fostered child or providing accommodation for a child on behalf of a local authority, local education authority, health authority or voluntary organisation;

(f) local education authority providing accommodation for any child;

(g) person employed in a teaching or administrative capacity at any educational establishment (whether or not maintained by a local education authority) at which a child is accommodated on behalf of a local authority or local education authority;

(h) person who is the occupier of any premises in which any person acts as a child minder (within the meaning of Part X) or provides day care for young children (within the meaning of that Part);

(i) person carrying on any home of a kind mentioned in subsection (1)(j).

(6) Any person inspecting any home or other premises under this section may—

(a) inspect the children there; and

(b) make such examination into the state and management of the home or premises and the treatment of the children there as he thinks fit.

(7) Any person authorised by the Secretary of State to exercise the power to inspect records conferred by subsection (4)—

(a) shall be entitled at any reasonable time to have access to, and inspect and check the operation of, any computer and any associated apparatus or material which is or has been in use in connection with the records in question; and

(b) may require—

(i) the person by whom or on whose behalf the computer is or has been so used; or

(ii) any person having charge of, or otherwise concerned with the operation of, the computer, apparatus or material,

to afford him such reasonable assistance as he may require.

(8) A person authorised to inspect any premises under this section shall have a right to enter the premises for that purpose, and for any purpose specified in subsection (4), at any reasonable time.

(9) Any person exercising that power shall, if so required, produce some duly authenticated document showing his authority to do so.

(10) Any person who intentionally obstructs another in the exercise of that power shall be guilty of an offence and liable on summary conviction to a fine not exceeding level 3 on the standard scale.

(11) The Secretary of State may by order provide for subsections (1), (4) and (6) not to apply in relation to such homes, or other premises, as may be specified in the order.

(12) Without prejudice to section 104, any such order may make different provision with respect to each of those subsections.

DEFINITIONS

"adoption agency": s.105(1).
"child": s.105(1).
"childminder": s.71.
"child . . . looked after by a local authority": s.22(1).
"children's home": s.63.
"day care": ss.18, 71.
"health authority": s.105(1).
"independent school": s.105(1).
"local authority": s.105(1).
"local education authority": s.105(1).
"mental nursing home": s.105(1).
"nursing home": s.105(1).
"privately fostered child": s.66.
"protected child": s.105(1).
"residential care home": s.105(1).
"voluntary home": s.60(3).
"voluntary organisation": s.105(1).

GENERAL NOTE
This section re-enacts C.C.A. 1980, ss. 74 and 75, and provides the Secretary of State
with powers to inspect premises where children are being cared for by people other than
those with parental responsibility or relatives (subs. (1)) and the children therein (subs. (6)).
The inspection power is supplemented by powers to direct specified people to give specific
information (subss. (4) and (5)), to inspect records (subs. (7)) and to enter (subs. (8)). It is
an offence intentionally to obstruct entry (subs. (10)). If entry is refused, a warrant can be
obtained under s.102. The Secretary of State may make regulations to exempt premises
from the duties in subss. (1), (4) and (6) (subs. (11) and (12)).

Inquiries

81.—(1) The Secretary of State may cause an inquiry to be held into
any matter connected with—
  (a) the functions of the social services committee of a local authority,
    in so far as those functions relate to children;
  (b) the functions of an adoption agency;
  (c) the functions of a voluntary organisation, in so far as those functions
    relate to children;
  (d) a registered children's home or voluntary home;
  (e) a residential care home, nursing home or mental nursing home, so
    far as it provides accommodation for children;
  (f) a home provided by the Secretary of State under section 82(5);
  (g) the detention of a child under section 53 of the Children and Young
    Persons Act 1933.

(2) Before an inquiry is begun, the Secretary of State may direct that
it shall be held in private.

(3) Where no direction has been given, the person holding the inquiry
may if he thinks fit hold it, or any part of it, in private.

(4) Subsections (2) to (5) of section 250 of the Local Government Act
1972 (powers in relation to local inquiries) shall apply in relation to an
inquiry under this section as they apply in relation to a local inquiry under
that section.

(5) In this section "functions" includes powers and duties which a
person has otherwise than by virtue of any enactment.

DEFINITIONS
  "adoption agency": s.105(1).
  "child": s.105(1).
  "functions": s.81(5).
  "local authority": s.105(1).
  "mental nursing home": s.105(1).
  "nursing home": s.105(1).
  "registered children's home": s.63.
  "residential care home": s.105(1).
  "voluntary home": s.60(3).
  "voluntary organisation": s.105(1).

GENERAL NOTE
This section re-enacts with minor amendments C.C.A. 1980, s.76. The scope of the power
is broadened to include all homes covered by the Act and also all functions relating to
children looked after by voluntary organisations. The power to hold inquiries has not been
heavily used; most child death inquiries are held by individual local authorities. The
Cleveland Inquiry was held under s.76 and s.84 of the National Health Service Act 1977.
Unregistered children's homes may be the subject of inquiries; see Courts and Legal Services
Bill, Sched. 10, para. 8.

Financial support by Secretary of State

82.—(1) The Secretary of State may (with the consent of the Treasury)
defray or contribute towards—

(a) any fees or expenses incurred by any person undergoing approved child care training;

(b) any fees charged, or expenses incurred, by any person providing approved child care training or preparing material for use in connection with such training; or

(c) the cost of maintaining any person undergoing such training.

(2) The Secretary of State may make grants to local authorities in respect of expenditure incurred by them in providing secure accommodation in community homes other than assisted community homes.

(3) Where—

(a) a grant has been made under subsection (2) with respect to any secure accommodation; but

(b) the grant is not used for the purpose for which it was made or the accommodation is not used as, or ceases to be used as, secure accommodation,

the Secretary of State may (with the consent of the Treasury) require the authority concerned to repay the grant, in whole or in part.

(4) The Secretary of State may make grants to voluntary organisations towards—

(a) expenditure incurred by them in connection with the establishment, maintenance or improvement of voluntary homes which, at the time when the expenditure was incurred—

(i) were assisted community homes; or

(ii) were designated as such; or

(b) expenses incurred in respect of the borrowing of money to defray any such expenditure.

(5) The Secretary of State may arrange for the provision, equipment and maintenance of homes for the accommodation of children who are in need of particular facilities and services which—

(a) are or will be provided in those homes; and

(b) in the opinion of the Secretary of State, are unlikely to be readily available in community homes.

(6) In this Part—

"child care training" means training undergone by any person with a view to, or in the course of—

(a) his employment for the purposes of any of the functions mentioned in section 83(9) or in connection with the adoption of children or with the accommodation of children in a residential care home, nursing home or mental nursing home; or

(b) his employment by a voluntary organisation for similar purposes;

"approved child care training" means child care training which is approved by the Secretary of State; and

"secure accommodation" means accommodation provided for the purpose of restricting the liberty of children.

(7) Any grant made under this section shall be of such amount, and shall be subject to such conditions, as the Secretary of State may (with the consent of the Treasury) determine.

DEFINITIONS

"approved child care training": s.82(6).

"child care training": s.82(6).

"community home", "assisted community home": s.53.

"functions": s.105(1).

"mental nursing home": s.105(1).

"nursing home": s.105(1).

"residential care home": s.105(1).

"secure accommodation": ss.25, 82(6).

"voluntary home": s.60(3).

"voluntary organisation": s.105(1).

GENERAL NOTE
This section re-enacts with minor amendments C.C.A. 1980, ss.78 and 80. It empowers the Secretary of State to make grants as follows: for approved child care training (subs. (1)); to local authorities for secure accommodation (subs. (2)); and to voluntary organisations for voluntary homes (subs. (4)). Grants under subs. (2) may be reclaimed (subs. (3)); grants under subs. (4) may be reclaimed under s.58.

The Secretary of State may also arrange for homes to be provided for children who need particular facilities (subs. (5)). Such facilities—child treatment centres—are already provided.

Research and returns of information

83.—(1) The Secretary of State may conduct, or assist other persons in conducting, research into any matter connected with—

(a) his functions, or the functions of local authorities, under the enactments mentioned in subsection (9);

(b) the adoption of children; or

(c) the accommodation of children in a residential care home, nursing home or mental nursing home.

(2) Any local authority may conduct, or assist other persons in conducting, research into any matter connected with—

(a) their functions under the enactments mentioned in subsection (9);

(b) the adoption of children; or

(c) the accommodation of children in a residential care home, nursing home or mental nursing home.

(3) Every local authority shall, at such times and in such form as the Secretary of State may direct, transmit to him such particulars as he may require with respect to—

(a) the performance by the local authority of all or any of their functions—

(i) under the enactments mentioned in subsection (9); or

(ii) in connection with the accommodation of children in a residential care home, nursing home or mental nursing home; and

(b) the children in relation to whom the authority have exercised those functions.

(4) Every voluntary organisation shall, at such times and in such form as the Secretary of State may direct, transmit to him such particulars as he may require with respect to children accommodated by them or on their behalf.

(5) The Secretary of State may direct the clerk of each magistrates' court to which the direction is expressed to relate to transmit—

(a) to such person as may be specified in the direction; and

(b) at such times and in such form as he may direct,

such particulars as he may require with respect to proceedings of the court which relate to children.

(6) The Secretary of State shall in each year lay before Parliament a consolidated and classified abstract of the information transmitted to him under subsections (3) to (5).

(7) The Secretary of State may institute research designed to provide information on which requests for information under this section may be based.

(8) The Secretary of State shall keep under review the adequacy of the provision of child care training and for that purpose shall receive and consider any information from or representations made by—

(a) the Central Council for Education and Training in Social Work;

(b) such representatives of local authorities as appear to him to be appropriate; or

(c) such other persons or organisations as appear to him to be appropriate,

concerning the provision of such training.
  (9) The enactments are—
    (a) this Act;
    (b) the Children and Young Persons Acts 1933 to 1969;
    (c) section 116 of the Mental Health Act 1983 (so far as it relates to children looked after by local authorities);
    (d) section 10 of the Mental Health (Scotland) Act 1984 (so far as it relates to children for whom local authorities have responsibility).

DEFINITIONS
  "child care training": s.82(6).
  "functions": s.105(1).
  "local authority": s.105(1).
  "mental nursing home": s.105(1).
  "nursing home": s.105(1).
  "residential care home": s.105(1).
  "voluntary organisation": s.105(1)

GENERAL NOTE
  Subss. (1), (2) and (9) re-enact with amendments C.C.A. 1980, s.77. They empower the Secretary of State and local authorities to conduct or assist others in research on child care.
  Subss. (3) to (6) re-enact with amendments C.C.A. 1980, s.79. They require local authorities, voluntary organisations and magistrates' court clerks to provide information to the Secretary of State (or another specified person in the case of magistrates' courts) who must lay an abstract of the information before Parliament. Triennial reports to Parliament are no longer required. Subs. (8) requires the Secretary of State to monitor the adequacy of child care training.

Local authority failure to comply with statutory duty: default power of Secretary of State

  84.—(1) If the Secretary of State is satisfied that any local authority has failed, without reasonable excuse, to comply with any of the duties imposed on them by or under this Act he may make an order declaring that authority to be in default with respect to that duty.
  (2) An order under subsection (1) shall give the Secretary of State's reasons for making it.
  (3) An order under subsection (1) may contain such directions for the purpose of ensuring that the duty is complied with, within such period as may be specified in the order, as appear to the Secretary of State to be necessary.
  (4) Any such direction shall, on the application of the Secretary of State, be enforceable by mandamus.

GENERAL NOTE
  This section provides a new power which will enable the Secretary of State to issue a direction, enforceable by mandamus (subs. (4)), where a local authority is in default of its duties under the Act (subs. (1)). It is envisaged that the power will only be used in "extreme circumstances, but . . . it may be necessary to use it . . . for example, where a local authority fails to make the requisite provision for a class of children." (*per* Solicitor General (Standing Committee B, col. 492, June 8, 1989)).
  A similar power is found in the Education Act 1944, s.99, but the power is rarely used. Ministers seem reluctant to use it and see its value in the threat it provides (see J. Logie *Enforcing statutory duties: The courts and default powers* [1988] J.S.W.L. 185). Where the minister unreasonably refuses to act, it may be possible to challenge his decision by judicial review. Also, although it has been held that the existence of a default power prevents other judicial action (*Pasmore* v. *Oswaldtwistle Urban District Council* [1898] A.C. 387) this does not apply to applications for judicial review (*R.* v. *Secretary of State for the Environment* ex p. *Ward* [1984] 1 W.L.R. 834). However, it will be difficult to challenge a local authority's decisions about its duties under this Act by judicial review (see notes on s.22). Despite this

new power, the main method for obtaining redress will be via the complaints procedure in s.26.

PART XII

MISCELLANEOUS AND GENERAL

Notification of children accommodated in certain establishments

Children accommodated by health authorities and local education authorities

85.—(1) Where a child is provided with accommodation by any health authority or local education authority ("the accommodating authority")—

(a) for a consecutive period of at least three months; or
(b) with the intention, on the part of that authority, of accommodating him for such a period,

the accommodating authority shall notify the responsible authority.

(2) Where subsection (1) applies with respect to a child, the accommodating authority shall also notify the responsible authority when they cease to accommodate the child.

(3) In this section "the responsible authority" means—

(a) the local authority appearing to the accommodating authority to be the authority within whose area the child was ordinarily resident immediately before being accommodated; or
(b) where it appears to the accommodating authority that a child was not ordinarily resident within the area of any local authority, the local authority within whose area the accommodation is situated.

(4) Where a local authority have been notified under this section, they shall—

(a) take such steps as are reasonably practicable to enable them to determine whether the child's welfare is adequately safeguarded and promoted while he is accommodated by the accommodating authority; and
(b) consider the extent to which (if at all) they should exercise any of their functions under this Act with respect to the child.

DEFINITIONS
"child": s.105(1).
"functions": s.105(1).
"health authority": s.105(1).
"local authority": s.105(1).
"local education authority": s.105(1).
"the accommodating authority": s.85(1).
"the responsible authority": s.85(3)

GENERAL NOTE
This section imposes new responsibilities on local authorities to safeguard the welfare of children accommodated for more than three consecutive months by health authorities or local education authorities (subs. (4)). Health authorities and L.E.A.s are under a duty to notify the responsible authority of such children (subs. (1)) and when they cease to accommodate them (subs. (2)). Local authorities have further duties in relation to the after-care of such children under s.24. This follows the recommendations of the R.C.C.L. Ch. 11, paras. 8–11, which noted the large number of such children and the concerns expressed that children in long-stay hospitals particularly had no contact with their families.

Subs. (3)

The obligation falls on the authority for the child's home area unless subs. (3)(b) applies, *e.g.* a severely handicapped child who has never lived outside a hospital.

Subs. (4)

This would seem to require at the least consultation with the accommodating authority, participation in a review of the child's care and a consideration of whether there should be further action. The powers and duties in Pt. III give local authorities wide scope. D.H.S.S. guidance HC(78)28/LAC(78)16 already encourages health authorities to review the cases of such children jointly with local authorities.

Children accommodated in residential care, nursing or mental nursing homes

86.—(1) Where a child is provided with accommodation in any residential care home, nursing home or mental nursing home—

(a) for a consecutive period of at least three months; or

(b) with the intention, on the part of the person taking the decision to accommodate him, of accommodating him for such period,

the person carrying on the home shall notify the local authority within whose area the home is carried on.

(2) Where subsection (1) applies with respect to a child, the person carrying on the home shall also notify that authority when he ceases to accommodate the child in the home.

(3) Where a local authority have been notified under this section, they shall—

(a) take such steps as are reasonably practicable to enable them to determine whether the child's welfare is adequately safeguarded and promoted while he is accommodated in the home; and

(b) consider the extent to which (if at all) they should exercise any of their functions under this Act with respect to the child.

(4) If the person carrying on any home fails, without reasonable excuse, to comply with this section he shall be guilty of an offence.

(5) A person authorised by a local authority may enter any residential care home, nursing home or mental nursing home within the authority's area for the purpose of establishing whether the requirements of this section have been complied with.

(6) Any person who intentionally obstructs another in the exercise of the power of entry shall be guilty of an offence.

(7) Any person exercising the power of entry shall, if so required, produce some duly authenticated document showing his authority to do so.

(8) Any person committing an offence under this section shall be liable on summary conviction to a fine not exceeding level 3 on the standard scale.

DEFINITIONS

"child": s.105(1).
"local authority": s.105(1).
"mental nursing home": s.105(1).
"nursing home": s.105(1).
"residential care home": s.105(1).

GENERAL NOTE

This section imposes a duty, comparable to that in s.85, on those carrying on residential care homes, nursing homes and mental nursing homes to notify the local authority about children they are accommodating (subss. (1) and (2)) and on the local authority in whose areas the home is situated to safeguard the children's welfare (subs. (3)). The local authority also has a duty in relation to the after-care of such children under s.24. Failure to notify the authority without reasonable cause is an offence (summary conviction: fine level 3) (subss. (4) and (8)). A person authorised by the local authority has a power of entry to establish whether the section has been complied with (subs. (5)). It is an offence (level 3) to intentionally obstruct such entry (subss. (6) and (8)). Where entry is refused, a warrant could be obtained under s.102, or, if an emergency protection order was sought, s.48(9).

Subs. (5)
A comparable power of entry exists under s.60(5) (see notes to that section).

Welfare of children accommodated in independent schools

87.—(1) It shall be the duty of—
    (a) the proprietor of any independent school which provides accommodation for any child; and
    (b) any person who is not the proprietor of such a school but who is responsible for conducting it,
to safeguard and promote the child's welfare.

(2) Subsection (1) does not apply in relation to a school which is a children's home or a residential care home.

(3) Where accommodation is provided for a child by an independent school within the area of a local authority, the authority shall take such steps as are reasonably practicable to enable them to determine whether the child's welfare is adequately safeguarded and promoted while he is accommodated by the school.

(4) Where a local authority are of the opinion that there has been a failure to comply with subsection (1) in relation to a child provided with accommodation by a school within their area, they shall notify the Secretary of State.

(5) Any person authorised by a local authority may, for the purpose of enabling the authority to discharge their duty under this section, enter at any reasonable time any independent school within their area which provides accommodation for any child.

(6) Any person entering an independent school in exercise of the power conferred by subsection (5) may carry out such inspection of premises, children and records as is prescribed by regulations made by the Secretary of State for the purposes of this section.

(7) Any person exercising that power shall, if asked to do so, produce some duly authenticated document showing his authority to do so.

(8) Any person authorised by the regulations to inspect records—
    (a) shall be entitled at any reasonable time to have access to, and inspect and check the operation of, any computer and any associated apparatus or material which is or has been in use in connection with the records in question; and
    (b) may require—
        (i) the person by whom or on whose behalf the computer is or has been so used; or
        (ii) any person having charge of, or otherwise concerned with the operation of, the computer, apparatus or material,
        to afford him such assistance as he may reasonably require.

(9) Any person who intentionally obstructs another in the exercise of any power conferred by this section or the regulations shall be guilty of an offence and liable on summary conviction to a fine not exceeding level 3 on the standard scale.

(10) In this section "proprietor" has the same meaning as in the Education Act 1944.

DEFINITIONS
  "child": 105(1).
  "children's home": s.63.
  "independent school": s.105(1).
  "local authority": s.105(1).

"proprietor": s.87(10).
"school": s.105(1).
"residential care home": s.105(1).

GENERAL NOTE

This section imposes two new duties:— (1) a duty on the proprietors of independent schools which are not either residential care homes or children's homes (subs. (2)) to safeguard and promote the welfare of children they accommodate (subs. (1)) and (2) a duty on the local authority in whose area the school is situated to take reasonable steps to determine whether the duty is being complied with (subs. (3)).

Where the local authority considers that the proprietors have breached their duty it must inform the Secretary of State, who may send a notice of complaint under the Education Act 1944, s.71 (as amended in Sched. 13, para. 9). This could lead to the closure of the school. Where a child is suffering (or likely to suffer) significant harm, the local authority will be able to take action by removing him under an emergency protection order (s.44) or arranging for him to be accommodated by the local authority with the parents' agreement until they are able to collect him (s.20).

The provision dovetails with those in the Registered Homes Act 1984 and Pts. VI–IX and XII of this Act so that the welfare of all children provided with accommodation away from home is safeguarded. This section only applies to schools with more than 50 boarders; smaller schools are required to register as children's homes (s.63(6)). The local authority has a power to enter premises at any reasonable time and may carry out inspection as permitted by the regulations (subss. (5) and (6)). No indication was given during the debate of the content of the regulations. However, s.62(6) gives local authorities a statutory right to inspect voluntary homes, children accommodated in them and relevant records. It is an offence (level 3) intentionally to obstruct entry or an inspection permitted by the regulations (subs. (9)).

Subs. (1)

Which provides accommodation: Accommodation outside the curtilage of the school but provided by the school is included. However, where the school merely arranges for children to be boarded with local landladies it does not provide accommodation. If they cared or intended to care for more than 28 days, such people would be private foster parents within Pt. IX and have a duty to register with the local authority. The local authority would also have a duty to safeguard the welfare of any children privately fostered. There is no requirement to register as a private foster parent if the children are over 16 unless they are disabled (s.71). However, where the accommodation is provided by the school, the local authority's responsibility will last until the child is 18. The local authority has no special responsibility for day schools but may take action to remove individual children where there are grounds for an emergency protection order.

Subs. (5)

Enter at any reasonable time: See s.62(6). Any time when the children are up may be reasonable unless it disrupts the school unduly, *e.g.*, the inspection of children during a public exam.

Adoption

Amendments of adoption legislation

88.—(1) The Adoption Act 1976 shall have effect subject to the amendments made by Part I of Schedule 10.

(2) The Adoption (Scotland) Act 1978 shall have effect subject to the amendments made by Part II of Schedule 10.

GENERAL NOTE

This section and Sched. 10 amend adoption law. The changes do three things. First, they harmonise U.K. adoption law following the reforms in Northern Ireland introduced by the Adoption (Northern Ireland) Order 1987. This is designed to enable adoption agencies in different parts of the U.K. to work in closer co-operation with one another. Secondly, they make consequential amendments, particularly replacing the terms "parental rights" and "custody." Thirdly, they introduce reforms designed to improve adoption law. The Lord Chancellor has announced a full review of adoption law by the Law Commission which may be expected to lead to further reform in due course. The most significant changes are listed below:

(1) *Age limits*: A parent applicant need only be 18 years (Adoption Act 1976, s.14(18), Sched. 10, para. 4).

(2) *Freeing for adoption*: If parents do not agree, the child must be in care of the local authority (Adoption Act 1976, s.18(2A), Sched. 10, para. 6(1)). The court must consider whether a non-marital father intends to apply for parental responsibility or a residence order (Adoption Act 1976, s.18(7), Sched. 10, para. 6(3)). Revocation of a freeing order returns parental responsibility to the parents. It does not revive orders under s.8 of this Act. (Adoption Act 1976, s.20(3), Sched. 10, para. 8(3)).

(3) *Notification of intention to adopt*: This cannot be made more than two years before the adoption order (s.22(1A), Sched. 10, para. 10(1)). "Protected child" is redefined to take account of this Act (Pts. VI–IX and XII and the Adoption Act 1976, s.32, para. 18).

(4) *Removal from adoption applicant*: S.20(8) of this Act does not entitle a parent to remove a child from those who have cared for him for five years (Adoption Act 1976, s.28(2A), Sched. 10, para. 14(1)).

(5) *Access to birth records*: Adoption Act 1976, s.51, is amended to make further provision for counselling and enabling people who were adopted in England or Wales to have access to birth records, even though they now live overseas (Sched. 10, para. 20).

(6) *Adoption contact register*: Adoption Act 1976, s.51A, provides for the Registrar General to establish a register which will enable adopted persons (and their natural relatives) to register their names and addresses and thus facilitate tracing (Sched. 10, para. 21).

(7) *Adoption Allowances*: Adoption Act 1976, s.57A, empowers the Secretary of State to make regulations about such payments which will replace approval for Schemes under s.57(4) (Sched. 10, para. 25).

(8) *Guardians ad litem*: Adoption Act 1976, s.65A, empowers the Secretary of State to make regulations about guardian ad litem panels. S.65A(2) is identical to s.41(9) of this Act, thus panels regulations can apply to guardians under both Acts (Sched. 10, para. 29).

(9) *Scotland:* Pt. II of Sched. 10 makes minor amendments to the Adoption (Scotland) Act 1978.

Paternity tests

Tests to establish paternity

89. In section 20 of the Family Law Reform Act 1969 (power of court to require use of tests to determine paternity), the following subsections shall be inserted after subsection (1)—

"(1A) Where—
    (a) an application is made for a direction under this section; and
    (b) the person whose paternity is in issue is under the age of eighteen when the application is made,
the application shall specify who is to carry out the tests.

(1B) In the case of a direction made on an application to which subsection (1A) applies the court shall—
    (a) specify, as the person who is to carry out the tests, the person specified in the application; or
    (b) where the court considers that it would be inappropriate to specify that person (whether because to specify him would be incompatible with any provision made by or under regulations made under section 22 of this Act or for any other reason), decline to give the direction applied for."

GENERAL NOTE

This section amends the Family Law Reform Act 1969, s.20 to take account of developments in blood tests for proof of paternity. There are now two alternative tests: first immunological testing, costing under £50, and second D.N.A. profiling, costing over £300. Applicants may choose which they prefer but the court will retain its overriding discretion to refuse the order sought. The wording of s.20 is further clarified by the Courts and Legal Services Bill, Sched. 10, para. 3.

Criminal care and supervision orders

Care and supervision orders in criminal proceedings

90.—(1) The power of a court to make an order under subsection (2) of section 1 of the Children and Young Persons Act 1969 (care proceedings in juvenile courts) where it is of the opinion that the condition mentioned in paragraph (f) of that subsection ("the offence condition") is satisfied is hereby abolished.

(2) The powers of the court to make care orders—

    (a) under section 7(7)(a) of the Children and Young Persons Act 1969 (alteration in treatment of young offenders etc.); and

    (b) under section 15(1) of that Act, on discharging a supervision order made under section 7(7)(b) of that Act,

are hereby abolished.

(3) The powers given by that Act to include requirements in supervision orders shall have effect subject to amendments made by Schedule 12.

GENERAL NOTE

This section abolishes the power of the court to make a care order in respect of juvenile offenders in care, or criminal proceedings.

C.Y.P.A. 1969, s.1(2)(f), the offence condition, was scarcely used and did not fit with the notion that a care or supervision order should only be made on proof of substantial harm. Its abolition was recommended in the R.C.C.L., para. 15.20. Conduct which led to care proceedings on this ground may still lead to a care order under s.31, but it will be necessary to satisfy the significant harm test in s.31(2). It may be difficult to argue that minor criminal activity, particularly shoplifting or criminal damage, indicates significant harm because it is so widespread.

C.Y.P.A. 1969, s.7(7), care orders in criminal proceedings are abolished and replaced by supervision orders with a residence requirement (six months maximum) under s.12AA of the C.Y.P.A. 1969 (see Sched. 12, paras. 22–25). This new sentence can only be imposed where a further serious offence (punishable by imprisonment for someone over 21) is committed by someone already subject to a supervision order with a requirement under s.12A(3) of the C.Y.P.A. 1969 or a residence requirement. The court must also be satisfied that the offence is due to the conditions in which the offender was living (C.Y.P.A. 1969, s.12AA(6)). The court will have to have a Social Inquiry Report and consult the local authority (s.12AA(3), (7) and (8)). The offender must be legally represented unless the conditions in C.Y.P.A. 1969, s.12AA(9) and (10) apply.

The intention is to "put another step on the escalator of criminal penalties . . . to prevent (young offenders) from reaching the point on the escalator which amounts to custody. One can draw a clear distinction. Being required to live in a residential accommodation will not involve the total deprivation of liberty that would be involved in being placed in a custodial institution" (*per* David Mellor, Minister of Health (Standing Committee B, col. 502–3, June 13, 1989)). It is not, however, clear that this will work in practice. The order may be seen to be too lenient and those who might otherwise have been committed to care will be pushed up the tariff to a custodial sentence, thus increasing rather than inhibiting custodial sentences. Although the order may be repeated (see C.Y.P.A. 1969, s.12AA(6)(ii) and (7)) it seems unlikely that this disposal will be used in respect of young offenders who are already being looked after by local authorities and will thus add to the disparity in the treatment of this group of disadvantaged young offenders. Also, the Secretary of State has a power under s.25(7) to make regulations to extend secure accommodation to specific descriptions of children. This could include children living in residential accommodation under C.Y.P.A. 1969, s.12AA. No indication was made to Parliament about the use of secure accommodation for such cases.

Young offenders subject to orders under C.Y.P.A. 1969, s.12AA are being looked after by the local authority within s.21 of this Act. They are therefore owed the duties in Pt. III including the duty to provide after-care under s.24. In *Leeds City Council* v. *West Yorkshire Metropolitan Police* [1983] A.C. 29, the House of Lords held that the local authority was not a guardian of a child under a care order for the purpose of being required to pay a fine ordered against him under s.55(1) of the C.Y.P.A. 1933. It would necessarily seem that the local authority would similarly not be liable for a child in its accommodation under s.12AA of the C.Y.P.A. 1969.

Effect and duration of orders etc.

Effect and duration of orders etc.

91.—(1) The making of a residence order with respect to a child who is the subject of a care order discharges the care order.

(2) The making of a care order with respect to a child who is the subject of any section 8 order discharges that order.

(3) The making of a care order with respect to a child who is the subject of a supervision order discharges that other order.

(4) The making of a care order with respect to a child who is a ward of court brings that wardship to an end.

(5) The making of a care order with respect to a child who is the subject of a school attendance order made under section 37 of the Education Act 1944 discharges the school attendance order.

(6) Where an emergency protection order is made with respect to a child who is in care, the care order shall have effect subject to the emergency protection order.

(7) Any order made under section 4(1) or 5(1) shall continue in force until the child reaches the age of eighteen, unless it is brought to an end earlier.

(8) Any—

(a) agreement under section 4; or

(b) appointment under section 5(3) or (4),

shall continue in force until the child reaches the age of eighteen, unless it is brought to an end earlier.

(9) An order under Schedule 1 has effect as specified in that Schedule.

(10) A section 8 order shall, if it would otherwise still be in force, cease to have effect when the child reaches the age of sixteen, unless it is to have effect beyond that age by virtue of section 9(6).

(11) Where a section 8 order has effect with respect to a child who has reached the age of sixteen, it shall, if it would otherwise still be in force, cease to have effect when he reaches the age of eighteen.

(12) Any care order, other than an interim care order, shall continue in force until the child reaches the age of eighteen, unless it is brought to an end earlier.

(13) Any order made under any other provision of this Act in relation to a child shall, if it would otherwise still be in force, cease to have effect when he reaches the age of eighteen.

(14) On disposing of any application for an order under this Act, the court may (whether or not it makes any other order in response to the application) order that no application for an order under this Act of any specified kind may be made with respect to the child concerned by any person named in the order without leave of the court.

(15) Where an application ("the previous application") has been made for—

(a) the discharge of a care order;

(b) the discharge of a supervision order;

(c) the discharge of an education supervision order;

(d) the substitution of a supervision order for a care order; or

(e) a child assessment order,

no further application of a kind mentioned in paragraphs (a) to (e) may be made with respect to the child concerned, without leave of the court, unless the period between the disposal of the previous application and the making of the further application exceeds six months.

(16) Subsection (15) does not apply to applications made in relation to interim orders.

(17) Where—

(a) a person has made an application for an order under section 34;

(b) the application has been refused; and

(c) a period of less than six months has elapsed since the refusal,

that person may not make a further application for such an order with respect to the same child, unless he has obtained the leave of the court.

DEFINITIONS

"care order": s.31(11).

"child assessment order": s.43.

"education supervision order": s.36.

"emergency protection order": s.44.

"interim care order": ss.31(11), 38.

"residence order": s.8(1).

"section 8 order": s.8(1).

"supervision order": ss.31(11), 35.

GENERAL NOTE

This section states the effect and duration of orders:

Section 8 orders: All section 8 orders are discharged by the making of a care order (subs. (2)), or when the child is 16, unless s.9(6) applies (subs. (10)). These orders end at 18 (subs. (11)).

Care orders (s.31). These continue until the child is 18 unless discharged (subs. (12)). Care orders discharge supervision orders (subs. (3)), wardship (subs. (4)), school attendance orders (subs. (5)). Care orders are discharged by the making of a residence order (subs. (1)). Care orders have effect subject to any emergency protection orders made in respect of the child (subs. (6)). They cease to have effect if the child goes to live in Northern Ireland, etc., in accordance with regulations (see s.101(4)). Care orders end at 18 (subs. (12)).

Parental responsibility agreements and orders (s.4) and *guardianship appointments* (s.5) continue until the child is 18 unless ended earlier (subs. (8)).

Maintenance orders (Sched. 1) last until the child is 17 but may last longer where Sched. 1, para. 3(2) applies (subs. (9)).

Other orders (ss.16, 34, 35, 38, 43, 44, etc.), end when the child is 18, if not before (subs. (13)).

This section also lists the restrictions on further applications, implementing the recommendations in Law Com. 172 para. 6.31 (subss. (14) to (17)). The court has a wide power to order that further applications require leave (subs. (14)). Applications for the discharge of care, supervision, education supervision orders, the substitution of a supervision order for a care order, or the making of a child assessment order, all require leave if a previous application has been made within six months (subs. (15)). The same applies where an application has been made unsuccessfully for contact under s.34 (subs. (17)). There are no restrictions in relation to interim orders (subs. (16)).

Subs. (5).

School attendance order: is an order made by a local education authority under the Education Act 1944, s.37(1), requiring parents to have the child registered at and attend a school named in the order.

Subs. (14)

It is not clear how willing the courts will be to make such orders. The protection of this provision will only be necessary where there is a danger of vindictive or harassing applications by someone such as a parent who does not otherwise require leave. S.1 applies, so the court will need to be satisfied that it is necessary and in the child's welfare to require leave.

Jurisdiction and procedure etc.

Jurisdiction of courts

92.—(1) The name "domestic proceedings", given to certain proceedings in magistrates' courts, is hereby changed to "family proceedings" and the names "domestic court" and "domestic court panel" are hereby changed to "family proceedings court" and "family panel", respectively.

(2) Proceedings under this Act shall be treated as family proceedings in relation to magistrates' courts.

(3) Subsection (2) is subject to the provisions of section 65(1) and (2) of the Magistrates' Courts Act 1980 (proceedings which may be treated as not being family proceedings), as amended by this Act.

(4) A magistrates' court shall not be competent to entertain any application, or make any order, involving the administration or application of—

(a) any property belonging to or held in trust for a child; or
(b) the income of any such property.

(5) The powers of a magistrates' court under section 63(2) of the Act of 1980 to suspend or rescind orders shall not apply in relation to any order made under this Act.

(6) Part I of Schedule 11 makes provision, including provision for the Lord Chancellor to make orders, with respect to the jurisdiction of courts and justices of the peace in relation to—

(a) proceedings under this Act; and
(b) proceedings under certain other enactments.

(7) For the purposes of this Act "the court" means the High Court, a county court or a magistrates' court.

(8) Subsection (7) is subject to the provision made by or under Part I of Schedule 11 and to any express provision as to the jurisdiction of any court made by any other provision of this Act.

(9) The Lord Chancellor may by order make provision for the principal registry of the Family Division of the High Court to be treated as if it were a county court for such purposes of this Act, or of any provision made under this Act, as may be specified in the order.

(10) Any order under subsection (9) may make such provision as the Lord Chancellor thinks expedient for the purpose of applying (with or without modifications) provisions which apply in relation to the procedure in county courts to the principal registry when it acts as if it were a county court.

(11) Part II of Schedule 11 makes amendments consequential on this section.

DEFINITIONS
"family panel": s.92(1).
"family proceedings": s.92(2).
"family proceedings court": s.92(1).
"specified": Sched. 11, para. 4(2).
"the court": s.92(7).

GENERAL NOTE
Under this section that part of the magistrates' court which will hear proceedings under this Act will now be known as the family proceedings court. This section should be read with Sched. 11. Proceedings which were heard in the domestic court under the Magistrates' Courts Act 1980, s.65(1)(2) (as amended), are now to be heard in the family proceedings court but the court will continue to have no jurisdiction over issues concerning trusts or income arising from trust property (subss. (3) and (4)). Orders made in the magistrates' court can no longer be suspended or rescinded under the Magistrates' Courts Act 1980, s.63(2), and will have to be varied or discharged in accordance with s.91 of this Act (subs. (5)). Other details of jurisdiction are contained in Sched. 11 and any rules will be made under subss. (6), (9) and (10).

The Solicitor General stated

"The Children Bill is only the beginning of a rolling programme to review the substantive law and the arrangements for its application. The wider programme, which involves more than provisions for children, will be informed by the need for legal consistency, the desirability of all proceedings for one family being heard together, and the need to move away from adversarial to inquisitorial procedures." (Standing Committee B, col. 456, June 8, 1989).

Sched. 11, together with s.92, provides the structure for the new court system which will handle cases under this Act, the Adoption Act 1976 and the inherent jurisdiction of the High Court. The Lord Chancellor has power to make orders concerning the initiation of cases (para. 1), their transfer (para. 2) and the effect of contravention of the rules (paras. 1 and 4). In most matters, the magistrates' court, the county court and the High Court will all have jurisdiction and cases will be directed to the appropriate level of court, according to their complexity.

The Government has indicated that it would expect some cases to be started in the family proceedings court (magistrates' court) with transfer to a specified county court, or even the High Court, in three circumstances: first, if there are other proceedings, for example divorce proceedings, currently being heard in the other court; secondly, if the case is complex, *e.g.*, it involves contested medical evidence, or thirdly, if transfer could prevent delay (*per* Solicitor General (*Hansard*, H.C., Vol. 158, col. 549–551)). It is intended that the magistrates' clerk should be able to transfer cases at any stage and a party may apply to a county court registrar for a transfer up. There will be no appeal against a decision to transfer from the magistrates' court (s.94(2)) but the Lord Chancellor may, by order, make provision for other appeals about transfer (s.94(10)).

The Lord Chancellor is also empowered to order that a single justice may grant an emergency protection order or make orders about the transfer of proceedings (para. 3). Sched. 11 contains further consequential amendments and empowers the Lord Chancellor to make further changes (para. 4).

Rules of court

93.—(1) An authority having power to make rules of court may make such provision for giving effect to—
  (a) this Act;
  (b) the provisions of any statutory instrument made under this Act; or
  (c) any amendment made by this Act in any other enactment,
as appears to that authority to be necessary or expedient.
  (2) The rules may, in particular, make provision—
      (a) with respect to the procedure to be followed in any relevant proceedings (including the manner in which any application is to be made or other proceedings commenced);
      (b) as to the persons entitled to participate in any relevant proceedings, whether as parties to the proceedings or by being given the opportunity to make representations to the court;
      (c) with respect to the documents and information to be furnished, and notices to be given, in connection with any relevant proceedings;
      (d) applying (with or without modification) enactments which govern the procedure to be followed with respect to proceedings brought on a complaint made to a magistrates' court to relevant proceedings in such a court brought otherwise than on a complaint;
      (e) with respect to preliminary hearings;
      (f) for the service outside the United Kingdom, in such circumstances and in such manner as may be prescribed, of any notice of proceedings in a magistrates' court;
      (g) for the exercise by magistrates' courts, in such circumstances as may be prescribed, of such powers as may be prescribed (even though a party to the proceedings in question is outside England and Wales);
      (h) enabling the court, in such circumstances as may be prescribed, to proceed on any application even though the respondent has not been given notice of the proceedings;
      (i) authorising a single justice to discharge the functions of a magistrates' court with respect to such relevant proceedings as may be prescribed;
      (j) authorising a magistrates' court to order any of the parties to

such relevant proceedings as may be prescribed, in such circumstances as may be prescribed, to pay the whole or part of the costs of all or any of the other parties.

(3) In subsection (2)—

"notice of proceedings" means a summons or such other notice of proceedings as is required; and "given", in relation to a summons, means "served";

"prescribed" means prescribed by the rules; and

"relevant proceedings" means any application made, or proceedings brought, under any of the provisions mentioned in paragraphs (a) to (c) of subsection (1) and any part of such proceedings.

(4) This section and any other power in this Act to make rules of court are not to be taken as in any way limiting any other power of the authority in question to make rules of court.

(5) When making any rules under this section an authority shall be subject to the same requirements as to consultation (if any) as apply when the authority makes rules under its general rule making power.

DEFINITIONS

"notice of proceedings": s.93(3).
"prescribed": s.93(3).
"relevant proceedings": s.93(3).
"the court": s.92(7).

GENERAL NOTE

This section enables rules of court to be made to govern practice and procedure in proceedings brought under this Act. Indications have been given about:—

(1) *Party status* (subs. (2)(b)).

David Mellor, Minister of Health, stated at the third reading in the Commons that the undertakings in Cm. 62 1987 would be implemented (*Hansard*, H.C., Vol. 151, col. 112). It appears that the status quo in care proceedings will be maintained and anyone seeking a residence order in such proceedings will be a party. Children will not automatically be parties in other types of family proceedings (*per* Solicitor General (Standing Committee B, col. 480, June 8, 1989)).

(2) *Documents* (subs. (2)(c)).

Advanced disclosure is likely to be required. S.42 provides for guardians ad litem to have access to all local authority documentation. Rules made under this section may provide for access to other bodies' files, *e.g.*, the files of N.S.P.C.C. (see Solicitor General (*Hansard*, H.C., Vol. 158, col. 629)).

(3) *Preliminary hearings* (subs. (2)(e)).

These may occur as part of the timetabling process under ss.10 and 29.

This section is not affected by the separate rule making power in s.52(1).

Appeals

94.—(1) An appeal shall lie to the High Court against—

(a) the making by a magistrates' court of any order under this Act; or

(b) any refusal by a magistrates' court to make such an order.

(2) Where a magistrates' court has power, in relation to any proceedings under this Act, to decline jurisdiction because it considers that the case can more conveniently be dealt with by another court, no appeal shall lie against any exercise by that magistrates' court of that power.

(3) Subsection (1) does not apply in relation to an interim order for periodical payments made under Schedule 1.

(4) On an appeal under this section, the High Court may make such orders as may be necessary to give effect to its determination of the appeal.

(5) Where an order is made under subsection (4) the High Court may also make such incidental or consequential orders as appear to it to be just.

(6) Where an appeal from a magistrates' court relates to an order for the making of periodical payments, the High Court may order that its determination of the appeal shall have effect from such date as it thinks fit to specify in the order.

(7) The date so specified must not be earlier than the earliest date allowed in accordance with rules of court made for the purposes of this section.

(8) Where, on an appeal under this section in respect of an order requiring a person to make periodical payments, the High Court reduces the amount of those payments or discharges the order—

(a) it may order the person entitled to the payments to pay to the person making them such sum in respect of payments already made as the High Court thinks fit; and

(b) if any arrears are due under the order for periodical payments, it may remit payment of the whole, or part, of those arrears.

(9) Any order of the High Court made on an appeal under this section (other than one directing that an application be re-heard by a magistrates' court) shall, for the purposes—

(a) of the enforcement of the order; and

(b) of any power to vary, revive or discharge orders,

be treated as if it were an order of the magistrates' court from which the appeal was brought and not an order of the High Court.

(10) The Lord Chancellor may by order make provision as to the circumstances in which appeals may be made against decisions taken by courts on questions arising in connection with the transfer, or proposed transfer, of proceedings by virtue of any order under paragraph 2 of Schedule 11.

(11) Except to the extent provided for in any order made under subsection (10), no appeal may be made against any decision of a kind mentioned in that subsection.

GENERAL NOTE

This section makes new provision for appeals. Appeals in care proceedings will now be heard by the High Court, not, as previously, the Crown Court. Local authorities will have the same rights of appeal as other parties to care proceedings (subs. (1)). There will be no appeal to the High Court from a refusal by the magistrates to exercise jurisdiction because the case could more conveniently be heard elsewhere (subs. (2)), nor will there be an appeal against an interim periodical payments order (subs. (3)). Subss. (4) to (8) set out the powers of the High Court when hearing an appeal. The court has the power to make any order which reflects its conclusions and any necessary consequential orders. Orders in periodical payments appeals may be backdated in accordance with court rules (subss. (6), (7)) and may include orders for repayment or remission of arrears (subs. (8)). Orders made by the appeal court, except orders for rehearing, operate as orders of the original court (subs. (9)). Rules may be made to provide for appeals against tranfer of cases (subs. (10)). No other appeal may be made on such matters (subs. (11)).

This section should be read with s.40, which deals with the effect of care and supervision orders where appeals are pending.

Attendance of child at hearing under Part IV or V

95.—(1) In any proceedings in which a court is hearing an application for an order under Part IV or V, or is considering whether to make any such order, the court may order the child concerned to attend such stage or stages of the proceedings as may be specified in the order.

(2) The power conferred by subsection (1) shall be exercised in accordance with rules of court.

(3) Subsections (4) to (6) apply where—

(a) an order under subsection (1) has not been complied with; or

(b) the court has reasonable cause to believe that it will not be complied with.

(4) The court may make an order authorising a constable, or such person as may be specified in the order—

(a) to take charge of the child and to bring him to the court; and

(b) to enter and search any premises specified in the order if he has reasonable cause to believe that the child may be found on the premises.

(5) The court may order any person who is in a position to do so to bring the child to the court.

(6) Where the court has reason to believe that a person has information about the whereabouts of the child it may order him to disclose it to the court.

DEFINITIONS
"child": s.105(1).
"the court": s.92(7).

GENERAL NOTE

Two distinct philosophies have operated in the juvenile court on the one part, and in the county court and the High Court on the other, about the child's attendance at court. In the juvenile court, the child's attendance was required, but he could be excused if he were below the age of five, indisposed, or, in the case of an interim order, legally represented. (see C.Y.P.A. 1969, ss.2(9) and 22(1) and *Northampton County Council* v. *H.* [1988] 2 W.L.R. 389). In other courts, except in adoption proceedings, the child's attendance was generally considered inappropriate. The court will now have a complete discretion as to whether to order the child's attendance for all or part of any hearing for an order under Pts. IV or V (subs. (1)), which must be exercised in accordance with rules of court (subs. (2)).

"[The] principal reforms on representation of the child and court procedure and practice should make it unnecessary for the child to attend the hearing in many cases" (*per* Solicitor-General (*Hansard*, H.C., Vol. 158, cols. 630, 631)).

Where the child is a party, he should be able to attend if he wishes to do so. Subs. (1) only gives the court a discretion to require his attendance, not to forbid it.

Where an order for attendance is not complied with (or there is reasonable cause to believe it will not be), the court may order a constable or other specified person to search premises, take charge of the child and bring him before the court (subs. (4)) or order any person who is in a position to do so to bring the child before the court (subs. (5)), or to disclose information to it (subs. (6)). These subsections reproduce in a decriminalised form C.Y.P.A. 1969, s.2(4)(5).

Evidence given by, or with respect to, children

96.—(1) Subsection (2) applies where a child who is called as a witness in any civil proceedings does not, in the opinion of the court, understand the nature of an oath.

(2) The child's evidence may be heard by the court if, in its opinion—

(a) he understands that it is his duty to speak the truth; and

(b) he has sufficient understanding to justify his evidence being heard.

(3) The Lord Chancellor may by order make provision for the admissibility of evidence which would otherwise be inadmissible under any rule of law relating to hearsay.

(4) An order under subsection (3) may only be made with respect to—

(a) civil proceedings in general or such civil proceedings, or class of civil proceedings, as may be prescribed; and

(b) evidence in connection with the upbringing, maintenance or welfare of a child.

(5) An order under subsection (3)—

(a) may, in particular, provide for the admissibility of statements which are made orally or in a prescribed form or which are recorded by any prescribed method of recording;

(b) may make different provision for different purposes and in relation to different descriptions of court; and

(c) may make such amendments and repeals in any enactment relating to evidence (other than in this Act) as the Lord Chancellor considers necessary or expedient in consequence of the provision made by the order.

(6) Subsection (5)(b) is without prejudice to section 104(4).

(7) In this section—

"civil proceedings" and "court" have the same meaning as they have in the Civil Evidence Act 1968 by virtue of section 18 of that Act; and

"prescribed" means prescribed by an order under subsection (3).

DEFINITIONS
"child": s.105(1).
"civil proceedings": s.96(7).
"prescribed": s.96(7).
"the court": s.92(7).

GENERAL NOTE
This section makes two major changes to the law of evidence in civil proceedings. First, it allows the unsworn evidence of a child of tender years to be heard if subs. (2) is satisfied. It thus brings civil proceedings in line with criminal proceedings (see C.Y.P.A. 1933, s.38, as amended by Criminal Justice Act 1988, s.34). Secondly, it empowers the Lord Chancellor to make orders overriding the rules relating to hearsay in all or any civil proceedings in respect of evidence about the upbringing, maintenance or welfare of a child (subss. (3) and (4)). It will thus enable the Lord Chancellor to reverse the effect of *Re H., Re K* (Minors), *The Times*, June 9, 1989, and *Bradford City Metropolitan Borough Council* v. *K, The Times*, August 18, 1989, which restricted the admissibility of hearsay (particularly of allegations to a third party by the child not called as a witness to wardship cases).

S.96(3) to (7) came into force on Royal Assent (s.108(2)). However, *Re H., Re K* is on appeal to the House of Lords, and the Lord Chancellor may not exercise his power to make orders until the Lords have given their opinion.

Subs. (1)
Understand the nature of an oath: A child may only be sworn (or affirm) if he appreciates the particular nature of the case and realises that taking the oath involves more than the ordinary duty of telling the truth (*per* May L.J. *R.* v. *Campbell*, *The Times*, December 10, 1982). The dividing line between children who are normally considered old enough and those normally considered too young lies between the ages of eight and ten (*R.* v. *Hayes* [1977] 1 W.L.R. 234) and it has been said that it is undesirable for children of five to be called to give evidence (*R.* v. *Wallwork* (1958) 122 J.P. 299), but attitudes may be changing (see Spencer [1988] New L.J. 147 and [1989] New L.J. 1309).

Subs. (2)
It was suggested that this formulation might prevent hearing the evidence of very young children who, although honest, do not comprehend concepts such as duty and truth. However, the Solicitor-General preferred a novel interpretation which subsumed subs. (2)(a) in (2)(b) (*Hansard*, H.C., Vol. 158, col. 771).

Subss. (4) and (5)
This allows an order under subs. (3) to apply to all or only some civil proceedings relating to children. It may prescribe the form or means of recording which can be used for permitted hearsay evidence. No indication was given of the proposed content of the order but it can, at least, be expected to allow statements by children recorded in welfare officers' reports to be admitted in residence and contact proceedings. When wardship ceases to be available to local authorities it will also need to allow hearsay in these cases; a narrow approach will lead to more children having to give evidence.

Privacy for children involved in certain proceedings

97.—(1) Rules made under section 144 of the Magistrates' Courts Act 1980 may make provision for a magistrates' court to sit in private in proceedings in which any powers under this Act may be exercised by the court with respect to any child.

(2) No person shall publish any material which is intended, or likely, to identify—

    (a) any child as being involved in any proceedings before a magistrates' court in which any power under this Act may be exercised by the court with respect to that or any other child; or

    (b) an address or school as being that of a child involved in any such proceedings.

(3) In any proceedings for an offence under this section it shall be a defence for the accused to prove that he did not know, and had no reason to suspect, that the published material was intended, or likely, to identify the child.

(4) The court or the Secretary of State may, if satisfied that the welfare of the child requires it, by order dispense with the requirements of subsection (2) to such extent as may be specified in the order.

(5) For the purposes of this section—
    "publish" includes—

        (a) broadcast by radio, television or cable television; or

        (b) cause to be published; and
    "material" includes any picture or representation.

(6) Any person who contravenes this section shall be guilty of an offence and liable, on summary conviction, to a fine not exceeding level 4 on the standard scale.

(7) Subsection (1) is without prejudice to—

    (a) the generality of the rule making power in section 144 of the Act of 1980; or

    (b) any other power of a magistrates' court to sit in private.

(8) Section 71 of the Act of 1980 (newspaper reports of certain proceedings) shall apply in relation to any proceedings to which this section applies subject to the provisions of this section.

DEFINITIONS
    "child": s.105(1).
    "material": s.97(5).
    "publish": s.97(5).
    "school": s.105(1).

GENERAL NOTE
    This section clarifies the rules relating to the power of magistrates to sit in private and to the publication of material about children involved in civil cases. It will enable children to be given the same privacy in all proceedings in the family proceedings court as they had in the domestic court in proceedings under the G.M.A. 1971. The restriction on reporting children's cases is similar to that in C.Y.P.A. 1933, s.39, which also applied to radio, television and cable broadcasting. It is an offence (level 4) to contravene this section, but there is now a defence for a person who did not know and had no reason to suspect that the published material was intended or likely to identify the child (subs. (3)).

    The court or the Secretary of State may permit publication where the welfare of the child requires it (subs. (4)). This might be appropriate to allow full publication to quell rumours or, more commonly, where the child is missing and publication may help those searching for him.

Subss. (2) and (5)
    Publish: In defamation proceedings this word has a wide meaning and includes any communication to a third party which is not privileged (see *Winfield and Jolowicz on Tort* (13th edit. 1989) 314 *et seq.*) A similarly wide definition may be appropriate here despite the possibility of a criminal penalty, because of the interests of the child and the availability of the defence in subs. (2). However, the wording of the definition and the recent approach of the High Court to publication in children's cases may suggest a narrower approach (see *Re C (No. 2)*, *The Times*, April 27, 1989).

Self-incrimination

98.—(1) In any proceedings in which a court is hearing an application for an order under Part IV or V, no person shall be excused from—

(a) giving evidence on any matter; or

(b) answering any question put to him in the course of his giving evidence,

on the ground that doing so might incriminate him or his spouse of an offence.

(2) A statement or admission made in such proceedings shall not be admissible in evidence against the person making it or his spouse in proceedings for an offence other than perjury.

GENERAL NOTE

This section removes the privilege against self-incrimination in proceedings under Pts. IV and V of the Act. In its place it grants the witness indemnity, so that his statements cannot be used for his prosecution except for perjury. Similar provisions exist in relation to disclosure of the child's whereabouts under ss.48 and 50 of this Act and the Family Law Act 1986, s.33. There should no longer be any reason for delaying care proceedings until the completion of any criminal trial of the alleged perpetrator.

Legal Aid

99.—(1) The Legal Aid Act 1988 is amended as mentioned in subsections (2) to (4).

(2) In section 15 (availability of, and payment for, representation under provisions relating to civil legal aid), for the words "and (3)" in subsection (1) there shall be substituted "to (3B)"; and the following subsections shall be inserted after subsection (3)—

"(3A) Representation under this Part shall not be available—

(a) to any local authority; or

(b) to any other body which falls within a prescribed description,

for the purposes of any proceedings under the Children Act 1989.

(3B) Regardless of subsection (2) or (3), representation under this Part must be granted where a child who is brought before a court under section 25 of the 1989 Act (use of accommodation for restricting liberty) is not, but wishes to be, legally represented before the court."

(3) In section 19(5) (scope of provisions about criminal legal aid), at the end of the definition of "criminal proceedings" there shall be added "and also includes proceedings under section 15 of the Children and Young Persons Act 1969 (variation and discharge of supervision orders) and section 16(8) of that Act (appeals in such proceedings)".

(4) Sections 27, 28 and 30(1) and (2) (provisions about legal aid in care, and other, proceedings in relation to children) shall cease to have effect.

(5) The Lord Chancellor may by order make such further amendments in the Legal Aid Act 1988 as he considers necessary or expedient in consequence of any provision made by or under this Act.

DEFINITION

"child": s.105(1).

GENERAL NOTE

This section makes changes to the Legal Aid Act 1988 to facilitate the granting of legal aid in proceedings brought under this Act. Henceforth, civil legal aid will be available in care proceedings. The Government is concerned that legal aid should be granted swiftly in children's cases. The Solicitor General stated that "the Government intends to waive the merits test for those who are automatically parties in care proceedings and to grant legal aid in advance of the means test, and to waive the means test entirely for children who are the subject of a care application" (*Hansard*, H.C. Vol. 158, col. 159).

Civil legal aid will also be available without either a means or a merits test to any child in proceedings under s.25 relating to secure accommodation (subs. (2)). Criminal legal aid will be available in proceedings relating to (criminal) supervision orders under the C.Y.P.A. 1969, s.15 (subs. (4)). The Lord Chancellor is given power to make further consequential amendments (subs. (5)).

Restrictions on use of wardship jurisdiction

100.—(1) Section 7 of the Family Law Reform Act 1969 (which gives the High Court power to place a ward of court in the care, or under the supervision, of a local authority) shall cease to have effect.

(2) No court shall exercise the High Court's inherent jurisdiction with respect to children—

(a) so as to require a child to be placed in the care, or put under the supervision, of a local authority;

(b) so as to require a child to be accommodated by or on behalf of a local authority;

(c) so as to make a child who is the subject of a care order a ward of court; or

(d) for the purpose of conferring on any local authority power to determine any question which has arisen, or which may arise, in connection with any aspect of parental responsibility for a child.

(3) No application for any exercise of the court's inherent jurisdiction with respect to children may be made by a local authority unless the authority have obtained the leave of the court.

(4) The court may only grant leave if it is satisfied that—

(a) the result which the authority wish to achieve could not be achieved through the making of any order of a kind to which subsection (5) applies; and

(b) there is reasonable cause to believe that if the court's inherent jurisdiction is not exercised with respect to the child he is likely to suffer significant harm.

(5) This subsection applies to any order—

(a) made otherwise than in the exercise of the court's inherent jurisdiction; and

(b) which the local authority is entitled to apply for (assuming, in the case of any application which may only be made with leave, that leave is granted).

DEFINITIONS
   "local authority": s.105(1).
   "parental responsibility": s.3.
   "significant harm": s.31(9), (10).
   "the court": s.92(7).

GENERAL NOTE
   This section completes the new scheme for compulsory measures of care by effectively ending local authorities' use of wardship to remove children from their families or commit them to local authority care. The R.C.C.L. did not recommend changes to wardship but did expect that reform would reduce the need to use it (para. 15.38). The Law Commission canvassed its retention, restriction or abolition (see Working Paper 101 1987 *Wards of Court*) but did not go on to make firm proposals in a report. However, unless some restrictions on the inherent jurisdiction were introduced, it would have been impossible to impose one standard, the "significant harm" test, to justify intervention.
   Local authority use of wardship is restricted in three ways. First, the court's powers to commit a child to care in s.7 of the Family Law Reform Act 1969 is abolished (subs. (1)). Secondly, the inherent jurisdiction of the High Court cannot be exercised to require a child to be placed in care, supervised by the local authority, accommodated by the local authority, it cannot be exercised to give the local authority power to make parental decisions in respect of a child, or to make a child subject to a care order a ward (subs. (2)). Finally, if the local authority wishes to apply to the court for an order under the inherent jurisdiction it must obtain leave (subs. (3)) and satisfy the conditions in subss. (4) and (5). Leave will only be granted if the result could not be achieved by the local authority applying for an order other

than in wardship *and* there is reasonable cause to believe that the child will suffer significant harm if the jurisdiction is not exercised.

Apart from these restrictions the inherent jurisdiction remains intact. Anyone other than a local authority who can show sufficient interest will be able to ward any child who is not in local authority care. Where the restrictions in *A.* v. *Liverpool City Council* [1982] A.C. 363 and subs. (2) do not apply, wardship can be used to review the decision of a local authority, although an application for judicial review may be required. The High Court can still make orders, *e.g.*, injunctions, under its inherent jurisdiction otherwise than in wardship. Where the child is harmed because of the failure of the local authority to act it may be possible to get the Secretary of State to require action under s.84.

The removal of wardship will certainly make it more difficult for those local authorities which have relied on it to make some arrangements for children they are looking after.

(1) *Prevention of removal from accommodation.*

If s.44 is satisfied, the local authority will be able to obtain an emergency protection order. Where s.31(2) is satisfied it will be able to obtain a care order.

If the child has been with the carers for more than three years *they* will be able to apply for a residence order without leave (s.10(5)).

If the child has been with the carers for less than three years they will need leave of the court and consent of the authority before making an application for a residence order (ss.9(3) and 10(8)). A local authority which readily gives consent may undermine the confidence of those who need it to accommodate their children. The local authority will be able to support a child under a residence order as they could support those children subject to custodianship orders (Sched. 1, para. 15).

(2) *Facilitating adoption placements.*

Contact with the child may be controlled under s.34 but repeated applications for orders may theoretically be made every six months.

Parental responsibility may be ended by a freeing order under the Adoption Act 1976, s.18, but the child must be in care of the local authority if the order is contested.

The Adoption Act 1976 also provides limited protection for would-be adoption applicants to prevent removal of the child pending an adoption hearing. These supplement the powers to control the child's placement by a care order or residence order. It seems likely that there will be more hearings in such cases but they need not take longer overall.

Where an access condition is appropriate in an adoption order, this could be provided without recourse to wardship by the imposition of a contact order under s.10. In other cases local authority action may be simplified because there will be no need to consult the High Court about plans and because residence orders can be made in favour of third parties under s.10.

(3) *Child abuse cases.*

Unless and until satisfactory provision is made for hearsay evidence outside wardship under s.96 it will be impossible to prove some cases, and in others it will be necessary to call the child to give evidence. Ss.40 and 94 enable a child to be protected pending an appeal against refusal to grant or discharge of a care order.

(4) *Disputes with parents and difficult decisions.*

Subject to subss. (4) and (5) where the child is in care, the local authority will not be able to submit to the High Court's jurisdiction and have the court make difficult decisions such as whether the child has an abortion (*Re P* [1986] 1 F.L.R. 272). Nor will it be able to have a dispute with parents of a child in care settled by the court.

Subs. (1)

The High Court will still be able to make a care order but the grounds in s.31(2) will have to be satisfied. Cases will normally start in the magistrates' court and will be transferred to the High Court where appropriate (Sched. 11).

Subs. (2)

A child who is made a ward in proceedings may be accommodated by the local authority at the request of the current carer with the consent of the court. The High Court may still exercise its inherent jurisdiction without making the child a ward, *e.g.*, to grant injunctions against third parties (*per* Solicitor General (Standing Committee B, col. 488, June 8, 1989)).

Subs. (4)

If the child is accommodated by the local authority, the authority will be able to seek a "prohibited steps" or "specific issue" order but not so as to require a child to remain in local authority accommodation nor be supervised by the local authority (s.9(5)). Issues about medical treatment over which a parent has power could thus be decided by the court. S.9(1) precludes "prohibited steps" and "specific issue" orders in respect of children in care. S.8 defines these orders by reference to parental responsibility. Parents do not have a right to make decisions about the medical treatment of mature children under 16 years of age (*Gillick* v. *West Norfolk Area Health Authority* [1986] A.C. 112), nor, apparently, to consent to non therapeutic treatment (*Re D* [1976] Fam. 185). The court may consent to sterilisation of a minor who is incapable of making the decision (*Re B* [1987] A.C. 199) and could do so without making the child a ward.

Effect of orders as between England and Wales and Northern Ireland, the Channel Islands or the Isle of Man

101.—(1) The Secretary of State may make regulations providing—
    (a) for prescribed orders which—
        (i) are made by a court in Northern Ireland; and
        (ii) appear to the Secretary of State to correspond in their effect to orders which may be made under any provision of this Act,
    to have effect in prescribed circumstances, for prescribed purposes of this Act, as if they were orders of a prescribed kind made under this Act;
    (b) for prescribed orders which—
        (i) are made by a court in England and Wales; and
        (ii) appear to the Secretary of State to correspond in their effect to orders which may be made under any provision in force in Northern Ireland,
    to have effect in prescribed circumstances, for prescribed purposes of the law of Northern Ireland, as if they were orders of a prescribed kind made in Northern Ireland.

(2) Regulations under subsection (1) may provide for the order concerned to cease to have effect for the purposes of the law of Northern Ireland, or (as the case may be) the law of England and Wales, if prescribed conditions are satisfied.

(3) The Secretary of State may make regulations providing for prescribed orders which—
    (a) are made by a court in the Isle of Man or in any of the Channel Islands; and
    (b) appear to the Secretary of State to correspond in their effect to orders which may be made under this Act,
to have effect in prescribed circumstances for prescribed purposes of this Act, as if they were orders of a prescribed kind made under this Act.

(4) Where a child who is in the care of a local authority is lawfully taken to live in Northern Ireland, the Isle of Man or any of the Channel Islands, the care order in question shall cease to have effect if the conditions prescribed in regulations made by the Secretary of State are satisfied.

(5) Any regulations made under this section may—
    (a) make such consequential amendments (including repeals) in—
        (i) section 25 of the Children and Young Persons Act 1969 (transfers between England and Wales and Northern Ireland); or
        (ii) section 26 (transfers between England and Wales and Channel Islands or Isle of Man) of that Act,
    as the Secretary of State considers necessary or expedient; and
    (b) modify any provision of this Act, in its application (by virtue of the regulations) in relation to an order made otherwise than in England and Wales.

DEFINITION
"care order": s.31(11).

GENERAL NOTE
This section empowers the Secretary of State to make regulations providing that orders made by Northern Ireland courts have effect in England and Wales (subs. (1)) and that orders made by courts in England and Wales have effect in Northern Ireland (subs. (2)); also that care orders shall cease to have effect if the child lawfully goes to Northern Ireland, etc. (subs. (4)). Orders made in courts in the Channel Isles and the Isle of Man may also have the effect prescribed by regulations (subs. (5)). Ss.25 and 26 of the C.Y.P.A. 1969 can be amended by regulations.

Search warrants

Power of constable to assist in exercise of certain powers to search for children or inspect premises

102.—(1) Where, on an application made by any person for a warrant under this section, it appears to the court—

(a) that a person attempting to exercise powers under any enactment mentioned in subsection (6) has been prevented from doing so by being refused entry to the premises concerned or refused access to the child concerned; or

(b) that any such person is likely to be so prevented from exercising any such powers,

it may issue a warrant authorising any constable to assist that person in the exercise of those powers, using reasonable force if necessary.

(2) Every warrant issued under this section shall be addressed to, and executed by, a constable who shall be accompanied by the person applying for the warrant if—

(a) that person so desires; and

(b) the court by whom the warrant is issued does not direct otherwise.

(3) A court granting an application for a warrant under this section may direct that the constable concerned may, in executing the warrant, be accompanied by a registered medical practitioner, registered nurse or registered health visitor if he so chooses.

(4) An application for a warrant under this section shall be made in the manner and form prescribed by rules of court.

(5) Where—

(a) an application for a warrant under this section relates to a particular child; and

(b) it is reasonably practicable to do so,

the application and any warrant granted on the application shall name the child; and where it does not name him it shall describe him as clearly as possible.

(6) The enactments are—

(a) sections 62, 64, 67, 76, 80, 86 and 87;

(b) paragraph 8(1)(b) and (2)(b) of Schedule 3;

(c) section 33 of the Adoption Act 1976 (duty of local authority to secure that protected children are visited from time to time).

DEFINITION
"the court": s.92(7).

GENERAL NOTE
This section re-enacts the provisions relating to search warrants which may be granted to facilitate the inspection of premises by the Secretary of State, a local authority or any duly authorised person. This power is additional to that to grant warrants in connection with emergency protection orders under s.48. The grounds for a warrant and its provisions are identical to those in s.48(9) to (13) but the provisions in subs. (6) relate to general supervisory powers, not emergency protection. Where a search revealed a child at risk and the local authority wished to remove the child (rather than arrange for the parents to do so), an emergency protection order would be necessary.

General

Offences by bodies corporate

103.—(1) This section applies where any offence under this Act is committed by a body corporate.

(2) If the offence is proved to have been committed with the consent or connivance of or to be attributable to any neglect on the part of any director, manager, secretary or other similar officer of the body corporate, or any person who was purporting to act in any such capacity, he (as well as the body corporate) shall be guilty of the offence and shall be liable to be proceeded against and punished accordingly.

GENERAL NOTE

This section explains that where certain officers of a corporate body are involved in committing an offence under the Act, they *and* the corporate body are liable to be prosecuted.

Regulations and orders

104.—(1) Any power of the Lord Chancellor or the Secretary of State under this Act to make an order, regulations, or rules, except an order under section 54(2), 56(4)(a), 57(3), 84 or 97(4) or paragraph 1(1) of Schedule 4, shall be exercisable by statutory instrument.

(2) Any such statutory instrument, except one made under section 17(4), 107 or 108(2), shall be subject to annulment in pursuance of a resolution of either House of Parliament.

(3) An order under section 17(4) shall not be made unless a draft of it has been laid before, and approved by a resolution of, each House of Parliament.

(4) Any statutory instrument made under this Act may—
  (a) make different provision for different cases;
  (b) provide for exemptions from any of its provisions; and
  (c) contain such incidental, supplemental and transitional provisions as the person making it considers expedient.

Interpretation

105.—(1) In this Act—
  "adoption agency" means a body which may be referred to as an adoption agency by virtue of section 1 of the Adoption Act 1976;
  "bank holiday" means a day which is a bank holiday under the Banking and Financial Dealings Act 1971;
  "care order" has the meaning given by section 31(11) and also includes any order which by or under any enactment has the effect of, or is deemed to be, a care order for the purposes of this Act; and any reference to a child who is in the care of an authority is a reference to a child who is in their care by virtue of a care order;
  "child" means, subject to paragraph 16 of Schedule 1, a person under the age of eighteen;
  "child assessment order" has the meaning given by section 43(2);
  "child minder" has the meaning given by section 71;
  "child of the family", in relation to the parties to a marriage, means—
    (a) a child of both of those parties;
    (b) any other child, not being a child who is placed with those parties as foster parents by a local authority or voluntary organ-

isation, who has been treated by both of those parties as a child of their family;

"children's home" has the same meaning as in section 63;

"community home" has the meaning given by section 53;

"contact order" has the meaning given by section 8(1);

"day care" has the same meaning as in section 18;

"disabled," in relation to a child, has the same meaning as in section 17(11);

"district health authority" has the same meaning as in the National Health Service Act 1977;

"domestic premises" has the meaning given by section 71(12);

"education supervision order" has the meaning given in section 36;

"emergency protection order" means an order under section 44;

"family assistance order" has the meaning given in section 16(2);

"family proceedings" has the meaning given by section 8(3);

"functions" includes powers and duties;

"guardian of a child" means a guardian (other than a guardian of the estate of a child) appointed in accordance with the provisions of section 5;

"harm" has the same meaning as in section 31(9) and the question of whether harm is significant shall be determined in accordance with section 31(10);

"health authority" means any district health authority and any special health authority established under the National Health Service Act 1977;

"health service hospital" has the same meaning as in the National Health Service Act 1977;

"hospital" has the same meaning as in the Mental Health Act 1983, except that it does not include a special hospital within the meaning of that Act;

"ill-treatment" has the same meaning as in section 31(9);

"independent school" has the same meaning as in the Education Act 1944;

"local authority" means, in relation to England and Wales, the council of a county, a metropolitan district, a London Borough or the Common Council of the City of London and, in relation to Scotland, a local authority within the meaning of section 1(2) of the Social Work (Scotland) Act 1968;

"local authority foster parent" has the same meaning as in section 23(3);

"local education authority" has the same meaning as in the Education Act 1944;

"local housing authority" has the same meaning as in the Housing Act 1985;

"mental nursing home" has the same meaning as in the Registered Homes Act 1984;

"nursing home" has the same meaning as in the Act of 1984;

"parental responsibility" has the meaning given in section 3;

"parental responsibility agreement" has the meaning given in section 4(1);

"prescribed" means prescribed by regulations made under this Act;

"privately fostered child" and "to foster a child privately" have the same meaning as in section 66;

"prohibited steps order" has the meaning given by section 8(1);

"protected child" has the same meaning as in Part III of the Adoption Act 1976;

"registered children's home" has the same meaning as in section 63;

"registered pupil" has the same meaning as in the Education Act 1944;

"relative", in relation to a child, means a grandparent, brother, sister, uncle or aunt (whether of the full blood or half blood or by affinity) or step-parent;

"residence order" has the meaning given by section 8(1);

"residential care home" has the same meaning as in the Registered Homes Act 1984;

"responsible person", in relation to a child who is the subject of a supervision order, has the meaning given in paragraph 1 of Schedule 3;

"school" has the same meaning as in the Education Act 1944 or, in relation to Scotland, in the Education (Scotland) Act 1980;

"service", in relation to any provision made under Part III, includes any facility;

"signed", in relation to any person, includes the making by that person of his mark;

"special educational needs" has the same meaning as in the Education Act 1981;

"special health authority" has the same meaning as in the National Health Service Act 1977;

"specific issue order" has the meaning given by section 8(1);

"supervision order" has the meaning given by section 31(11);

"supervised child" and "supervisor", in relation to a supervision order or an education supervision order, mean respectively the child who is (or is to be) under supervision and the person under whose supervision he is (or is to be) by virtue of the order;

"upbringing", in relation to any child, includes the care of the child but not his maintenance;

"voluntary home" has the meaning given by section 60;

"voluntary organisation" means a body (other than a public or local authority) whose activities are not carried on for profit.

(2) References in this Act to a child whose father and mother were, or (as the case may be) were not, married to each other at the time of his birth must be read with section 1 of the Family Law Reform Act 1987 (which extends the meaning of such references).

(3) References in this Act to—

(a) a person with whom a child lives, or is to live, as the result of a residence order; or

(b) a person in whose favour a residence order is in force,

shall be construed as references to the person named in the order as the person with whom the child is to live.

(4) References in this Act to a child who is looked after by a local authority have the same meaning as they have (by virtue of section 22) in Part III.

(5) References in this Act to accommodation provided by or on behalf of a local authority are references to accommodation so provided in the exercise of functions which stand referred to the social services committee of that or any other local authority under the Local Authority Social Services Act 1970.

(6) In determining the "ordinary residence" of a child for any purpose of this Act, there shall be disregarded any period in which he lives in any place—

(a) which is a school or other institution;

(b) in accordance with the requirements of a supervision order under this Act or an order under section 7(7)(b) of the Children and Young Persons Act 1969; or

(c) while he is being provided with accommodation by or on behalf of a local authority.

(7) References in this Act to children who are in need shall be construed in accordance with section 17.

(8) Any notice or other document required under this Act to be served on any person may be served on him by being delivered personally to him, or being sent by post to him in a registered letter or by the recorded delivery service at his proper address.

(9) Any such notice or other document required to be served on a body corporate or a firm shall be duly served if it is served on the secretary or clerk of that body or a partner of that firm.

(10) For the purposes of this section, and of section 7 of the Interpretation Act 1978 in its application to this section, the proper address of a person—

(a) in the case of a secretary or clerk of a body corporate, shall be that of the registered or principal office of that body;

(b) in the case of a partner of a firm, shall be that of the principal office of the firm; and

(c) in any other case, shall be the last known address of the person to be served.

Financial provisions

106.—(1) Any—

(a) grants made by the Secretary of State under this Act; and

(b) any other expenses incurred by the Secretary of State under this Act,

shall be payable out of money provided by Parliament.

(2) Any sums received by the Secretary of State under section 58, or by way of the repayment of any grant made under section 82(2) or (4) shall be paid into the Consolidated Fund.

Application to Channel Islands

107. Her Majesty may by Order in Council direct that any of the provisions of this Act shall extend to any of the Channel Islands with such exceptions and modifications as may be specified in the Order.

Short title, commencement extent etc.

108.—(1) This Act may be cited as the Children Act 1989.

(2) Sections 89 and 96(3) to (7), and paragraph 35 of Schedule 12, shall come into force on the passing of this Act and paragraph 36 of Schedule 12 shall come into force at the end of the period of two months beginning with the day on which this Act is passed but otherwise this Act shall come into force on such date as may be appointed by order made by the Lord Chancellor or the Secretary of State, or by both acting jointly.

(3) Different dates may be appointed for different provisions of this Act and in relation to different cases.

(4) The minor amendments set out in Schedule 12 shall have effect.

(5) The consequential amendments set out in Schedule 13 shall have effect.

(6) The transitional provisions and savings set out in Schedule 14 shall have effect.

(7) The repeals set out in Schedule 15 shall have effect.

(8) An order under subsection (2) may make such transitional provisions or savings as appear to the person making the order to be necessary or expedient in connection with the provisions brought into force by the order, including—

(a) provisions adding to or modifying the provisions of Schedule 14; and

(b) such adaptations—
    (i) of the provisions brought into force by the order; and
    (ii) of any provisions of this Act then in force,
as appear to him necessary or expedient in consequence of the partial operation of this Act.

(9) The Lord Chancellor may by order make such amendments or repeals, in such enactments as may be specified in the order, as appear to him to be necessary or expedient in consequence of any provision of this Act.

(10) This Act shall, in its application to the Isles of Scilly, have effect subject to such exceptions, adaptations and modifications as the Secretary of State may by order prescribe.

(11) The following provisions of this Act extend to Scotland—
    section 19;
    section 25(8);
    section 50(13);
    Part X;
    section 80(1)(h) and (i), (2) to (4), (5)(a), (b) and (h) and (6) to (12);
    section 88;
    section 104 (so far as necessary);
    section 105 (so far as necessary);
    subsections (1) to (3), (8) and (9) and this subsection;
    in Schedule 2, paragraph 24;
    in Schedule 12, paragraphs 1, 7 to 10, 18, 27, 30(a) and 41 to 44;
    in Schedule 13, paragraphs 18 to 23, 32, 46, 47, 50, 57, 62, 63, 68(a) and (b) and 71;
    in Schedule 14, paragraphs 1, 33 and 34;
    in Schedule 15, the entries relating to—
        (a) the Custody of Children Act 1891;
        (b) the Nurseries and Child Minders Regulation Act 1948;
        (c) section 53(3) of the Children and Young Persons Act 1963;
        (d) section 60 of the Health Services and Public Health Act 1968;
        (e) the Social Work (Scotland) Act 1968;
        (f) the Adoption (Scotland) Act 1978;
        (g) the Child Care Act 1980;
        (h) the Foster Children (Scotland) Act 1984;
        (i) the Child Abduction and Custody Act 1985; and
        (j) the Family Law Act 1986.

(12) The following provisions of this Act extend to Northern Ireland—
    section 50;
    section 101(1)(b), (2) and (5)(a)(i);
    subsections (1) to (3), (8) and (9) and this subsection;
    in Schedule 2, paragraph 24;
    in Schedule 12, paragraphs 7 to 10, 18 and 27;
    in Schedule 13, paragraphs 21, 22, 46, 47, 57, 62, 63, 68(c) to (e) and 69 to 71;
    in Schedule 14, paragraphs 18, 28 to 30 and 38(a); and
    in Schedule 15, the entries relating to the Guardianship of Minors Act 1971, the Children Act 1975, the Child Care Act 1980, and the Family Law Act 1986.

SCHEDULES

SCHEDULE 1

FINANCIAL PROVISION FOR CHILDREN

Orders for financial relief against parents

1.—(1) On an application made by a parent or guardian of a child, or by any person in whose favour a residence order is in force with respect to a child, the court may—
   (a) in the case of an application to the High Court or a county court, make one or more of the orders mentioned in sub-paragraph (2);
   (b) in the case of an application to a magistrates' court, make one or both of the orders mentioned in paragraphs (a) and (c) of that sub-paragraph.
   (2) The orders referred to in sub-paragraph (1) are—
      (a) an order requiring either or both parents of a child—
         (i) to make to the applicant for the benefit of the child; or
         (ii) to make to the child himself,
         such periodical payments, for such term, as may be specified in the order;
      (b) an order requiring either or both parents of a child—
         (i) to secure to the applicant for the benefit of the child; or
         (ii) to secure to the child himself,
         such periodical payments, for such term, as may be so specified;
      (c) an order requiring either or both parents of a child—
         (i) to pay to the applicant for the benefit of the child; or
         (ii) to pay to the child himself,
         such lump sum as may be so specified;
      (d) an order requiring a settlement to be made for the benefit of the child, and to the satisfaction of the court, of property—
         (i) to which either parent is entitled (either in possession or in reversion); and
         (ii) which is specified in the order;
      (e) an order requiring either or both parents of a child—
         (i) to transfer to the applicant, for the benefit of the child; or
         (ii) to transfer to the child himself,
         such property to which the parent is, or the parents are, entitled (either in possession or in reversion) as may be specified in the order.
   (3) The powers conferred by this paragraph may be exercised at any time.
   (4) An order under sub-paragraph (2)(a) or (b) may be varied or discharged by a subsequent order made on the application of any person by or to whom payments were required to be made under the previous order.
   (5) Where a court makes an order under this paragraph—
      (a) it may at any time make a further such order under sub-paragraph (2)(a), (b) or (c) with respect to the child concerned if he has not reached the age of eighteen;
      (b) it may not make more than one order under sub-paragraph (2)(d) or (e) against the same person in respect of the same child.
   (6) On making, varying or discharging a residence order the court may exercise any of its powers under this Schedule even though no application has been made to it under this Schedule.

Orders for financial relief for persons over eighteen

2.—(1) If, on an application by a person who has reached the age of eighteen, it appears to the court—
   (a) that the applicant is, will be or (if an order were made under this paragraph) would be receiving instruction at an educational establishment or undergoing training for a trade, profession or vocation, whether or not while in gainful employment; or
   (b) that there are special circumstances which justify the making of an order under this paragraph,
the court may make one or both of the orders mentioned in sub-paragraph (2).
   (2) The orders are—
      (a) an order requiring either or both of the applicant's parents to pay to the

applicant such periodical payments, for such term, as may be specified in the order;

(b) an order requiring either or both of the applicant's parents to pay to the applicant such lump sum as may be so specified.

(3) An application may not be made under this paragraph by any person if, immediately before he reached the age of sixteen, a periodical payments order was in force with respect to him.

(4) No order shall be made under this paragraph at a time when the parents of the applicant are living with each other in the same household.

(5) An order under sub-paragraph (2)(a) may be varied or discharged by a subsequent order made on the application of any person by or to whom payments were required to be made under the previous order.

(6) In sub-paragraph (3) "periodical payments order" means an order made under—

(a) this Schedule;

(b) section 6(3) of the Family Law Reform Act 1969;

(c) section 23 or 27 of the Matrimonial Causes Act 1973;

(d) Part I of the Domestic Proceedings and Magistrates' Courts Act 1978, for the making or securing of periodical payments.

(7) The powers conferred by this paragraph shall be exercisable at any time.

(8) Where the court makes an order under this paragraph it may from time to time while that order remains in force make a further such order.

Duration of orders for financial relief

3.—(1) The term to be specified in an order for periodical payments made under paragraph 1(2)(a) or (b) in favour of a child may begin with the date of the making of an application for the order in question or any later date but—

(a) shall not in the first instance extend beyond the child's seventeenth birthday unless the court thinks it right in the circumstances of the case to specify a later date; and

(b) shall not in any event extend beyond the child's eighteenth birthday.

(2) Paragraph (b) of sub-paragraph (1) shall not apply in the case of a child if it appears to the court that—

(a) the child is, or will be or (if an order were made without complying with that paragraph) would be receiving instruction at an educational establishment or under-going training for a trade, profession or vocation, whether or not while in gainful employment; or

(b) there are special circumstances which justify the making of an order without complying with that paragraph.

(3) An order for periodical payments made under paragraph 1(2)(a) or 2(2)(a) shall, notwithstanding anything in the order, cease to have effect on the death of the person liable to make payments under the order.

(4) Where an order is made under paragraph 1(2)(a) or (b) requiring periodical payments to be made or secured to the parent of a child, the order shall cease to have effect if—

(a) any parent making or securing the payments; and

(b) any parent to whom the payments are made or secured,

live together for a period of more than six months.

Matters to which court is to have regard in making orders for financial relief

4.—(1) In deciding whether to exercise its powers under paragraph 1 or 2, and if so in what manner, the court shall have regard to all the circumstances including—

(a) the income, earning capacity, property and other financial resources which each person mentioned in sub-paragraph (4) has or is likely to have in the foreseeable future;

(b) the financial needs, obligations and responsibilities which each person mentioned in sub-paragraph (4) has or is likely to have in the foreseeable future;

(c) the financial needs of the child;

(d) the income, earning capacity (if any), property and other financial resources of the child;

(e) any physical or mental disability of the child;

(f) the manner in which the child was being, or was expected to be, educated or trained.

(2) In deciding whether to exercise its powers under paragraph 1 against a person who is not the mother or father of the child, and if so in what manner, the court shall in addition have regard to—

(a) whether that person had assumed responsibility for the maintenance of the child and, if so, the extent to which and basis on which he assumed that responsibility and the length of the period during which he met that responsibility;

(b) whether he did so knowing that the child was not his child;

(c) the liability of any other person to maintain the child.

(3) Where the court makes an order under paragraph 1 against a person who is not the father of the child, it shall record in the order that the order is made on the basis that the person against whom the order is made is not the child's father.

(4) The persons mentioned in sub-paragraph (1) are—

(a) in relation to a decision whether to exercise its powers under paragraph 1, any parent of the child;

(b) in relation to a decision whether to exercise its powers under paragraph 2, the mother and father of the child;

(c) the applicant for the order;

(d) any other person in whose favour the court proposes to make the order.

Provisions relating to lump sums

5.—(1) Without prejudice to the generality of paragraph 1, an order under that paragraph for the payment of a lump sum may be made for the purpose of enabling any liabilities or expenses—

(a) incurred in connection with the birth of the child or in maintaining the child; and

(b) reasonably incurred before the making of the order,

to be met.

(2) The amount of any lump sum required to be paid by an order made by a magistrates' court under paragraph 1 or 2 shall not exceed £1000 or such larger amount as the Secretary of State may from time to time by order fix for the purposes of this sub-paragraph.

(3) The power of the court under paragraph 1 or 2 to vary or discharge an order for the making or securing of periodical payments by a parent shall include power to make an order under that provision for the payment of a lump sum by that parent.

(4) The amount of any lump sum which a parent may be required to pay by virtue of sub-paragraph (3) shall not, in the case of an order made by a magistrates' court, exceed the maximum amount that may at the time of the making of the order be required to be paid under sub-paragraph (2), but a magistrates' court may make an order for the payment of a lump sum not exceeding that amount even though the parent was required to pay a lump sum by a previous order under this Act.

(5) An order made under paragraph 1 or 2 for the payment of a lump sum may provide for the payment of that sum by instalments.

(6) Where the court provides for the payment of a lump sum by instalments the court, on an application made either by the person liable to pay or the person entitled to receive that sum, shall have power to vary that order by varying—

(a) the number of instalments payable;

(b) the amount of any instalment payable;

(c) the date on which any instalment becomes payable.

Variation etc. of orders for periodical payments

6.—(1) In exercising its powers under paragraph 1 or 2 to vary or discharge an order for the making or securing of periodical payments the court shall have regard to all the circumstances of the case, including any change in any of the matters to which the court was required to have regard when making the order.

(2) The power of the court under paragraph 1 or 2 to vary an order for the making or securing of periodical payments shall include power to suspend any provision of the order temporarily and to revive any provision so suspended.

(3) Where on an application under paragraph 1 or 2 for the variation or discharge of an order for the making or securing of periodical payments the court varies the payments required to be made under that order, the court may provide that the payments as so varied shall be made from such date as the court may specify, not being earlier than the date of the making of the application.

(4) An application for the variation of an order made under paragraph 1 for the making or securing of periodical payments to or for the benefit of a child may, if the child has reached the age of sixteen, be made by the child himself.

(5) Where an order for the making or securing of periodical payments made under paragraph 1 ceases to have effect on the date on which the child reaches the age of sixteen,

or at any time after that date but before or on the date on which he reaches the age of eighteen, the child may apply to the court which made the order for an order for its revival.

(6) If on such an application it appears to the court that—

    (a) the child is, will be or (if an order were made under this sub-paragraph) would be receiving instruction at an educational establishment or undergoing training for a trade, profession or vocation, whether or not while in gainful employment; or

    (b) there are special circumstances which justify the making of an order under this paragraph,

the court shall have power by order to revive the order from such date as the court may specify, not being earlier than the date of the making of the application.

(7) Any order which is revived by an order under sub-paragraph (5) may be varied or discharged under that provision, on the application of any person by whom or to whom payments are required to be made under the revived order.

(8) An order for the making or securing of periodical payments made under paragraph 1 may be varied or discharged, after the death of either parent, on the application of a guardian of the child concerned.

Variation of orders for secured periodical payments after death of parent

7.—(1) Where the parent liable to make payments under a secured periodical payments order has died, the persons who may apply for the variation or discharge of the order shall include the personal representatives of the deceased parent.

(2) No application for the variation of the order shall, except with the permission of the court, be made after the end of the period of six months from the date on which representation in regard to the estate of that parent is first taken out.

(3) The personal representatives of a deceased person against whom a secured periodical payments order was made shall not be liable for having distributed any part of the estate of the deceased after the end of the period of six months referred to in sub-paragraph (2) on the ground that they ought to have taken into account the possibility that the court might permit an application for variation to be made after that period by the person entitled to payments under the order.

(4) Sub-paragraph (3) shall not prejudice any power to recover any part of the estate so distributed arising by virtue of the variation of an order in accordance with this paragraph.

(5) Where an application to vary a secured periodical payments order is made after the death of the parent liable to make payments under the order, the circumstances to which the court is required to have regard under paragraph 6(1) shall include the changed circumstances resulting from the death of the parent.

(6) In considering for the purposes of sub-paragraph (2) the question when representation was first taken out, a grant limited to settled land or to trust property shall be left out of account and a grant limited to real estate or to personal estate shall be left out of account unless a grant limited to the remainder of the estate has previously been made or is made at the same time.

(7) In this paragraph "secured periodical payments order" means an order for secured periodical payments under paragraph 1(2)(b).

Financial relief under other enactments

8.—(1) This paragraph applies where a residence order is made with respect to a child at a time when there is in force an order ("the financial relief order") made under any enactment other than this Act and requiring a person to contribute to the child's maintenance.

(2) Where this paragraph applies, the court may, on the application of—

    (a) any person required by the financial relief order to contribute to the child's maintenance; or

    (b) any person in whose favour a residence order with respect to the child is in force,

make an order revoking the financial relief order, or varying it by altering the amount of any sum payable under that order or by substituting the applicant for the person to whom any such sum is otherwise payable under that order.

Interim orders

9.—(1) Where an application is made under paragraph 1 or 2 the court may, at any time before it disposes of the application, make an interim order—

(a) requiring either or both parents to make such periodical payments, at such times and for such term as the court thinks fit; and

(b) giving any direction which the court thinks fit.

(2) An interim order made under this paragraph may provide for payments to be made from such date as the court may specify, not being earlier than the date of the making of the application under paragraph 1 or 2.

(3) An interim order made under this paragraph shall cease to have effect when the application is disposed of or, if earlier, on the date specified for the purposes of this paragraph in the interim order.

(4) An interim order in which a date has been specified for the purposes of sub-paragraph (3) may be varied by substituting a later date.

Alteration of maintenance agreements

10.—(1) In this paragraph and in paragraph 11 "maintenance agreement" means any agreement in writing made with respect to a child, whether before or after the commencement of this paragraph, which—

(a) is or was made between the father and mother of the child; and

(b) contains provision with respect to the making or securing of payments, or the disposition or use of any property, for the maintenance or education of the child,

and any such provisions are in this paragraph, and paragraph 11, referred to as "financial arrangements".

(2) Where a maintenance agreement is for the time being subsisting and each of the parties to the agreement is for the time being either domiciled or resident in England and Wales, then, either party may apply to the court for an order under this paragraph.

(3) If the court to which the application is made is satisfied either—

(a) that, by reason of a change in the circumstances in the light of which any financial arrangements contained in the agreement were made (including a change foreseen by the parties when making the agreement), the agreement should be altered so as to make different financial arrangements; or

(b) that the agreement does not contain proper financial arrangements with respect to the child,

then that court may by order make such alterations in the agreement by varying or revoking any financial arrangements contained in it as may appear to it to be just having regard to all the circumstances.

(4) If the maintenance agreement is altered by an order under this paragraph, the agreement shall have effect thereafter as if the alteration had been made by agreement between the parties and for valuable consideration.

(5) Where a court decides to make an order under this paragraph altering the maintenance agreement—

(a) by inserting provision for the making or securing by one of the parties to the agreement of periodical payments for the maintenance of the child; or

(b) by increasing the rate of periodical payments required to be made or secured by one of the parties for the maintenance of the child,

then, in deciding the term for which under the agreement as altered by the order the payments or (as the case may be) the additional payments attributable to the increase are to be made or secured for the benefit of the child, the court shall apply the provisions of sub-paragraphs (1) and (2) of paragraph 3 as if the order were an order under paragraph 1(2)(a) or (b).

(6) A magistrates' court shall not entertain an application under sub-paragraph (2) unless both the parties to the agreement are resident in England and Wales and at least one of the parties is resident in the commission area (within the meaning of the Justices of the Peace Act 1979) for which the court is appointed, and shall not have power to make any order on such an application except—

(a) in a case where the agreement contains no provision for periodical payments by either of the parties, an order inserting provision for the making by one of the parties of periodical payments for the maintenance of the child;

(b) in a case where the agreement includes provision for the making by one of the parties of periodical payments, an order increasing or reducing the rate of, or terminating, any of those payments.

(7) For the avoidance of doubt it is hereby declared that nothing in this paragraph affects any power of a court before which any proceedings between the parties to a maintenance agreement are brought under any other enactment to make an order containing financial arrangements or any right of either party to apply for such an order in such proceedings.

11.—(1) Where a maintenance agreement provides for the continuation, after the death of one of the parties, of payments for the maintenance of a child and that party dies domiciled in England and Wales, the surviving party or the personal representatives of the deceased party may apply to the High Court or a county court for an order under paragraph 10.

(2) If a maintenance agreement is altered by a court on an application under this paragraph, the agreement shall have effect thereafter as if the alteration had been made, immediately before the death, by agreement between the parties and for valuable consideration.

(3) An application under this paragraph shall not, except with leave of the High Court or a county court, be made after the end of the period of six months beginning with the day on which representation in regard to the estate of the deceased is first taken out.

(4) In considering for the purposes of sub-paragraph (3) the question when representation was first taken out, a grant limited to settled land or to trust property shall be left out of account and a grant limited to real estate or to personal estate shall be left out of account unless a grant limited to the remainder of the estate has previously been made or is made at the same time.

(5) A county court shall not entertain an application under this paragraph, or an application for leave to make an application under this paragraph, unless it would have jurisdiction to hear and determine proceedings for an order under section 2 of the Inheritance (Provision for Family and Dependants) Act 1975 in relation to the deceased's estate by virtue of section 25 of the County Courts Act 1984 (jurisdiction under the Act of 1975).

(6) The provisions of this paragraph shall not render the personal representatives of the deceased liable for having distributed any part of the estate of the deceased after the expiry of the period of six months referred to in sub-paragraph (3) on the ground that they ought to have taken into account the possibility that a court might grant leave for an application by virtue of this paragraph to be made by the surviving party after that period.

(7) Sub-paragraph (6) shall not prejudice any power to recover any part of the estate so distributed arising by virtue of the making of an order in pursuance of this paragraph.

Enforcement of orders for maintenance

12.—(1) Any person for the time being under an obligation to make payments in pursuance of any order for the payment of money made by a magistrates' court under this Act shall give notice of any change of address to such person (if any) as may be specified in the order.

(2) Any person failing without reasonable excuse to give such a notice shall be guilty of an offence and liable on summary conviction to a fine not exceeding level 2 on the standard scale.

(3) An order for the payment of money made by a magistrates' court under this Act shall be enforceable as a magistrates' court maintenance order within the meaning of section 150(1) of the Magistrates' Courts Act 1980.

Direction for settlement of instrument by conveyancing counsel

13. Where the High Court or a county court decides to make an order under this Act for the securing of periodical payments or for the transfer or settlement of property, it may direct that the matter be referred to one of the conveyancing counsel of the court to settle a proper instrument to be executed by all necessary parties.

Financial provision for child resident in country outside England and Wales

14.—(1) Where one parent of a child lives in England and Wales and the child lives outside England and Wales with—
(a) another parent of his;
(b) a guardian of his; or
(c) a person in whose favour a residence order is in force with respect to the child,
the court shall have power, on an application made by any of the persons mentioned in paragraphs (a) to (c), to make one or both of the orders mentioned in paragraph 1(2)(a) and (b) against the parent living in England and Wales.

(2) Any reference in this Act to the powers of the court under paragraph 1(2) or to an order made under paragraph 1(2) shall include a reference to the powers which the court has by virtue of sub-paragraph (1) or (as the case may be) to an order made by virtue of sub-paragraph (1).

Local authority contribution to child's maintenance

15.—(1) Where a child lives, or is to live, with a person as the result of a residence order, a local authority may make contributions to that person towards the cost of the accommodation and maintenance of the child.

(2) Sub-paragraph (1) does not apply where the person with whom the child lives, or is to live, is a parent of the child or the husband or wife of a parent of the child.

Interpretation

16.—(1) In this Schedule "child" includes, in any case where an application is made under paragraph 2 or 6 in relation to á person who has reached the age of eighteen, that person.

(2) In this Schedule, except paragraphs 2 and 15, "parent" includes any party to a marriage (whether or not subsisting) in relation to whom the child concerned is a child of the family; and for this purpose any reference to either parent or both parents shall be construed as references to any parent of his and to all of his parents.

DEFINITIONS
"child": s.105, Sched. 1, para. 16.
"parent": Sched. 1, para. 16.

GENERAL NOTE
See notes to s.15.

Section 17, 23 and 29   SCHEDULE 2

LOCAL AUTHORITY SUPPORT FOR CHILDREN AND FAMILIES

PART I

PROVISION OF SERVICES FOR FAMILIES

Identification of children in need and provision of information

1.—(1) Every local authority shall take reasonable steps to identify the extent to which there are children in need within their area.

(2) Every local authority shall—
    (a) publish information—
        (i) about services provided by them under sections 17, 18, 20 and 24; and
        (ii) where they consider it appropriate, about the provision by others (including, in particular, voluntary organisations) of services which the authority have power to provide under those sections; and
    (b) take such steps as are reasonably practicable to ensure that those who might benefit from the services receive the information relevant to them.

Maintenance of a register of disabled children

2.—(1) Every local authority shall open and maintain a register of disabled children within their area.

(2) The register may be kept by means of a computer.

Assessment of children's needs

3. Where it appears to a local authority that a child within their area is in need, the authority may assess his needs for the purposes of this Act at the same time as any assessment of his needs is made under— *
    (a) the Chronically Sick and Disabled Persons Act 1970;
    (b) the Education Act 1981;
    (c) the Disabled Persons (Services, Consultation and Representation) Act 1986; or
    (d) any other enactment.

Prevention of neglect and abuse

4.—(1) Every local authority shall take reasonable steps, through the provision of services under Part III of this Act, to prevent children within their area suffering ill-treatment or neglect.

(2) Where a local authority believe that a child who is at any time within their area—

(a) is likely to suffer harm; but

(b) lives or proposes to live in the area of another local authority

they shall inform that other local authority.

(3) When informing that other local authority they shall specify—

(a) the harm that they believe he is likely to suffer; and

(b) (if they can) where the child lives or proposes to live.

Provision of accommodation in order to protect child

5.—(1) Where—

(a) it appears to a local authority that a child who is living on particular premises is suffering, or is likely to suffer, ill treatment at the hands of another person who is living on those premises; and

(b) that other person proposes to move from the premises,

the authority may assist that other person to obtain alternative accommodation.

(2) Assistance given under this paragraph may be in cash.

(3) Subsections (7) to (9) of section 17 shall apply in relation to assistance given under this paragraph as they apply in relation to assistance given under that section.

Provision for disabled children

6. Every local authority shall provide services designed—

(a) to minimise the effect on disabled children within their area of their disabilities; and

(b) to give such children the opportunity to lead lives which are as normal as possible.

Provision to reduce need for care proceedings etc.

7. Every local authority shall take reasonable steps designed—

(a) to reduce the need to bring—

(i) proceedings for care or supervision orders with respect to children within their area;

(ii) criminal proceedings against such children;

(iii) any family or other proceedings with respect to such children which might lead to them being placed in the authority's care; or

(iv) proceedings under the inherent jurisdiction of the High Court with respect to children;

(b) to encourage children within their area not to commit criminal offences; and

(c) to avoid the need for children within their area to be placed in secure accommodation.

Provision for children living with their families

8. Every local authority shall make such provision as they consider appropriate for the following services to be available with respect to children in need within their area while they are living with their families—

(a) advice, guidance and counselling;

(b) occupational, social, cultural or recreational activities;

(c) home help (which may include laundry facilities);

(d) facilities for, or assistance with, travelling to and from home for the purpose of taking advantage of any other service provided under this Act or of any similar service;

(e) assistance to enable the child concerned and his family to have a holiday.

Family centres

9.—(1) Every local authority shall provide such family centres as they consider appropriate in relation to children within their area.

(2) "Family centre" means a centre at which any of the persons mentioned in sub-paragraph (3) may—

    (a) attend for occupational, social, cultural or recreational activities;

    (b) attend for advice, guidance or counselling; or

    (c) be provided with accommodation while he is receiving advice, guidance or counselling.

(3) The persons are—

    (a) a child;

    (b) his parents;

    (c) any person who is not a parent of his but who has parental responsibility for him;

    (d) any other person who is looking after him.

Maintenance of the family home

10. Every local authority shall take such steps as are reasonably practicable, where any child within their area who is in need and whom they are not looking after is living apart from his family—

    (a) to enable him to live with his family; or

    (b) to promote contact between him and his family,

if, in their opinion, it is necessary to do so in order to safeguard or promote his welfare.

Duty to consider racial groups to which children in need belong

11. Every local authority shall, in making any arrangements—

    (a) for the provision of day care within their area; or

    (b) designed to encourage persons to act as local authority foster parents,

have regard to the different racial groups to which children within their area who are in need belong.

Part II

Children Looked After By Local Authorities

Regulations as to placing of children with local authority foster parents

12. Regulations under section 23(2)(a) may, in particular, make provision—

    (a) with regard to the welfare of children placed with local authority foster parents;

    (b) as to the arrangements to be made by local authorities in connection with the health and education of such children;

    (c) as to the records to be kept by local authorities;

    (d) for securing that a child is not placed with a local authority foster parent unless that person is for the time being approved as a local authority foster parent by such local authority as may be prescribed;

    (e) for securing that where possible the local authority foster parent with whom a child is to be placed is—

        (i) of the same religious persuasion as the child; or

        (ii) gives an undertaking that the child will be brought up in that religious persuasion;

    (f) for securing that children placed with local authority foster parents, and the premises in which they are accommodated, will be supervised and inspected by a local authority and that the children will be removed from those premises if their welfare appears to require it;

    (g) as to the circumstances in which local authorities may make arrangements for duties imposed on them by the regulations to be discharged, on their behalf.

Regulations as to arrangements under section 23(2)(f)

13. Regulations under section 23(2)(f) may, in particular, make provision as to—

    (a) the persons to be notified of any proposed arrangements;

    (b) the opportunities such persons are to have to make representations in relation to the arrangements proposed;

    (c) the persons to be notified of any proposed changes in arrangements;

    (d) the records to be kept by local authorities;

(e) the supervision by local authorities of any arrangements made.

Regulations as to conditions under which child in care is allowed to live with parent, etc.

14. Regulations under section 23(5) may, in particular, impose requirements on a local authority as to—
  (a) the making of any decision by a local authority to allow a child to live with any person falling within section 23(4) (including requirements as to those who must be consulted before the decision is made, and those who must be notified when it has been made);
  (b) the supervision or medical examination of the child concerned;
  (c) the removal of the child, in such circumstances as may be prescribed, from the care of the person with whom he has been allowed to live.

Promotion and maintenance of contact between child and family

15.—(1) Where a child is being looked after by a local authority, the authority shall, unless it is not reasonably practicable or consistent with his welfare, endeavour to promote contact between the child and—
  (a) his parents;
  (b) any person who is not a parent of his but who has parental responsibility for him; and
  (c) any relative, friend or other person connected with him.
  (2) Where a child is being looked after by a local authority—
  (a) the authority shall take such steps as are reasonably practicable to secure that—
      (i) his parents; and
      (ii) any person who is not a parent of his but who has parental responsibility for him,
    are kept informed of where he is being accommodated; and
  (b) every such person shall secure that the authority is kept informed of his or her address.
  (3) Where a local authority ("the receiving authority") take over the provision of accommodation for a child from another local authority ("the transferring authority") under section 20(2)—
  (a) the receiving authority shall (where reasonably practicable) inform—
      (i) the child's parents; and
      (ii) any person who is not a parent of his but who has parental responsibility for him;
  (b) sub-paragraph (2)(a) shall apply to the transferring authority, as well as the receiving authority, until at least one such person has been informed of the change; and
  (c) sub-paragraph (2)(b) shall not require any person to inform the receiving authority of his address until he has been so informed.
  (4) Nothing in this paragraph requires a local authority to inform any person of the whereabouts of a child if—
  (a) the child is in the care of the authority; and
  (b) the authority has reasonable cause to believe that informing the person would prejudice the child's welfare.
  (5) Any person who fails (without reasonable excuse) to comply with sub-paragraph (2)(b) shall be guilty of an offence and liable on summary conviction to a fine not exceeding level 2 on the standard scale.
  (6) It shall be a defence in any proceedings under sub-paragraph (5) to prove that the defendant was residing at the same address as another person who was the child's parent or had parental responsibility for the child and had reasonable cause to believe that the other person had informed the appropriate authority that both of them were residing at that address.

Visits to or by children: expenses

16.—(1) This paragraph applies where—
  (a) a child is being looked after by a local authority; and
  (b) the conditions mentioned in sub-paragraph (3) are satisfied.
  (2) The authority may—
  (a) make payments to—
      (i) a parent of the child;

(ii) any person who is not a parent of his but who has parental responsibility for him; or

(iii) any relative, friend or other person connected with him,

in respect of travelling, subsistence or other expenses incurred by that person in visiting the child; or

(b) make payments to the child, or to any person on his behalf, in respect of travelling, subsistence or other expenses incurred by or on behalf of the child in his visiting—

(i) a parent of his;

(ii) any person who is not a parent of his but who has parental responsibility for him; or

(iii) any relative, friend or other person connected with him.

(3) The conditions are that—

(a) it appears to the authority that the visit in question could not otherwise be made without undue financial hardship; and

(b) the circumstances warrant the making of the payments.

Appointment of visitor for child who is not being visited

17.—(1) Where it appears to a local authority in relation to any child that they are looking after that—

(a) communication between the child and—

(i) a parent of his, or

(ii) any person who is not a parent of his but who has parental responsibility for him,

has been infrequent; or

(b) he has not visited or been visited by (or lived with) any such person during the preceding twelve months,

and that it would be in the child's best interests for an independent person to be appointed to be his visitor for the purposes of this paragraph, they shall appoint such a visitor.

(2) A person so appointed shall—

(a) have the duty of visiting, advising and befriending the child; and

(b) be entitled to recover from the authority who appointed him any reasonable expenses incurred by him for the purposes of his functions under this paragraph.

(3) A person's appointment as a visitor in pursuance of this paragraph shall be determined if—

(a) he gives notice in writing to the authority who appointed him that he resigns the appointment; or

(b) the authority give him notice in writing that they have terminated it.

(4) The determination of such an appointment shall not prejudice any duty under this paragraph to make a further appointment.

(5) Where a local authority propose to appoint a visitor for a child under this paragraph, the appointment shall not be made if—

(a) the child objects to it; and

(b) the authority are satisfied that he has sufficient understanding to make an informed decision.

(6) Where a visitor has been appointed for a child under this paragraph, the local authority shall determine the appointment if—

(a) the child objects to its continuing; and

(b) the authority are satisfied that he has sufficient understanding to make an informed decision.

(7) The Secretary of State may make regulations as to the circumstances in which a person appointed as a visitor under this paragraph is to be regarded as independent of the local authority appointing him.

Power to guarantee apprenticeship deeds etc.

18.—(1) While a child is being looked after by a local authority, or is a person qualifying for advice and assistance, the authority may undertake any obligation by way of guarantee under any deed of apprenticeship or articles of clerkship which he enters into.

(2) Where a local authority have undertaken any such obligation under any deed or articles they may at any time (whether or not they are still looking after the person concerned) undertake the like obligation under any supplemental deed or articles.

Arrangements to assist children to live abroad

19.—(1) A local authority may only arrange for, or assist in arranging for, any child in their care to live outside England and Wales with the approval of the court.

(2) A local authority may, with the approval of every person who has parental responsibility for the child arrange for, or assist in arranging for, any other child looked after by them to live outside England and Wales.

(3) The court shall not give its approval under sub-paragraph (1) unless it is satisfied that—

(a) living outside England and Wales would be in the child's best interests;
(b) suitable arrangements have been, or will be, made for his reception and welfare in the country in which he will live;
(c) the child has consented to living in that country; and
(d) every person who has parental responsibility for the child has consented to his living in that country.

(4) Where the court is satisfied that the child does not have sufficient understanding to give or withhold his consent, it may disregard sub-paragraph (3)(c) and give its approval if the child is to live in the country concerned with a parent, guardian, or other suitable person.

(5) Where a person whose consent is required by sub-paragraph (3)(d) fails to give his consent, the court may disregard that provision and give its approval if it is satisfied that that person—

(a) cannot be found;
(b) is incapable of consenting; or
(c) is withholding his consent unreasonably.

(6) Section 56 of the Adoption Act 1976 (which requires authority for the taking or sending abroad for adoption of a child who is a British subject) shall not apply in the case of any child who is to live outside England and Wales with the approval of the court given under this paragraph.

(7) Where a court decides to give its approval under this paragraph it may order that its decision is not to have effect during the appeal period.

(8) In sub-paragraph (7) "the appeal period" means—

(a) where an appeal is made against the decision, the period between the making of the decision and the determination of the appeal; and
(b) otherwise, the period during which an appeal may be made against the decision.

Death of children being looked after by local authorities

20.—(1) If a child who is being looked after by a local authority dies, the authority—

(a) shall notify the Secretary of State;
(b) shall, so far as is reasonably practicable, notify the child's parents and every person who is not a parent of his but who has parental responsibility for him;
(c) may, with the consent (so far as it is reasonably practicable to obtain it) of every person who has parental responsibility for the child, arrange for the child's body to be buried or cremated; and
(d) may, if the conditions mentioned in sub-paragraph (2) are satisfied, make payments to any person who has parental responsibility for the child, or any relative, friend or other person connected with the child, in respect of travelling, subsistence or other expenses incurred by that person in attending the child's funeral.

(2) The conditions are that—

(a) it appears to the authority that the person concerned could not otherwise attend the child's funeral without undue financial hardship; and
(b) that the circumstances warrant the making of the payments.

(3) Sub-paragraph (1) does not authorise cremation where it does not accord with the practice of the child's religious persuasion.

(4) Where a local authority have exercised their power under sub-paragraph (1)(c) with respect to a child who was under sixteen when he died, they may recover from any parent of the child any expenses incurred by them.

(5) Any sums so recoverable shall, without prejudice to any other method of recovery, be recoverable summarily as a civil debt.

(6) Nothing in this paragraph affects any enactment regulating or authorising the burial, cremation or anatomical examination of the body of a deceased person.

PART III

CONTRIBUTIONS TOWARDS MAINTENANCE OF CHILDREN LOOKED AFTER BY LOCAL AUTHORITIES

Liability to contribute

21.—(1) Where a local authority are looking after a child (other than in the cases mentioned in sub-paragraph (7)) they shall consider whether they should recover contributions towards the child's maintenance from any person liable to contribute ("a contributor").

(2) An authority may only recover contributions from a contributor if they consider it reasonable to do so.

(3) The persons liable to contribute are—
    (a) where the child is under sixteen, each of his parents;
    (b) where he has reached the age of sixteen, the child himself.

(4) A parent is not liable to contribute during any period when he is in receipt of income support or family credit under the Social Security Act 1986.

(5) A person is not liable to contribute towards the maintenance of a child in the care of a local authority in respect of any period during which the child is allowed by the authority (under section 23(5)) to live with a parent of his.

(6) A contributor is not obliged to make any contribution towards a child's maintenance except as agreed or determined in accordance with this Part of this Schedule.

(7) The cases are where the child is looked after by a local authority under—
    (a) section 21;
    (b) an interim care order;
    (c) section 53 of the Children and Young Persons Act 1933.

Agreed contributions

22.—(1) Contributions towards a child's maintenance may only be recovered if the local authority have served a notice ("a contribution notice") on the contributor specifying—
    (a) the weekly sum which they consider that he should contribute; and
    (b) arrangements for payment.

(2) The contribution notice must be in writing and dated.

(3) Arrangements for payment shall, in particular, include—
    (a) the date on which liability to contribute begins (which must not be earlier than the date of the notice);
    (b) the date on which liability under the notice will end (if the child has not before that date ceased to be looked after by the authority); and
    (c) the date on which the first payment is to be made.

(4) The authority may specify in a contribution notice a weekly sum which is a standard contribution determined by them for all children looked after by them.

(5) The authority may not specify in a contribution notice a weekly sum greater than that which they consider—
    (a) they would normally be prepared to pay if they had placed a similar child with local authority foster parents; and
    (b) it is reasonably practicable for the contributor to pay (having regard to his means).

(6) An authority may at any time withdraw a contribution notice (without prejudice to their power to serve another).

(7) Where the authority and the contributor agree—
    (a) the sum which the contributor is to contribute; and
    (b) arrangements for payment,
(whether as specified in the contribution notice or otherwise) and the contributor notifies the authority in writing that he so agrees, the authority may recover summarily as a civil debt any contribution which is overdue and unpaid.

(8) A contributor may, by serving a notice in writing on the authority, withdraw his agreement in relation to any period of liability falling after the date of service of the notice.

(9) Sub-paragraph (7) is without prejudice to any other method of recovery.

Contribution orders

23.—(1) Where a contributor has been served with a contribution notice and has—
    (a) failed to reach any agreement with the local authority as mentioned in paragraph 22(7) within the period of one month beginning with the day on which the contribution notice was served; or

(b) served a notice under paragraph 22(8) withdrawing his agreement,
the authority may apply to the court for an order under this paragraph.

(2) On such an application the court may make an order ("a contribution order") requiring the contributor to contribute a weekly sum towards the child's maintenance in accordance with arrangements for payment specified by the court.

(3) A contribution order—

(a) shall not specify a weekly sum greater than that specified in the contribution notice; and

(b) shall be made with due regard to the contributor's means.

(4) A contribution order shall not—

(a) take effect before the date specified in the contribution notice; or

(b) have effect while the contributor is not liable to contribute (by virtue of paragraph 21); or

(c) remain in force after the child has ceased to be looked after by the authority who obtained the order.

(5) An authority may not apply to the court under sub-paragraph (1) in relation to a contribution notice which they have withdrawn.

(6) Where—

(a) a contribution order is in force;

(b) the authority serve another contribution notice; and

(c) the contributor and the authority reach an agreement under paragraph 22(7) in respect of that other contribution notice,

the effect of the agreement shall be to discharge the order from the date on which it is agreed that the agreement shall take effect.

(7) Where an agreement is reached under sub-paragraph (6) the authority shall notify the court—

(a) of the agreement; and

(b) of the date on which it took effect.

(8) A contribution order may be varied or revoked on the application of the contributor or the authority.

(9) In proceedings for the variation of a contribution order, the authority shall specify—

(a) the weekly sum which, having regard to paragraph 22, they propose that the contributor should contribute under the order as varied; and

(b) the proposed arrangements for payment.

(10) Where a contribution order is varied, the order—

(a) shall not specify a weekly sum greater than that specified by the authority in the proceedings for variation; and

(b) shall be made with due regard to the contributor's means.

(11) An appeal shall lie in accordance with rules of court from any order made under this paragraph.

Enforcement of contribution orders etc.

24.—(1) A contribution order made by a magistrates' court shall be enforceable as a magistrates' court maintenance order (within the meaning of section 150(1) of the Magistrates' Courts Act 1980).

(2) Where a contributor has agreed, or has been ordered, to make contributions to a local authority, any other local authority within whose area the contributor is for the time being living may—

(a) at the request of the local authority who served the contribution notice; and

(b) subject to agreement as to any sum to be deducted in respect of services rendered,

collect from the contributor any contributions due on behalf of the authority who served the notice.

(3) In sub-paragraph (2) the reference to any other local authority includes a reference to—

(a) a local authority within the meaning of section 1(2) of the Social Work (Scotland) Act 1968; and

(b) a Health and Social Services Board established under Article 16 of the Health and Personal Social Services (Northern Ireland) Order 1972.

(4) The power to collect sums under sub-paragraph (2) includes the power to—

(a) receive and give a discharge for any contributions due; and

(b) (if necessary) enforce payment of any contributions,

even though those contributions may have fallen due at a time when the contributor was living elsewhere.

(5) Any contribution collected under sub-paragraph (2) shall be paid (subject to any agreed deduction) to the local authority who served the contribution notice.

(6) In any proceedings under this paragraph, a document which purports to be—

(a) a copy of an order made by a court under or by virtue of paragraph 23; and

(b) certified as a true copy by the clerk of the court,

shall be evidence of the order.

(7) In any proceedings under this paragraph, a certificate which—

(a) purports to be signed by the clerk or some other duly authorised officer of the local authority who obtained the contribution order; and

(b) states that any sum due to the authority under the order is overdue and unpaid,

shall be evidence that the sum is overdue and unpaid.

Regulations

25. The Secretary of State may make regulations—

(a) as to the considerations which a local authority must take into account in deciding—

(i) whether it is reasonable to recover contributions; and

(ii) what the arrangements for payment should be;

(b) as to the procedures they must follow in reaching agreements with—

(i) contributors (under paragraphs 22 and 23); and

(ii) any other local authority (under paragraph 23).

GENERAL NOTE

Pt. I: see notes to s.17.

Pt. II: see notes to s.23.

Pt. III: see notes to s.29.

Sections 35 and 36   SCHEDULE 3

SUPERVISION ORDERS

PART I

GENERAL

Meaning of "responsible person"

1. In this Schedule, "the responsible person", in relation to a supervised child, means—

(a) any person who has parental responsibility for the child; and

(b) any other person with whom the child is living.

Power of supervisor to give directions to supervised child

2.—(1) A supervision order may require the supervised child to comply with any directions given from time to time by the supervisor which require him to do all or any of the following things—

(a) to live at a place or places specified in the directions for a period or periods so specified;

(b) to present himself to a person or persons specified in the directions at a place or places and on a day or days so specified;

(c) to participate in activities specified in the directions on a day or days so specified.

(2) It shall be for the supervisor to decide whether, and to what extent, he exercises his power to give directions and to decide the form of any directions which he gives.

(3) Sub-paragraph (1) does not confer on a supervisor power to give directions in respect of any medical or psychiatric examination or treatment (which are matters dealt with in paragraphs 4 and 5).

Imposition of obligations on responsible person

3.—(1) With the consent of any responsible person, a supervision order may include a requirement—

   (a) that he take all reasonable steps to ensure that the supervised child complies with any direction given by the supervisor under paragraph 2;

   (b) that he take all reasonable steps to ensure that the supervised child complies with any requirement included in the order under paragraph 4 or 5;

   (c) that he comply with any directions given by the supervisor requiring him to attend at a place specified in the directions for the purpose of taking part in activities so specified.

(2) A direction given under sub-paragraph (1)(c) may specify the time at which the responsible person is to attend and whether or not the supervised child is required to attend with him.

(3) A supervision order may require any person who is a responsible person in relation to the supervised child to keep the supervisor informed of his address, if it differs from the child's.

Psychiatric and medical examinations

4.—(1) A supervision order may require the supervised child—

   (a) to submit to a medical or psychiatric examination; or

   (b) to submit to any such examination from time to time as directed by the supervisor.

(2) Any such examination shall be required to be conducted—

   (a) by, or under the direction of, such registered medical practitioner as may be specified in the order;

   (b) at a place specified in the order and at which the supervised child is to attend as a non-resident patient; or

   (c) at—

      (i) a health service hospital; or

      (ii) in the case of a psychiatric examination, a hospital or mental nursing home,

   at which the supervised child is, or is to attend as, a resident patient.

(3) A requirement of a kind mentioned in sub-paragraph (2)(c) shall not be included unless the court is satisfied, on the evidence of a registered medical practitioner, that—

   (a) the child may be suffering from a physical or mental condition that requires, and may be susceptible to, treatment; and

   (b) a period as a resident patient is necessary if the examination is to be carried out properly.

(4) No court shall include a requirement under this paragraph in a supervision order unless it is satisfied that—

   (a) where the child has sufficient understanding to make an informed decision, he consents to its inclusion; and

   (b) satisfactory arrangements have been, or can be, made for the examination.

Psychiatric and medical treatment

5.—(1) Where a court which proposes to make or vary a supervision order is satisfied, on the evidence of a registered medical practitioner approved for the purposes of section 12 of the Mental Health Act 1983, that the mental condition of the supervised child—

   (a) is such as requires, and may be susceptible to, treatment; but

   (b) is not such as to warrant his detention in pursuance of a hospital order under Part III of that Act,

the court may include in the order a requirement that the supervised child shall, for a period specified in the order, submit to such treatment as is so specified.

(2) The treatment specified in accordance with sub-paragraph (1) must be—

   (a) by, or under the direction of, such registered medical practitioner as may be specified in the order;

   (b) as a non-resident patient at such a place as may be so specified; or

   (c) as a resident patient in a hospital or mental nursing home.

(3) Where a court which proposes to make or vary a supervision order is satisfied, on the evidence of a registered medical practitioner, that the physical condition of the supervised child is such as requires, and may be susceptible to, treatment, the court may include in the order a requirement that the supervised child shall, for a period specified in the order, submit to such treatment as is so specified.

(4) The treatment specified in accordance with sub-paragraph (3) must be—

    (a) by, or under the direction of, such registered medical practitioner as may be specified in the order;

    (b) as a non-resident patient at such place as may be so specified; or

    (c) as a resident patient in a health service hospital.

(5) No court shall include a requirement under this paragraph in a supervision order unless it is satisfied—

    (a) where the child has sufficient understanding to make an informed decision, that he consents to its inclusion; and

    (b) that satisfactory arrangements have been, or can be, made for the treatment.

(6) If a medical practitioner by whom or under whose direction a supervised person is being treated in pursuance of a requirement included in a supervision order by virtue of this paragraph is unwilling to continue to treat or direct the treatment of the supervised child or is of the opinion that—

    (a) the treatment should be continued beyond the period specified in the order;

    (b) the supervised child needs different treatment;

    (c) he is not susceptible to treatment; or

    (d) he does not require further treatment,

the practitioner shall make a report in writing to that effect to the supervisor.

(7) On receiving a report under this paragraph the supervisor shall refer it to the court, and on such a reference the court may make an order cancelling or varying the requirement.

Part II

Miscellaneous

Life of supervision order

6.—(1) Subject to sub-paragraph (2) and section 91, a supervision order shall cease to have effect at the end of the period of one year beginning with the date on which it was made.

(2) A supervision order shall also cease to have effect if an event mentioned in section 25(1)(a) or (b) of the Child Abduction and Custody Act 1985 (termination of existing orders) occurs with respect to the child.

(3) Where the supervisor applies to the court to extend, or further extend, a supervision order the court may extend the order for such period as it may specify.

(4) A supervision order may not be extended so as to run beyond the end of the period of three years beginning with the date on which it was made.

Limited life of directions

7.—(1) The total number of days in respect of which a supervised child or (as the case may be) responsible person may be required to comply with directions given under paragraph 2 or 3 shall not exceed 90 or such lesser number (if any) as the supervision order may specify.

(2) For the purpose of calculating that total number of days, the supervisor may disregard any day in respect of which directions previously given in pursuance of the order were not complied with.

Information to be given to supervisor etc.

8.—(1) A supervision order may require the supervised child—

    (a) to keep the supervisor informed of any change in his address; and

    (b) to allow the supervisor to visit him at the place where he is living.

(2) The responsible person in relation to any child with respect to whom a supervision order is made shall—

    (a) if asked by the supervisor, inform him of the child's address (if it is known to him); and

    (b) if he is living with the child, allow the supervisor reasonable contact with the child.

Selection of supervisor

9.—(1) A supervision order shall not designate a local authority as the supervisor unless—

    (a) the authority agree; or

(b) the supervised child lives or will live within their area.

(2) A court shall not place a child under the supervision of a probation officer unless—

    (a) the appropriate authority so request; and

    (b) a probation officer is already exercising or has exercised, in relation to another member of the household to which the child belongs, duties imposed on probation officers—

        (i) by paragraph 8 of Schedule 3 to the Powers of Criminal Courts Act 1973; or

        (ii) by rules under paragraph 18(1)(b) of that Schedule.

(3) In sub-paragraph (2) "the appropriate authority" means the local authority appearing to the court to be the authority in whose area the supervised child lives or will live.

(4) Where a supervision order places a person under the supervision of a probation officer, the officer shall be selected in accordance with arrangements made by the probation committee for the area in question.

(5) If the selected probation officer is unable to carry out his duties, or dies, another probation officer shall be selected in the same manner.

Effect of supervision order on earlier orders

10. The making of a supervision order with respect to any child brings to an end any earlier care or supervision order which—

(a) was made with respect to that child; and

(b) would otherwise continue in force.

Local authority functions and expenditure

11.—(1) The Secretary of State may make regulations with respect to the exercise by a local authority of their functions where a child has been placed under their supervision by a supervision order.

(2) Where a supervision order requires compliance with directions given by virtue of this section, any expenditure incurred by the supervisor for the purposes of the directions shall be defrayed by the local authority designated in the order.

PART III

EDUCATION SUPERVISION ORDERS

Effect of orders

12.—(1) Where an education supervision order is in force with respect to a child, it shall be the duty of the supervisor—

    (a) to advise, assist and befriend, and give directions to—

        (i) the supervised child; and

        (ii) his parents,

    in such a way as will, in the opinion of the supervisor, secure that he is properly educated;

    (b) where any such directions given to—

        (i) the supervised child; or

        (ii) a parent of his,

    have not been complied with, to consider what further steps to take in the exercise of the supervisor's powers under this Act.

(2) Before giving any directions under sub-paragraph (1) the supervisor shall, so far as is reasonably practicable, ascertain the wishes and feelings of—

(a) the child; and

(b) his parents,

including, in particular, their wishes as to the place at which the child should be educated.

(3) When settling the terms of any such directions, the supervisor shall give due consideration—

(a) having regard to the child's age and understanding, to such wishes and feelings of his as the supervisor has been able to ascertain; and

(b) to such wishes and feelings of the child's parents as he has been able to ascertain.

(4) Directions may be given under this paragraph at any time while the education supervision order is in force.

13.—(1) Where an education supervision order is in force with respect to a child, the duties of the child's parents under sections 36 and 39 of the Education Act 1944 (duty to secure education of children and to secure regular attendance of registered pupils) shall be superseded by their duty to comply with any directions in force under the education supervision order.

(2) Where an education supervision order is made with respect to a child—

(a)   any school attendance order—

(i)   made under section 37 of the Act of 1944 with respect to the child; and

(ii)   in force immediately before the making of the education supervision order,

shall cease to have effect; and

(b)   while the education supervision order remains in force, the following provisions shall not apply with respect to the child—

(i)   section 37 of that Act (school attendance orders);

(ii)   section 76 of that Act (pupils to be educated in accordance with wishes of their parents);

(iii)   sections 6 and 7 of the Education Act 1980 (parental preference and appeals against admission decisions);

(c)   a supervision order made with respect to the child in criminal proceedings, while the education supervision order is in force, may not include an education requirement of the kind which could otherwise be included under section 12C of the Children and Young Persons Act 1969;

(d)   any education requirement of a kind mentioned in paragraph (c), which was in force with respect to the child immediately before the making of the education supervision order, shall cease to have effect.

Effect where child also subject to supervision order

14.—(1) This paragraph applies where an education supervision order and a Supervision order, or order under section 7(7)(b) of the Children and Young Persons Act 1969, are in force at the same time with respect to the same child.

(2) Any failure to comply with a direction given by the supervisor under the education supervision order shall be disregarded if it would not have been reasonably practicable to comply with it without failing to comply with a direction given under the other order.

Duration of orders

15.—(1) An education supervision order shall have effect for a period of one year, beginning with the date on which it is made.

(2) An education supervision order shall not expire if, before it would otherwise have expired, the court has (on the application of the authority in whose favour the order was made) extended the period during which it is in force.

(3) Such an application may not be made earlier than three months before the date on which the order would otherwise expire.

(4) The period during which an education supervision order is in force may be extended under sub-paragraph (2) on more than one occasion.

(5) No one extension may be for a period of more than three years.

(6) An education supervision order shall cease to have effect on—

(a)   the child's ceasing to be of compulsory school age; or

(b)   the making of a care order with respect to the child;

and sub-paragraphs (1) to (4) are subject to this sub-paragraph.

Information to be given to supervisor etc.

16.—(1) An education supervision order may require the child—

(a)   to keep the supervisor informed of any change in his address; and

(b)   to allow the supervisor to visit him at the place where he is living.

(2) A person who is the parent of a child with respect to whom an education supervision order has been made shall—

(a)   if asked by the supervisor, inform him of the child's address (if it is known to him); and

(b)   if he is living with the child, allow the supervisor reasonable contact with the child.

Discharge of orders

17.—(1) The court may discharge any education supervision order on the application of—

(a) the child concerned;
(b) a parent of his; or
(c) the local education authority concerned.

(2) On discharging an education supervision order, the court may direct the local authority within whose area the child lives, or will live, to investigate the circumstances of the child.

Offences

18.—(1) If a parent of a child with respect to whom an education supervision order is in force persistently fails to comply with a direction given under the order he shall be guilty of an offence.

(2) It shall be a defence for any person charged with such an offence to prove that—
(a) he took all reasonable steps to ensure that the direction was complied with;
(b) the direction was unreasonable; or
(c) he had complied with—
(i) a requirement included in a supervision order made with respect to the child; or
(ii) directions given under such a requirement,
and that it was not reasonably practicable to comply both with the direction and with the requirement or directions mentioned in this paragraph.

(3) A person guilty of an offence under this paragraph shall be liable on summary conviction to a fine not exceeding level 3 on the standard scale.

Persistent failure of child to comply with directions

19.—(1) Where a child with respect to whom an education supervision order is in force persistently fails to comply with any direction given under the order, the local education authority concerned shall notify the appropriate local authority.

(2) Where a local authority have been notified under sub-paragraph (1) they shall investigate the circumstances of the child.

(3) In this paragraph "the appropriate local authority" has the same meaning as in section 36.

Miscellaneous

20. The Secretary of State may by regulations make provision modifying, or displacing, the provisions of any enactment about education in relation to any child with respect to whom an education supervision order is in force to such extent as appears to the Secretary of State to be necessary or expedient in consequence of the provision made by this Act with respect to such orders.

Interpretation

21. In this Part of this Schedule "parent" has the same meaning as in the Education Act 1944 (as amended by Schedule 13).

GENERAL NOTE
Pts. I and II: see notes to s.35.
Pt. III: see notes to s.36.

Section 53(6)   SCHEDULE 4

MANAGEMENT AND CONDUCT OF COMMUNITY HOMES

PART I

INSTRUMENTS OF MANAGEMENT

Instruments of management for controlled and assisted community homes

1.—(1) The Secretary of State may by order make an instrument of management providing for the constitution of a body of managers for any voluntary home which is designated as a controlled or assisted community home.

(2) Sub-paragraph (3) applies where two or more voluntary homes are designated as controlled community homes or as assisted community homes.

(3) If—

(a) those homes are, or are to be, provided by the same voluntary organisation; and

(b) the same local authority is to be represented on the body of managers for those homes,

a single instrument of management may be made by the Secretary of State under this paragraph constituting one body of managers for those homes or for any two or more of them.

(4) The number of persons who, in accordance with an instrument of management, constitute the body of managers for a voluntary home shall be such number (which must be a multiple of three) as may be specified in the instrument.

(5) The instrument shall provide that the local authority specified in the instrument shall appoint—

(a) in the case of a voluntary home which is designated as a controlled community home, two-thirds of the managers; and

(b) in the case of a voluntary home which is designated as an assisted community home, one-third of them.

(6) An instrument of management shall provide that the foundation managers shall be appointed, in such manner and by such persons as may be specified in the instrument—

(a) so as to represent the interests of the voluntary organisation by which the home is, or is to be, provided; and

(b) for the purpose of securing that—

(i) so far as is practicable, the character of the home as a voluntary home will be preserved; and

(ii) subject to paragraph 2(3), the terms of any trust deed relating to the home are observed.

(7) An instrument of management shall come into force on such date as it may specify.

(8) If an instrument of management is in force in relation to a voluntary home the home shall be (and be known as) a controlled community home or an assisted community home, according to its designation.

(9) In this paragraph—

"foundation managers", in relation to a voluntary home, means those of the managers of the home who are not appointed by a local authority in accordance with sub-paragraph (5); and

"designated" means designated in accordance with section 53.

2.—(1) An instrument of management shall contain such provisions as the Secretary of State considers appropriate.

(2) Nothing in the instrument of management shall affect the purposes for which the premises comprising the home are held.

(3) Without prejudice to the generality of sub-paragraph (1), an instrument of management may contain provisions—

(a) specifying the nature and purpose of the home (or each of the homes) to which it relates;

(b) requiring a specified number or proportion of the places in that home (or those homes) to be made available to local authorities and to any other body specified in the instrument; and

(c) relating to the management of that home (or those homes) and the charging of fees with respect to—

(i) children placed there; or

(ii) places made available to any local authority or other body.

(4) Subject to sub-paragraphs (1) and (2), in the event of any inconsistency between the provisions of any trust deed and an instrument of management, the instrument of management shall prevail over the provisions of the trust deed in so far as they relate to the home concerned.

(5) After consultation with the voluntary organisation concerned and with the local authority specified in its instrument of management, the Secretary of State may by order vary or revoke any provisions of the instrument.

PART II

MANAGEMENT OF CONTROLLED AND ASSISTED COMMUNITY HOMES

3.—(1) The management, equipment and maintenance of a controlled community home shall be the responsibility of the local authority specified in its instrument of management.

(2) The management, equipment and maintenance of an assisted community home shall be the responsibility of the voluntary organisation by which the home is provided.

(3) In this paragraph—

"home" means a controlled community home or (as the case may be) assisted community home; and

"the managers", in relation to a home, means the managers constituted by its instrument of management; and

"the responsible body", in relation to a home, means the local authority or (as the case may be) voluntary organisation responsible for its management, equipment and maintenance.

(4) The functions of a home's responsible body shall be exercised through the managers.

(5) Anything done, liability incurred or property acquired by a home's managers shall be done, incurred or acquired by them as agents of the responsible body.

(6) In so far as any matter is reserved for the decision of a home's responsible body by—

(a) sub-paragraph (8);

(b) the instrument of management;

(c) the service by the body on the managers, or any of them, of a notice reserving any matter,

that matter shall be dealt with by the body and not by the managers.

(7) In dealing with any matter so reserved, the responsible body shall have regard to any representations made to the body by the managers.

(8) The employment of persons at a home shall be a matter reserved for the decision of the responsible body.

(9) Where the instrument of management of a controlled community home so provides, the responsible body may enter into arrangements with the voluntary organisation by which that home is provided whereby, in accordance with such terms as may be agreed between them and the voluntary organisation, persons who are not in the employment of the responsible body shall undertake duties at that home.

(10) Subject to sub-paragraph (11)—

(a) where the responsible body for an assisted community home proposes to engage any person to work at that home or to terminate without notice the employment of any person at that home, it shall consult the local authority specified in the instrument of management and, if that authority so direct, the responsible body shall not carry out its proposal without their consent; and

(b) that local authority may, after consultation with the responsible body, require that body to terminate the employment of any person at that home.

(11) Paragraphs (a) and (b) of sub-paragraph (10) shall not apply—

(a) in such cases or circumstances as may be specified by notice in writing given by the local authority to the responsible body; and

(b) in relation to the employment of any persons or class of persons specified in the home's instrument of management.

(12) The accounting year of the managers of a home shall be such as may be specified by the responsible body.

(13) Before such date in each accounting year as may be so specified, the managers of a home shall submit to the responsible body estimates, in such form as the body may require, of expenditure and receipts in respect of the next accounting year.

(14) Any expenses incurred by the managers of a home with the approval of the responsible body shall be defrayed by that body.

(15) The managers of a home shall keep—

(a) proper accounts with respect to the home; and

(b) proper records in relation to the accounts.

(16) Where an instrument of management relates to more than one home, one set of accounts and records may be kept in respect of all the homes to which it relates.

PART III

REGULATIONS

4.—(1) The Secretary of State may make regulations—

(a) as to the placing of children in community homes;

(b) as to the conduct of such homes; and

(c) for securing the welfare of children in such homes.

(2) The regulations may, in particular—

(a) prescribe standards to which the premises used for such homes are to conform;

(b) impose requirements as to the accommodation, staff and equipment to be provided in such homes, and as to the arrangements to be made for protecting the health of children in such homes;

(c) provide for the control and discipline of children in such homes;

(d) impose requirements as to the keeping of records and giving of notices in respect of children in such homes;

(e) impose requirements as to the facilities which are to be provided for giving religious instruction to children in such homes;

(f) authorise the Secretary of State to give and revoke directions requiring—

(i) the local authority by whom a home is provided or who are specified in the instrument of management for a controlled community home, or

(ii) the voluntary organisation by which an assisted community home is provided,

to accommodate in the home a child looked after by a local authority for whom no places are made available in that home or to take such action in relation to a child accommodated in the home as may be specified in the directions;

(g) provide for consultation with the Secretary of State as to applicants for appointment to the charge of a home;

(h) empower the Secretary of State to prohibit the appointment of any particular applicant except in the cases (if any) in which the regulations dispense with such consultation by reason that the person to be appointed possesses such qualifications as may be prescribed;

(i) require the approval of the Secretary of State for the provision and use of accommodation for the purpose of restricting the liberty of children in such homes and impose other requirements (in addition to those imposed by section 25) as to the placing of a child in accommodation provided for that purpose, including a requirement to obtain the permission of any local authority who are looking after the child;

(j) provide that, to such extent as may be provided for in the regulations, the Secretary of State may direct that any provision of regulations under this paragraph which is specified in the direction and makes any such provision as is referred to in paragraph (a) or (b) shall not apply in relation to a particular home or the premises used for it, and may provide for the variation or revocation of any such direction by the Secretary of State.

(3) Without prejudice to the power to make regulations under this paragraph conferring functions on—

(a) the local authority or voluntary organisation by which a community home is provided; or

(b) the managers of a controlled or assisted community home,

regulations under this paragraph may confer functions in relation to a controlled or assisted community home on the local authority named in the instrument of management for the home.

DEFINITIONS

"designated": Sched. 4, para. 1(9).

"foundation managers": Sched. 4, para. 1(9).

"home": Sched. 4, para. 3(3).

"the managers": Sched. 4, para. 3(3).

"the responsible body": Sched. 4, para. 3(3).

GENERAL NOTE

See notes to s.53.

      SCHEDULE 5

VOLUNTARY HOMES AND VOLUNTARY ORGANISATIONS

PART I

REGISTRATION OF VOLUNTARY HOMES

General

1.—(1) An application for registration under this paragraph shall—
    (a) be made by the persons intending to carry on the home to which the application relates; and
    (b) be made in such manner, and be accompanied by such particulars, as the Secretary of State may prescribe.
(2) On an application duly made under sub-paragraph (1) the Secretary of State may—
    (a) grant or refuse the application, as he thinks fit; or
    (b) grant the application subject to such conditions as he considers appropriate.
(3) The Secretary of State may from time to time—
    (a) vary any condition for the time being in force with respect to a voluntary home by virtue of this paragraph; or
    (b) impose an additional condition,
either on the application of the person carrying on the home or without such an application.
(4) Where at any time it appears to the Secretary of State that the conduct of any voluntary home—
    (a) is not in accordance with regulations made under paragraph 7; or
    (b) is otherwise unsatisfactory,
he may cancel the registration of the home and remove it from the register.
(5) Any person who, without reasonable excuse, carries on a voluntary home in contravention of—
    (a) section 60; or
    (b) a condition to which the registration of the home is for the time being subject by virtue of this Part,
shall be guilty of an offence.
(6) Any person guilty of such an offence shall be liable on summary conviction to a fine not exceeding—
    (a) level 5 on the standard scale, if his offence is under sub-paragraph (5)(a); or
    (b) level 4, if it is under sub-paragraph (5)(b).
(7) Where the Secretary of State registers a home under this paragraph, or cancels the registration of a home, he shall notify the local authority within whose area the home is situated.

Procedure

2.—(1) Where—
    (a) a person applies for registration of a voluntary home; and
    (b) the Secretary of State proposes to grant his application,
the Secretary of State shall give him written notice of his proposal and of the conditions subject to which he proposes to grant the application.
(2) The Secretary of State need not give notice if he proposes to grant the application subject only to conditions which—
    (a) the applicant specified in the application; or
    (b) the Secretary of State and the applicant have subsequently agreed.
(3) Where the Secretary of State proposes to refuse such an application he shall give notice of his proposal to the applicant.
(4) The Secretary of State shall give any person carrying on a voluntary home notice of a proposal to—
    (a) cancel the registration of the home;
    (b) vary any condition for the time being in force with respect to the home by virtue of paragraph 1; or
    (c) impose any additional condition.
(5) A notice under this paragraph shall give the Secretary of State's reasons for his proposal.

Right to make representations

3.—(1) A notice under paragraph 2 shall state that within 14 days of service of the notice any person on whom it is served may (in writing) require the Secretary of State to give him an opportunity to make representations to the Secretary of State concerning the matter.

(2) Where a notice has been served under paragraph 2, the Secretary of State shall not determine the matter until either—

    (a) any person on whom the notice was served has made representations to him concerning the matter; or

    (b) the period during which any such person could have required the Secretary of State to give him an opportunity to make representations has elapsed without the Secretary of State being required to give such an opportunity; or

    (c) the conditions specified in sub-paragraph (3) are satisfied.

(3) The conditions are that—

    (a) a person on whom the notice was served has required the Secretary of State to give him an opportunity to make representations to the Secretary of State;

    (b) the Secretary of State has allowed him a reasonable period to make his representations; and

    (c) he has failed to make them within that period.

(4) The representations may be made, at the option of the person making them, either in writing or orally.

(5) If he informs the Secretary of State that he desires to make oral representations, the Secretary of State shall give him an opportunity of appearing before, and of being heard by, a person appointed by the Secretary of State.

Decision of Secretary of State

4.—(1) If the Secretary of State decides to adopt the proposal, he shall serve notice in writing of his decision on any person on whom he was required to serve notice of his proposal.

(2) A notice under this paragraph shall be accompanied by a notice explaining the right of appeal conferred by paragraph 5.

(3) A decision of the Secretary of State, other than a decision to grant an application for registration subject only to such conditions as are mentioned in paragraph 2(2) or to refuse an application for registration, shall not take effect—

    (a) if no appeal is brought, until the end of the period of 28 days referred to in paragraph 5(3); and

    (b) if an appeal is brought, until it is determined or abandoned.

Appeals

5.—(1) An appeal against a decision of the Secretary of State under Part VII shall lie to a Registered Homes Tribunal.

(2) An appeal shall be brought by notice in writing given to the Secretary of State.

(3) No appeal may be brought by a person more than 28 days after service on him of notice of the decision.

(4) On an appeal, the Tribunal may confirm the Secretary of State's decision or direct that it shall not have effect.

(5) A Tribunal shall also have power on an appeal to—

    (a) vary any condition for the time being in force by virtue of Part VII with respect to the home to which the appeal relates;

    (b) direct that any such condition shall cease to have effect; or

    (c) direct that any such condition as it thinks fit shall have effect with respect to the home.

Notification of particulars with respect to voluntary homes

6.—(1) It shall be the duty of the person in charge of any voluntary home established after the commencement of this Act to send to the Secretary of State within three months from the establishment of the home such particulars with respect to the home as the Secretary of State may prescribe.

(2) It shall be the duty of the person in charge of any voluntary home (whether established before or after the commencement of this Act) to send to the Secretary of State such particulars with respect to the home as may be prescribed.

(3) The particulars must be sent—
    (a) in the case of a home established before the commencement of this Act, in every year, or
    (b) in the case of a home established after the commencement of this Act, in every year subsequent to the year in which particulars are sent under sub-paragraph (1),
by such date as the Secretary of State may prescribe.

(4) Where the Secretary of State by regulations varies the particulars which are to be sent to him under sub-paragraph (1) or (2) by the person in charge of a voluntary home—
    (a) that person shall send to the Secretary of State the prescribed particulars within three months from the date of the making of the regulations;
    (b) where any such home was established before, but not more than three months before, the making of the regulations, compliance with paragraph (a) shall be sufficient compliance with the requirement of sub-paragraph (1) to send the prescribed particulars within three months from the establishment of the home;
    (c) in the year in which the particulars are varied, compliance with paragraph (a) by the person in charge of any voluntary home shall be sufficient compliance with the requirement of sub-paragraph (2) to send the prescribed particulars before the prescribed date in that year.

(5) If the person in charge of a voluntary home fails, without reasonable excuse, to comply with any of the requirements of this paragraph he shall be guilty of an offence.

(6) Any person guilty of such an offence shall be liable on summary conviction to a fine not exceeding level 2 on the standard scale.

PART II

REGULATIONS AS TO VOLUNTARY HOMES

Regulations as to conduct of voluntary homes

7.—(1) The Secretary of State may make regulations—
    (a) as to the placing of children in voluntary homes;
    (b) as to the conduct of such homes; and
    (c) for securing the welfare of children in such homes.

(2) The regulations may, in particular—
    (a) prescribe standards to which the premises used for such homes are to conform,
    (b) impose requirements as to the accommodation, staff and equipment to be provided in such homes, and as to the arrangements to be made for protecting the health of children in such homes;
    (c) provide for the control and discipline of children in such homes;
    (d) require the furnishing to the Secretary of State of information as to the facilities provided for—
        (i) the parents of children in the homes; and
        (ii) persons who are not parents of such children but who have parental responsibility for them; and
        (iii) other persons connected with such children,
    to visit and communicate with the children;
    (e) authorise the Secretary of State to limit the number of children who may be accommodated in any particular voluntary home;
    (f) prohibit the use of accommodation for the purpose of restricting the liberty of children in such homes;
    (g) impose requirements as to the keeping of records and giving of notices with respect to children in such homes;
    (h) impose requirements as to the facilities which are to be provided for giving religious instruction to children in such homes;
    (i) require notice to be given to the Secretary of State of any change of the person carrying on or in charge of a voluntary home or of the premises used by such a home.

(3) The regulations may provide that a contravention of, or failure to comply with, any specified provision of the regulations without reasonable excuse shall be an offence against the regulations.

(4) Any person guilty of such an offence shall be liable to a fine not exceeding level 4 on the standard scale.

Disqualification

8. The Secretary of State may by regulation make provision with respect to the disqualification of persons in relation to voluntary homes of a kind similar to that made in relation to children's homes by section 65.

GENERAL NOTE
See notes to s.60.

Section 63(11)   SCHEDULE 6

REGISTERED CHILDREN'S HOMES

PART I

REGISTRATION

Application for registration

1.—(1) An application for the registration of a children's home shall be made—
    (a) by the person carrying on, or intending to carry on, the home; and
    (b) to the local authority for the area in which the home is, or is to be, situated.
(2) The application shall be made in the prescribed manner and shall be accompanied by—
    (a) such particulars as may be prescribed; and
    (b) such reasonable fee as the local authority may determine.
(3) In this Schedule "prescribed" means prescribed by regulations made by the Secretary of State.
(4) If a local authority are satisfied that a children's home with respect to which an application has been made in accordance with this Schedule complies or (as the case may be) will comply—
    (a) with such requirements as may be prescribed, and
    (b) with such other requirements (if any) as appear to them to be appropriate,
they shall grant the application, either unconditionally or subject to conditions imposed under paragraph 2.
(5) Before deciding whether or not to grant an application a local authority shall comply with any prescribed requirements.
(6) Regulations made for the purposes of sub-paragraph (5) may, in particular, make provision as to the inspection of the home in question.
(7) Where an application is granted, the authority shall notify the applicant that the home has been registered under this Act as from such date as may be specified in the notice.
(8) If the authority are not satisfied as mentioned in sub-paragraph (4), they shall refuse the application.
(9) For the purposes of this Act, an application which has not been granted or refused within the period of twelve months beginning with the date when it is served on the authority shall be deemed to have been refused by them, and the applicant shall be deemed to have been notified of their refusal at the end of that period.
(10) Where a school to which section 63(1) applies is registered it shall not cease to be a registered children's home by reason only of a subsequent change in the number of children for whom it provides accommodation.

Conditions imposed on registration

2.—(1) A local authority may grant an application for registration subject to such conditions relating to the conduct of the home as they think fit.
(2) A local authority may from time to time—
    (a) vary any condition for the time being in force with respect to a home by virtue of this paragraph; or
    (b) impose an additional condition,
either on the application of the person carrying on the home or without such an application.

(3) If any condition imposed or varied under this paragraph is not complied with, the person carrying on the home shall, if he has no reasonable excuse, be guilty of an offence and liable on summary conviction to a fine not exceeding level 4 on the standard scale.

Annual review of registration

3.—(1) In this Part "the responsible authority", in relation to a registered children's home means the local authority who registered it.

(2) The responsible authority for a registered children's home shall, at the end of the period of twelve months beginning with the date of registration, and annually thereafter, review its registration for the purpose of determining whether the registration should continue in force or be cancelled under paragraph 4(3).

(3) If on any such annual review the responsible authority are satisfied that the home is being carried on in accordance with the relevant requirements they shall determine that, subject to sub-paragraph (4), the registration should continue in force.

(4) The responsible authority shall give to the person carrying on the home notice of their determination under sub-paragraph (3) and the notice shall require him to pay to the authority with respect to the review such reasonable fee as the authority may determine.

(5) It shall be a condition of the home's continued registration that the fee is so paid before the expiry of the period of twenty-eight days beginning with the date on which the notice is received by the person carrying on the home.

(6) In this Schedule "the relevant requirements" means any requirements of Part VIII and of any regulations made under paragraph 10, and any conditions imposed under paragraph 2.

Cancellation of registration

4.—(1) The person carrying on a registered children's home may at any time make an application, in such manner and including such particulars as may be prescribed, for the cancellation by the responsible authority of the registration of the home.

(2) If the authority are satisfied, in the case of a school registered by virtue of section 63(6), that it is no longer a school to which that provision applies, the authority shall give to the person carrying on the home notice that the registration of the home has been cancelled as from the date of the notice.

(3) If on any annual review under paragraph 3, or at any other time, it appears to the responsible authority that a registered home is being carried on otherwise than in accordance with the relevant requirements, they may determine that the registration of the home should be cancelled.

(4) The responsible authority may at any time determine that the registration of a home should be cancelled on the ground—

(a) that the person carrying on the home has been convicted of an offence under this Part or any regulations made under paragraph 10; or

(b) that any other person has been convicted of such an offence in relation to the home.

Procedure

5.—(1) Where—

(a) a person applies for the registration of a children's home; and

(b) the local authority propose to grant his application,

they shall give him written notice of their proposal and of the conditions (if any) subject to which they propose to grant his application.

(2) The authority need not give notice if they propose to grant the application subject only to conditions which—

(a) the applicant specified in the application; or

(b) the authority and the applicant have subsequently agreed.

(3) The authority shall give an applicant notice of a proposal to refuse his application.

(4) The authority shall give any person carrying on a registered children's home notice of a proposal—

(a) to cancel the registration;

(b) to vary any condition for the time being in force with respect to the home by virtue of Part VIII; or

(c) to impose any additional condition.

(5) A notice under this paragraph shall give the local authority's reasons for their proposal.

Right to make representations

6.—(1) A notice under paragraph 5 shall state that within 14 days of service of the notice any person on whom it is served may in writing require the local authority to give him an opportunity to make representations to them concerning the matter.

(2) Where a notice has been served under paragraph 5, the local authority shall not determine the matter until—

(a) any person on whom the notice was served has made representations to them concerning the matter;

(b) the period during which any such person could have required the local authority to give him an opportunity to make representations has elapsed without their being required to give such an opportunity; or

(c) the conditions specified in sub-paragraph (3) below are satisfied.

(3) The conditions are—

(a) that a person on whom the notice was served has required the local authority to give him an opportunity to make representations to them concerning the matter;

(b) that the authority have allowed him a reasonable period to make his representations; and

(c) that he has failed to make them within that period.

(4) The representations may be made, at the option of the person making them, either in writing or orally.

(5) If he informs the local authority that he desires to make oral representations, the authority shall give him an opportunity of appearing before and of being heard by a committee or sub-committee of theirs.

Decision of local authority

7.—(1) If the local authority decide to adopt a proposal of theirs to grant an application, they shall serve notice in writing of their decision on any person on whom they were required to serve notice of their proposal.

(2) A notice under this paragraph shall be accompanied by an explanation of the right of appeal conferred by paragraph 8.

(3) A decision of a local authority, other than a decision to grant an application for registration subject only to such conditions as are mentioned in paragraph 5(2) or to refuse an application for registration, shall not take effect—

(a) if no appeal is brought, until the end of the period of 28 days referred to in paragraph 8(3); and

(b) if an appeal is brought, until it is determined or abandoned.

Appeals

8.—(1) An appeal against a decision of a local authority under Part VIII shall lie to a Registered Homes Tribunal.

(2) An appeal shall be brought by notice in writing given to the local authority.

(3) No appeal shall be brought by a person more than 28 days after service on him of notice of the decision.

(4) On an appeal the Tribunal may confirm the local authority's decision or direct that it shall not have effect.

(5) A Tribunal shall also have power on an appeal—

(a) to vary any condition in force with respect to the home to which the appeal relates by virtue of paragraph 2;

(b) to direct that any such condition shall cease to have effect; or

(c) to direct that any such condition as it thinks fit shall have effect with respect to the home.

(6) A local authority shall comply with any direction given by a Tribunal under this paragraph.

Prohibition on further applications

9.—(1) Where an application for the registration of a home is refused, no further application may be made within the period of six months beginning with the date when the applicant is notified of the refusal.

(2) Sub-paragraph (1) shall have effect, where an appeal against the refusal of an application is determined or abandoned, as if the reference to the date when the applicant

is notified of the refusal were a reference to the date on which the appeal is determined or abandoned.

(3) Where the registration of a home is cancelled, no application for the registration of the home shall be made within the period of six months beginning with the date of cancellation.

(4) Sub-paragraph (3) shall have effect, where an appeal against the cancellation of the registration of a home is determined or abandoned, as if the reference to the date of cancellation were a reference to the date on which the appeal is determined or abandoned.

PART II

REGULATIONS

10.—(1) The Secretary of State may make regulations—
  (a) as to the placing of children in registered children's homes;
  (b) as to the conduct of such homes; and
  (c) for securing the welfare of the children in such homes.
(2) The regulations may in particular—
  (a) prescribe standards to which the premises used for such homes are to conform;
  (b) impose requirements as to the accommodation, staff and equipment to be provided in such homes;
  (c) impose requirements as to the arrangements to be made for protecting the health of children in such homes;
  (d) provide for the control and discipline of children in such homes;
  (e) require the furnishing to the responsible authority of information as to the facilities provided for—
      (i) the parents of children in such homes;
      (ii) persons who are not parents of such children but who have parental responsibility for them; and
      (iii) other persons connected with such children,
    to visit and communicate with the children;
  (f) impose requirements as to the keeping of records and giving of notices with respect to children in such homes;
  (g) impose requirements as to the facilities which are to be provided for giving religious instruction to children in such homes;
  (h) make provision as to the carrying out of annual reviews under paragraph 3;
  (i) authorise the responsible authority to limit the number of children who may be accommodated in any particular registered home;
  (j) prohibit the use of accommodation for the purpose of restricting the liberty of children in such homes;
  (k) require notice to be given to the responsible authority of any change of the person carrying on or in charge of a registered home or of the premises used by such a home;
  (l) make provision similar to that made by regulations under section 26.
(3) The regulations may provide that a contravention of or failure to comply with any specified provision of the regulations, without reasonable excuse, shall be an offence against the regulations.

(4) Any person guilty of such an offence shall be liable on summary conviction to a fine not exceeding level 4 on the standard scale.

DEFINITIONS
  "prescribed": Sched. 6, para. 1(3).
  "the responsible authority": Sched. 6, para. 3(1).

GENERAL NOTE
  See note on s.63(11).

Section 63(12) SCHEDULE 7

FOSTER PARENTS: LIMITS ON NUMBER OF FOSTER CHILDREN

Interpretation

1. For the purposes of this Schedule, a person fosters a child if—
  (a) he is a local authority foster parent in relation to the child;

(b) he is a foster parent with whom the child has been placed by a voluntary organisation; or

(c) he fosters the child privately.

The usual fostering limit

2. Subject to what follows, a person may not foster more than three children ("the usual fostering limit").

Siblings

3. A person may exceed the usual fostering limit if the children concerned are all siblings with respect to each other.

Exemption by local authority

4.—(1) A person may exceed the usual fostering limit if he is exempted from it by the local authority within whose area he lives.

(2) In considering whether to exempt a person, a local authority shall have regard, in particular, to—

(a) the number of children whom the person proposes to foster;

(b) the arrangements which the person proposes for the care and accommodation of the fostered children;

(c) the intended and likely relationship between the person and the fostered children;

(d) the period of time for which he proposes to foster the children; and

(e) whether the welfare of the fostered children (and of any other children who are or will be living in the accommodation) will be safeguarded and promoted.

(3) Where a local authority exempt a person, they shall inform him by notice in writing—

(a) that he is so exempted;

(b) of the children, described by name, whom he may foster; and

(c) of any condition to which the exemption is subject.

(4) A local authority may at any time by notice in writing—

(a) vary or cancel an exemption; or

(b) impose, vary or cancel a condition to which the exemption is subject,

and, in considering whether to do so, they shall have regard in particular to the considerations mentioned in sub-paragraph (2).

(5) The Secretary of State may make regulations amplifying or modifying the provisions of this paragraph in order to provide for cases where children need to be placed with foster parents as a matter of urgency.

Effect of exceeding fostering limit

5.—(1) A person shall cease to be treated as fostering and shall be treated as carrying on a children's home if—

(a) he exceeds the usual fostering limit; or

(b) where he is exempted under paragraph 4,—

(i) he fosters any child not named in the exemption; and

(ii) in so doing, he exceeds the usual fostering limit.

(2) Sub-paragraph (1) does not apply if the children concerned are all siblings in respect of each other.

Complaints etc.

6.—(1) Every local authority shall establish a procedure for considering any representations (including any complaint) made to them about the discharge of their functions under paragraph 4 by a person exempted or seeking to be exempted under that paragraph.

(2) In carrying out any consideration of representations under sub-paragraph (1), a local authority shall comply with any regulations made by the Secretary of State for the purposes of this paragraph.

DEFINITION
  "usual fostering limit": Sched. 7, para. 2.

GENERAL NOTE
See notes to s.63(12).

Section 66(5) SCHEDULE 8

PRIVATELY FOSTERED CHILDREN

Exemptions

1. A child is not a privately fostered child while he is being looked after by a local authority.

2.—(1) A child is not a privately fostered child while he is in the care of any person—
  (a) in premises in which any—
        (i) parent of his;
        (ii) person who is not a parent of his but who has parental responsibility for him; or
        (iii) person who is a relative of his and who has assumed responsibility for his care,
      is for the time being living;
  (b) in any children's home;
  (c) in accommodation provided by or on behalf of any voluntary organisation;
  (d) in any school in which he is receiving full-time education;
  (e) in any health service hospital;
  (f) in any residential care home, nursing home or mental nursing home; or
  (g) in any home or institution not specified in this paragraph but provided, equipped and maintained by the Secretary of State.

(2) Sub-paragraph (1)(b) to (g) does not apply where the person caring for the child is doing so in his personal capacity and not in the course of carrying out his duties in relation to the establishment mentioned in the paragraph in question.

3. A child is not a privately fostered child while he is in the care of any person in compliance with—
  (a) an order under section 7(7)(b) of the Children and Young Persons Act 1969; or
  (b) a supervision requirement within the meaning of the Social Work (Scotland) Act 1968.

4. A child is not a privately fostered child while he is liable to be detained, or subject to guardianship, under the Mental Health Act 1983.

5. A child is not a privately fostered child while—
  (a) he is placed in the care of a person who proposes to adopt him under arrangements made by an adoption agency within the meaning of—
        (i) section 1 of the Adoption Act 1976;
        (ii) section 1 of the Adoption (Scotland) Act 1978; or
        (iii) Article 3 of the Adoption (Northern Ireland) Order 1987; or
  (b) he is a protected child.

Power of local authority to impose requirements

6.—(1) Where a person is fostering any child privately, or proposes to foster any child privately, the appropriate local authority may impose on him requirements as to—
  (a) the number, age and sex of the children who may be privately fostered by him;
  (b) the standard of the accommodation and equipment to be provided for them;
  (c) the arrangements to be made with respect to their health and safety; and
  (d) particular arrangements which must be made with respect to the provision of care for them,
and it shall be his duty to comply with any such requirement before the end of such period as the authority may specify unless, in the case of a proposal, the proposal is not carried out.

(2) A requirement may be limited to a particular child, or class of child.

(3) A requirement (other than one imposed under sub-paragraph (1)(a)) may be limited by the authority so as to apply only when the number of children fostered by the person exceeds a specified number.

(4) A requirement shall be imposed by notice in writing addressed to the person on whom it is imposed and informing him of—
  (a) the reason for imposing the requirement;
  (b) his right under paragraph 8 to appeal against it; and

(c) the time within which he may do so.

(5) A local authority may at any time vary any requirement, impose any additional requirement or remove any requirement.

(6) In this Schedule—

    (a) "the appropriate local authority" means—

        (i) the local authority within whose area the child is being fostered; or

        (ii) in the case of a proposal to foster a child, the local authority within whose area it is proposed that he will be fostered; and

    (b) "requirement", in relation to any person, means a requirement imposed on him under this paragraph.

Regulations requiring notification of fostering etc.

7.—(1) The Secretary of State may by regulations make provision as to—

    (a) the circumstances in which notification is required to be given in connection with children who are, have been or are proposed to be fostered privately; and

    (b) the manner and form in which such notification is to be given.

(2) The regulations may, in particular—

    (a) require any person who is, or proposes to be, involved (whether or not directly) in arranging for a child to be fostered privately to notify the appropriate authority;

    (b) require any person who is—

        (i) a parent of a child; or

        (ii) a person who is not a parent of his but who has parental responsibility for a child,

    and who knows that it is proposed that the child should be fostered privately, to notify the appropriate authority;

    (c) require any parent of a privately fostered child, or person who is not a parent of such a child but who has parental responsibility for him, to notify the appropriate authority of any change in his address;

    (d) require any person who proposes to foster a child privately, to notify the appropriate authority of his proposal;

    (e) require any person who is fostering a child privately, or proposes to do so, to notify the appropriate authority of—

        (i) any offence of which he has been convicted;

        (ii) any disqualification imposed on him under section 68; or

        (iii) any prohibition imposed on him under section 69;

    (f) require any person who is fostering a child privately, to notify the appropriate authority of any change in his address;

    (g) require any person who is fostering a child privately to notify the appropriate authority in writing of any person who begins, or ceases, to be part of his household;

    (h) require any person who has been fostering a child privately, but has ceased to do so, to notify the appropriate authority (indicating, where the child has died, that that is the reason).

Appeals

8.—(1) A person aggrieved by—

    (a) a requirement imposed under paragraph 6;

    (b) a refusal of consent under section 68;

    (c) a prohibition imposed under section 69;

    (d) a refusal to cancel such a prohibition;

    (e) a refusal to make an exemption under paragraph 4 of Schedule 7;

    (f) a condition imposed in such an exemption; or

    (g) a variation or cancellation of such an exemption,

may appeal to the court.

(2) The appeal must be made within fourteen days from the date on which the person appealing is notified of the requirement, refusal, prohibition, condition, variation or cancellation.

(3) Where the appeal is against—

    (a) a requirement imposed under paragraph 6;

    (b) a condition of an exemption imposed under paragraph 4 of Schedule 7; or

    (c) a variation or cancellation of such an exemption,

the requirement, condition, variation or cancellation shall not have effect while the appeal is pending.

(4) Where it allows an appeal against a requirement or prohibition, the court may, instead of cancelling the requirement or prohibition—

(a) vary the requirement, or allow more time for compliance with it; or

(b) if an absolute prohibition has been imposed, substitute for it a prohibition on using the premises after such time as the court may specify unless such specified requirements as the local authority had power to impose under paragraph 6 are complied with.

(5) Any requirement or prohibition specified or substituted by a court under this paragraph shall be deemed for the purposes of Part IX (other than this paragraph) to have been imposed by the local authority under paragraph 6 or (as the case may be) section 69.

(6) Where it allows an appeal against a refusal to make an exemption, a condition imposed in such an exemption or a variation or cancellation of such an exemption, the court may—

(a) make an exemption;

(b) impose a condition; or

(c) vary the exemption.

(7) Any exemption made or varied under sub-paragraph (6), or any condition imposed under that sub-paragraph, shall be deemed for the purposes of Schedule 7 (but not for the purposes of this paragraph) to have been made, varied or imposed under that Schedule.

(8) Nothing in sub-paragraph (1)(e) to (g) confers any right of appeal on—

(a) a person who is, or would be if exempted under Schedule 7, a local authority foster parent; or

(b) a person who is, or would be if so exempted, a person with whom a child is placed by a voluntary organisation.

Extension of Part IX to certain school children during holidays

9.—(1) Where a child under sixteen who is a pupil at a school which is not maintained by a local education authority lives at the school during school holidays for a period of more than two weeks, Part IX shall apply in relation to the child as if—

(a) while living at the school, he were a privately fostered child; and

(b) paragraphs 2(1)(d) and 6 were omitted.

(2) Sub-paragraph (3) applies to any person who proposes to care for and accommodate one or more children at a school in circumstances in which some or all of them will be treated as private foster children by virtue of this paragraph.

(3) That person shall, not less than two weeks before the first of those children is treated as a private foster child by virtue of this paragraph during the holiday in question, give written notice of his proposal to the local authority within whose area the child is ordinarily resident ("the appropriate authority"), stating the estimated number of the children.

(4) A local authority may exempt any person from the duty of giving notice under sub-paragraph (3).

(5) Any such exemption may be granted for a special period or indefinitely and may be revoked at any time by notice in writing given to the person exempted.

(6) Where a child who is treated as a private foster child by virtue of this paragraph dies, the person caring for him at the school shall, not later than 48 hours after the death, give written notice of it—

(a) to the appropriate local authority; and

(b) where reasonably practicable, to each parent of the child and to every person who is not a parent of his but who has parental responsibility for him.

(7) Where a child who is treated as a foster child by virtue of this paragraph ceases for any other reason to be such a child, the person caring for him at the school shall give written notice of the fact to the appropriate local authority.

Prohibition of advertisements relating to fostering

10. No advertisement indicating that a person will undertake, or will arrange for, a child to be privately fostered shall be published, unless it states that person's name and address.

Avoidance of insurances on lives of privately fostered children

11. A person who fosters a child privately and for reward shall be deemed for the purposes of the Life Assurance Act 1774 to have no interest in the life of the child.

Section 71(16)   SCHEDULE 9

CHILD MINDING AND DAY CARE FOR YOUNG CHILDREN

Applications for registration

1.—(1) An application for registration under section 71 shall be of no effect unless it contains—
   (a) a statement with respect to the applicant which complies with the requirements of regulations made for the purposes of this paragraph by the Secretary of State; and
   (b) a statement with respect to any person assisting or likely to be assisting in looking after children on the premises in question, or living or likely to be living there, which complies with the requirements of such regulations.

(2) Where a person provides, or proposes to provide, day care for children under the age of eight on different premises situated within the area of the same local authority, he shall make a separate application with respect to each of those premises.

(3) An application under section 71 shall be accompanied by such fee as may be prescribed.

(4) On receipt of an application for registration under section 71 from any person who is acting, or proposes to act, in any way which requires him to be registered under that section, a local authority shall register him if the application is properly made and they are not otherwise entitled to refuse to do so.

Disqualification from registration

2.—(1) A person may not be registered under section 71 if he is disqualified by regulations made by the Secretary of State for the purposes of this paragraph.

(2) The regulations may, in particular, provide for a person to be disqualified where—
   (a) an order of a prescribed kind has been made at any time with respect to him;
   (b) an order of a prescribed kind has been made at any time with respect to any child who has been in his care;
   (c) a requirement of a prescribed kind has been imposed at any time with respect to such a child, under or by virtue of any enactment;
   (d) he has at any time been refused registration under Part X or any other prescribed enactment or had any such registration cancelled;
   (e) he has been convicted of any offence of a prescribed kind, or has been placed on probation or discharged absolutely or conditionally for any such offence;
   (f) he has at any time been disqualified from fostering a child privately;
   (g) a prohibition has been imposed on him at any time under section 61, section 10 of the Foster Children (Scotland) Act 1984 or any other prescribed enactment;
   (h) his rights and powers with respect to a child have at any time been vested in a prescribed authority under a prescribed enactment.

(3) A person who lives—
   (a) in the same household as a person who is himself disqualified by the regulations; or
   (b) in a household at which any such person is employed,
shall be disqualified unless he has disclosed the fact to the appropriate local authority and obtained their written consent.

(4) A person who is disqualified shall not provide day care, or be concerned in the management of, or have any financial interest in, any provision of day care unless he has—
   (a) disclosed the fact to the appropriate local authority; and
   (b) obtained their written consent.

(5) No person shall employ, in connection with the provision of day care, a person who is disqualified, unless he has—
   (a) disclosed to the appropriate local authority the fact that that person is so disqualified; and

(b) obtained their written consent.

(6) In this paragraph "enactment" means any enactment having effect, at any time, in any part of the United Kingdom.

Exemption of certain schools

3.—(1) Section 71 does not apply in relation to any child looked after in any—
(a) school maintained or assisted by a local education authority;
(b) school under the management of an education authority;
(c) school in respect of which payments are made by the Secretary of State under section 100 of the Education Act 1944;
(d) independent school;
(e) grant-aided school;
(f) grant maintained school;
(g) self-governing school;
(h) play centre maintained or assisted by a local education authority under section 53 of the Act of 1944, or by an education authority under section 6 of the Education (Scotland) Act 1980.

(2) The exemption provided by sub-paragraph (1) only applies where the child concerned is being looked after in accordance with provision for day care made by—
(a) the person carrying on the establishment in question as part of the establishment's activities; or
(b) a person employed to work at that establishment and authorised to make that provision as part of the establishment's activities.

(3) In sub-paragraph (1)—
"assisted" and "maintained" have the same meanings as in the Education Act 1944;
"grant maintained" has the same meaning as in section 52(3) of the Education Reform Act 1988; and
"grant-aided school", "self-governing school" and (in relation to Scotland) "independent school" have the same meaning as in the Education (Scotland) Act 1980.

Exemption for other establishments

4.—(1) Section 71(1)(b) does not apply in relation to any child looked after in—
(a) a registered children's home;
(b) a voluntary home;
(c) a community home;
(d) a residential care home, nursing home or mental nursing home required to be registered under the Registered Homes Act 1984;
(e) a health service hospital;
(f) a home provided, equipped and maintained by the Secretary of State; or
(g) an establishment which is required to be registered under section 61 of the Social Work (Scotland) Act 1968.

(2) The exemption provided by sub-paragraph (1) only applies where the child concerned is being looked after in accordance with provision for day care made by—
(a) the department, authority or other person carrying on the establishment in question as part of the establishment's activities; or
(b) a person employed to work at that establishment and authorised to make that provision as part of the establishment's activities.

(3) In this paragraph "a health service hospital" includes a health service hospital within the meaning of the National Health Service (Scotland) Act 1978.

Exemption for occasional facilities

5.—(1) Where day care for children under the age of eight is provided in particular premises on less than six days in any year, that provision shall be disregarded for the purposes of section 71 if the person making it has notified the appropriate local authority in writing before the first occasion on which the premises concerned are so used in that year.

(2) In sub-paragraph (1) "year" means the year beginning with the day on which the day care in question is (after the commencement of this paragraph) first provided in the premises concerned and any subsequent year.

Certificates of registration

6.—(1) Where a local authority register a person under section 71 they shall issue him with a certificate of registration.

(2) The certificate shall specify—
    (a) the registered person's name and address;
    (b) in a case falling within section 71(1)(b), the address or situation of the premises concerned; and
    (c) any requirements imposed under section 72 or 73.

(3) Where, due to a change of circumstances, any part of the certificate requires to be amended, the authority shall issue an amended certificate.

(4) Where the authority are satisfied that the certificate has been lost or destroyed, they shall issue a copy, on payment by the registered person of such fee as may be prescribed.

Fees for annual inspection of premises

7.—(1) Where—
    (a) a person is registered under section 71, and
    (b) the local authority concerned make an annual inspection of the premises in question under section 76,
they shall serve on that person a notice informing him that the inspection is to be carried out and requiring him to pay to them such fee as may be prescribed.

(2) It shall be a condition of the continued registration of that person under section 71 that the fee is so paid before the expiry of the period of twenty-eight days beginning with the date on which the inspection is carried out.

Co-operation between authorities

8.—(1) Where it appears to a local authority that any local education authority or, in Scotland, education authority could, by taking any specified action, help in the exercise of any of their functions under Part X, they may request the help of that local education authority, or education authority, specifying the action in question.

(2) An authority whose help is so requested shall comply with the request if it is compatible with their own statutory or other duties and obligations and does not unduly prejudice the discharge of any of their functions.

DEFINITIONS
    "assisted": Sched. 9, para. 3(3).
    "grant aided": Sched. 9, para. 3(3).
    "grant maintained", "maintained": Sched. 9, para. 3(3).
    "health service hospital": Sched. 9, para. 4(3).
    "independent school": Sched. 9, para. 3(3).
    "self governing school": Sched. 9, para. 3(3).
    "year": Sched. 9, para. 5(2).

GENERAL NOTE
    See notes to s.71.

Section 88   SCHEDULE 10

AMENDMENTS OF ADOPTION LEGISLATION

PART I

AMENDMENTS OF ADOPTION ACT 1976 (c. 36)

1. In section 2 (local authorities' social services) for the words from "relating to" to the end there shall be substituted—
    "(a) under the Children Act 1989, relating to family assistance orders, local authority support for children and families, care and supervision and emergency protection of children, community homes, voluntary homes and organisations, registered children's homes, private arrangements for fostering children, child minding and

day care for young children and children accommodated by health authorities and local education authorities or in residential care, nursing or mental nursing homes or in independent schools; and

(b) under the National Health Service Act 1977, relating to the provision of care for expectant and nursing mothers."

2. In section 11 (restrictions on arranging adoptions and placing of children) for subsection (2) there shall be substituted—

"(2) An adoption society which is—

(a) approved as respects Scotland under section 3 of the Adoption (Scotland) Act 1978; or

(b) registered as respects Northern Ireland under Article 4 of the Adoption (Northern Ireland) Order 1987,

but which is not approved under section 3 of this Act, shall not act as an adoption society in England and Wales except to the extent that the society considers it necessary to do so in the interests of a person mentioned in section 1 of the Act of 1978 or Article 3 of the Order of 1987."

3.—(1) In section 12 (adoption orders), in subsection (1) for the words "vesting the parental rights and duties relating to a child in" there shall be substituted "giving parental responsibility for a child to".

(2) In subsection (2) of that section for the words "the parental rights and duties so far as they relate" there shall be substituted "parental responsibility so far as it relates".

(3) In subsection (3) of that section for paragraph (a) there shall be substituted—

"(a) the parental responsibility which any person has for the child immediately before the making of the order;

(aa) any order under the Children Act 1989";

and in paragraph (b) for the words from "for any period" to the end there shall be substituted "or upbringing for any period after the making of the order."

4. For section 14(1) (adoption by married couple) there shall be substituted—

"(1) An adoption order shall not be made on the application of more than one person except in the circumstances specified in subsections (1A) and (1B).

(1A) An adoption order may be made on the application of a married couple where both the husband and the wife have attained the age of 21 years.

(1B) An adoption order may be made on the application of a married couple where—

(a) the husband or the wife—

(i) is the father or mother of the child; and

(ii) has attained the age of 18 years:

and

(b) his or her spouse has attained the age of 21 years."

5.—(1) In section 16 (parental agreement), in subsection (1) for the words from "in England" to "Scotland)" there shall be substituted—

"(i) in England and Wales, under section 18;

(ii) in Scotland, under section 18 of the Adoption (Scotland) Act 1978; or

(iii) in Northern Ireland, under Article 17(1) or 18(1) of the Adoption (Northern Ireland) Order 1987."

(2) In subsection (2)(c) of that section for the words "the parental duties in relation to" there shall be substituted "his parental responsibility for".

6.—(1) In section 18 (freeing child for adoption), after subsection (2) there shall be inserted—

"(2A) For the purposes of subsection (2) a child is in the care of an adoption agency if the adoption agency is a local authority and he is in their care."

(2) In subsection (5) of that section, for the words from "the parental rights" to "vest in" there shall be substituted "parental responsibility for the child is given to", and for the words "and (3)" there shall be substituted "to (4)".

(3) For subsections (7) and (8) of that section there shall be substituted—

"(7) Before making an order under this section in the case of a child whose father does not have parental responsibility for him, the court shall satisfy itself in relation to any person claiming to be the father that—

(a) he has no intention of applying for—

(i) an order under section 4(1) of the Children Act 1989, or

(ii) a residence order under section 10 of that Act, or

(b) if he did make any such application, it would be likely to be refused.

(8) Subsections (5) and (7) of section 12 apply in relation to the making of an order under this section as they apply in relation to the making of an order under that section."

7. In section 19(2) (progress reports to former parents) for the words "in which the parental rights and duties were vested" there shall be substituted "to which parental responsibility was given".

8.—(1) In section 20 (revocation of section 18 order), in subsections (1) and (2) for the words "the parental rights and duties", in both places where they occur, there shall be substituted "parental responsibility".

(2) For subsection (3) of that section there shall be substituted—

"(3) The revocation of an order under section 18 ("a section 18 order") operates—

(a) to extinguish the parental responsibility given to the adoption agency under the section 18 order;

(b) to give parental responsibility for the child to—

(i) the child's mother; and

(ii) where the child's father and mother were married to each other at the time of his birth, the father; and

(c) to revive—

(i) any parental responsibility agreement,

(ii) any order under section 4(1) of the Children Act 1989, and

(iii) any appointment of a guardian in respect of the child (whether made by a court or otherwise),

extinguished by the making of the section 18 order.

(3A) Subject to subsection (3)(c), the revocation does not—

(a) operate to revive—

(i) any order under the Children Act 1989, or

(ii) any duty referred to in section 12(3)(b),

extinguished by the making of the section 18 order; or

(b) affect any person's parental responsibility so far as it relates to the period between the making of the section 18 order and the date of revocation of that order."

9. For section 21 (transfer of parental rights and duties between adoption agencies) there shall be substituted—

"Variation of section 18 order so as to substitute one adoption agency for another

21.—(1) On an application to which this section applies, an authorised court may vary an order under section 18 so as to give parental responsibility for the child to another adoption agency ('the substitute agency') in place of the agency for the time being having parental responsibility for the child under the order ('the existing agency').

(2) This section applies to any application made jointly by—

(a) the existing agency; and

(b) the would-be substitute agency.

(3) Where an order under section 18 is varied under this section, section 19 shall apply as if the substitute agency had been given responsibility for the child on the making of the order."

10.—(1) In section 22 (notification to local authority of adoption application), after subsection (1) there shall be inserted the following subsections—

"(1A) An application for such an adoption order shall not be made unless the person wishing to make the application has, within the period of two years preceding the making of the application, given notice as mentioned in subsection (1).

(1B) In subsections (1) and (1A) the references to the area in which the applicant or person has his home are references to the area in which he has his home at the time of giving the notice."

(2) In subsection (4) of that section for the word "receives" there shall be substituted "receive" and for the words "in the care of" there shall be substituted "looked after by".

11. In section 25(1) (interim orders) for the words "vesting the legal custody of the child in" there shall be substituted "giving parental responsibility for the child to".

12. In—

(a) section 27(1) and (2) (restrictions on removal where adoption agreed or application made under section 18); and

(b) section 28(1) and (2) (restrictions on removal where applicant has provided home for 5 years),

for the words "actual custody", in each place where they occur, there shall be substituted "home".

13. After section 27(2) there shall be inserted—

"(2A) For the purposes of subsection (2) a child is in the care of an adoption agency if the adoption agency is a local authority and he is in their care."

14.—(1) After section 28(2) there shall be inserted—

"(2A) The reference in subsections (1) and (2) to any enactment does not include a reference to section 20(8) of the Children Act 1989".

(2) For subsection (3) of that section there shall be substituted—

"(3) In any case where subsection (1) or (2) applies and—

(a) the child was being looked after by a local authority before he began to have his home with the applicant or, as the case may be, the prospective adopter, and

(b) the child is still being looked after by a local authority,

the authority which are looking after the child shall not remove him from the home of the applicant or the prospective adopter except in accordance with section 30 or 31 or with the leave of a court."

(3) In subsection (5) of that section—

(a) for the word "receives" there shall be substituted "receive"; and

(b) for the words "in the care of another local authority or of a voluntary organisation" there shall be substituted "looked after by another local authority".

15. In section 29 (return of child taken away in breach of section 27 or 28) for subsections (1) and (2) there shall be substituted—

"(1) An authorised court may, on the application of a person from whose home a child has been removed in breach of—

(a) section 27 or 28,

(b) section 27 or 28 of the Adoption (Scotland) Act 1978, or

(c) Article 28 or 29 of the Adoption (Northern Ireland) Order 1987,

order the person who has so removed the child to return the child to the applicant.

(2) An authorised court may, on the application of a person who has reasonable grounds for believing that another person is intending to remove a child from his home in breach of—

(a) section 27 or 28,

(b) section 27 or 28 of the Adoption (Scotland) Act 1978, or

(c) Article 28 or 29 of the Adoption (Northern Ireland) Order 1987,

by order direct that other person not to remove the child from the applicant's home in breach of any of those provisions."

16.—(1) In section 30 (return of children placed for adoption by adoption agencies), in subsection (1) there shall be substituted—

(a) for the words "delivered into the actual custody of" the words "placed with";

(b) in paragraph (a) for the words "retain the actual custody of the child" the words "give the child a home"; and

(c) in paragraph (b) for the words "actual custody" the word "home".

(2) In subsection (3) of that section for the words "in his actual custody" there shall be substituted "with him".

17.—(1) In section 31 (application of section 30 where child not placed for adoption), in subsection (1) for the words from "child", where it first occurs, to "except" there shall be substituted "child—

(a) who is (when the notice is given) being looked after by a local authority; but

(b) who was placed with that person otherwise than in pursuance of such arrangements as are mentioned in section 30(1),

that section shall apply as if the child had been placed in pursuance of such arrangements".

(2) In subsection (2) of that section for the words "for the time being in the care of" there shall be substituted "(when the notice is given) being looked after by".

(3) In subsection (3) of that section—

(a) for the words "remains in the actual custody of" there shall be substituted "has his home with"; and

(b) for the words "section 45 of the Child Care Act 1980" there shall be substituted "Part III of Schedule 2 to the Children Act 1989".

(4) At the end of that section there shall be added—

"(4) Nothing in this section affects the right of any person who has parental responsibility for a child to remove him under section 20(8) of the Children Act 1989".

18.—(1) In section 32 (meaning of "protected child"), in subsection (2) for the words "section 37 of the Adoption Act 1958" there shall be substituted—

"(a) section 32 of the Adoption (Scotland) Act 1978; or

(b) Article 33 of the Adoption (Northern Ireland) Order 1987."

(2) In subsection (3) of that section for paragraph (a) there shall be substituted—

"(a) he is in the care of any person—

(i) in any community home, voluntary home or registered children's home;

(ii) in any school in which he is receiving full-time education;

(iii) in any health service hospital";

and at the end of that subsection there shall be added—

"(d) he is in the care of any person in any home or institution not specified in this subsection but provided, equipped and maintained by the Secretary of State."

(3) After that subsection there shall be inserted—

"(3A) In subsection (3) 'community home', 'voluntary home', 'registered children's home', 'school' and 'health service hospital' have the same meaning as in the Children Act 1989."

(4) For subsection (4) of that section there shall be substituted—

"(4) A protected child ceases to be a protected child—

(a) on the grant or refusal of the application for an adoption order;

(b) on the notification to the local authority for the area where the child has his home that the application for an adoption order has been withdrawn;

(c) in a case where no application is made for an adoption order, on the expiry of the period of two years from the giving of the notice;

(d) on the making of a residence order, a care order or a supervision order under the Children Act 1989 in respect of the child;

(e) on the appointment of a guardian for him under that Act;

(f) on his attaining the age of 18 years; or

(g) on his marriage,

whichever first occurs.

(5) In Subsection (4)(d) the references to a care order and a supervision order do not include references to an interim care order or interim supervision order."

19.—(1) In section 35 (notices and information to be given to local authorities), in subsection (1) for the words "who has a protected child in his actual custody" there shall be substituted "with whom a protected child has his home".

(2) In subsection (2) of that section for the words "in whose actual custody he was" there shall be substituted "with whom he had his home".

20.—(1) In section 51 (disclosure of birth records of adopted children), in subsection (1) for the words "subsections (4) and (6)" there shall be substituted "what follows".

(2) For subsections (3) to (7) of that section there shall be substituted—

"(3) Before supplying any information to an applicant under subsection (1), the Registrar General shall inform the applicant that counselling services are available to him—

(a) if he is in England and Wales—

(i) at the General Register Office;

(ii) from the local authority in whose area he is living;

(iii) where the adoption order relating to him was made in England and Wales, from the local authority in whose area the court which made the order sat; or

(iv) from any other local authority;

(b) if he is in Scotland—

(i) from the regional or islands council in whose area he is living;

(ii) where the adoption order relating to him was made in Scotland, from the council in whose area the court which made the order sat; or

(iii) from any other regional or islands council;

(c) if he is in Northern Ireland—

(i) from the Board in whose area he is living;

(ii) where the adoption order relating to him was made in Northern Ireland, from the Board in whose area the court which made the order sat; or

(iii) from any other Board;

(d) if he is in the United Kingdom and his adoption was arranged by an adoption society—

(i) approved under section 3,

(ii) approved under section 3 of the Adoption (Scotland) Act 1978,

(iii) registered under Article 4 of the Adoption (Northern Ireland) Order 1987,

from that society.

(4) Where an adopted person who is in England and Wales—

(a) applies for information under—

    (i) subsection (1), or

    (ii) Article 54 of the Adoption (Northern Ireland) Order 1987, or

  (b) is supplied with information under section 45 of the Adoption (Scotland) Act 1978,

it shall be the duty of the persons and bodies mentioned in subsection (5) to provide counselling for him if asked by him to do so.

    (5) The persons and bodies are—

  (a) the Registrar General;

  (b) any local authority falling within subsection (3)(a)(ii) to (iv);

  (c) any adoption society falling within subsection (3)(d) in so far as it is acting as an adoption society in England and Wales.

    (6) If the applicant chooses to receive counselling from a person or body falling within subsection (3), the Registrar General shall send to the person or body the information to which the applicant is entitled under subsection (1).

    (7) Where a person—

  (a) was adopted before 12th November 1975, and

  (b) applies for information under subsection (1),

the Registrar General shall not supply the information to him unless he has attended an interview with a counsellor arranged by a person or body from whom counselling services are available as mentioned in subsection (3).

    (8) Where the Registrar General is prevented by subsection (7) from supplying information to a person who is not living in the United Kingdom, he may supply the information to any body which—

  (a) the Registrar General is satisfied is suitable to provide counselling to that person, and

  (b) has notified the Registrar General that it is prepared to provide such counselling.

    (9) In this section—

    "a Board" means a Health and Social Services Board established under Article 16 of the Health and Personal Social Services (Northern Ireland) Order 1972; and

    "prescribed" means prescribed by regulations made by the Registrar General."

  21. After section 51 there shall be inserted—

"Adoption Contact Register

  51A.—(1) The Registrar General shall maintain at the General Register Office a register to be called the Adoption Contact Register.

    (2) The register shall be in two parts—

  (a) Part I: Adopted Persons; and

  (b) Part II: Relatives.

    (3) The Registrar General shall, on payment of such fee as may be prescribed, enter in Part I of the register the name and address of any adopted person who fulfils the conditions in subsection (4) and who gives notice that he wishes to contact any relative of his.

    (4) The conditions are that—

  (a) a record of the adopted person's birth is kept by the Registrar General; and

  (b) the adopted person has attained the age of 18 years and—

    (i) has been supplied by the Registrar General with information under section 51; or

    (ii) has satisfied the Registrar General that he has such information as is necessary to enable him to obtain a certified copy of the record of his birth.

    (5) The Registrar General shall, on payment of such fee as may be prescribed, enter in Part II of the register the name and address of any person who fulfills the conditions in subsection (6) and who gives notice that he wishes to contact an adopted person.

    (6) The conditions are that—

  (a) a record of the adopted person's birth is kept by the Registrar General; and

  (b) the person giving notice under subsection (5) has attained the age of 18 years and has satisfied the Registrar General that—

    (i) he is a relative of the adopted person; and

    (ii) he has such information as is necessary to enable him to obtain a certified copy of the record of the adopted person's birth.

    (7) The Registrar General shall, on receiving notice from any person named in an entry in the register that he wishes the entry to be cancelled, cancel the entry.

    (8) Any notice given under this section must be in such form as may be determined by the Registrar General.

(9) The Registrar General shall transmit to an adopted person whose name is entered in Part I of the register the name and address of any relative in respect of whom there is an entry in Part II of the register.

(10) Any entry cancelled under subsection (7) ceases from the time of cancellation to be an entry for the purposes of subsection (9).

(11) The register shall not be open to public inspection or search and the Registrar General shall not supply any person with information entered in the register (whether in an uncancelled or a cancelled entry) except in accordance with this section.

(12) The register may be kept by means of a computer.

(13) In this section—

    (a) "relative" means any person (other than an adoptive relative) who is related to the adopted person by blood (including half-blood) or marriage;

    (b) "address" includes any address at or through which the person concerned may be contacted; and

    (c) "prescribed" means prescribed by the Secretary of State."

22.—(1) In section 55 (adoption of children abroad), in subsection (1) after the word "Scotland" there shall be inserted "or Northern Ireland" and for the words "vesting in him the parental rights and duties relating to the child" there shall be substituted "giving him parental responsibility for the child".

(2) In subsection (3) of that section for the words "word '(Scotland)' " there shall be substituted "words '(Scotland)' or '(Northern Ireland)' ".

23.—(1) In section 56 (restriction on removal of children for adoption outside Great Britain),—

    (a) in subsections (1) and (3) for the words "transferring the actual custody of a child to", in both places where they occur, there shall be substituted "placing a child with"; and

    (b) in subsection (3)(a) for the words "in the actual custody of" there shall be substituted "with".

(2) In subsection (1) of that section—

    (a) for the words from "or under" to "abroad" there shall be substituted "section 49 of the Adoption (Scotland) Act 1978 or Article 57 of the Adoption (Northern Ireland) Order 1987"; and

    (b) for the words "British Islands" there shall be substituted "United Kingdom, the Channel Islands and the Isle of Man".

24.—(1) In section 57 (prohibition on certain payments) in subsection (1)(c), for the words "transfer by that person of the actual custody of a child" there shall be substituted "handing over of a child by that person".

(2) In subsection (3A)(b) of that section, for the words "in the actual custody of" there shall be substituted "with".

25. After section 57 there shall be inserted—

"Permitted allowances

57A.—(1) The Secretary of State may make regulations for the purpose of enabling adoption agencies to pay allowances to persons who have adopted, or intend to adopt, children in pursuance of arrangements made by the agencies.

(2) Section 57(1) shall not apply to any payment made by an adoption agency in accordance with the regulations.

(3) The regulations may, in particular, make provision as to—

    (a) the procedure to be followed by any agency in determining whether a person should be paid an allowance;

    (b) the circumstances in which an allowance may be paid;

    (c) the factors to be taken into account in determining the amount of an allowance;

    (d) the procedure for review, variation and termination of allowances; and

    (e) the information about allowances to be supplied by any agency to any person who is intending to adopt a child.

(4) Any scheme approved under section 57(4) shall be revoked as from the coming into force of this section.

(5) Section 57(1) shall not apply in relation to any payment made—

    (a) in accordance with a scheme revoked under subsection (4) or section 57(5)(b); and

    (b) to a person to whom such payments were made before the revocation of the scheme.

(6) Subsection (5) shall not apply where any person to whom any payments may lawfully be made by virtue of subsection (5) agrees to receive (instead of such payments) payments complying with regulations made under this section."

26.—(1) In section 59 (effect of determination and orders made in Scotland and overseas in adoption proceedings), in subsection (1) for the words "Great Britain" there shall be substituted "the United Kingdom".

(2) For subsection (2) of that section there shall be substituted—

"(2) Subsections (2) to (4) of section 12 shall apply in relation to an order freeing a child for adoption (other than an order under section 18) as if it were an adoption order; and, on the revocation in Scotland or Northern Ireland of an order freeing a child for adoption, subsections (3) and (3A) of section 20 shall apply as if the order had been revoked under that section."

27. In section 60 (evidence of adoption in Scotland and Northern Ireland), in paragraph (a) for the words "section 22(2) of the Adoption Act 1958" there shall be substituted "section 45(2) of the Adoption (Scotland) Act 1978" and in paragraph (b) for the words from "section 23(4)" to "in force" there shall be substituted "Article 63(1) of the Adoption (Northern Ireland) Order 1987".

28. In section 62(5)(b) (courts), for the words from "section 8" to "child" there shall be substituted—

    "(i) section 12 or 18 of the Adoption (Scotland) Act 1978; or

    (ii) Article 12, 17 or 18 of the Adoption (Northern Ireland) Order 1987".

29. After section 65 (guardians ad litem and reporting officers) there shall be inserted—

"Panels for selection of guardians ad litem and reporting officers

65A.—(1) The Secretary of State may by regulations provide for the establishment of panels of persons from whom guardians ad litem and reporting officers appointed under rules made under section 65 must be selected.

(2) The regulations may, in particular, make provision—

    (a) as to the constitution, administration and procedures of panels;

    (b) requiring two or more specified local authorities to make arrangements for the joint management of a panel;

    (c) for the defrayment by local authorities of expenses incurred by members of panels;

    (d) for the payment by local authorities of fees and allowances for members of panels;

    (e) as to the qualifications for membership of a panel;

    (f) as to the training to be given to members of panels;

    (g) as to the co-operation required of specified local authorities in the provision of panels in specified areas; and

    (h) for monitoring the work of guardians ad litem and reporting officers.

(3) Rules of court may make provision as to the assistance which any guardian ad litem or reporting officer may be required by the court to give to it."

30.—(1) Section 72(1) (interpretation) shall be amended as follows.

(2) In the definition of "adoption agency" for the words from "section 1" to the end there shall be substituted"—

(a) section 1 of the Adoption (Scotland) Act 1978; and

(b) Article 3 of the Adoption (Northern Ireland) Order 1987."

(3) For the definition of "adoption order" there shall be substituted—

    " 'adoption order'—

        (a) means an order under section 12(1); and

        (b) in sections 12(3) and (4), 18 to 20, 27, 28 and 30 to 32 and in the definition of 'British adoption order' in this subsection includes an order under section 12 of the Adoption (Scotland) Act 1978 and Article 12 of the Adoption (Northern Ireland) Order 1987 (adoption orders in Scotland and Northern Ireland respectively); and

        (c) in sections 27, 28 and 30 to 32 includes an order under section 55, section 49 of the Adoption (Scotland) Act 1978 and Article 57 of the Adoption (Northern Ireland) Order 1987 (orders in relation to children being adopted abroad)."

(4) For the definition of "British adoption order" there shall be substituted—

    " 'British adoption order' means—

        (a) an adoption order as defined in this subsection, and

        (b) an order under any provision for the adoption of a child effected under the law of any British territory outside the United Kingdom."

(5) For the definition of "guardian" there shall be substituted—

    " 'guardian' has the same meaning as in the Children Act 1989."

(6) In the definition of "order freeing a child for adoption" for the words from "section 27(2)" to the end there shall be substituted "sections 27(2) and 59 includes an order under—

(a) section 18 of the Adoption (Scotland) Act 1978; and

(b) Article 17 or 18 of the Adoption (Northern Ireland) Order 1987".

(7) After the definition of "overseas adoption" there shall be inserted—

" 'parent' means, in relation to a child, any parent who has parental responsibility for the child under the Children Act 1989;

'parental responsibility' and 'parental responsibility agreement' have the same meaning as in the Children Act 1989."

(8) After the definition of "United Kingdom national" there shall be inserted—

" 'upbringing' has the same meaning as in the Children Act 1989."

(9) For section 72(1A) there shall be substituted the following subsections—

"(1A) In this Act, in determining with what person, or where, a child has his home, any absence of the child at a hospital or boarding school and any other temporary absence shall be disregarded.

(1B) In this Act, references to a child who is in the care of or looked after by a local authority have the same meaning as in the Children Act 1989."

31. For section 74(3) and (4) (extent) there shall be substituted—

"(3) This Act extends to England and Wales only."

PART II

AMENDMENTS OF ADOPTION (SCOTLAND) ACT 1978 (C. 28)

32. In section 11 (restrictions on arranging of adoptions and placing of children) for subsection (2) there shall be substituted—

"(2) An adoption society which is—

(a) approved as respects England and Wales under section 3 of the Adoption Act 1976; or

(b) registered as respects Northern Ireland under Article 4 of the Adoption (Northern Ireland) Order 1987,

but which is not approved under section 3 of this Act, shall not act as an adoption society in Scotland except to the extent that the society considers it necessary to do so in the interests of a person mentioned in section 1 of that Act or, as the case may be, Article 3 of that Order."

33. For section 14(1) (adoption by married couple) there shall be substituted—

"(1) Subject to section 53(1) of the Children Act 1975 (which provides for the making of a custody order instead of an adoption order in certain cases), an adoption order shall not be made on the application of more than one person except in the circumstances specified in subsections (1A) and (1B).

(1A) An adoption order may be made on the application of a married couple where both the husband and the wife have attained the age of 21 years.

(1B) An adoption order may be made on the application of a married couple where—

(a) the husband or the wife—

(i) is the father or mother of the child; and

(ii) has attained the age of 18 years; and

(b) his or her spouse has attained the age of 21 years."

34. In section 16(1)(a) (parental agreement) for the words from "in England" to "revoked", in the second place where it occurs, there shall be substituted—

"(i) in Scotland under section 18;

(ii) in England and Wales under section 18 of the Adoption Act 1976; or

(iii) in Northern Ireland under Article 17(1) or 18(1) of the Adoption (Northern Ireland) Order 1987,

and not revoked."

35. In section 18(5) (effect of order freeing child for adoption) for the words "and (3)" there shall be substituted "to (4)".

36. In section 20(3)(c) (revocation of section 18 order) the words "section 12(3)(b) of the Adoption Act 1976 or of" shall cease to have effect.

37. For section 21 (transfer of parental rights and duties between adoption agencies) there shall be substituted—

"Variation of section 18 order so as to substitute one adoption agency for another

21.—(1) On an application to which this section applies an authorised court may vary an order under section 18 so as to transfer the parental rights and duties relating to the child from the adoption agency in which they are vested under the order ('the existing agency') to another adoption agency ('the substitute agency').

(2) This section applies to any application made jointly by the existing agency and the would-be substitute agency.

(3) Where an order under section 18 is varied under this section, section 19 shall apply as if the parental rights and duties relating to the child had vested in the substitute agency on the making of the order."

38. In section 22(4) (notification to local authority of adoption application) for the word "receives" there shall be substituted "receive".

39. In section 29 (return of child taken away in breach of section 27 or 28) after the word "1976" in each place where it occurs there shall be inserted "or Article 28 or 29 of the Adoption (Northern Ireland) Order 1987".

40. In section 32 (meaning of "protected child"), at the end of subsection (2) there shall be added "or Article 33 of the Adoption (Northern Ireland) Order 1987".

41. In section 45 (adopted children register)—

    (a) for the words from "or an approved" in subsection (5) to the end of subsection (6) there shall be substituted—

"Board or adoption society falling within subsection (6) which is providing counselling for that adopted person.

(6) Where the Registrar General for Scotland furnishes an adopted person with information under subsection (5), he shall advise that person that counselling services are available—

    (a) if the person is in Scotland—

        (i) from the local authority in whose area he is living;

        (ii) where the adoption order relating to him was made in Scotland, from the local authority in whose area the court which made the order sat; or

        (iii) from any other local authority in Scotland;

    (b) if the person is in England and Wales—

        (i) from the local authority in whose area he is living;

        (ii) where the adoption order relating to him was made in England and Wales, from the local authority in whose area the court which made the order sat; or

        (iii) from any other local authority in England and Wales;

    (c) if the person is in Northern Ireland—

        (i) from the Board in whose area he is living;

        (ii) where the adoption order relating to him was made in Northern Ireland, from the Board in whose area the court which made the order sat; or

        (iii) from any other Board;

    (d) if the person is in the United Kingdom and his adoption was arranged by an adoption society—

        (i) approved under section 3;

        (ii) approved under section 3 of the Adoption Act 1976; or

        (iii) registered under Article 4 of the Adoption (Northern Ireland) Order 1987,

from that society.

(6A) Where an adopted person who is in Scotland—

    (a) is furnished with information under subsection (5); or

    (b) applies for information under—

        (i) section 51(1) of the Adoption Act 1976; or

        (ii) Article 54 of the Adoption (Northern Ireland) Order 1987,

any body mentioned in subsection (6B) to which the adopted person applies for counselling shall have a duty to provide counselling for him.

(6B) The bodies referred to in subsection (6A) are—

    (a) any local authority falling within subsection (6)(a); and

    (b) any adoption society falling within subsection (6)(d) so far as it is acting as an adoption society in Scotland.";

    (b) in subsection (7)—

        (i) for the word "under" there shall be substituted "from a local authority, Board or adoption society falling within";

(ii) for the words "or adoption society which is providing that counselling" there shall be substituted ", Board or adoption society"; and

(iii) after the word "authority" where it second occurs there shall be inserted ", Board"; and

(c) after subsection (9) there shall be inserted the following subsection—

"(10) In this section—

"Board" means a Health and Social Services Board established under Article 16 of the Health and Personal Social Services (Northern Ireland) Order 1972; and

"local authority", in relation to England and Wales, means the council of a county (other than a metropolitan county), a metropolitan district, a London borough or the Common Council of the City of London."

42. In section 49 (adoption of children abroad)—

(a) in subsection (1) after the word "Scotland" there shall be inserted "or Northern Ireland"; and

(b) in subsection (3) for the words "word 'England' " there shall be substituted "words '(England)' or '(Northern Ireland)'".

43. In section 50(1) (restriction on removal of children for adoption outside Great Britain) after the word "1976" there shall be inserted "or Article 57 of the Adoption (Northern Ireland) Order 1987".

44. In section 53(1) (effect of determination and orders made in England and Wales and overseas in adoption proceedings)—

(a) in subsection (1) for the words "Great Britain" there shall be substituted "the United Kingdom"; and

(b) for subsection (2) there shall be substituted—

"(2) Subsections (2) to (4) of section 12 shall apply in relation to an order freeing a child for adoption (other than an order under section 18) as if it were an adoption order; and on the revocation in England and Wales or Northern Ireland of an order freeing a child for adoption subsection (3) of section 20 shall apply as if the order had been revoked under that section."

45. In section 54(b) (evidence of adoption in Northern Ireland) for the words from "section 23(4)" to "in force" there shall be substituted "Article 63(1) of the Adoption (Northern Ireland) Order 1987".

46. In section 65(1) (interpretation)—

(a) in the definition of "adoption agency", at the end there shall be added "and an adoption agency within the meaning of Article 3 of the Adoption (Northern Ireland) Order 1987 (adoption agencies in Northern Ireland)";

(b) for the definition of "adoption order" there shall be substituted—

" 'adoption order'—

(a) means an order under section 12(1); and

(b) in sections 12(3) and (4), 18 to 20, 27, 28 and 30 to 32 and in the definition of "British adoption order" in this subsection includes an order under section 12 of the Adoption Act 1976 and Article 12 of the Adoption (Northern Ireland) Order 1987 (adoption orders in England and Wales and Northern Ireland respectively); and

(c) in sections 27, 28 and 30 to 32 includes an order under section 49, section 55 of the Adoption Act 1976 and Article 57 of the Adoption (Northern Ireland) Order 1987 (orders in relation to children being adopted abroad);";

(c) for the definition of "British adoption order" there shall be substituted—

" 'British adoption order' means—

(a) an adoption order as defined in this subsection; and

(b) an order under any provision for the adoption of a child effected under the law of any British territory outside the United Kingdom;";

(d) in the definition of "order freeing a child for adoption" for the words from "section 27(2)" to the end there shall be substituted "sections 27(2) and 53 includes an order under—

(a) section 18 of the Adoption Act 1976; and

(b) Article 17 or 18 of the Adoption (Northern Ireland) Order 1987;".

GENERAL NOTE
See notes to s.88.

SCHEDULE 11

JURISDICTION

PART I

GENERAL

Commencement of proceedings

1.—(1) The Lord Chancellor may by order specify proceedings under this Act or the Adoption Act 1976 which may only be commenced in—
(a) a specified level of court;
(b) a court which falls within a specified class of court; or
(c) a particular court determined in accordance with, or specified in, the order.
(2) The Lord Chancellor may by order specify circumstances in which specified proceedings under this Act or the Adoption Act 1976 (which might otherwise be commenced elsewhere) may only be commenced in—
(a) a specified level of court;
(b) a court which falls within a specified class of court; or
(c) a particular court determined in accordance with, or specified in, the order.
(3) The Lord Chancellor may by order make provision by virtue of which, where specified proceedings with respect to a child under—
(a) this Act;
(b) the Adoption Act 1976; or
(c) the High Court's inherent jurisdiction with respect to children,
have been commenced in or transferred to any court (whether or not by virtue of an order under this Schedule), any other specified family proceedings which may affect, or are otherwise connected with, the child may, in specified circumstances, only be commenced in that court.
(4) A class of court specified in an order under this Schedule may be described by reference to a description of proceedings and may include different levels of court.

Transfer of proceedings

2.—(1) The Lord Chancellor may by order provide that in specified circumstances the whole, or any specified part of, specified proceedings to which this paragraph applies shall be transferred to—
(a) a specified level of court;
(b) a court which falls within a specified class of court; or
(c) a particular court determined in accordance with, or specified in, the order.
(2) Any order under this paragraph may provide for the transfer to be made at any stage, or specified stage, of the proceedings and whether or not the proceedings, or any part of them, have already been transferred.
(3) The proceedings to which this paragraph applies are—
    (a) any proceedings under this Act;
    (b) any proceedings under the Adoption Act 1976;
    (c) any other proceedings which—
        (i) are family proceedings for the purposes of this Act, other than proceedings under the inherent jurisdiction of the High Court; and
        (ii) may affect, or are otherwise connected with, the child concerned.
(4) Proceedings to which this paragraph applies by virtue of sub-paragraph (3)(c) may only be transferred in accordance with the provisions of an order made under this paragraph for the purpose of consolidating them with proceedings under—
    (a) this Act;
    (b) the Adoption Act 1976; or
    (c) the High Court's inherent jurisdiction with respect to children.
(5) An order under this paragraph may make such provision as the Lord Chancellor thinks appropriate for excluding proceedings to which this paragraph applies from the operation of any enactment which would otherwise govern the transfer of those proceedings, or any part of them.

Hearings by single justice

3.—(1) In such circumstances as the Lord Chancellor may by order specify—
    (a) the jurisdiction of a magistrates' court to make an emergency protection order;
    (b) any specified question with respect to the transfer of specified proceedings to or from a magistrates' court in accordance with the provisions of an order under paragraph 2,
may be exercised by a single justice.

(2) Any provision made under this paragraph shall be without prejudice to any other enactment or rule of law relating to the functions which may be performed by a single justice of the peace.

General

4.—(1) For the purposes of this Schedule—
    (a) the commencement of proceedings under this Act includes the making of any application under this Act in the course of proceedings (whether or not those proceedings are proceedings under this Act); and
    (b) there are three levels of court, that is to say the High Court, any county court and any magistrates' court.

(2) In this Schedule "specified" means specified by an order made under this Schedule.

(3) Any order under paragraph 1 may make provision as to the effect of commencing proceedings in contravention of any of the provisions of the order.

(4) An order under paragraph 2 may make provision as to the effect of a failure to comply with any of the provisions of the order.

(5) An order under this Schedule may—
    (a) make such consequential, incidental or transitional provision as the Lord Chancellor considers expedient, including provision amending any other enactment so far as it concerns the jurisdiction of any court or justice of the peace;
    (b) make provision for treating proceedings which are—
        (i) in part proceedings of a kind mentioned in paragraph (a) or (b) of paragraph 2(3); and
        (ii) in part proceedings of a kind mentioned in paragraph (c) of paragraph 2(3),
as consisting entirely of proceedings of one or other of those kinds, for the purposes of the application of any order made under paragraph 2.

PART II

CONSEQUENTIAL AMENDMENTS

The Administration of Justice Act 1964 (c. 42)

5. In section 38 of the Administration of Justice Act 1964 (interpretation), the definition of "domestic court", which is spent, shall be omitted.

The Domestic Proceedings and Magistrates' Courts Act 1978 (c. 22)

6. In the Domestic Proceedings and Magistrates' Courts Act 1978—
    (a) for the words "domestic proceedings", wherever they occur in sections 16(5)(c) and 88(1), there shall be substituted "family proceedings";
    (b) for the words "domestic court panel", wherever they occur in section 16(5)(b), there shall be substituted "family panel".

The Justices of the Peace Act 1979 (c. 55)

7. In the Justices of the Peace Act 1979—
    (a) for the words "domestic proceedings", wherever they occur in section 16(5), there shall be substituted "family proceedings";
    (b) for the words "domestic court", wherever they occur in section 17(3), there shall be substituted "family proceedings court";
    (c) for the words "domestic courts", wherever they occur in sections 38(2) and 58(1) and (5), there shall be substituted "family proceedings courts".

The Magistrates' Courts Act 1980 (c. 43)

8. In the Magistrates' Courts Act 1980—
   (a) in section 65(1) (meaning of family proceedings), the following paragraph shall be inserted after paragraph (m)—
   "(n) the Children Act 1989";
   (b) in section 65(2)(a) for the words "and (m)" there shall be substituted "(m) and (n)";
   (c) for the words "domestic proceedings", wherever they occur in sections 65(1), (2) and (3), 66(1) and (2), 67(1), (2) and (7), 69(1), (2), (3) and (4), 70(2) and (3), 71(1) and (2), 72(1), 73, 74(1), 121(8) and 150(1), there shall be substituted "family proceedings";
   (d) for the words "domestic court panel", wherever they occur in sections 66(2), 67(2), (4), (5), (7) and (8) and 68(1), (2) and (3), there shall be substituted "family panel";
   (e) for the words "domestic court panels", wherever they occur in section 67(3), (4), (5) and (6), there shall be substituted "family panels";
   (f) for the words "domestic courts", wherever they occur in sections 67(1) and (3) and 68(1), there shall be substituted "family proceedings courts";
   (g) for the words "domestic court", wherever they occur in section 67(2) and (5), there shall be substituted "family proceedings court".

The Supreme Court Act 1981 (c. 54)

9. In paragraph 3 of Schedule 1 to the Supreme Court Act 1981 (distribution of business to the Family Division of the High Court), the following sub-paragraph shall be added at the end—
   "(e) proceedings under the Children Act 1989".

The Matrimonial and Family Proceedings Act 1984 (c. 42)

10. In section 44 of the Matrimonial and Family Proceedings Act 1984 (domestic proceedings in magistrates' courts to include applications to alter maintenance agreements) for the words "domestic proceedings", wherever they occur, there shall be substituted "family proceedings".

The Insolvency Act 1986 (c. 45)

11.—(1) In section 281(5)(b) of the Insolvency Act 1986 (discharge not to release bankrupt from bankruptcy debt arising under any order made in family proceedings or in domestic proceedings), the words "or in domestic proceedings" shall be omitted.
   (2) In section 281(8) of that Act (interpretation), for the definitions of "domestic proceedings" and "family proceedings" there shall be substituted—
   "family proceedings" means—
      (a) family proceedings within the meaning of the Magistrates' Courts Act 1980 and any proceedings which would be such proceedings but for section 65(1)(ii) of that Act (proceedings for variation of order for periodical payments); and
      (b) family proceedings within the meaning of Part V of the Matrimonial and Family Proceedings Act 1984."

DEFINITION
"specified": Sched. 11, para. 4(1).

GENERAL NOTE
See notes to s.92.

Section 108(4)   SCHEDULE 12

MINOR AMENDMENTS

The Custody of Children Act 1891 (c. 3)

1. The Custody of Children Act 1891 (which contains miscellaneous obsolete provisions with respect to the custody of children) shall cease to have effect.

The Children and Young Persons Act 1933 (c. 12)

2. In section 1(2)(a) of the Children and Young Persons Act 1933 (cruelty to persons under sixteen), after the words "young person" there shall be inserted ", or the legal guardian of a child or young person,".

3. Section 40 of that Act shall cease to have effect.

The Education Act 1944 (c. 31)

4. In section 40(1) of the Education Act 1944 (enforcement of school attendance), the words from "or to imprisonment" to the end shall cease to have effect.

The Marriage Act 1949 (c. 76)

5.—(1) In section 3 of the Marriage Act 1949 (consent required to the marriage of a child by common licence or superintendent registrar's certificate), in subsection (1) for the words "the Second Schedule to this Act" there shall be substituted "subsection (1A) of this section".

(2) After that subsection there shall be inserted—

"(1A) The consents are—

    (a) subject to paragraphs (b) to (d) of this subsection, the consent of—

        (i) each parent (if any) of the child who has parental responsibility for him; and

        (ii) each guardian (if any) of the child;

    (b) where a residence order is in force with respect to the child, the consent of the person or persons with whom he lives, or is to live, as a result of the order (in substitution for the consents mentioned in paragraph (a) of this subsection);

    (c) where a care order is in force with respect to the child, the consent of the local authority designated in the order (in addition to the consents mentioned in paragraph (a) of this subsection);

    (d) where neither paragraph (b) nor (c) of this subsection applies but a residence order was in force with respect to the child immediately before he reached the age of sixteen, the consent of the person or persons with whom he lived, or was to live, as a result of the order (in substitution for the consents mentioned in paragraph (a) of this subsection).

(1B) In this section 'guardian of a child', 'parental responsibility', 'residence order' and 'care order' have the same meaning as in the Children Act 1989."

The Births and Deaths Registration Act 1953 (c. 20)

6.—(1) Sections 10 and 10A of the Births and Deaths Registration Act 1953 (registration of father, and re-registration, where parents not married) shall be amended as follows.

(2) In sections 10(1) and 10A(1) for paragraph (d) there shall be substituted—

"(d) at the request of the mother or that person on production of—

    (i) a copy of a parental responsibility agreement made between them in relation to the child; and

    (ii) a declaration in the prescribed form by the person making the request stating that the agreement was made in compliance with section 4 of the Children Act 1989 and has not been brought to an end by an order of a court; or

(e) at the request of the mother or that person on production of—

    (i) a certified copy of an order under section 4 of the Children Act 1989 giving that person parental responsibility for the child; and

    (ii) a declaration in the prescribed form by the person making the request stating that the order has not been brought to an end by an order of a court; or

(f) at the request of the mother or that person on production of—

    (i) a certified copy of an order under paragraph 1 of Schedule 1 to the Children Act 1989 which requires that person to make any financial provision for the child and which is not an order falling within paragraph 4(3) of that Schedule; and

    (ii) a declaration in the prescribed form by the person making the request stating that the order has not been discharged by an order of a court; or

(g) at the request of the mother or that person on production of—
    (i) a certified copy of any of the orders which are mentioned in subsection (1A) of this section which has been made in relation to the child; and
    (ii) a declaration in the prescribed form by the person making the request stating that the order has not been brought to an end or discharged by an order of a court."

(3) After sections 10(1) and 10A(1) there shall be inserted—
    "(1A) The orders are—
      (a) an order under section 4 of the Family Law Reform Act 1987 that that person shall have all the parental rights and duties with respect to the child;
      (b) an order that that person shall have custody or care and control or legal custody of the child made under section 9 of the Guardianship of Minors Act 1971 at a time when such an order could only be made in favour of a parent;
      (c) an order under section 9 or 11B of that Act which requires that person to make any financial provision in relation to the child;
      (d) an order under section 4 of the Affiliation Proceedings Act 1957 naming that person as putative father of the child."

(4) In section 10(2) for the words "or (d)" there shall be substituted "to (g)".

(5) In section 10(3) for the words from " 'relevant order' " to the end there shall be substituted " 'parental responsibility agreement' has the same meaning as in the Children Act 1989".

(6) In section 10A(2) in paragraphs (b) and (c) for the words "paragraph (d)" in both places where they occur there shall be substituted "any of paragraphs (d) to (g)."

The Army Act 1955 (c. 18)

7. In section 151 of the Army Act 1955 (deductions from pay for maintenance of wife or child), in subsection (1A)(a) for the words "in the care of a local authority in England or Wales" there shall be substituted "being looked after by a local authority in England or Wales (within the meaning of the Children Act 1989)".

8.—(1) Schedule 5A to that Act (powers of court on trial of civilian) shall be amended as follows.

(2) For paragraphs 7(3) and (4) there shall be substituted—
    "(3) While an authorisation under a reception order is in force the order shall (subject to sub-paragraph (4) below) be deemed to be a care order for the purposes of the Children Act 1989, and the authorised authority shall be deemed to be the authority designated in that deemed care order.
    (3A) In sub-paragraph (3) above "care order" means a care order which is not an interim care order under section 38 of the Children Act 1989.
    (4) The Children Act 1989 shall apply to a reception order which is deemed to be a care order by virtue of sub-paragraph (3) above as if sections 31(8) (designated local authority), 91 (duration of care order etc.) and 101 (effect of orders as between different jurisdictions) were omitted."

(3) In sub-paragraph (5)(c) for the words from "attains" to the end there shall be substituted "attains 18 years of age".

(4) In paragraph 8(1) for the words "Children and Young Persons Act 1969" there shall be substituted "Children Act 1989".

The Air Force Act 1955 (c. 19)

9. Section 151(1A) of the Air Force Act 1955 (deductions from pay for maintenance of wife or child) shall have effect subject to the amendment that is set out in paragraph 7 in relation to section 151(1A) of the Army Act 1955.

10. Schedule 5A to that Act (powers of court on trial of civilian) shall have effect subject to the amendments that are set out in paragraph 8(2) to (4) in relation to Schedule 5A to the Army Act 1955.

The Sexual Offences Act 1956 (c. 69)

11. In section 19(3) of the Sexual Offences Act 1956 (abduction of unmarried girl under eighteen from parent or guardian) for the words "the lawful care or charge of" there shall be substituted "parental responsibility for or care of".

12. In section 20(2) of that Act (abduction of unmarried girl under sixteen from parent or guardian) for the words "the lawful care or charge of" there shall be substituted "parental responsibility for or care of".

13. In section 21(3) of that Act (abduction of defective from parent or guardian) for the words "the lawful care or charge of" there shall be substituted "parental responsibility for or care of".

14. In section 28 of that Act (causing or encouraging prostitution of, intercourse with, or indecent assault on, girl under sixteen) for subsections (3) and (4) there shall be substituted—

"(3) The persons who are to be treated for the purposes of this section as responsible for a girl are (subject to subsection (4) of this section)—

(a) her parents;

(b) any person who is not a parent of hers but who has parental responsibility for her; and

(c) any person who has care of her.

(4) An individual falling within subsection (3)(a) or (b) of this section not to be treated as responsible for a girl if—

(a) a residence order under the Children Act 1989 is in force with respect to her and he is not named in the order as the person with whom she is to live; or

(b) a care order under that Act is in force with respect to her."

15. Section 38 of that Act (power of court to divest person of authority over girl or boy in case of incest) shall cease to have effect.

16.—(1) In section 43 of that Act (power to search for and recover woman detained for immoral purposes), in subsection (5) for the words "the lawful care or charge of" there shall be substituted "parental responsibility for or care of".

(2) In subsection (6) of that section, for the words "section forty of the Children and Young Persons Act 1933" there shall be substituted "Part V of the Children Act 1989".

17. After section 46 of that Act there shall be inserted—

"Meaning of 'parental responsibility'

46A. In this Act 'parental responsibility' has the same meaning as in the Children Act 1989."

The Naval Discipline Act 1957 (c. 53)

18. Schedule 4A to the Naval Discipline Act 1957 (powers of court on trial of civilian) shall have effect subject to the amendments that are set out in paragraph 8(2) to (4) in relation to Schedule 5A to the Army Act 1955.

The Children and Young Persons Act 1963 (c. 37)

19. Section 3 of the Children and Young Persons Act 1963 (children and young persons beyond control) shall cease to have effect.

The Children and Young Persons Act 1969 (c. 54)

20. In section 5 of the Children and Young Persons Act 1969 (restrictions on criminal proceedings for offences by young persons), in subsection (2), for the words "section 1 of this Act" there shall be substituted "Part IV of the Children Act 1989".

21. After section 7(7) of that Act (alteration in treatment of young offenders, etc.) there shall be inserted—

"(7B) An order under subsection (7)(c) of this section shall not require a person to enter into a recognisance—

(a) for an amount exceeding £1,000; or

(b) for a period exceeding—

(i) three years; or

(ii) where the young person concerned will attain the age of eighteen in a period shorter than three years, that shorter period.

(7C) Section 120 of the Magistrates' Courts Act 1980 shall apply to a recognisance entered into in pursuance of an order under subsection (7)(c) of this section as it applies to a recognisance to keep the peace."

22. In section 12A of that Act (young offenders) for subsections (1) and (2) there shall be substituted—

"(1) This subsection applies to any supervision order made under section 7(7) of this Act unless it requires the supervised person to comply with directions given by the supervisor under section 12(2) of this Act."

23. After that section there shall be inserted—

"Requirement for young offender to live in local authority accommodation

12AA.—(1) Where the conditions mentioned in subsection (6) of this section are satisfied, a supervision order may impose a requirement ('a residence requirement') that a child or young person shall live for a specified period in local authority accommodation.

(2) A residence requirement shall designate the local authority who are to receive the child or young person and that authority shall be the authority in whose area the child or young person resides.

(3) The court shall not impose a residence requirement without first consulting the designated authority.

(4) A residence requirement may stipulate that the child or young person shall not live with a named person.

(5) The maximum period which may be specified in a residence requirement is six months.

(6) The conditions are that—

(a) a supervision order has previously been made in respect of the child or young person;

(b) that order imposed—

(i) a requirement under section 12A(3) of this Act; or

(ii) a residence requirement;

(c) he is found guilty of an offence which—

(i) was committed while that order was in force;

(ii) if it had been committed by a person over the age of twenty-one, would have been punishable with imprisonment; and

(iii) in the opinion of the court is serious; and

(d) the court is satisfied that the behaviour which constituted the offence was due, to a significant extent, to the circumstances in which he was living,

except that the condition in paragraph (d) of this subsection does not apply where the condition in paragraph (b)(ii) is satisfied.

(7) For the purposes of satisfying itself as mentioned in subsection (6)(d) of this section, the court shall obtain a social inquiry report which makes particular reference to the circumstances in which the child or young person was living.

(8) Subsection (7) of this section does not apply if the court already has before it a social inquiry report which contains sufficient information about the circumstances in which the child or young person was living.

(9) A court shall not include a residence requirement in respect of a child or young person who is not legally represented at the relevant time in that court unless—

(a) he has applied for legal aid for the purposes of the proceedings and the application was refused on the ground that it did not appear that his resources were such that he required assistance; or

(b) he has been informed of his right to apply for legal aid for the purposes of the proceedings and has had the opportunity to do so, but nevertheless refused or failed to apply.

(10) In subsection (9) of this section—

(a) 'the relevant time' means the time when the court is considering whether or not to impose the requirement; and

(b) 'the proceedings' means—

(i) the whole proceedings; or

(ii) the part of the proceedings relating to the imposition of the requirement.

(11) A supervision order imposing a residence requirement may also impose any of the requirements mentioned in sections 12, 12A, 12B or 12C of this Act.

(12) In this section 'social inquiry report' has the same meaning as in section 2 of the Criminal Justice Act 1982."

24.—(1) In section 15 of that Act (variation and discharge of supervision orders), in subsections (1)(a), (2A), (3)(e) and (4) after the word "12A", in each place where it occurs, there shall be inserted "12AA".

(2) In subsection (4) of that section for the words "(not being a juvenile court)" there shall be substituted "other than a juvenile court".

25.—(1) In section 16 of that Act (provisions supplementary to section 15), in subsection (3) for the words "either direct" to the end there shall be substituted—

"(i) direct that he be released forthwith; or
(ii) remand him."

(2) In subsection (4) of that section—

(a) in paragraph (a) for the words "an interim order made by virtue of" there shall be substituted "a remand under";

(b) in paragraph (b) for the words "makes an interim order in respect of" there shall be substituted "remands", and

(c) for the words "make an interim order in respect of" there shall be substituted "remand".

(3) In subsections (5)(b) and (c) and (6)(a) after the word "12A", in each place where it occurs, there shall be inserted "12AA".

26. For section 23 of that Act (remand to care of local authorities etc.) there shall be substituted—

"Remand to local authority accommodation, committal of young persons of unruly character, etc.

23.—(1) Where a court—

(a) remands or commits for trial a child charged with homicide or remands a child convicted of homicide; or

(b) remands a young person charged with or convicted of one or more offences or commits him for trial or sentence,

and he is not released on bail, then, unless he is a young person who is certified by the court to be of unruly character, the court shall remand him to local authority accommodation.

(2) A court remanding a person to local authority accommodation shall designate the authority who are to receive him and that authority shall be the authority in whose area it appears to the court that—

(a) he resides; or

(b) the offence or one of the offences was committed.

(3) Where a person is remanded to local authority accommodation, it shall be lawful for any person acting on behalf of the designated authority to detain him.

(4) The court shall not certify a young person as being of unruly character unless—

(a) he cannot safely be remanded to local authority accommodation; and

(b) the conditions prescribed by order made by the Secretary of State under this subsection are satisfied in relation to him.

(5) Where the court certifies that a young person is of unruly character, it shall commit him—

(a) to a remand centre, if it has been notified that such a centre is available for the reception from the court of such persons; and

(b) to a prison, if it has not been so notified.

(6) Where a young person is remanded to local authority accommodation, a court may, on the application of the designated authority, certify him to be of unruly character in accordance with subsection (4) of this section (and on so doing he shall cease to be remanded to local authority accommodation and subsection (5) of this section shall apply).

(7) For the purposes of subsection (6) of this section, "a court" means—

(a) the court which remanded the young person; or

(b) any magistrates' court having jurisdiction in the place where that person is for the time being,

and in this section "court" and "magistrates' court" include a justice.

(8) This section has effect subject to—

(a) section 37 of the Magistrates' Courts Act 1980 (committal to the Crown Court with a view to a sentence of detention in a young offender institution); and

(b) section 128(7) of that Act (remands to the custody of a constable for periods of not more than three days),

but section 128(7) shall have effect in relation to a child or young person as if for the reference to three clear days there were substituted a reference to twenty-four hours."

27.—(1) In section 32 of that Act (detention of absentees), for subsection (1A) there shall be substituted the following subsections—

"(1A) If a child or young person is absent, without the consent of the responsible person—

(a) from a place of safety to which he has been taken under section 16(3) of this Act; or

(b) from local authority accommodation—

(i) in which he is required to live under section 12AA of this Act; or

(ii) to which he has been remanded under section 23(1) of this Act,
he may be arrested by a constable anywhere in the United Kingdom or Channel Islands
without a warrant.

(1B) A person so arrested shall be conducted to—

(a) the place of safety;

(b) the local authority accommodation; or

(c) such other place as the responsible person may direct,

at the responsible person's expense.

(1C) In this section 'the responsible person' means the person who made the
arrangements under section 16(3) of this Act or, as the case may be, the authority
designated under section 12AA or 23 of this Act."

(2) In subsection (2B) of that section for the words "person referred to in subsection
(1A)(a) or (b) (as the case may be) of this section" there shall be substituted "responsible
person".

28. In section 34(1) of that Act (transitional modifications of Part I for persons of specified
ages)—

(a) in paragraph (a), for the words "13(2) or 28(4) or (5)" there shall be substituted "or
13(2)"; and

(b) in paragraph (e), for the words "section 23(2) or (3)" there shall be substituted
"section 23(4) to (6)".

29. In section 70(1) of that Act (interpretation)—

(a) after the definition of "local authority" there shall be inserted—

" 'local authority accommodation' means accommodation provided by or on
behalf of a local authority (within the meaning of the Children Act
1989)"; and

(b) in the definition of "reside" for "12(4) and (5)" there shall be substituted
"12B(1) and (2)".

30. In section 73 of that Act (extent, etc.)—

(a) in subsection (4)(a) for "32(1), (3) and (4)" there shall be substituted "32(1) to
(1C) and (2A) to (4)"; and

(b) in subsection (6) for "32(1), (1A)" there shall be substituted "32(1) to (1C)".

The Matrimonial Causes Act 1973 (c. 18)

31. For section 41 of the Matrimonial Causes Act 1973 (restrictions on decrees for
dissolution, annulment or separation affecting children) there shall be substituted—

"Restrictions on decrees for dissolution, annulment or separation affecting children

41.—(1) In any proceedings for a decree of divorce or nullity of marriage, or a
decree of judicial separation, the court shall consider—

(a) whether there are any children of the family to whom this section
applies; and

(b) where there are any such children, whether (in the light of the arrangements which have been, or are proposed to be, made for their upbringing
and welfare) it should exercise any of its powers under the Children Act
1989 with respect to any of them.

(2) Where, in any case to which this section applies, it appears to the court that—

(a) the circumstances of the case require it, or are likely to require it, to
exercise any of its powers under the Act of 1989 with respect to any
such child;

(b) it is not in a position to exercise that power or (as the case may be)
those powers without giving further consideration to the case; and

(c) there are exceptional circumstances which make it desirable in the
interests of the child that the court should give a direction under this
section,

it may direct that the decree of divorce or nullity is not to be made absolute, or that
the decree of judicial separation is not to be granted, until the court orders otherwise.

(3) This section applies to—

(a) any child of the family who has not reached the age of sixteen at the
date when the court considers the case in accordance with the requirements of this section; and

(b) any child of the family who has reached that age at that date and in
relation to whom the court directs that this section shall apply."

32. In section 42 of that Act, subsection (3) (declaration by court that party to marriage
unfit to have custody of children of family) shall cease to have effect.

33. In section 52(1) of that Act (interpretation), in the definition of "child of the family", for the words "has been boarded-out with those parties" there shall be substituted "is placed with those parties as foster parents".

The National Health Service Act 1977 (c. 49)

34. In Schedule 8 to the National Health Service Act 1977 (functions of local social services authorities), the following sub-paragraph shall be added at the end of paragraph 2—

"(4A) This paragraph does not apply in relation to persons under the age of 18."

The Child Care Act 1980 (c. 5)

35. Until the repeal of the Child Care Act 1980 by this Act takes effect, the definition of "parent" in section 87 of that Act shall have effect as if it applied only in relation to Part I and sections 13, 24, 64 and 65 of that Act (provisions excluded by section 2(1)(f) of the Family Law Reform Act 1987 from the application of the general rule in that Act governing the meaning of references to relationships between persons).

The Education Act 1981 (c. 60)

36. The following section shall be inserted in the Education Act 1981, after section 3—

"Provision outside England and Wales for certain children
3A.—(1) A local authority may make such arrangements as they think fit to enable any child in respect of whom they maintain a statement under section 7 to attend an establishment outside England and Wales which specialises in providing for children with special needs.

(2) In subsection (1) above "children with special needs" means children who have particular needs which would be special educational needs if those children were in England and Wales.

(3) Where an authority make arrangements under this section with respect to a child, those arrangements may, in particular, include contributing to or paying—
  (a) fees charged by the establishment;
  (b) expenses reasonably incurred in maintaining him while he is at the establishment or travelling to or from it;
  (c) those travelling expenses;
  (d) expenses reasonably incurred by any accompanying him while he is travelling or staying at the establishment.

(4) This section is not to be taken as in any way limiting any other powers of a local education authority."

The Child Abduction Act 1984 (c. 37)

37.—(1) Section 1 of the Child Abduction Act 1984 (offence of abduction by parent, etc.) shall be amended as follows.

(2) For subsections (2) to (4) there shall be substituted—
  "(2) A person is connected with a child for the purposes of this section if—
  (a) he is a parent of the child; or
  (b) in the case of a child whose parents were not married to each other at the time of his birth, there are reasonable grounds for believing that he is the father of the child; or
  (c) he is a guardian of the child; or
  (d) he is a person in whose favour a residence order is in force with respect to the child; or
  (e) he has custody of the child.
  (3) In this section 'the appropriate consent', in relation to a child, means—
  (a) the consent of each of the following—
    (i) the child's mother;
    (ii) the child's father, if he has parental responsibility for him;
    (iii) any guardian of the child;
    (iv) any person in whose favour a residence order is in force with respect to the child;
    (v) any person who has custody of the child; or

    (b) the leave of the court granted under or by virtue of any provision of Part II of the Children Act 1989; or

    (c) if any person has custody of the child, the leave of the court which awarded custody to him.

    (4) A person does not commit an offence under this section by taking or sending a child out of the United Kingdom without obtaining the appropriate consent if—

    (a) he is a person in whose favour there is a residence order in force with respect to the child, and

    (b) he takes or sends him out of the United Kingdom for a period of less than one month.

    (4A) Subsection (4) above does not apply if the person taking or sending the child out of the United Kingdom does so in breach of an order under Part II of the Children Act 1989.''

    (3) In subsection (5) for the words from "but" to the end there shall be substituted—

    "(5A) Subsection (5)(c) above does not apply if—

    (a) the person who refused to consent is a person—

        (i) in whose favour there is a residence order in force with respect to the child; or

        (ii) who has custody of the child; or

    (b) the person taking or sending the child out of the United Kingdom is, by so acting, in breach of an order made by a court in the United Kingdom.''

    (4) For subsection (7) there shall be substituted—

    "(7) For the purposes of this section—

    (a) 'guardian of a child', 'residence order' and 'parental responsibility' have the same meaning as in the Children Act 1989; and

    (b) a person shall be treated as having custody of a child if there is in force an order of a court in the United Kingdom awarding him (whether solely or jointly with another person) custody, legal custody or care and control of the child.''

    (5) In subsection (8) for the words from "or voluntary organisation" to "custodianship proceedings or" there shall be substituted "detained in a place of safety, remanded to a local authority accommodation or the subject of".

    38.—(1) In section 2 of that Act (offence of abduction of child by other persons), in subsection (1) for the words from "Subject" to "above" there shall be substituted "Subject to subsection (3) below, a person, other than one mentioned in subsection (2) below."

    (2) For subsection (2) of that section there shall be substituted—

    "(2) The persons are—

    (a) where the father and mother of the child in question were married to each other at the time of his birth, the child's father and mother;

    (b) where the father and mother of the child in question were not married to each other at the time of his birth, the child's mother; and

    (c) any other person mentioned in section 1(2)(c) to (e) above.

    (3) In proceedings against any person for an offence under this section, it shall be a defence for that person to prove—

    (a) where the father and mother of the child in question were not married to each other at the time of his birth—

        (i) that he is the child's father; or

        (ii) that, at the time of the alleged offence, he believed, on reasonable grounds, that he was the child's father; or

    (b) that, at the time of the alleged offence, he believed that the child had attained the age of sixteen.''

    39. At the end of section 3 of that Act (construction of references to taking, sending and detaining) there shall be added "and

    (d) references to a child's parents and to a child whose parents were (or were not) married to each other at the time of his birth shall be construed in accordance with section 1 of the Family Law Reform Act 1987 (which extends their meaning).''

    40.—(1) The Schedule to that Act (modifications of section 1 for children in certain cases) shall be amended as follows.

    (2) In paragraph 1(1) for the words "or voluntary organisation" there shall be substituted "within the meaning of the Children Act 1989".

    (3) For paragraph 2(1) there shall be substituted—

    "(1) This paragraph applies in the case of a child who is—

    (a) detained in a place of safety under section 16(3) of the Children and Young Persons Act 1969; or

    (b) remanded to local authority accommodation under section 23 of that Act.''

(4) In paragraph 3(1)—
  (a) in paragraph (a) for the words "section 14 of the Children Act 1975" there shall be substituted "section 18 of the Adoption Act 1976"; and
  (b) in paragraph (d) for the words "section 25 of the Children Act 1975 or section 53 of the Adoption Act 1958" there shall be substituted "section 55 of the Adoption Act 1976".

(5) In paragraph 3(2)(a)—
  (a) in sub-paragraph (i), for the words from "order or," to "Children Act 1975" there shall be substituted "section 18 order or, if the section 18 order has been varied under section 21 of that Act so as to give parental responsibility to another agency", and
  (b) in sub-paragraph (ii), for the words "(c) or (e)" there shall be substituted "or (c)".

(6) At the end of paragraph 3 there shall be added—
  "(3) Sub-paragraph (2) above shall be construed as if the references to the court included, in any case where the court is a magistrates' court, a reference to any magistrates' court acting for the same area as that court".

(7) For paragraph 5 there shall be substituted—
  "5. In this Schedule—
  (a) 'adoption agency' and 'adoption order' have the same meaning as in the Adoption Act 1976; and
  (b) 'area', in relation to a magistrates' court, means the petty sessions area (within the meaning of the Justices of the Peace Act 1979) for which the court is appointed."

The Foster Children (Scotland) Act 1984 (c. 56)

41. In section 1 of the Foster Children (Scotland) Act 1984 (definition of foster child)—
  (a) for the words "he is— (a) "there shall be substituted "(a) he is"; and
  (b) the words "for a period of more than 6 days" and the words from "The period" to the end shall cease to have effect.

42. In section 2(2) of that Act (exceptions to section 1), for paragraph (f) there shall be substituted—
  "(f) if he has been in that person's care for a period of less than 28 days and that person does not intend to undertake his care for any longer period."

43. In section 7(1) of that Act (persons disqualified from keeping foster children)—
  (a) the word "or" at the end of paragraph (e) shall be omitted; and
  (b) after paragraph (f) there shall be inserted "or
    (g) he is disqualified from fostering a child privately (within the meaning of the Children Act 1989) by regulations made under section 68 of that Act,".

The Disabled Persons (Services, Consultation and Representation) Act 1986 (c. 33)

44. In section 2(5) of the Disabled Persons (Services, Consultation and Representation) Act 1986 (circumstances in which authorised representative has right to visit etc. disabled person), after paragraph (d) there shall be inserted—
  "(dd) in accommodation provided by any educational establishment."

The Legal Aid Act 1988 (c. 34)

45. In paragraph 2 of Part I of Schedule 2 to the Legal Aid Act 1988 (proceedings in magistrates' courts to which the civil legal aid provisions of Part IV of the Act apply), the following sub-paragraph shall be added at the end—
  "(g) proceedings under the Children Act 1989."

Section 108(5)   SCHEDULE 13

CONSEQUENTIAL AMENDMENTS

The Wills Act 1837 (c. 26)

1. In section 1 of the Wills Act 1837 (interpretation), in the definition of "will", for the words "and also to a disposition by will and testament or devise of the custody and tuition

of any child" there shall be substituted "and also to an appointment by will of a guardian of a child".

The Children and Young Persons Act 1933 (c. 12)

2. In section 1(1) of the Children and Young Persons Act 1933 (cruelty to persons under sixteen) for the words "has the custody, charge or care of" there shall be substituted "has responsibility for".

3. In the following sections of that Act—
    (a) 3(1) (allowing persons under sixteen to be in brothels);
    (b) 4(1) and (2) (causing or allowing persons under sixteen to be used for begging);
    (c) 11 (exposing children under twelve to risk of burning); and
    (d) 25(1) (restrictions on persons under eighteen going abroad for the purpose of performing for profit),

for the words "the custody, charge or care of" there shall, in each case, be substituted "responsibility for".

4. In section 10(1A) of that Act (vagrants preventing children from receiving education), for the words from "to bring the child" to the end there shall be substituted "to make an application in respect of the child or young person for an education supervision order under section 36 of the Children Act 1989".

5. For section 17 of that Act (interpretation of Part I) there shall be substituted the following section—

"Interpretation of Part I

17.—(1) For the purposes of this Part of this Act, the following shall be presumed to have responsibility for a child or young person—
    (a) any person who—
        (i) has parental responsibility for him (within the meaning of the Children Act 1989); or
        (ii) is otherwise legally liable to maintain him; and
    (b) any person who has care of him.

(2) A person who is presumed to be responsible for a child or young person by virtue of subsection (1)(a) shall not be taken to have ceased to be responsible for him by reason only that he does not have care of him."

6.—(1) In section 34 of that Act (attendance at court of parent of child or young person charged with an offence etc.), in subsection (1) after the word "offence" there shall be inserted "is the subject of an application for a care or supervision order under Part IV of the Children Act 1989".

(2) In subsection (7) of that section after the words "Children and Young Persons Act 1969" there shall be inserted "or Part IV of the Children Act 1989".

(3) After subsection (7) of that section there shall be inserted—

"(7A) If it appears that at the time of his arrest the child or young person is being provided with accommodation by or on behalf of a local authority under section 20 of the Children Act 1989, the local authority shall also be informed as described in subsection (3) above as soon as it is reasonably practicable to do so."

7. In section 107(1) of that Act (interpretation)—
    (a) in the definition of "guardian", for the words "charge of or control over" there shall be substituted "care of";
    (b) for the definition of legal guardian there shall be substituted—
        " 'legal guardian', in relation to a child or young person, means a guardian of a child as defined in the Children Act 1989".

The Education Act 1944 (c. 31)

8.—(1) Section 40 of the Education Act 1944 (enforcement of school attendance) shall be amended as follows.

(2) For subsection (2) there shall be substituted—

"(2) Proceedings for such offences shall not be instituted except by a local education authority.

(2A) Before instituting such proceedings the local education authority shall consider whether it would be appropriate, instead of or as well as instituting the proceedings, to apply for an education supervision order with respect to the child."

(3) For subsections (3) and (4) there shall be substituted—
    "(3) The court—

(a) by which a person is convicted of an offence against section 37 of this Act; or

(b) before which a person is charged with an offence under section 39 of this Act,

may direct the local education authority instituting the proceedings to apply for an education supervision order with respect to the child unless the authority, having consulted the appropriate local authority, decide that the child's welfare will be satisfactorily safeguarded even though no education supervision order is made.

(3A) Where, following such a direction, a local education authority decide not to apply for an education supervision order they shall inform the court of the reasons for their decision.

(3B) Unless the court has directed otherwise, the information required under subsection (3A) shall be given to the court before the end of the period of eight weeks beginning with the date on which the direction was given.

(4) Where—

(a) a local education authority apply for an education supervision order with respect to a child who is the subject of a school attendance order; and

(b) the court decides that section 36(3) of the Children Act 1989 prevents it from making the order;

the court may direct that the school attendance order shall cease to be in force."

(4) After subsection (4) there shall be inserted—

"(5) In this section—

'appropriate local authority' has the same meaning as in section 36(9) of the Children Act 1989; and

'education supervision order' means an education supervision order under that Act."

9. In section 71 of that Act (complaints with respect to independent schools), the following paragraph shall be added after paragraph (d), in subsection (1)—

"(e) there has been a failure, in relation to a child provided with accommodation by the school, to comply with the duty imposed by section 87 of the Children Act 1989 (welfare of children accommodated in independent schools);".

10. After section 114(1C) of that Act (interpretation) there shall be inserted the following subsections—

"(1D) In this Act, unless the context otherwise requires, 'parent', in relation to a child or young person, includes any person—

(a) who is not a parent of his but who has parental responsibility for him, or

(b) who has care of him,

except for the purposes of the enactments mentioned in subsection (1E) of this section, where it only includes such a person if he is an individual.

(1E) The enactments are—

(a) sections 5(4), 15(2) and (6), 31 and 65(1) of, and paragraph 7(6) of Schedule 2 to, the Education (No. 2) Act 1986; and

(b) sections 53(8), 54(2), 58(5)(k), 60 and 61 of the Education Reform Act 1988.

(1F) For the purposes of subsection (1D) of this section—

(a) 'parental responsibility' has the same meaning as in the Children Act 1989; and

(b) in determining whether an individual has care of a child or young person any absence of the child or young person at a hospital or boarding school and any other temporary absence shall be disregarded."

The National Assistance Act 1948 (c. 29)

11.—(1) In section 21(1)(a) of the National Assistance Act 1948 (persons for whom local authority is to provide residential accommodation) after the word "persons" there shall be inserted "aged eighteen or over".

(2) In section 29(1) of that Act (welfare arrangements for blind, deaf, dumb and crippled persons) after the words "that is to say persons" and after the words "and other persons" there shall, in each case, be inserted "aged eighteen or over".

The Reserve and Auxiliary Forces (Protection of Civil Interests) Act 1951 (c. 65)

12. For section 2(1)(d) of the Reserve and Auxiliary Forces (Protection of Civil Interests) Act 1951 (cases in which leave of the appropriate court is required before enforcing certain orders for the payment of money), there shall be substituted—

"(d) an order for alimony, maintenance or other payment made under sections 21 to 33 of the Matrimonial Causes Act 1973 or made, or having effect as if made, under Schedule 1 to the Children Act 1989."

The Mines and Quarries Act 1954 (c. 70)

13. In section 182(1) of the Mines and Quarries Act 1954 (interpretation), in the definition of "parent", for the words from "or guardian" to first "young person" there shall be substituted "of a young person or any person who is not a parent of his but who has parental responsibility for him (within the meaning of the Children Act 1989)".

The Administration of Justice Act 1960 (c. 65)

14. In section 12 of the Administration of Justice Act 1960 (publication of information relating to proceedings in private), in subsection (1) for paragraph (a) there shall be substituted—
"(a) where the proceedings—
    (i) relate to the exercise of the inherent jurisdiction of the High Court with respect to minors;
    (ii) are brought under the Children Act 1989; or
    (iii) otherwise relate wholly or mainly to the maintenance or upbringing of a minor;".

The Factories Act 1961 (c. 34)

15. In section 176(1) of the Factories Act 1961 (interpretation), in the definition of "parent", for the words from "or guardian" to first "young person" there shall be substituted "of a child or young person or any person who is not a parent of his but who has parental responsibility for him (within the meaning of the Children Act 1989)".

The Criminal Justice Act 1967 (c. 80)

16. In section 67(1A)(c) of the Criminal Justice Act 1967 (computation of sentences of imprisonment passed in England and Wales) for the words "in the care of a local authority" there shall be substituted "remanded to local authority accommodation".

The Health Services and Public Health Act 1968 (c. 46)

17.—(1) In section 64(3)(a) of the Health Services and Public Health Act 1968 (meaning of "relevant enactments" in relation to power of Minister of Health or Secretary of State to provide financial assistance), for sub-paragraph (xix) inserted by paragraph 19 of Schedule 5 to the Child Care Act 1980 there shall be substituted—
    "(xx) the Children Act 1989."
(2) In section 65(3)(b) of that Act (meaning of "relevant enactments" in relation to power of local authority to provide financial and other assistance), for sub-paragraph (xx) inserted by paragraph 20 of Schedule 5 to the Child Care Act 1980 there shall be substituted—
    "(xxi) the Children Act 1989."

The Social Work (Scotland) Act 1968 (c. 49)

18. In section 2(2) of the Social Work (Scotland) Act 1968 (matters referred to social work committee) after paragraph (j) there shall be inserted—
"(k) section 19 and Part X of the Children Act 1989,".
19. In section 5(2)(c) of that Act (power of Secretary of State to make regulations) for the words "and (j)" there shall be substituted "to (k)".
20. In section 21(3) of that Act (mode of provision of accommodation and maintenance) for the words "section 21 of the Child Care Act 1980" there shall be substituted "section 23 of the Children Act 1989".
21. In section 74(6) of that Act (parent of child in residential establishment moving to England or Wales) for the words from "Children and Young Persons Act 1969" to the end there shall be substituted "Children Act 1989, but as if section 31(8) were omitted".

22. In section 75(2) of that Act (parent of child subject to care order etc. moving to Scotland), for the words "Children and Young Persons Act 1969" there shall be substituted "Children Act 1989".

23. In section 86(3) of that Act (meaning of ordinary residence for purpose of adjustments between authority providing accommodation and authority of area of residence), the words "the Child Care Act 1980 or" shall be omitted and after the words "education authority" there shall be inserted "or placed with local authority foster parents under the Children Act 1989".

The Civil Evidence Act 1968 (c. 64)

24. In section 12(5)(b) of the Civil Evidence Act 1968 (findings of paternity etc. as evidence in civil proceedings - meaning of "relevant proceedings") for sub-paragraph (iv) there shall be substituted—

"(iv) paragraph 23 of Schedule 2 to the Children Act 1989."

The Administration of Justice Act 1970 (c. 31)

25. In Schedule 8 to the Administration of Justice Act 1970 (maintenance orders for purposes of Maintenance Orders Act 1958 and the 1970 Act), in paragraph 6 for the words "section 47 or 51 of the Child Care Act 1980" there shall be substituted "paragraph 23 of Schedule 2 to the Children Act 1989".

The Local Authority Social Services Act 1970 (c. 42)

26.—(1) In Schedule 1 to the Local Authority Social Services Act 1970 (enactments conferring functions assigned to social service committee)—
  (a) in the entry relating to the Mental Health Act 1959, for the words "sections 8 and 9" there shall be substituted "section 8"; and
  (b) in the entry relating to the Children and Young Persons Act 1969, for the words "sections 1, 2 and 9" there shall be substituted "section 9".

(2) At the end of that Schedule there shall be added—

"Children Act 1989. The whole Act, in so far as it confers functions on a local authority within the meaning of that Act.	Welfare reports. Consent to application for residence order in respect of child in care. Family assistance orders. Functions under Part III of the Act (local authority support for children and families). Care and supervision. Protection of children. Functions in relation to community homes, voluntary homes and voluntary organisations, registered children's homes, private arrangements for fostering children, child minding and day care for young children. Inspection of children's homes on behalf of Secretary of State. Research and returns of information. Functions in relation to children accommodated by health authorities and local education authorities or in residential care, nursing or mental nursing homes or in independent schools."

The Chronically Sick and Disabled Persons Act 1970 (c. 44)

27. After section 28 of the Chronically Sick and Disabled Persons Act 1970 there shall be inserted—

"Application of Act to authorities having functions under the Children Act 1989
28A. This Act applies with respect to disabled children in relation to whom a local authority have functions under Part III of the Children Act 1989 as it applies in relation to persons to whom section 29 of the National Assistance Act 1948 applies."

The Courts Act 1971 (c. 23)

28. In Part I of Schedule 9 to the Courts Act 1971 (substitution of references to Crown Court), in the entry relating to the Children and Young Persons Act 1969, for the words "Sections 2(12), 3(8), 16(8), 21(4)(5)" there shall be substituted "Section 16(8).".

The Attachment of Earnings Act 1971 (c. 32)

29. In Schedule 1 to the Attachment of Earnings Act 1971 (maintenance orders to which that Act applies), in paragraph 7, for the words "section 47 or 51 of the Child Care Act 1980" there shall be substituted "paragraph 23 of Schedule 2 to the Children Act 1989".

The Tribunals and Inquiries Act 1971 (c. 62)

30. In Schedule 1 to the Tribunals and Inquiries Act 1971 (tribunals under direct supervision of the Council on Tribunals) for paragraph 4 there shall be substituted—

"Registration of voluntary homes and children's homes under the Children Act 1989
4. Registered Homes Tribunals constituted under Part III of the Registered Homes Act 1984."

The Local Government Act 1972 (c. 70)

31.—(1) In section 102(1) of the Local Government Act 1972 (appointment of committees) for the words "section 31 of the Child Care Act 1980" there shall be substituted "section 53 of the Children Act 1989".
(2) In Schedule 12A to that Act (access to information: exempt information), in Part III (interpretation), in paragraph 1(1)(b) for the words "section 20 of the Children and Young Persons Act 1969" there shall be substituted "section 31 of the Children Act 1989".

The Employment of Children Act 1973 (c. 24)

32.—(1) In section 2 of the Employment of Children Act 1973 (supervision by education authorities), in subsection (2)(a) for the words "guardian or a person who has actual custody of" there shall be substituted "any person responsible for".
(2) After that subsection there shall be inserted—
"(2A) For the purposes of subsection (2)(a) above a person is responsible for a child—
(a) in England and Wales, if he has parental responsibility for the child or care of him; and
(b) in Scotland, if he is his guardian or has actual custody of him.".

The Domicile and Matrimonial Proceedings Act 1973 (c. 45)

33.—(1) In Schedule 1 to the Domicile and Matrimonial Proceedings Act 1973 (proceedings in divorce etc. stayed by reference to proceedings in other jurisdiction), paragraph 11(1) shall be amended as follows—
(a) at the end of the definition of "lump sum" there shall be added "or an order made in equivalent circumstances under Schedule 1 to the Children Act 1989 and of a kind mentioned in paragraph 1(2)(c) of that Schedule";
(b) in the definition of "relevant order", at the end of paragraph (b), there shall be added "or an order made in equivalent circumstances under Schedule 1 to the Children Act 1989 and of a kind mentioned in paragraph 1(2)(a) or (b) of that Schedule";
(c) in paragraph (c) of that definition, after the word "children)" there shall be inserted "or a section 8 order under the Children Act 1989"; and
(d) in paragraph (d) of that definition for the words "the custody, care or control" there shall be substituted "care".
(2) In paragraph 11(3) of that Schedule—

(a) the word "four" shall be omitted; and
(b) for the words "the custody of a child and the education of a child" there shall be substituted "or any provision which could be made by a section 8 order under the Children Act 1989".

The Powers of Criminal Courts Act 1973 (c. 62)

34. In Schedule 3 to the Powers of Criminal Courts Act 1973 (the probation and after-care service and its functions), in paragraph 3(2A) after paragraph (b) there shall be inserted—
"and
(c) directions given under paragraph 2 or 3 of Schedule 3 to the Children Act 1989".

The Rehabilitation of Offenders Act 1974 (c. 53)

35.—(1) Section 7(2) of the Rehabilitation of Offenders Act 1974 (limitations on rehabilitation under the Act) shall be amended as follows.
(2) For paragraph (c) there shall be substituted—
"(c) in any proceedings relating to adoption, the marriage of any minor, the exercise of the inherent jurisdiction of the High Court with respect to minors or the provision by any person of accommodation, care or schooling for minors;
(cc) in any proceedings brought under the Children Act 1989;"
(3) For paragraph (d) there shall be substituted—
"(d) in any proceedings relating to the variation or discharge of a supervision order under the Children and Young Persons Act 1969, or on appeal from any such proceedings."

The Domestic Proceedings and Magistrates' Courts Act 1978 (c. 22)

36. For section 8 of the Domestic Proceedings and Magistrates' Courts Act 1978 (orders for the custody of children) there shall be substituted—

"Restrictions on making of orders under this Act: welfare of children
8. Where an application is made by a party to a marriage for an order under section 2, 6 or 7 of this Act, then, if there is a child of the family who is under the age of eighteen, the court shall not dismiss or make a final order on the application until it has decided whether to exercise any of its powers under the Children Act 1989 with respect to the child."
37. In section 19(3A)(b) (interim orders) for the words "subsections (2) and" there shall be substituted "subsection".
38. For section 20(12) of that Act (variation and revocation of orders for periodical payments) there shall be substituted—
"(12) An application under this section may be made—
(a) where it is for the variation or revocation of an order under section 2, 6, 7 or 19 of this Act for periodical payments, by either party to the marriage in question; and
(b) where it is for the variation of an order under section 2(1)(c), 6 or 7 of this Act for periodical payments to or in respect of a child, also by the child himself, if he has attained the age of sixteen."
39.—(1) For section 20A of that Act (revival of orders for periodical payments) there shall be substituted—

"Revival of orders for periodical payments
20A.—(1) Where an order made by a magistrates' court under this Part of this Act for the making of periodical payments to or in respect of a child (other than an interim maintenance order) ceases to have effect—
(a) on the date on which the child attains the age of sixteen, or
(b) at any time after that date but before or on the date on which he attains the age of eighteen,
the child may apply to the court which made the order for an order for its revival.
(2) If on such an application it appears to the court that—
(a) the child is, will be or (if an order were made under this subsection) would be receiving instruction at an educational establishment or undergoing training for a trade, profession or vocation, whether or not while in gainful employment, or
(b) there are special circumstances which justify the making of an order under this subsection,

the court shall have power by order to revive the order from such date as the court may specify, not being earlier than the date of the making of the application.

(3) Any order revived under this section may be varied or revoked under section 20 in the same way as it could have been varied or revoked had it continued in being."

40. In section 23(1) of that Act (supplementary provisions with respect to the variation and revocation of orders) for the words "14(3), 20 or 21" there shall be substituted "20" and for the words "section 20 of this Act" there shall be substituted "that section".

41.—(1) In section 25 of that Act (effect on certain orders of parties living together), in subsection (1)(a) for the words "6 or 11(2)" there shall be substituted "or 6".

(2) In subsection (2) of that section—

(a) in paragraph (a) for the words "6 or 11(2)" there shall be substituted "or 6"; and

(b) after paragraph (a) there shall be inserted "or".

42. In section 29(5) of that Act (appeals) for the words "sections 14(3), 20 and 21" there shall be substituted "section 20".

43. In section 88(1) of that Act (interpretation)—

(a) in the definition of "child", for the words from "an illegitimate" to the end there shall be substituted "a child whose father and mother were not married to each other at the time of his birth"; and

(b) in the definition of "child of the family", for the words "being boarded-out with those parties" there shall be substituted "placed with those parties as foster parents".

The Magistrates' Courts Act 1980 (c. 43)

44.—(1) In section 59(2) of the Magistrates' Courts Act 1980 (periodical payments through justices' clerk) for the words "the Guardianship of Minors Acts 1971 and 1973" there shall be substituted "(or having effect as if made under) Schedule 1 to the Children Act 1989".

(2) For section 62(5) of that Act (payments to children) there shall be substituted—

"(5) In this section references to the person with whom a child has his home—

(a) in the case of any child who is being looked after by a local authority (within the meaning of section 22 of the Children Act 1989), are references to that local authority; and

(b) in any other case, are references to the person who, disregarding any absence of the child at a hospital or boarding school and any other temporary absence, has care of the child.".

The Supreme Court Act 1981 (c. 54)

45.—(1) In section 18 of the Supreme Court Act 1981 (restrictions on appeals to Court of Appeal)—

(a) in subsection (1)(h)(i), for the word "custody" there shall be substituted "residence"; and

(b) in subsection (1)(h)(ii) for the words "access to", in both places, there shall be substituted "contact with".

(2) In section 41 of that Act (wards of court), the following subsection shall be inserted after subsection (2)—

"(2A) Subsection (2) does not apply with respect to a child who is the subject of a care order (as defined by section 105 of the Children Act 1989)."

(3) In Schedule 1 to that Act (distribution of business in High Court), for paragraph 3(b)(ii) there shall be substituted—

" '(ii) the exercise of the inherent jurisdiction of the High Court with respect to minors, the maintenance of minors and any proceedings under the Children Act 1989, except proceedings solely for the appointment of a guardian of a minor's estate;".

The Armed Forces Act 1981 (c. 55)

46. In section 14 of the Armed Forces Act 1981 (temporary removal to, and detention in, place of safety abroad or in the United Kingdom of service children in need of care and control), in subsection (9A) for the words "the Children and Young Persons Act 1933, the Children and Young Persons Act 1969" there shall be substituted "the Children Act 1989".

The Civil Jurisdiction and Judgments Act 1982 (c. 27)

47. In paragraph 5(a) of Schedule 5 to the Civil Jurisdiction and Judgments Act 1982 (maintenance and similar payments excluded from Schedule 4 to that Act) for the words

"section 47 or 51 of the Child Care Act 1980" there shall be substituted "paragraph 23 of Schedule 2 to the Children Act 1989".

The Mental Health Act 1983 (c. 20)

48.—(1) For section 27 of the Mental Health Act 1983 (children and young persons in care of local authority) there shall be substituted the following section—

"Children and young persons in care

27. Where—
   (a) a patient who is a child or young person is in the care of a local authority by virtue of a care order within the meaning of the Children Act 1989; or
   (b) the rights and powers of a parent of a patient who is a child or young person are vested in a local authority by virtue of section 16 of the Social Work (Scotland) Act 1968,

the authority shall be deemed to be the nearest relative of the patient in preference to any person except the patient's husband or wife (if any)."

(2) Section 28 of that Act (nearest relative of minor under guardianship, etc.) is amended as mentioned in sub-paragraphs (3) and (4).

(3) For subsection (1) there shall be substituted—

"(1) Where—
   (a) a guardian has been appointed for a person who has not attained the age of eighteen years; or
   (b) a residence order (as defined by section 8 of the Children Act 1989) is in force with respect to such a person,

the guardian (or guardians, where there is more than one) or the person named in the residence order shall, to the exclusion of any other person, be deemed to be his nearest relative."

(4) For subsection (3) there shall be substituted—

"(3) In this section "guardian" does not include a guardian under this Part of this Act."

(5) In section 131(2) of that Act (informal admission of patients aged sixteen or over) for the words from "notwithstanding" to the end there shall be substituted "even though there are one or more persons who have parental responsibility for him (within the meaning of the Children Act 1989)".

The Registered Homes Act 1984 (c. 23)

49.—(1) In section 1(5) of the Registered Homes Act 1984 (requirement of registration) for paragraphs (d) and (e) there shall be substituted—

"(d) any community home, voluntary home or children's home within the meaning of the Children Act 1989."

(2) In section 39 of that Act (preliminary) for paragraphs (a) and (b) there shall be substituted—

"(a) the Children Act 1989."

The Mental Health (Scotland) Act 1984 (c. 36)

50. For section 54 of the Mental Health (Scotland) Act 1984 (children and young persons in care of local authority) there shall be substituted the following section—

"Children and young persons in care of local authority

54. Where—
   (a) the rights and powers of a parent of a patient who is a child or young person are vested in a local authority by virtue of section 16 of the Social Work (Scotland) Act 1968; or
   (b) a patient who is a child or young person is in the care of a local authority by virtue of a care order made under the Children Act 1989,

the authority shall be deemed to be the nearest relative of the patient in preference to any person except the patient's husband or wife (if any)."

The Matrimonial and Family Proceedings Act 1984 (c. 42)

51. In section 38(2)(b) of the Matrimonial and Family Proceedings Act 1984 (transfer of family proceedings from High Court to county court) after the words "a ward of court"

there shall be inserted "or any other proceedings which relate to the exercise of the inherent jurisdiction of the High Court with respect to minors".

The Police and Criminal Evidence Act 1984 (c. 60)

52. In section 37(14) of the Police and Criminal Evidence Act 1984 (duties of custody officer before charge) after the words "Children and Young Persons Act 1969" there shall be inserted "or in Part IV of the Children Act 1989".

53.—(1) In section 38 of that Act (duties of custody officer after charge), in subsection (6) for the words from "make arrangements" to the end there shall be substituted "secure that the arrested juvenile is moved to local authority accommodation".

(2) After that subsection there shall be inserted—

"(6A) In this section 'local authority accommodation' means accommodation provided by or on behalf of a local authority (within the meaning of the Children Act 1989).

(6B) Where an arrested juvenile is moved to local authority accommodation under subsection (6) above, it shall be lawful for any person acting on behalf of the authority to detain him.".

(3) In subsection (8) of that section for the words "Children and Young Persons Act 1969" there shall be substituted "Children Act 1989".

54. In section 39(4) of that Act (responsibilities in relation to persons detained) for the words "transferred to the care of a local authority in pursuance of arrangements made" there shall be substituted "moved to local authority accommodation".

55. In Schedule 2 to that Act (preserved powers of arrest) in the entry relating to the Children and Young Persons Act 1969 for the words "Sections 28(2) and" there shall be substituted "Section".

The Surrogacy Arrangements Act 1985 (c. 49)

56. In section 1(2)(b) of the Surrogacy Arrangements Act 1985 (meaning of "surrogate mother", etc.) for the words "the parental rights being exercised" there shall be substituted "parental responsibility being met".

The Child Abduction and Custody Act 1985 (c. 60)

57.—(1) In section 9(a) and 20(2)(a) of the Child Abduction and Custody Act 1985 (orders with respect to which court's powers suspended), for the words "any other order under section 1(2) of the Children and Young Persons Act 1969" there shall be substituted "a supervision order under section 31 of the Children Act 1989".

(2) At the end of section 27 of that Act (interpretation), there shall be added—

"(4) In this Act a decision relating to rights of access in England and Wales means a decision as to the contact which a child may, or may not, have with any person."

(3) In Part I of Schedule 3 to that Act (orders in England and Wales which are custody orders for the purposes of the Act), for paragraph 1 there shall be substituted—

"1. The following are the orders referred to in section 27(1) of this Act—

(a) a care order under the Children Act 1989 (as defined by section 31(11) of that Act, read with section 105(1) and Schedule 14);

(b) a residence order (as defined by section 8 of the Act of 1989); and

(c) any order made by a court in England and Wales under any of the following enactments—

(i) section 9(1), 10(1)(a) or 11(a) of the Guardianship of Minors Act 1971;

(ii) section 42(1) or (2) or 43(1) of the Matrimonial Causes Act 1973;

(iii) section 2(2)(b), 4(b) or (5) of the Guardianship Act 1973 as applied by section 34(5) of the Children Act 1975;

(iv) section 8(2)(a), 10(1) or 19(1)(ii) of the Domestic Proceedings and Magistrates Courts Act 1978;

(v) section 26(1)(b) of the Adoption Act 1976."

The Disabled Persons (Services, Consultation and Representation) Act 1986 (c. 33)

58. In section 1(3) of the Disabled Persons (Services, Consultation and Representation) Act 1986 (circumstances in which regulations may provide for the appointment of authorised representatives of disabled persons)—

(a) in paragraph (a), for the words "parent or guardian of a disabled person under the age of sixteen" there shall be substituted—

"(i) the parent of a disabled person under the age of sixteen, or

(ii) any other person who is not a parent of his but who has parental responsibility for him"; and

(b) in paragraph (b), for the words "in the care of" there shall be substituted "looked after by".

59.—(1) Section 2 of that Act (circumstances in which authorised representative has right to visit etc. disabled person) shall be amended as follows.

(2) In subsection (3)(a) for the words from second "the" to "by" there shall be substituted "for the words 'if so requested by the disabled person' there shall be substituted 'if so requested by any person mentioned in section 1 (3)(a)(i) or (ii)'. "

(3) In subsection (5) after paragraph (b) there shall be inserted—

"(bb) in accommodation provided by or on behalf of a local authority under Part III of the Children Act 1989, or".

(4) After paragraph (c) of subsection (5) there shall be inserted—

"(cc) in accommodation provided by a voluntary organisation in accordance with arrangements made by a local authority under section 17 of the Children Act 1989, or".

60. In section 5(7)(b) of that Act (disabled persons leaving special education) for the word "guardian" there shall be substituted "other person who is not a parent of his but who has parental responsibility for him".

61.—(1) In section 16 of that Act (interpretation) in the definition of "disabled person", in paragraph (a) for the words from "means" to "applies" there shall be substituted "means—

"(i) in the case of a person aged eighteen or over, a person to whom section 29 of the 1948 Act applies, and

(ii) in the case of a person under the age of eighteen, a person who is disabled within the meaning of Part III of the Children Act 1989".

(2) After the definition of "parent" in that section there shall be inserted—

" 'parental responsibility' has the same meaning as in the Children Act 1989".

(3) In the definition of "the welfare enactments" in that section, in paragraph (a) after the words "the 1977 Act" there shall be inserted "and Part III of the Children Act 1989".

(4) At the end of that section there shall be added—

"(2) In this Act any reference to a child who is looked after by a local authority has the same meaning as in the Children Act 1989."

The Family Law Act 1986 (c. 55)

62.—(1) The Family Law Act 1986 shall be amended as follows.

(2) Subject to paragraphs 63 to 71, in Part I—

(a) for the words "custody order", in each place where they occur, there shall be substituted "Part I order";

(b) for the words "proceedings with respect to the custody of", in each place where they occur, there shall be substituted "Part I proceedings with respect to"; and

(c) for the words "matters relating to the custody of", in each place where they occur, there shall be substituted "Part I matters relating to."

(3) For section 42(7) (general interpretation of Part I) there shall be substituted—

"(7) In this Part—

(a) references to Part I proceedings in respect of a child are references to any proceedings for a Part I order or an order corresponding to a Part I order and include, in relation to proceedings outside the United Kingdom, references to proceedings before a tribunal or other authority having power under the law having effect there to determine Part I matters; and

(b) references to Part I matters are references to matters that might be determined by a Part I order or an order corresponding to a Part I order."

63.—(1) In section 1 (orders to which Part I of the Act of 1986 applies), in subsection (1)—

(a) for paragraph (a) there shall be substituted—

"(a) a section 8 order made by a court in England and Wales under the Children Act 1989, other than an order varying or discharging such an order"; and

(b) for paragraph (d) there shall be substituted the following paragraphs—

"(d) an order made by a court in England and Wales in the exercise of the inherent jurisdiction of the High Court with respect to children—

     (i) so far as it gives care of a child to any person or provides for contact with, or the education of, a child; but

     (ii) excluding an order varying or revoking such an order;

(e) an order made by the High Court in Northern Ireland in the exercise of its jurisdiction relating to wardship—

     (i) so far as it gives care and control of a child to any person or provides for the education of or access to a child; but

     (ii) excluding an order relating to a child of whom care or care and control is (immediately after the making of the order) vested in the Department of Health and Social Services or a Health and Social Services Board."

(2) In subsection (2) of that section, in paragraph (c) for "(d)" there shall be substituted "(e)".

(3) For subsections (3) to (5) of that section there shall be substituted—

  "(3) In this Part, 'Part I order'—

(a) includes any order which would have been a custody order by virtue of this section in any form in which it was in force at any time before its amendment by the Children Act 1989; and

(b) (subject to sections 32 and 40 of this Act) excludes any order which would have been excluded from being a custody order by virtue of this section in any such form."

64. For section 2 there shall be substituted the following sections—

"Jurisdiction: general

    2.—(1) A court in England and Wales shall not have jurisdiction to make a section 1(1)(a) order with respect to a child in or in connection with matrimonial proceedings in England and Wales unless the condition in section 2A of this Act is satisfied.

    (2) A court in England and Wales shall not have jurisdiction to make a section 1(1)(a) order in a non-matrimonial case (that is to say, where the condition in section 2A of this Act is not satisfied) unless the condition in section 3 of this Act is satisfied.

    (3) A court in England and Wales shall not have jurisdiction to make a section 1(1)(d) order unless—

(a) the condition in section 3 of this Act is satisfied, or

(b) the child concerned is present in England and Wales on the relevant date and the court considers that the immediate exercise of its powers is necessary for his protection.

Jurisdiction in or in connection with matrimonial proceedings

    2A.—(1) The condition referred to in section 2(1) of this Act is that the matrimonial proceedings are proceedings in respect of the marriage of the parents of the child concerned and—

(a) the proceedings—

     (i) are proceedings for divorce or nullity of marriage, and

     (ii) are continuing;

(b) the proceedings—

     (i) are proceedings for judicial separation,

     (ii) are continuing,

    and the jurisdiction of the court is not excluded by subsection (2) below; or

(c) the proceedings have been dismissed after the beginning of the trial but—

     (i) the section 1(1)(a) order is being made forthwith, or

     (ii) the application for the order was made on or before the dismissal.

    (2) For the purposes of subsection (1)(b) above, the jurisdiction of the court is excluded if, after the grant of a decree of judicial separation, on the relevant date, proceedings for divorce or nullity in respect of the marriage are continuing in Scotland or Northern Ireland.

    (3) Subsection (2) above shall not apply if the court in which the other proceedings there referred to are continuing has made—

(a) an order under section 13(6) or 21(5) of this Act (not being an order made by virtue of section 13(6)(a)(i)), or

(b) an order under section 14(2) or 22(2) of this Act which is recorded as being made for the purpose of enabling Part I proceedings to be taken in England and Wales with respect to the child concerned.

    (4) Where a court—

(a) has jurisdiction to make a section 1(1)(a) order in or in connection with matrimonial proceedings, but

(b) considers that it would be more appropriate for Part I matters relating to the child to be determined outside England and Wales,

the court may by order direct that, while the order under this subsection is in force, no section 1(1)(a) order shall be made by any court in or in connection with those proceedings."

65.—(1) In section 3 (habitual residence or presence of child concerned) in subsection (1) for "section 2" there shall be substituted "section 2(2)".

(2) In subsection (2) of that section for the words "proceedings for divorce, nullity or judicial separation" there shall be substituted "matrimonial proceedings".

66.—(1) In section 6 (duration and variation of Part I orders), for subsection (3) there shall be substituted the following subsections—

"(3) A court in England and Wales shall not have jurisdiction to vary a Part I order if, on the relevant date, matrimonial proceedings are continuing in Scotland or Northern Ireland in respect of the marriage of the parents of the child concerned.

(3A) Subsection (3) above shall not apply if—

(a) the Part I order was made in or in connection with proceedings for divorce or nullity in England and Wales in respect of the marriage of the parents of the child concerned; and

(b) those proceedings are continuing.

(3B) Subsection (3) above shall not apply if—

(a) the Part I order was made in or in connection with proceedings for judicial separation in England and Wales;

(b) those proceedings are continuing; and

(c) the decree of judicial separation has not yet been granted."

(2) In subsection (5) of that section for the words from "variation of" to "if the ward" there shall be substituted "variation of a section 1(1)(d) order if the child concerned."

(3) For subsections (6) and (7) of that section there shall be substituted the following subsections—

"(6) Subsection (7) below applies where a Part I order which is—

(a) a residence order (within the meaning of the Children Act 1989) in favour of a person with respect to a child,

(b) an order made in the exercise of the High Court's inherent jurisdiction with respect to children by virtue of which a person has care of a child, or

(c) an order—

(i) of a kind mentioned in section 1(3)(a) of this Act,

(ii) under which a person is entitled to the actual possession of a child,

ceases to have effect in relation to that person by virtue of subsection (1) above.

(7) Where this subsection applies, any family assistance order made under section 16 of the Children Act 1989 with respect to the child shall also cease to have effect.

(8) For the purposes of subsection (7) above the reference to a family assistance order under section 16 of the Children Act 1989 shall be deemed to include a reference to an order for the supervision of a child made under—

(a) section 7(4) of the Family Law Reform Act 1969,

(b) section 44 of the Matrimonial Causes Act 1973,

(c) section 2(2)(a) of the Guardianship Act 1973,

(d) section 34(5) or 36(3)(b) of the Children Act 1975, or

(e) section 9 of the Domestic Proceedings and Magistrates' Courts Act 1978;

but this subsection shall cease to have effect once all such orders for the supervision of children have ceased to have effect in accordance with Schedule 14 to the Children Act 1989."

67. For section 7 (interpretation of Chapter II) there shall be substituted—

"Interpretation of Chapter II

7. In this Chapter—

(a) 'child' means a person who has not attained the age of eighteen;

(b) 'matrimonial proceedings' means proceedings for divorce, nullity of marriage or judicial separation;

(c) 'the relevant date' means, in relation to the making or variation of an order—

(i) where an application is made for an order to be made or varied, the date of the application (or first application, if two or more are determined together), and

(ii) where no such application is made, the date on which the court is considering whether to make or, as the case may be, vary the order; and

(d) 'section 1(1)(a) order' and 'section 1(1)(d) order' mean orders falling within section 1 (1)(a) and (d) of this Act respectively."

68. In each of the following sections—

(a) section 11(2)(a) (provisions supplementary to sections 9 and 10),

(b) section 13(5)(a) (jurisdiction ancillary to matrimonial proceedings),

(c) section 20(3)(a) (habitual residence or presence of child),

(d) section 21(4)(a) (jurisdiction in divorce proceedings, etc.), and

(e) section 23(4)(a) (duration and variation of custody orders),

for "4(5)" there shall be substituted "2A(4)".

69. In each of the following sections—

(a) section 19(2) (jurisdiction in cases other than divorce, etc.),

(b) section 20(6) (habitual residence or presence of child), and

(c) section 23(5) (duration and variation of custody orders),

for "section 1(1)(d)" there shall be substituted "section 1(1)(e)".

70. In section 34(3) (power to order recovery of child) for paragraph (a) there shall be substituted—

"(a) section 14 of the Children Act 1989".

71.—(1) In section 42 (general interpretation of Part I), in subsection (4)(a) for the words "has been boarded out with those parties" there shall be substituted "is placed with those parties as foster parents".

(2) In subsection (6) of that section, in paragraph (a) after the word "person" there shall be inserted "to be allowed contact with or".

The Local Government Act 1988 (c. 9)

72. In Schedule 1 to the Local Government Act 1988 (competition) at the end of paragraph 2(4) (cleaning of buildings: buildings to which competition provisions do not apply) for paragraph (c) there shall be substituted—

"(c) section 53 of the Children Act 1989".

Amendments of local Acts

73.—(1) Section 16 of the Greater London Council (General Powers) Act 1981 (exemption from provisions of Part IV of the Act of certain premises) shall be amended as follows.

(2) After paragraph (g) there shall be inserted—

"(gg) used as a children's home as defined in section 63 of the Children Act 1989".

(3) In paragraph (h)—

(a) for the words "section 56 of the Child Care Act 1980" there shall be substituted "section 60 of the Children Act 1989";

(b) for the words "section 57" there shall be substituted "section 60"; and

(c) for the words "section 32" there shall be substituted "section 53".

(4) In paragraph (i), for the words "section 8 of the Foster Children Act 1980" there shall be substituted "section 67 of the Children Act 1989".

74.—(1) Section 10(2) of the Greater London Council (General Powers) Act 1984 (exemption from provisions of Part IV of the Act of certain premises) shall be amended as follows.

(2) In paragraph (d)—

(a) for the words "section 56 of the Child Care Act 1980" there shall be substituted "section 60 of the Children Act 1989";

(b) for the words "section 57" there shall be substituted "section 60"; and

(c) for the words "section 31" there shall be substituted "section 53".

(3) In paragraph (e), for the words "section 8 of the Foster Children Act 1980" there shall be substituted "section 67 of the Children Act 1989".

(4) In paragraph (1) for the words "section 1 of the Children's Homes Act 1982" there shall be substituted "section 63 of the Children Act 1989".

Section 108(6)   SCHEDULE 14

TRANSITIONALS AND SAVINGS

Pending proceedings, etc.

1.—(1) Subject to sub-paragraph (4), nothing in any provision of this Act (other than the repeals mentioned in sub-paragraph (2)) shall affect any proceedings which are pending immediately before the commencement of that provision.

(2) The repeals are those of—

(a) section 42(3) of the Matrimonial Causes Act 1973 (declaration by court that party to marriage unfit to have custody of children of family); and

(b) section 38 of the Sexual Offences Act 1956 (power of court to divest person of authority over girl or boy in cases of incest).

(3) For the purposes of the following provisions of this Schedule, any reference to an order in force immediately before the commencement of a provision of this Act shall be construed as including a reference to an order made after that commencement in proceedings pending before that commencement.

(4) Sub-paragraph (3) is not to be read as making the order in question have effect from a date earlier than that on which it was made.

(5) An order under section 96(3) may make such provision with respect to the application of the order in relation to proceedings which are pending when the order comes into force as the Lord Chancellor considers appropriate.

2. Where, immediately before the day on which Part IV comes into force, there was in force an order under section 3(1) of the Children and Young Persons Act 1963 (order directing a local authority to bring a child or young person before a juvenile court under section 1 of the Children and Young Persons Act 1969), the order shall cease to have effect on that day.

CUSTODY ORDERS, ETC.

Cessation of declarations of unfitness, etc.

3. Where, immediately before the day on which Parts I and II come into force, there was in force—

(a) a declaration under section 42(3) of the Matrimonial Causes Act 1973 (declaration by court that party to marriage unfit to have custody of children of family); or

(b) an order under section 38(1) of the Sexual Offences Act 1956 divesting a person of authority over a girl or boy in a case of incest;

the declaration or, as the case may be, the order shall cease to have effect on that day.

The Family Law Reform Act 1987 (c. 42)

Conversion of orders under section 4

4. Where, immediately before the day on which Parts I and II come into force, there was in force an order under section 4(1) of the Family Law Reform Act 1987 (order giving father parental rights and duties in relation to a child), then, on and after that day, the order shall be deemed to be an order under section 4 of this Act giving the father parental responsibility for the child.

Orders to which paragraphs 6 to 11 apply

5.—(1) In paragraphs 6 to 11 "an existing order" means any order which—

(a) is in force immediately before the commencement of Parts I and II;

(b) was made under any enactment mentioned in sub-paragraph (2);

(c) determines all or any of the following—

  (i) who is to have custody of a child;

  (ii) who is to have care and control of a child;

  (iii) who is to have access to a child;

  (iv) any matter with respect to a child's education or upbringing; and

(d) is not an order of a kind mentioned in paragraph 15(1).

(2) The enactments are—

(a) the Domestic Proceedings and Magistrates' Courts Act 1978;
(b) the Children Act 1975;
(c) the Matrimonial Causes Act 1973;
(d) the Guardianship of Minors Acts 1971 and 1973;
(e) the Matrimonial Causes Act 1965;
(f) the Matrimonial Proceedings (Magistrates' Courts) Act 1960.

(3) For the purposes of this paragraph and paragraphs 6 to 11 "custody" includes legal custody and joint as well as sole custody but does not include access.

Parental responsibility of parents

6.—(1) Where—
(a) a child's father and mother were married to each other at the time of his birth; and
(b) there is an existing order with respect to the child,
each parent shall have parental responsibility for the child in accordance with section 2 as modified by sub-paragraph (3).

(2) Where—
(a) a child's father and mother were not married to each other at the time of his birth; and
(b) there is an existing order with respect to the child,
section 2 shall apply as modified by sub-paragraphs (3) and (4).

(3) The modification is that for section 2(8) there shall be substituted—
"(8) The fact that a person has parental responsibility for a child does not entitle him to act in a way which would be incompatible with any existing order or any order made under this Act with respect to the child".

(4) The modifications are that—
(a) for the purposes of section 2(2), where the father has custody or care and control of the child by virtue of any existing order, the court shall be deemed to have made (at the commencement of that section) an order under section 4(1) giving him parental responsibility for the child; and
(b) where by virtue of paragraph (a) a court is deemed to have made an order under section 4(1) in favour of a father who has care and control of a child by virtue of an existing order, the court shall not bring the order under section 4(1) to an end at any time while he has care and control of the child by virtue of the order.

Persons who are not parents but who have custody or care and control

7.—(1) Where a person who is not the parent or guardian of a child has custody or care and control of him by virtue of an existing order, that person shall have parental responsibility for him so long as he continues to have that custody or care and control by virtue of the order.

(2) Where sub-paragraph (1) applies, Parts I and II shall have effect as modified by this paragraph.

(3) The modifications are that—
(a) for section 2(8) there shall be substituted—
"(8) The fact that a person has parental responsibility for a child does not entitle him to act in a way which would be incompatible with any existing order or with any order made under this Act with respect to the child";
(b) at the end of section 10(4) there shall be inserted—
"(c) any person who has custody or care and control of a child by virtue of any existing order"; and
(c) at the end of section 34(1)(c) there shall be inserted—
"(cc) where immediately before the care order was made there was an existing order by virtue of which a person had custody or care and control of the child, that person."

Persons who have care and control

8.—(1) Sub-paragraphs (2) to (6) apply where a person has care and control of a child by virtue of an existing order, but they shall cease to apply when that order ceases to have effect.

(2) Section 5 shall have effect as if—
(a) for any reference to a residence order in favour of a parent or guardian there were

substituted a reference to any existing order by virtue of which the parent or guardian has care and control of the child; and

(b) for subsection (9) there were substituted—

"(9) Subsections (1) and (7) do not apply if the existing order referred to in paragraph (b) of those subsections was one by virtue of which a surviving parent of the child also had care and control of him."

(3) Section 10 shall have effect as if for subsection (5)(c)(i) there were substituted—

"(i) in any case where by virtue of an existing order any person or persons has or have care and control of the child, has the consent of that person or each of those persons".

(4) Section 20 shall have effect as if for subsection (9)(a) there were substituted "who has care and control of the child by virtue of an existing order."

(5) Section 23 shall have effect as if for subsection (4)(c) there were substituted—

"(c) where the child is in care and immediately before the care order was made there was an existing order by virtue of which a person had care and control of the child, that person."

(6) In Schedule 1, paragraphs 1(1) and 14(1) shall have effect as if for the words "in whose favour a residence order is in force with respect to the child" there were substituted "who has been given care and control of the child by virtue of an existing order".

Persons who have access

9.—(1) Sub-paragraphs (2) to (4) apply where a person has access by virtue of an existing order.

(2) Section 10 shall have effect as if after subsection (5) there were inserted—

"(5A) Any person who has access to a child by virtue of an existing order is entitled to apply for a contact order."

(3) Section 16(2) shall have effect as if after paragraph (b) there were inserted—

"(bb) any person who has access to the child by virtue of an existing order."

(4) Sections 43(11), 44(13) and 46(10), shall have effect as if in each case after paragraph (d) there were inserted—

"(dd) any person who has been given access to him by virtue of an existing order."

Enforcement of certain existing orders

10.—(1) Sub-paragraph (2) applies in relation to any existing order which, but for the repeal by this Act of—

(a) section 13(1) of the Guardianship of Minors Act 1971;

(b) section 43(1) of the Children Act 1975; or

(c) section 33 of the Domestic Proceedings and Magistrates' Courts Act 1978,

(provisions concerning the enforcement of custody orders) might have been enforced as if it were an order requiring a person to give up a child to another person.

(2) Where this sub-paragraph applies, the existing order may, after the repeal of the enactments mentioned in sub-paragraph (1)(a) to (c), be enforced under section 14 as if—

(a) any reference to a residence order were a reference to the existing order; and

(b) any reference to a person in whose favour the residence order is in force were a reference to a person to whom actual custody of the child is given by an existing order which is in force.

(3) In sub-paragraph (2) "actual custody", in relation to a child, means the actual possession of his person.

Discharge of existing orders

11.—(1) The making of a residence order or a care order with respect to a child who is the subject of an existing order discharges the existing order.

(2) Where the court makes any section 8 order (other than a residence order) with respect to a child with respect to whom any existing order is in force, the existing order shall have effect subject to the section 8 order.

(3) The court may discharge an existing order which is in force with respect to a child—

(a) in any family proceedings relating to the child or in which any question arises with respect to the child's welfare; or

(b) on the application of—

(i) any parent or guardian of the child;

(ii) the child himself; or

(iii) any person named in the order.

(4) A child may not apply for the discharge of an existing order except with the leave of the court.

(5) The power in sub-paragraph (3) to discharge an existing order includes the power to discharge any part of the order.

(6) In considering whether to discharge an order under the power conferred by sub-paragraph (3) the court shall, if the discharge of the order is opposed by any party to the proceedings, have regard in particular to the matters mentioned in section 1(3).

GUARDIANS

Existing guardians to be guardians under this Act

12.—(1) Any appointment of a person as guardian of a child which—

(a) was made—

(i) under sections 3 to 5 of the Guardianship of Minors Act 1971;

(ii) under section 38(3) of the Sexual Offences Act 1956; or

(iii) under the High Court's inherent jurisdiction with respect to children; and

(b) has taken effect before the commencement of section 5,

shall (subject to sub-paragraph (2)) be deemed, on and after the commencement of section 5, to be an appointment made and having effect under that section.

(2) Where an appointment of a person as guardian of a child has effect under section 5 by virtue of sub-paragraph (1)(a)(ii), the appointment shall not have effect for a period which is longer than any period specified in the order.

Appointment of guardian not yet in effect

13. Any appointment of a person to be a guardian of a child—

(a) which was made as mentioned in paragraph 12(1)(a)(i); but

(b) which, immediately before the commencement of section 5, had not taken effect,

shall take effect in accordance with section 5 (as modified, where it applies, by paragraph 8(2)).

Persons deemed to be appointed as guardians under existing wills

14. For the purposes of the Wills Act 1837 and of this Act any disposition by will and testament or devise of the custody and tuition of any child, made before the commencement of section 5 and paragraph 1 of Schedule 13, shall be deemed to be an appointment by will of a guardian of the child.

CHILDREN IN CARE

Children in compulsory care

15.—(1) Sub-paragraph (2) applies where, immediately before the day on which Part IV comes into force, a person was—

(a) in care by virtue of—

(i) a care order under section 1 of the Children and Young Persons Act 1969;

(ii) a care order under section 15 of that Act, on discharging a supervision order made under section 1 of that Act; or

(iii) an order or authorisation under section 25 or 26 of that Act;

(b) deemed, by virtue of—

(i) paragraph 7(3) of Schedule 5A to the Army Act 1955;

(ii) paragraph 7(3) of Schedule 5A to the Air Force Act 1955; or

(iii) paragraph 7(3) of Schedule 4A to the Naval Discipline Act 1957,

to be the subject of a care order under the Children and Young Persons Act 1969;

(c) in care—

(i) under section 2 of the Child Care Act 1980; or

(ii) by virtue of paragraph 1 of Schedule 4 to that Act (which extends the meaning of a child in care under section 2 to include children in care under section 1 of the Children Act 1948),

and a child in respect of whom a resolution under section 3 of the Act of 1980 or section 2 of the Act of 1948 was in force;

(d) a child in respect of whom a resolution had been passed under section 65 of the Child Care Act 1980;

(e) in care by virtue of an order under—

      (i) section 2(1)(e) of the Matrimonial Proceedings (Magistrates' Courts) Act 1960;

      (ii) section 7(2) of the Family Law Reform Act 1969;

      (iii) section 43(1) of the Matrimonial Causes Act 1973; or

      (iv) section 2(2)(b) of the Guardianship Act 1973;

      (v) section 10 of the Domestic Proceedings and Magistrates' Courts Act 1978,

(orders having effect for certain purposes as if the child had been received into care under section 2 of the Child Care Act 1980);

(f) in care by virtue of an order made, on the revocation of a custodianship order, under section 36 of the Children Act 1975; or

(g) in care by virtue of an order made, on the refusal of an adoption order, under section 26 of the Adoption Act 1976 or any order having effect (by virtue of paragraph 1 of Schedule 2 to that Act) as if made under that section.

(2) Where this sub-paragraph applies, then, on and after the day on which Part IV commences—

(a) the order or resolution in question shall be deemed to be a care order;

(b) the authority in whose care the person was immediately before that commencement shall be deemed to be the authority designated in that deemed care order; and

(c) any reference to a child in the care of a local authority shall include a reference to a person who is the subject of such a deemed care order,

and the provisions of this Act shall apply accordingly, subject to paragraph 16.

Modifications

16.—(1) Sub-paragraph (2) only applies where a person who is the subject of a care order by virtue of paragraph 15(2) is a person falling within sub-paragraph (1)(a) or (b) of that paragraph.

(2) Where the person would otherwise have remained in care until reaching the age of nineteen, by virtue of—

(a) section 20(3)(a) or 21(1) of the Children and Young Persons Act 1969; or

(b) paragraph 7(5)(c)(i) of—

      (i) Schedule 5A to the Army Act 1955;

      (ii) Schedule 5A to the Air Force Act 1955; or

      (iii) Schedule 4A to the Naval Discipline Act 1957,

this Act applies as if in section 91(12) for the word "eighteen" there were substituted "nineteen."

(3) Where a person who is the subject of a care order by virtue of paragraph 15(2) is a person falling within sub-paragraph (1)(b) of that paragraph, this Act applies as if section 101 were omitted.

(4) Sub-paragraph (5) only applies where a child who is the subject of a care order by virtue of paragraph 15(2) is a person falling within sub-paragraph (1)(e) to (g) of that paragraph.

(5) Where a court, on making the order, or at any time thereafter, gave directions under—

(a) section 4(4)(a) of the Guardianship Act 1973; or

(b) section 43(5)(a) of the Matrimonial Causes Act 1973,

as to the exercise by the authority of any powers, those directions shall continue to have effect (regardless of any conflicting provision in this Act) until varied or discharged by a court under this sub-paragraph.

Children placed with parent etc. while in compulsory care

17.—(1) This paragraph applies where a child is deemed by paragraph 15 to be in the care of a local authority under an order or resolution which is deemed by that paragraph to be a care order.

(2) If, immediately before the day on which Part III comes into force, the child was allowed to be under the charge and control of—

(a) a parent or guardian under section 21(2) of the Child Care Act 1980; or

(b) a person who, before the child was in the authority's care, had care and control of the child by virtue of an order falling within paragraph 5, on and after that day the provision made by and under section 23(5) shall apply as if the child had been placed with the person in question in accordance with that provision.

Orders for access to children in compulsory care

18.—(1) This paragraph applies to any access order—

(a) made under section 12C of the Child Care Act 1980 (access orders with respect to children in care of local authorities); and

(b) in force immediately before the commencement of Part IV.

(2) On and after the commencement of Part IV, the access order shall have effect as an order made under section 34 in favour of the person named in the order.

19.—(1) This paragraph applies where, immediately before the commencement of Part IV, an access order made under section 12C of the Act of 1980 was suspended by virtue of an order made under section 12E of that Act (suspension of access orders in emergencies).

(2) The suspending order shall continue to have effect as if this Act had not been passed.

(3) If—

(a) before the commencement of Part IV; and

(b) during the period for which the operation of the access order is suspended, the local authority concerned made an application for its variation or discharge to an appropriate juvenile court, its operation shall be suspended until the date on which the application to vary or discharge it is determined or abandoned.

Children in voluntary care

20.—(1) This paragraph applies where, immediately before the day on which Part III comes into force—

(a) a child was in the care of a local authority—

(i) under section 2(1) of the Child Care Act 1980; or

(ii) by virtue of paragraph 1 of Schedule 4 to that Act (which extends the meaning of references to children in care under section 2 to include references to children in care under section 1 of the Children Act 1948); and

(b) he was not a person in respect of whom a resolution under section 3 of the Act of 1980 or section 2 of the Act of 1948 was in force.

(2) Where this paragraph applies, the child shall, on and after the day mentioned in sub-paragraph (1), be treated for the purposes of this Act as a child who is provided with accommodation by the local authority under Part III, but he shall cease to be so treated once he ceases to be so accommodated in accordance with the provisions of Part III.

(3) Where—

(a) this paragraph applies; and

(b) the child, immediately before the day mentioned in sub-paragraph (1), was (by virtue of section 21(2) of the Act of 1980) under the charge and control of a person falling within paragraph 17(2)(a) or (b),

the child shall not be treated for the purposes of this Act as if he were being looked after by the authority concerned.

Boarded out children

21.—(1) Where, immediately before the day on which Part III comes into force, a child in the care of a local authority—

(a) was—

(i) boarded out with a person under section 21(1)(a) of the Child Care Act 1980; or

(ii) placed under the charge and control of a person, under section 21(2) of that Act; and

(b) the person with whom he was boarded out, or (as the case may be) placed, was not a person falling within paragraph 17(2)(a) or (b),

on and after that day, he shall be treated (subject to sub-paragraph (2)) as having been placed with a local authority foster parent and shall cease to be so treated when he ceases to be placed with that person in accordance with the provisions of this Act.

(2) Regulations made under section 23(2)(a) shall not apply in relation to a person who is a local authority foster parent by virtue of sub-paragraph (1) before the end of the period of twelve months beginning with the day on which Part III comes into force and accordingly that person shall for that period be subject—

(a) in a case falling within sub-paragraph (1)(a)(i), to terms and regulations mentioned in section 21(1)(a) of the Act of 1980; and

(b) in a case falling within sub-paragraph (1)(a)(ii), to terms fixed under section 21(2) of that Act and regulations made under section 22A of that Act,

as if that Act had not been repealed by this Act.

Children in care to qualify for advice and assistance

22. Any reference in Part III to a person qualifying for advice and assistance shall be construed as including a reference to a person within the area of the local authority in question who is under twenty-one and who was, at any time after reaching the age of sixteen but while still a child—

(a) a person falling within—
    (i) any of paragraphs (a) to (g) of paragraph 15(1); or
    (ii) paragraph 20(1); or

(b) the subject of a criminal care order (within the meaning of paragraph 34).

Emigration of children in care

23. Where—

(a) the Secretary of State has received a request in writing from a local authority that he give his consent under section 24 of the Child Care Act 1980 to the emigration of a child in their care; but

(b) immediately before the repeal of the Act of 1980 by this Act, he has not determined whether or not to give his consent,

section 24 of the Act of 1980 shall continue to apply (regardless of that repeal) until the Secretary of State has determined whether or not to give his consent to the request.

Contributions for maintenance of children in care

24.—(1) Where, immediately before the day on which Part III of Schedule 2 comes into force, there was in force an order made (or having effect as if made) under any of the enactments mentioned in sub-paragraph (2), then, on and after that day—

(a) the order shall have effect as if made under paragraph 23(2) of Schedule 2 against a person liable to contribute; and

(b) Part III of Schedule 2 shall apply to the order, subject to the modifications in sub-paragraph (3).

(2) The enactments are—

(a) section 11(4) of the Domestic Proceedings and Magistrates' Courts Act 1978;

(b) section 26(2) of the Adoption Act 1976;

(c) section 36(5) of the Children Act 1975;

(d) section 2(3) of the Guardianship Act 1973;

(e) section 2(1)(h) of the Matrimonial Proceedings (Magistrates' Courts) Act 1960,

(provisions empowering the court to make an order requiring a person to make periodical payments to a local authority in respect of a child in care).

(3) The modifications are that, in paragraph 23 of Schedule 2—

(a) in sub-paragraph (4), paragraph (a) shall be omitted;

(b) for sub-paragraph (6) there shall be substituted—

"(6) Where—
    (a) a contribution order is in force;
    (b) the authority serve a contribution notice under paragraph 22; and
    (c) the contributor and the authority reach an agreement under paragraph 22(7) in respect of the contribution notice,

the effect of the agreement shall be to discharge the order from the date on which it is agreed that the agreement shall take effect"; and

(c) at the end of sub-paragraph (10) there shall be inserted—

"and
    (c) where the order is against a person who is not a parent of the child, shall be made with due regard to—
        (i) whether that person had assumed responsibility for the maintenance of the child, and, if so, the extent to which and basis on which he assumed that responsibility and the length of the period during which he met that responsibility;
        (ii) whether he did so knowing that the child was not his child;
        (iii) the liability of any other person to maintain the child."

SUPERVISION ORDERS

Orders under section 1(3)(b) or 21 (2) of the 1969 Act

25.—(1) This paragraph applies to any supervision order—
(a) made—
> (i) under section 1(3)(b) of the Children and Young Persons Act 1969; or
> (ii) under section 21(2) of that Act on the discharge of a care order made under section 1(3)(c) of that Act; and

(b) in force immediately before the commencement of Part IV.
(2) On and after the commencement of Part IV, the order shall be deemed to be a supervision order made under section 31 and—
(a) any requirement of the order that the child reside with a named individual shall continue to have effect while the order remains in force, unless the court otherwise directs;
(b) any other requirement imposed by the court, or directions given by the supervisor, shall be deemed to have been imposed or given under the appropriate provisions of Schedule 3.
(3) Where, immediately before the commencement of Part IV, the order had been in force for a period of more than six months, it shall cease to have effect at the end of the period of six months beginning with the day on which Part IV comes into force unless—
(a) the court directs that it shall cease to have effect at the end of a different period (which shall not exceed three years);
(b) it ceases to have effect earlier in accordance with section 91; or
(c) it would have ceased to have had effect earlier had this Act not been passed.
(4) Where sub-paragraph (3) applies, paragraph 6 of Schedule 3 shall not apply.
(5) Where, immediately before the commencement of Part IV, the order had been in force for less than six months it shall cease to have effect in accordance with section 91 and paragraph 6 of Schedule 3 unless—
(a) the court directs that it shall cease to have effect at the end of a different period (which shall not exceed three years); or
(b) it would have ceased to have had effect earlier had this Act not been passed.

Other supervision orders

26.—(1) This paragraph applies to any order for the supervision of a child which was in force immediately before the commencement of Part IV and was made under—
(a) section 2(1)(f) of the Matrimonial Proceedings (Magistrates Courts) Act 1960;
(b) section 7(4) of the Family Law Reform Act 1969;
(c) section 44 of the Matrimonial Causes Act 1973;
(d) section 2(2)(a) of the Guardianship Act 1973;
(e) section 34(5) or 36(3)(b) of the Children Act 1975;
(f) section 26(1)(a) of the Adoption Act 1976; or
(g) section 9 of the Domestic Proceedings and Magistrates Courts Act 1978.
(2) The order shall not be deemed to be a supervision order made under any provision of this Act but shall nevertheless continue in force for a period of one year beginning with the day on which Part IV comes into force unless—
(a) the court directs that it shall cease to have effect at the end of a lesser period; or
(b) it would have ceased to have had effect earlier had this Act not been passed.

PLACE OF SAFETY ORDERS

27.—(1) This paragraph applies to—
(a) any order or warrant authorising the removal of a child to a place of safety which—
> (i) was made, or issued, under any of the enactments mentioned in sub-paragraph (2); and
> (ii) was in force immediately before the commencement of Part IV; and

(b) any interim order made under section 23(5) of the Children and Young Persons Act 1963 or section 28(6) of the Children and Young Persons Act 1969.
(2) The enactments are—
(a) section 40 of the Children and Young Persons Act 1933 (warrant to search for or remove child);

(b) section 28(1) of the Children and Young Persons Act 1969 (detention of child in place of safety);

(c) section 34(1) of the Adoption Act 1976 (removal of protected children from unsuitable surroundings);

(d) section 12(1) of the Foster Children Act 1980 (removal of foster children kept in unsuitable surroundings).

(3) The order or warrant shall continue to have effect as if this Act had not been passed.

(4) Any enactment repealed by this Act shall continue to have effect in relation to the order or warrant so far as is necessary for the purposes of securing that the effect of the order is what it would have been had this Act not been passed.

(5) Sub-paragraph (4) does not apply to the power to make an interim order or further interim order given by section 23(5) of the Children and Young Persons Act 1963 or section 28(6) of the Children and Young Persons Act 1969.

(6) Where, immediately before section 28 of the Children and Young Persons Act 1969 is repealed by this Act, a child is being detained under the powers granted by that section, he may continue to be detained in accordance with that section but subsection (6) shall not apply.

RECOVERY OF CHILDREN

28. The repeal by this Act of subsection (1) of section 16 of the Child Care Act 1980 (arrest of child absent from compulsory care) shall not affect the operation of that section in relation to any child arrested before the coming into force of the repeal.

29.—(1) This paragraph applies where—

(a) a summons has been issued under section 15 or 16 of the Child Care Act 1980 (recovery of children in voluntary or compulsory care); and

(b) the child concerned is not produced in accordance with the summons before the repeal of that section by this Act comes into force.

(2) The summons, any warrant issued in connection with it and section 15 or (as the case may be) section 16, shall continue to have effect as if this Act had not been passed.

30. The amendment by paragraph 27 of Schedule 12 of section 32 of the Children and Young Persons Act 1969 (detention of absentees) shall not affect the operation of that section in relation to—

(a) any child arrested; or

(b) any summons or warrant issued,

under that section before the coming into force of that paragraph.

VOLUNTARY ORGANISATIONS: PARENTAL RIGHTS RESOLUTIONS

31.—(1) This paragraph applies to a resolution—

(a) made under section 64 of the Child Care Act 1980 (transfer of parental rights and duties to voluntary organisations); and

(b) in force immediately before the commencement of Part IV.

(2) The resolution shall continue to have effect until the end of the period of six months beginning with the day on which Part IV comes into force unless it is brought to an end earlier in accordance with the provisions of the Act of 1980 preserved by this paragraph.

(3) While the resolution remains in force, any relevant provisions of, or made under, the Act of 1980 shall continue to have effect with respect to it.

(4) Sub-paragraph (3) does not apply to—

(a) section 62 of the Act of 1980 and any regulations made under that section (arrangements by voluntary organisations for emigration of children); or

(b) section 65 of the Act of 1980 (duty of local authority to assume parental rights and duties).

(5) Section 5(2) of the Act of 1980 (which is applied to resolutions under Part VI of that Act by section 64(7) of that Act) shall have effect with respect to the resolution as if the reference in paragraph (c) to an appointment of a guardian under section 5 of the Guardianship of Minors Act 1971 were a reference to an appointment of a guardian under section 5 of this Act.

FOSTER CHILDREN

32.—(1) This paragraph applies where—

(a) immediately before the commencement of Part VIII, a child was a foster child within the meaning of the Foster Children Act 1980; and

(b) the circumstances of the case are such that, had Parts VIII and IX then been in force, he would have been treated for the purposes of this Act as a child who was being provided with accommodation in a children's home and not as a child who was being privately fostered.

(2) If the child continues to be cared for and provided with accommodation as before, section 63(1) and (10) shall not apply in relation to him if—

(a) an application for registration of the home in question is made under section 63 before the end of the period of three months beginning with the day on which Part VIII comes into force; and

(b) the application has not been refused or, if it has been refused—

(i) the period for an appeal against the decision has not expired; or

(ii) an appeal against the refusal has been made but has not been determined or abandoned.

(3) While section 63(1) and (10) does not apply, the child shall be treated as a privately fostered child for the purposes of Part IX.

NURSERIES AND CHILD MINDING

33.—(1) Sub-paragraph (2) applies where, immediately before the commencement of Part X, any premises are registered under section 1(1)(a) of the Nurseries and Child-Minders Regulation Act 1948 (registration of premises, other than premises wholly or mainly used as private dwellings, where children are received to be looked after).

(2) During the transitional period, the provisions of the Act of 1948 shall continue to have effect with respect to those premises to the exclusion of Part X.

(3) Nothing in sub-paragraph (2) shall prevent the local authority concerned from registering any person under section 71(1)(b) with respect to the premises.

(4) In this paragraph "the transitional period" means the period ending with—

(a) the first anniversary of the commencement of Part X; or

(b) if earlier, the date on which the local authority concerned registers any person under section 71(1)(b) with respect to the premises.

34.—(1) Sub-paragraph (2) applies where, immediately before the commencement of Part X—

(a) a person is registered under section 1(1)(b) of the Act of 1948 (registration of persons who for reward receive into their homes children under the age of five to be looked after); and

(b) all the children looked after by him as mentioned in section 1(1)(b) of that Act are under the age of five.

(2) During the transitional period, the provisions of the Act of 1948 shall continue to have effect with respect to that person to the exclusion of Part X.

(3) Nothing in sub-paragraph (2) shall prevent the local authority concerned from registering that person under section 71(1)(a).

(4) In this paragraph "the transitional period" means the period ending with—

(a) the first anniversary of the commencement of Part X; or

(b) if earlier, the date on which the local authority concerned registers that person under section 71(1)(a).

CHILDREN ACCOMMODATED IN CERTAIN ESTABLISHMENTS

35. In calculating, for the purposes of section 85(1)(a) or 86(1)(a), the period of time for which a child has been accommodated any part of that period which fell before the day on which that section came into force shall be disregarded.

CRIMINAL CARE ORDERS

36.—(1) This paragraph applies where, immediately before the commencement of section 90(2) there was in force an order ("a criminal care order") made—

(a) under section 7(7)(a) of the Children and Young Persons Act 1969 (alteration in treatment of young offenders etc.); or

(b) under section 15(1) of that Act, on discharging a supervision order made under section 7(7)(b) of that Act.

(2) The criminal care order shall continue to have effect until the end of the period of six months beginning with the day on which section 90(2) comes into force unless it is brought to an end earlier in accordance with—

(a) the provisions of the Act of 1969 preserved by sub-paragraph (3)(a); or

(b) this paragraph.

(3) While the criminal care order remains in force, any relevant provisions—

(a) of the Act of 1969; and

(b) of the Child Care Act 1980,

shall continue to have effect with respect to it.

(4) While the criminal care order remains in force, a court may, on the application of the appropriate person, make—

(a) a residence order;

(b) a care order or a supervision order under section 31;

(c) an education supervision order under section 36 (regardless of subsection (6) of that section); or

(d) an order falling within sub-paragraph (5),

and shall, on making any of those orders, discharge the criminal care order.

(5) The order mentioned in sub-paragraph (4)(d) is an order having effect as if it were a supervision order of a kind mentioned in section 12AA of the Act of 1969 (as inserted by paragraph 23 of Schedule 12), that is to say, a supervision order—

(a) imposing a requirement that the child shall live for a specified period in local authority accommodation; but

(b) in relation to which the conditions mentioned in subsection (4) of section 12AA are not required to be satisfied.

(6) The maximum period which may be specified in an order made under sub-paragraph (4)(d) is six months and such an order may stipulate that the child shall not live with a named person.

(7) Where this paragraph applies, section 5 of the Rehabilitation of Offenders Act 1974 (rehabilitation periods for particular sentences) shall have effect regardless of the repeals in it made by this Act.

(8) In sub-paragraph (4) "appropriate person" means—

(a) in the case of an application for a residence order, any person (other than a local authority) who has the leave of the court;

(b) in the case of an application for an education supervision order, a local education authority; and

(c) in any other case, the local authority to whose care the child was committed by the order.

MISCELLANEOUS

Consents under the Marriage Act 1949 (c. 76)

37.—(1) In the circumstances mentioned in sub-paragraph (2), section 3 of and Schedule 2 to the Marriage Act 1949 (consents to marry) shall continue to have effect regardless of the amendment of that Act by paragraph 5 of Schedule 12.

(2) The circumstances are that—

(a) immediately before the day on which paragraph 5 of Schedule 12 comes into force, there is in force—

(i) an existing order, as defined in paragraph 5(1); or

(ii) an order of a kind mentioned in paragraph 16(1); and

(b) section 3 of and Schedule 2 to the Act of 1949 would, but for this Act, have applied to the marriage of the child who is the subject of the order.

The Children Act 1975 (c. 72)

38. The amendments of other enactments made by the following provisions of the Children Act 1975 shall continue to have effect regardless of the repeal of the Act of 1975 by this Act—

(a) section 68(4), (5) and (7) (amendments of section 32 of the Children and Young Persons Act 1969); and

(b) in Schedule 3—

(i) paragraph 13 (amendments of Births and Deaths Registration Act 1953);

(ii) paragraph 43 (amendment of Perpetuities and Accumulations Act 1964);

(iii) paragraphs 46 and 47 (amendments of Health Services and Public Health Act 1968); and

(iv) paragraph 77 (amendment of Parliamentary and Other Pensions Act 1972).

The Child Care Act 1980 (c. 5)

39. The amendment made to section 106(2)(a) of the Children and Young Persons Act 1963 by paragraph 26 of Schedule 5 to the Child Care Act 1980 shall continue to have effect regardless of the repeal of the Act of 1980 by this Act.

Legal aid

40. The Lord Chancellor may by order make such transitional and saving provisions as appear to him to be necessary or expedient, in consequence of any provision made by or under this Act, in connection with the operation of any provisions of the Legal Aid Act 1988 (including any provision of that Act which is amended or repealed by this Act).

      SCHEDULE 15

Repeals

Chapter	Short title	Extent of repeal
1891 c. 3.	The Custody of Children Act 1891.	The whole Act.
1933 c. 12.	The Children and Young Persons Act 1933.	In section 14(2), the words from "may also" to "together, and". In section 34(8), "(a)" and the words from "and (b)" to the end. Section 40. In section 107(1), the definitions of "care order" and "interim order".
1944 c. 31.	The Education Act 1944.	In section 40(1), the words from "or to imprisonment" to the end. In section 114(1), the definition of parent.
1948 c. 53.	The Nurseries and Child-Minders Regulation Act 1948.	The whole Act.
1949 c. 76.	The Marriage Act 1949.	In section 3(1), the words "unless the child is subject to a custodianship order, when the consent of the custodian and, where the custodian is the husband or wife of a parent of the child of that parent shall be required". Section 78(1A). Schedule 2.
1956 c. 69.	The Sexual Offences Act 1956.	Section 38.
1959 c. 72.	The Mental Health Act 1959.	Section 9.
1963 c. 37.	The Children and Young Persons Act 1963.	Section 3. Section 23. In section 29(1), the words "under section 1 of the Children and Young Persons Act 1969 or". Section 53(3). In Schedule 3, paragraph 11.
1964 c. 42.	The Administration of Justice Act 1964.	In section 38, the definition of "domestic court".
1968 c. 46.	The Health Services and Public Health Act 1968.	Section 60. In section 64(3)(a), sub-paragraphs (vi), (vii), (ix) and (xv). In section 63(3)(b), paragraphs (vii), (viii) and (x).
1968 c. 49.	The Social Work (Scotland) Act 1968.	Section 1(4)(a). Section 5(2)(d). In section 86(3), the words "the Child Care Act 1980 or". In Schedule 8, paragraph 20.
1969 c. 46.	The Family Law Reform Act 1969.	Section 7.
1969 c. 54.	The Children and Young Persons Act 1969.	Sections 1 to 3. In section 7, in subsection (7) the words "to subsection (7A) of this section and", paragraph (a) and the words from "and subsection (13) of section 2 of this Act" to the end; and subsection (7A). Section 7A. In section 8(3), the words from "and as if the reference to acquittal" to the end.

Chapter	Short title	Extent of repeal
1969 c. 54—*cont.*	The Children and Young Persons Act 1969—*cont.*	In section 9(1), the words "proceedings under section 1 of this Act or".
		Section 11A.
		Section 14A.
		In section 15, in subsection (1) the words "and may on discharging the supervision order make a care order (other than an interim order) in respect of the supervised person"; in subsection (2) the words "and the supervision order was not made by virtue of section 1 of this Act or on the occasion of the discharge of a care order"; in subsection (2A), the words "or made by a court on discharging a care order made under that subsection"; and in subsection (4), the words "or made by a court on discharging a care order made under that section".
		In section 16, in subsection (6)(a), the words "a care order or"; and in subsection (8) the words "or, in a case where a parent or guardian of his was a party to the proceedings on an application under the preceding section by virtue of an order under section 32A of this Act, the parent or guardian".
		In section 17, paragraphs (b) and (c).
		Sections 20 to 22.
		Section 27(4).
		Section 28.
		Sections 32A to 32C.
		In section 34(2) the words "under section 1 of this Act or", the words "2(3) or" and the words "and accordingly in the case of such a person the reference in section 1(1) of this Act to the said section 2(3) shall be construed as including a reference to this subsection".
		In section 70, in subsection (1), the definitions of "care order" and "interim order"; and in subsection (2) the words "21(2), 22(4) or (6) or 28(5)" and the words "care order or warrant".
		In Schedule 5, paragraphs 12(1), 37, 47 and 48.
1970 c. 34.	The Marriage (Registrar General's Licence) Act 1970.	In section 3(b), the words from "as amended" to "1969".
1970 c. 42.	The Local Authority Social Services Act 1970.	In Schedule 1, in the entry relating to the Children and Young Persons Act 1969, the words "welfare, etc. of foster children"; the entries relating to the Matrimonial Causes Act 1973, section 44, the Domestic Proceedings and Magistrates' Courts Act 1978, section 9, the Child Care Act 1980 and the Foster Children Act 1980.
1971 c. 3.	The Guardianship or Minors Act 1971.	The whole Act.

Chapter	Short title	Extent of repeal
1971 c. 23.	The Courts Act 1971.	In Schedule 8, paragraph 59(1).
1972 c. 18.	The Maintenance Orders (Reciprocal Enforcement) Act 1972.	Section 41.
1972 c. 70.	The Local Government Act 1972.	In Schedule 23, paragraphs 4 and 9(3).
1972 c. 71.	The Criminal Justice Act 1972.	Section 51(1).
1973 c. 18.	The Matrimonial Causes Act 1973.	Sections 42 to 44. In section 52(1), the definition of "custody". In Schedule 2, paragraph 11.
1973 c. 29.	The Guardianship Act 1973.	The whole Act.
1973 c. 45.	The Domicile and Matrimonial Proceedings Act 1973.	In Schedule 1, in paragraph 11(1) the definitions of "custody" and "education" and in paragraph 11(3) the word "four".
1973 c. 62.	The Powers of Criminal Courts Act 1973.	In section 13(1), the words "and the purposes of section 1(2)(bb) of the Children and Young Persons Act 1969". In Schedule 3, in paragraph 3(2A), the word "and" immediately preceding paragraph (b).
1974 c. 53.	The Rehabilitation of Offenders Act 1974.	In section 1(4)(b) the words "or in care proceedings under section 1 of the Children and Young Persons Act 1969". In section 5, in subsection 5(e), the words "a care order or"; and in subsection (10) the words "care order or".
1975 c. 72.	The Children Act 1975.	The whole Act.
1976 c. 36.	The Adoption Act 1976.	Section 11(5). Section 14(3). In section 15, in subsection (1), the words from "subject" to "cases)" and subsection (4). Section 26. In section 28(5), the words "or the organisation". Section 34. Section 36(1)(c). Section 37(1), (3) and (4). Section 55(4). In section 57, in subsection (2), the words from "and the court" to the end and subsections (4) to (10). In section 72(1), the definition of "place of safety", in the definition of "local authority" the words from "and" to the end and, in the definition of "specified order", the words "Northern Ireland or". In Schedule 3, paragraphs 8, 11, 19, 21, and 22.
1977 c. 45.	The Criminal Law Act 1977.	Section 58(3).
1977 c. 49.	The National Health Service Act 1977.	In section 21, in subsection (1)(a) the words "and young children".

Chapter	Short title	Extent of repeal
1977 c. 49—*cont.*	The National Health Service Act 1977—*cont.*	In Schedule 8, in paragraph 1(1), the words from "and of children" to the end; in paragraph 2(2) the words from "or (b) to persons who" to "arrangements"; and in paragraph 3(1) "(a)" and the words from "or (b) a child" to "school age". In Schedule 15, paragraphs 10 and 25.
1978 c. 22.	The Domestic Proceedings and Magistrates' Courts Act 1978.	Sections 9 to 15. In section 19, in subsection (1) the words "following powers, that is to say" and sub-paragraph (ii), subsections (2) and (4), in subsection (7) the words "and one interim custody order" and in subsection (9) the words "or 21". In section 20, subsection (4) and in subsection (9) the words "subject to the provisions of section 11(8) of this Act". Section 21. In section 24, the words "or 21" in both places where they occur. In section 25, in subsection (1) paragraph (b) and the word "or" immediately preceding it and in subsection (2) paragraphs (c) and (d). Section 29(4). Sections 33 and 34. Sections 36 to 53. Sections 64 to 72. Sections 73(1) and 74(1) and (3). In section 88(1), the definition of "actual custody". In Schedule 2, paragraphs 22, 23, 27, 29, 31, 36, 41 to 43, 46 to 50.
1978 c. 28.	The Adoption (Scotland) Act 1978.	In section 20(3)(c), the words "section 12(3)(b) of the Adoption Act 1976 or of ". In section 45(5), the word "approved". Section 49(4). In section 65(1), in the definition of "local authority", the words from "and" to the end and, in the definition of "specified order", the words "Northern Ireland or".
1978 c. 30.	The Interpretation Act 1978.	In Schedule 1, the entry with respect to the construction of certain expressions relating to children.
1980 c. 5.	The Child Care Act 1980.	The whole Act.
1980 c. 6.	The Foster Children Act 1980.	The whole Act.
1980 c. 43.	The Magistrates' Courts Act 1980.	In section 65(1), paragraphs (e) and (g) and the paragraph (m) inserted in section 65 by paragraph 82 of Schedule 2 to the Family Law Reform Act 1987. In section 81(8), in the definition of "guardian" the words "by deed or will" and in the definition of "sums adjudged to be paid by a conviction" the words from "as applied" to the end. In section 143(2), paragraph (i).

Chapter	Short title	Extent of repeal
1980 c. 43—*cont.*	The Magistrates' Courts Act 1980—*cont.*	In Schedule 7, paragraphs 78, 83, 91, 92, 110, 116, 117, 138, 157, 158, 165, 166 and 199 to 201.
1981 c. 60.	The Education Act 1981.	In Schedule 3, paragraph 9.
1982 c. 20.	The Children's Homes Act 1982.	The whole Act.
1982 c. 48.	The Criminal Justice Act 1982.	Sections 22 to 25. Section 27. In Schedule 14, paragraphs 45 and 46.
1983 c. 20.	The Mental Health Act 1983.	In section 26(5), paragraph (d) and the word "or" immediately preceding it. In section 28(1), the words "(including an order under section 38 of the Sexual Offences Act 1956)". In Schedule 4, paragraphs 12, 26(a), (b) and (c), 35, 44, 50 and 51.
1983 c. 41.	The Health and Social Services and 'Social Security Adjudications Act 1983.	Section 4(1). Sections 5 and 6. In section 11, in subsection (2) the words "the Child Care Act 1980 and the Children's Homes Act 1982". In section 19, subsections (1) to (5). Schedule 1. In Schedule 2, paragraphs 3, 9 to 14, 20 to 24, 27, 28, 34, 37 and 46 to 62. In Schedule 4, paragraphs 38 to 48. In Schedule 9, paragraphs 5, 16 and 17.
1984 c. 23.	The Registered Homes Act 1984.	In Schedule 1, in paragraph 5, sub-paragraph (a) and paragraphs 6, 7 and 8.
1984 c. 28.	The County Courts Act 1984.	In Schedule 2, paragraph 56.
1984 c. 37.	The Child Abduction Act 1984.	In section 3, the word "and" immediately preceding paragraph (c). In the Schedule, in paragraph 1(2) the words "or voluntary organisation" and paragraph 3(1)(e).
1984 c. 42.	The Matrimonial and Family Proceedings Act 1984.	In Schedule 1, paragraphs 19 and 23.
1984 c. 56.	The Foster Children (Scotland) Act 1984.	In section 1, the words "for a period of more than 6 days" and the words from "The period" to the end. In section 7(1), the word "or" at the end of paragraph (e). In Schedule 2, paragraphs 1 to 3 and 8.
1984 c. 60.	The Police and Criminal Evidence Act 1984.	In section 37(15), the words "and is not excluded from this Part of this Act by section 52 below". Section 39(5). Section 52. In section 118(1), in the definition of parent or guardian, paragraph (b) and the word "and" immediately preceding it. In Schedule 2, the entry relating to section 16 of the Children Care Act 1980. In Schedule 6, paragraphs 19(a) and 22.
1985 c. 23.	The Prosecution of Offences Act 1985.	Section 27.

Chapter	Short title	Extent of repeal
1985 c. 60.	The Child Abduction and Custody Act 1985.	Section 9(c). Section 20(2)(b) and (c). Section 25(3) and (5). In Schedule 3, paragraph 1(2).
1986 c. 28.	The Children and Young Persons (Amendment) Act 1986.	The whole Act.
1986 c. 33.	The Disabled Persons (Services, Consultation and Representation) Act 1986.	In section 16, in the definition of "guardian", paragraph (a).
1986 c. 45.	The Insolvency Act 1986.	In section 281(5)(b), the words "in domestic proceedings".
1986 c. 50.	The Social Security Act 1986.	In Schedule 10, paragraph 51.
1986 c. 55.	The Family Law Act 1986.	In section 1(2), in paragraph (a) the words "(a) or" and paragraph (b). Section 3(4) to (6). Section 4. Section 35(1). In section 42(6), in paragraph (b) the words "section 42(6) of the Matrimonial Causes Act 1973 or", in paragraph (c) the words "section 42(7) of that Act or" and in paragraph (d) the words "section 19(6) of the Domestic Proceedings and Magistrates' Courts Act 1978 or". In Schedule 1, paragraphs 10, 11, 13, 16, 17, 20 and 23.
1987 c. 42.	The Family Law Reform Act 1987.	Section 3. Sections 4 to 7. Sections 9 to 16. In Schedule 2, paragraphs 11, 14, 51, 67, 68, 94 and 95. In Schedule 3, paragraphs 11 and 12.
1988 c. 34.	The Legal Aid Act 1988.	Section 3(4)(c). Section 27. Section 28. In section 30, subsections (1) and (2). In Part I of Schedule 2, paragraph 2(a) and (e).

INDEX

References are to section and Schedule number

ABDUCTION,
offences, s.49
recovery of children, s.50
ADOPTION,
amendment of law, s.88, Sch. 10
panels of guardians ad litem and reporting
officers, Sch. 10
research into, s.83
ADOPTION AGENCY,
allowances, payment of, Sch. 10
functions, inquiry into, s.81
meaning, s.105
placement by, inspection of premises, s.80
substitution of, Sch. 10
ADOPTION CONTACT REGISTER,
maintenance of, Sch. 10
ADOPTION ORDER,
residence order instead of, s.8
ADVERTISEMENT,
fostering, of, Sch. 8
APPEALS,
care or supervision order cases, in, s.40
emergency protection order, in respect of,
s.45
High Court, to, s.94
privately fostered children, relating to,
Sch. 8
registration, relating to,
child minder, etc., of, s.77
registered children's homes, Sch. 6
voluntary homes, Sch. 5
APPRENTICESHIP DEEDS,
local authority, guaranteed by, Sch. 2

BLOOD TESTS,
paternity, establishing, s.89
BOARDING SCHOOL. *See* INDEPENDENT
SCHOOL.
BODIES CORPORATE,
offences by, s.103

CARE,
abduction of children in, s.49
contact with child in, s.34
generally, intro.
local authority, powers and duties of. *See*
LOCAL AUTHORITY.
order. *See* CARE ORDER.
parental contact during, s.34
proceedings, reduction of need for, Sch. 2
review of cases, s.26
transitional provisions, Sch. 14
CARE ORDER,
applications,
conditions for, s.31
period for disposal of, s.32
repeated, intervals between, s.91

CARE ORDER—*cont.*
contact order, discharging, s.8
criminal proceedings, in,
power to make, s.90
transitional provisions, Sch. 14
discharge of, s.39
duration of, s.91
effect of, s.33
emergency protection order, subject to,
s.91
family proceedings, powers of court in,
s.37
interim, s.38
local authority,
designated in, s.31
duties of, s.33
meaning, ss.31, 105
orders pending appeal, s.40
parental contact, order as to, s.34
power to make, s.31
residence order,
discharged by, ss.9, 91
discharging, ss.8, 91
school attendance order, discharging, s.91
section 8 order, discharging, s.91
supervision order,
discharging, s.91
substitution of, s.39
variation of, s.39
wardship, bringing to an end, s.91
CHANNEL ISLANDS,
application of Act to, s.107
orders, effect of, s.101
CHILD. *See also* ADOPTION; CARE, etc.
advice and assistance for, s.24
evidence given by, s.96
family, of, s.105
financial relief, order for, s.15, Sch. 1
harm to, ss.31, 43
hearing, attendance at, s.95
jurisdiction, restriction on removal from,
ss.13, 33
meaning, s.105, Sch. 1
name, restriction on changing, ss.13, 33
need, in, s.17, Sch. 2
ordinary residence, ss.30, 105
privacy of proceedings, s.97
relative of, meaning, s.105
representation of, s.41
welfare of, s.1
CHILD ASSESSMENT ORDER,
meaning, s.43
power to make, s.43
CHILD CARE TRAINING,
adequacy, keeping under review, s.83
grants for, s.82
meaning, s.82
CHILD MINDING,
child minder, person acting as, s.71

[1]

CHILD MINDING—*cont.*
  domestic premises, on, s.71
    inspection of, ss.76, 80, Sch. 9
  local authorities, co-operation between,
    Sch. 9
  offences, s.78
  registration,
    appeals, s.77
    applications, Sch. 9
    cancellation of, s.74
    certificate of, Sch. 9
    disqualification, Sch. 9
    emergency protection, s.75
    enforcement notice, s.78
    imposition of requirements, s.72
    refusal of, s.71
    requirement of, s.71
  review of services, s.19
  schools, etc., exemption of, Sch. 9
  Scotland, provisions applying to, s.79
  transitional provisions, Sch. 14
CHILDREN ACT 1989,
  background, intro.
  Channel Islands, application to, s.107
  commencement, s.108
  consequential amendments, Sch. 13
  financial provisions, s.106
  interpretation, s.105
  Isles of Scilly, application to, s.108
  minor amendments, Sch. 12
  repeals, Sch. 15
  savings, Sch. 14
  Scotland, extension of provisions to, s.108
  transitional provisions, Sch. 14
CHILDREN'S HOME,
  disqualification from interest or employ-
    ment in, s.65
  inspection of, s.80
  meaning, s.63
  registered. *See* REGISTERED CHILDREN'S
    HOME.
  unregistered, child not to be kept in, s.63
  welfare of children in, s.64
COMMUNITY HOME,
  accommodation in, providing, ss.20, 23,
    59
  assisted,
    body responsible for, s.54
    cessation, financial provisions on, s.58
    closure of, s.57
    disposal of premises, s.58
    disputes, determination of, s.55
    management of, Sch. 4
    meaning, s.53
    voluntary organisation, discontinuance
      by, s.56
  body responsible for, s.54
  controlled,
    body responsible for, s.54
    cessation, financial provisions on, s.58
    closure of, s.57
    disposal of premises, s.58
    disputes, determination of, s.55
    management of, Sch. 4
    meaning, s.53
    voluntary organisation, discontinuance
      by, s.56

COMMUNITY HOME—*cont.*
  direction that premises be no longer used
    for, s.54
  grants to, s.82
  management of, Sch. 4.
  meaning, s.53
  proprietor, meaning, s.58
  provision of, s.53
  regulations, Sch. 4.
CONTACT ORDERS,
  applicants for, s.10
  care order discharging, s.8
  cohabitation of parents, effect of, s.11
  effect of, s.8
  local authority, restriction on application
    by, s.9
  meaning, s.8
COUNTY COURT,
  Family Division treated as, s.92
COURT,
  hearing, attendance of child at, s.95
  jurisdiction, s.92
  meaning, s.96
  rules of, s.93
  welfare of child, considering, s.1
CRIMINAL PROCEEDINGS,
  care and supervision orders made in, s.90
  transitional provisions, Sch. 14
CUSTODY,
  transitional provisions, Sch. 14.

DAY CARE,
  domestic premises, on, s.71
    inspection of, ss.76, 80, Sch. 9
  generally, intro.
  local authorities, co-operation between,
    Sch. 9
  meaning, ss.18, 19, 71
  occasional facilities, Sch. 9
  offences, s.78
  provision of, s.18
  racial groups, taking account of, Sch. 2
  registration,
    appeals, s.77
    application for, Sch. 9
    cancellation of, s.74
    certificate of, Sch. 9
    disqualification, Sch. 9
    emergency protection, s.75
    imposition of requirements, s.73
    refusal of, s.71
    requirement of, s.71
  relevant establishment, s.19
  review of provisions, s.19
  schools, etc., exemption of, Sch. 9
  Scotland, provisions applying to, s.79
  transitional provisions, Sch. 14
DISABLED CHILDREN,
  accommodation and maintenance of, s.23
  private fostering, s.66
  register of, Sch. 2
  services, provision of, s.17, Sch. 2

EDUCATION SUPERVISION ORDERS,
  discharge of, Sch. 3
  duration of, Sch. 3

EDUCATION SUPERVISION ORDERS—*cont.*
　effect of, Sch. 3
　failure to comply with directions, Sch. 3
　meaning, s.36
　offences, s.3
　power to make, s.36
EMERGENCY PROTECTION ORDER,
　abduction of child subject to, s.49
　appeals, s.45
　application,
　　child assessment order application
　　　treated as, s.43
　　persons making, s.44
　care order subject to, s.91
　child in police protection, in respect of,
　　s.46
　discharge, application for, s.45
　duration of, s.45
　effect of, s.44
　extension of, s.45
　independent school, removal of child
　　from, s.87
　information about children in need of,
　　obtaining, s.48
　local authority, duty to investigate, s.47
　meaning, s.44
　power to make, s.44
　premises, authorising entry of, s.48
　single justice, hearing by, Sch. 11
　supervisor, meaning, s.105
EVIDENCE,
　child, of, s.96
　self-incrimination, abolition of privilege
　　against, s.98

FAMILY ASSISTANCE ORDERS,
　power to make, s.16
FAMILY CENTRES,
　meaning, Sch. 2
　provision of, Sch. 2
FAMILY PROCEEDINGS,
　care order, consideration of, s.37
　commencement, Sch. 11
　court, s.92
　guardians, appointment of, s.5
　meaning, ss.8, 92
　section 8 orders, making. *See* SECTION 8
　　ORDERS.
　supervision order, consideration on, s.37
　transfer, Sch. 11
　welfare reports, s.7
FINANCIAL RELIEF,
　children, in respect of, s.15, Sch. 1
　order,
　　duration of, s.91, Sch. 1
　　power to make, Sch. 1
FOSTER PARENTS,
　advertisements, prohibition of, Sch. 8
　disqualified person, living in same house-
　　hold as, s.68
　insurance of life of child, Sch. 8
　local authority,
　　meaning, ss.23, 79
　　provision of accommodation with, s.23,
　　　Sch. 2
　　racial groups, taking account of, Sch. 2
　　section 8 order, restriction on, s.9

FOSTER PARENTS—*cont.*
　meaning, s.51
　number of children, limits on, Sch. 7
　private,
　　disqualfication from being, s.68
　　offences, s.70
　　prohibition of, s.69
　privately fostered children,
　　appeals, Sch. 8
　　disabled, s.66
　　inspection of premises, s.80
　　local authority powers, Sch. 8
　　meaning, s.66, Sch. 8
　　notification, Sch. 8
　　offences, s.70
　　visiting, s.67
　　welfare of, s.67
　refuge, providing, s.51
　Scotland, provisions applying to, s.79
　transitional provisions, Sch. 14
　use of term, s.23
　voluntary organisations, placing of child
　　by, s.59

GUARDIAN,
　ad litem. *See* GUARDIAN AT LITEM.
　appointment of,
　　court, by, s.5
　　duration of, s.91
　　parent or other guardian, by, s.5
　　revocation of, s.6
　　termination of, s.6
　meaning, s.105
　disclaimer by, s.6
　section 8 order, application for, s.10
　transitional provisions, Sch. 14
GUARDIAN AD LITEM,
　appointment of, s.41
　local authority records, access to, s.42
　panel of, s.41, Sch. 10

HEALTH AUTHORITY,
　child accommodated by, notification, s.85
　child ceasing to be accommodated by, s.24
　emergency protection investigation,
　　assisting, s.47
　inspection of premises, s.80
　meaning, s.105
　other authorities, co-operation with, s.27
HIGH COURT,
　appeals to, s.94
　Family Division, treatment as county
　　court, s.92
　wardship jurisdiction, restrictions on use
　　of, s.100

INDEPENDENT SCHOOL,
　fostering requirements, extension of, Sch. 8
　inspection of premises, s.80
　meaning, s.105
　welfare of children accommodated in, s.87
INSURANCE,
　life of fostered child, of, Sch. 8

ISLE OF MAN,
  orders, effect of, s.101
ISLES OF SCILLY,
  provisions applying to, s.108

JURISDICTION,
  restriction on removal of child from, ss.13, 33

LEGAL AID,
  availability of, s.99
LOCAL AUTHORITY,
  accommodation for children, provision of,
    community home, in, s.20
    detention, in, s.21
    general duty, s.20
    inspection of, s.80
    meaning, ss.22, 105
    police protection, in, s.21
    protection of child, for, Sch. 2
    remand, on, s.21
    removal from, s.20
    secure, s.25
    wishes of child, and, s.20
  advice and assistance by, s.24
  apprenticeship deeds, guaranteeing, Sch. 2
  care. See CARE; CARE ORDER.
  children and families, provision of services for,
    assistance, providing, s.17
    child minding services, review of, s.19
    children in need, identification of, Sch. 2
    children living with families, Sch. 2
    day care, provision of, ss.18, 19. See also DAY CARE.
    general duty, s.17
  children looked after by,
    accommodation and maintenance, provision of, s.23
    assisting to live abroad, Sch. 2
    child and family, contact between, Sch. 2
    death of, Sch. 2
    foster parents, placing with, Sch. 2
    general duty in relation to, s.22
    maintenance, contributions to, Sch. 2
    parents, allowing to live with, Sch. 2
    visitor, appointment of, Sch. 2
    wishes of child, s.22
  community homes. See COMMUNITY HOMES.
  co-operation between, s.27, Sch. 9
  cost of providing services, recoupment of, s.29
  directions given to, s.22
  disabled children,
    provision of services for, s.17, Sch. 2
    register of, Sch. 2
  emergency protection, investigation in respect of, s.47
  family centres, provision of, Sch. 2
  foster parents. See FOSTER PARENTS.
  functions, inquiry into, s.81

LOCAL AUTHORITY—cont.
  grants to, s.82
  independent schools, steps to safeguard welfare in, s.87
  local education authorities,
    concurrent functions, s.30
    consultation with, s.28
    co-operation with, s.27
  maintenance of child, contribution to, Sch. 1
  meaning, s.105
  neglect and abuse, prevention of, Sch. 2
  notification of accommodation of children to, ss.85, 86
  other duties, provisions not affecting, s.30
  privately fostered child, requirements in respect of, s.67, Sch. 8
  racial groups, taking account of, Sch. 2
  records, access by guardian ad litem, s.42
  representations, procedure for, s.25
  research by, s.83
  review of cases, s.26
  Secretary of State, default powers, s.84
  section 8 orders, restriction on, s.9
  secure accommodation, provision of, s.25
  supervision orders. See SUPERVISION ORDERS.
  voluntary organisations, duties of regarding, s.62
  wardship, restriction on use of, s.100
LOCAL EDUCATION AUTHORITY,
  appropriate, meaning, s.28
  child accommodated by, notification, s.85
  child ceasing to be accommodated by, s.24
  education supervision order, designated in, s.36
  inspection of premsies, s.80
  local authority,
    concurrent functions, s.30
    consultation with, s.28
    co-operation with, s.27, Sch. 9
    emergency protection investigation, assisting, s.47
  meaning, s.105
LOCAL HOUSING AUTHORITY,
  emergency protection investigation, assisting, s.47
  meaning, s.105
  other authorities, co-operation with, s.27
LORD CHANCELLOR,
  regulations and orders by, s.104

MAGISTRATES' COURTS,
  appeals from. s.92
  contribution order, enforcement of, Sch. 2
  jurisdiction, s.92
  maintenance order, enforcement of, Sch. 1
  private, sitting in, s.97
  residence order, enforcement of, s.14
  single justice, hearings by, Sch. 11
MAINTENANCE AGREEMENT,
  alteration of, Sch. 1
  meaning, Sch. 1

Index

MAINTENANCE ORDER,
enforcement of, Sch. 1
MEDICAL EXAMINATION,
order for, ss.38, 44, Sch. 3
MENTAL NURSING HOME,
accommodation of child in, notification of, s.86
child ceasing to be accommodated in, s.24
functions, inquiry into, s.81
inspection of premises, s.80
meaning, s.105
research into, s.83

NAME,
child, of, restriction on changing, ss.13, 33
NANNY,
person acting as, s.71
NATIONAL SOCIETY FOR THE PREVENTION OF CRUELTY TO CHILDREN,
authorised person, as, s.31
NORTHERN IRELAND,
orders, effect of, s.101
provisions applying to, s.108
recovery orders, extension to, s.50
NURSING HOME,
accommodation of child in, notification of, s.86
child ceasing to be accommodated in, s.24
functions, inquiry into, s.81
inspection of premises, s.80
meaning, s.105
research into, s.83

ORDERS,
criteria for making, s.1
parts of United Kingdom, effect between, s.101
section 8. See SECTION 8 ORDERS.

PARENTAL RESPONSIBILITY,
agreement,
duration of, s.91
power to make, s.4
care order, during, s.33
delegation of, s.2
guardians, of, s.5
meaning, s.3
other obligations, and, s.3
person having, s.2
residence order, granted by, ss.8, 12
transitional provisions, Sch. 14.
unmarried father, of, ss.2, 4
PATERNITY TESTS,
use of, s.89
PLACE OF SAFETY ORDER,
replacement of, s.44
transitional provisions, Sch. 14
POLICE,
removal of child by, s.46
search warrants, s.102
PREMISES,
entry and search of, s.48
PROHIBITED STEPS ORDERS,
effect of, s.8

PROHIBITED STEPS ORDERS—cont.
meaning, s.8
restriction on making, s.9
PROTECTION OF CHILDREN,
accommodation, provision of, s.21
cancellation, etc., of registration of child minder, etc., on, s.75
child assessment orders. See CHILD ASSESSMENT ORDER.
discovery of children in need of, assisting, s.48
emergency protection order. See EMERGENCY PROTECTION ORDER.
local authority,
accommodation, provision of, Sch. 2
investigations, s.47
police, removal of child by, s.46
regulations, s.52
rules of court, s.52
PSYCHIATRIC EXAMINATION,
order for, ss.38, 44, Sch. 3.

RECOVERY ORDER,
power to make, s.50
transitional provisions, Sch. 14
REFUGE,
children at risk, for, s.51
REGISTERED CHILDREN'S HOME,
child ceasing to be accommodated in, s.24
children's home, meaning, s.63
disqualification from interest or employment in, s.65
functions, inquiry into, s.81
home, meaning, s.63
provision of accommodation in, ss.23, 59
refuge, as, s.51
registration of, s.63, Sch. 6
regulations, Sch. 6
welfare of children in, s.64
RESIDENCE,
ordinary, of child, s.30
RESIDENCE ORDERS,
adoption order, instead of, s.8
applicants for, s.10
care order,
discharged by, ss.8, 91
discharging, ss.9, 91
child in care, in respect of, s.9
cohabitation of parents, effect of, s.11
duration of, s.8
enforcement of, s.14
interim supervision order with, s.38
jurisdiction, removal of child from, s.13
local authority, restriction on application by, s.9
meaning, s.8
name of child, change of, s.13
parental responsibility, granting, ss.8, 12
two or more persons, in favour of, s.11
RESIDENTIAL CARE HOME,
accommodation of child in, notification of, s.86
child ceasing to be accommodated in, s.24
functions, inquiry into, s.81
inspection of premises, s.80
meaning, s.105
research into, s.83

[5]

SCHOOL ATTENDANCE ORDER,
care order, discharged by, s.91
SCOTLAND,
adoption, amendment of provisions, Sch. 10
child minding and day care, provisions on, s.79
fostering, provisions of, s.79
provisions applying to, s.108
recovery order, effect of, s.50
SEARCH,
warrants, ss.48, 102
SECRETARY OF STATE,
default powers, s.84
financial support by, s.82
information, requiring, ss.80, 83
inquiries, holding, s.81
inspection of premises by, s.80
regulations and orders by, s.104
research, assisting, s.83
SECTION 8 ORDERS,
application for,
applicants, s.10
leave for, s.10
care order discharging, s.91
child applying for, s.10
contact orders. See CONTACT ORDERS.
delay, avoiding, s.11
directions and conditions in, s.11
discharge, application for, s.10
duration of, ss.9, 91
family assistance order, and, s.16
family proceedings, made in, s.8
meaning, s.8
power of court to make, s.10
proceedings, made during, s.11
prohibited steps orders. See PROHIBITED STEPS ORDERS.
residence orders. See RESIDENCE ORDERS.
restrictions on, s.9
specific issue orders. See SPECIFIC ISSUE ORDERS.
variation, application for, s.10
SECURE ACCOMMODATION,
grants for, s.82
meaning, ss.25, 82
provision of, s.25
SOLICITOR,
child represented by, s.41
SPECIFIC ISSUE ORDERS,
meaning, s.8
restriction on making, s.9
SUPERVISION ORDERS,
applications,
period for disposal of, s.32
repeated, intervals between, s.91
care order,
discharge by, s.91
discharge of, Sch. 3
substituted for, s.39
criminal proceedings, in,
power to make, s.90
transitional provisions, Sch. 14
directions, Sch. 3
discharge of, ss.39, 91
duration of, s.91, Sch. 3
earlier orders, discharging, Sch. 3

SUPERVISION ORDERS—cont.
education. See EDUCATION SUPERVISION ORDER.
family proceedings, powers of court in, s.37
interim, s.38
meaning, s.31
orders pending appeal, s.40
power to make, s.31
responsible person, Sch. 3
supervisor,
directions, giving, Sch. 3
duties of, s.35
information to be given to, Sch. 3
meaning, s.105
selection of, Sch. 3
transitional provisions, Sch. 14
variation of, s.39

UNMARRIED FATHER,
parental responsibility, ss.2, 4

VOLUNTARY HOME,
disqualifiction of persons in relation to, Sch. 5
functions, inquiry into, s.81
meaning, s.60
particulars, notification of, Sch. 5
provision of accommodation in, ss.23, 59
refuge, as, s.51
registration of, s.60, Sch. 5
regulation of, s.60, Sch. 5
VOLUNTARY ORGANISATION,
child ceasing to be accommodated by, s.24
community home, provision of. See COMMUNITY HOME.
duties of, s.61
foster parents, placing child with, s.59
grants to, s.82
inspection of premises, s.80
local authorities, duties of, s.62
matters to be considered by, s.61
meaning, s.105
provision of accommodation by, s.59
representations, considering, s.59
review of cases by, s.59
transitional provisions, Sch. 14

WARDSHIP,
care order discharging, s.91
jurisdiction, restrictions on use of, s.100
WELFARE PRINCIPLE,
checklist, s.1
statement of, s.1
WELFARE REPORTS,
requests for, s.7
WORDS AND PHRASES,
accommodation, s.22
adoption agency, s.105
appeal period, s.40
appropriate authority, ss.46, 68
appropriate compensation, s.58
appropriate local education authority, s.28
approved child care training, s.82

WORDS AND PHRASES—*cont.*
authorised person, ss.31, 43, 44, 50
bank holiday, s.105
care order, ss.31, 105
child, s.105, Sch. 1
child assessment order, s.43
child care training, s.82
child minder, s.71
child of the family, s.105
children's home, s.63
civil proceedings, s.96
community home, s.53
contact order, s.8
contribution notice, Sch. 2
contribution order, Sch. 2
court, s.96
day care, ss.18, 19, 79
designated officer, s.50
development, ss.17, 31
disabled, s.17
disposal, s.58
district health authority, s.105
domestic premises, s.71
education authority, s.79
education supervision order, s.36
emergency protection order, s.44
enactment, s.68
family, s.17
family assistance order, s.16
family centre, Sch. 2
family panel, s.92
family proceedings, ss.8, 92
family proceedings court, s.92
financial relief order, Sch. 1
foster parent, s.51
functions, s.81
guardian, s.105
harm, s.31
health, ss.17, 31
health authority, s.105
health board, s.19
health service hospital, s.105
home, s.63
hospital, s.105
ill-treatment, s.31
independent school, s.105
local authority, s.105
local authority foster parent, ss.23, 79
local housing authority, s.105

WORDS AND PHRASES—*cont.*
maintenance agreement, Sch. 1
material, s.97
mental nursing home, s.105
nanny, s.71
notice of proceedings, s.93
nursing home, s.105
parental responsibility, s.3
parental responsibility agreement, s.4
periodical payments order, Sch. 1
person authorised to seek access, s.44
person qualifying for advice and assistance, s.24
premises, ss.58, 71
privately fostered child, s.66
prohibited steps order, s.8
proprietor, s.58
protected child, s.105
publish, s.97
recovery order, s.50
registered children's home, s.63
registered pupil, s.105
relative, s.105
relevant establishment, s.19
relevant period, s.38
relevant proceedings, s.93
relevant time, s.58
residence order, s.8
residential care home, s.105
responsible authority, ss.58, 85
responsible person, s.49, Sch. 3
review period, s.19
school, s.105
section 8 order, s.8
secure accommodation, ss.25, 82
secured periodical payments order, Sch. 1
service, s.105
signed, s.105
special educational needs, s.105
special health authority, s.105
specific issue order, s.8
specified proceedings, s.41
supervised activity, s.18
supervised child, s.105
supervision order, s.31
supervisor, s.105
upbringing, s.105
voluntary home, s.60
voluntary organisation, s.105